Français interactif

Table of Contents

THE UNIVERSITY OF TEXAS AT AUSTIN

Center for Open Educational Resources and Language Learning

Français interactif, *www.laits.utexas.edu/fi*, the web-based French program developed and in use at the University of Texas since 2004, and its companion site, **Tex's French Grammar** (2000) *www.laits.utexas.edu/tex/* are free open educational multimedia resources (OER), which require neither password nor fees. OER promote learning and scholarship for everyone, everywhere! **Français interactif**, used increasingly by students, teachers, and institutions throughout the world, includes 320 videos (American students in France, native French interviews, vocabulary and culture presentation videos) recorded vocabulary lists, phonetic lessons, online grammar lessons (600 pages) with self-correcting exercises and audio dialogues, online grammar tools (*verb conjugation reference, verb practice*), and diagnostic grammar tests. The accompanying textbook of classroom activities and homework is downloadable from the website in pdf format and available from the online publisher, *lulu.com*.

Français interactif was developed at the University of Texas Austin in the Department of French and Italian. It has been funded and created by Liberal Arts Instructional Technology Services at the University of Texas, and was financially supported by the U.S. Department of Education Fund for the Improvement of Post-Secondary Education (FIPSE Grant P116B070251) as an example of the open access initiative.

Third Edition

ISBN: 978-1-937963-00-2
Library of Congress Control Number: 2017958422
Manufactured in the United States of America.

Contributors

Produced by

Department of French and Italian
University of Texas at Austin
COERLL

Karen Kelton, Lower Division Coordinator, 2003-2006
Nancy Guilloteau, Lower Division Coordinator, 2006 -
Carl Blyth, Lower Division Coordinator, 1993 - 2002

Web, design, multimedia, cms:
- Eric Eubank
- Rachael Gilg
- Nathalie Steinfeld

Developers:
- Carl Blyth
- Nancy Guilloteau
- Karen Kelton

Audio recording:
- Mike Heidenreich

Audio recording
- Phonetics:
- Jean-Pierre Montreuil

- Vocabulary lists:
- François Lagarde
- Nora Megharbi
- Cécile Rey
- Nicholas Bacuez

Video voice-overs
- Rudy DeMattos
- Aicha Ennaciri
- Franck Guilloteau
- Nora Megharbi

Graduate student developers
- Nora Megharbi
- Charles Mignot
- Lindsy Myers

Graduate students
- Nicholas Bacuez
- Simone Barilleaux
- Katy Branch
- Claire Burkhart
- Christine Deden
- Rudy DeMattos
- Emilie Destruel
- Robyn Falline
- Carolyn Hardin
- Elizabeth Hythecker
- Karen Jones
- Sabrina Parent
- Rachel Pate
- Robert Reichle
- Cécile Rey
- Bea Schleppe
- Ellenor Shoemaker
- Melissa Skidmore
- Julia Tyurina
- Meredith Wright

Linguistic consultation
- David Birdsong
- Jean-Pierre Cauvin
- James Davis (Univ of Arkansas)
- Knud Lambrecht
- Jean-Pierre Montreuil
- Dina Sherzer

Support
- French and Italian, Former Chair: Dina Sherzer
- French and Italian, Chair: Daniela Bini
- Liberal Arts ITS, Director: Joe TenBarge

Interviewees
- Stéphanie Pellet
- Franck Guilloteau
- Virginie Royer
- Jean-Charles Bossert
- Karen Burke
- Blake Dublin
- Laila Kiblawi

Inspiration
- UT students in the Lyon Summer Program: Relations Internationales, Université Jean Moulin Lyon 3
- Audrey and Camille Guilloteau
- Tex and Tammy

Photos
- Kim Espinosa
- Shannon Kintner
- Jillian Owens
- Robert Reichle
- Ellenor Shoemaker

Illustrations
- Walter Moore

Awards

Français interactif was awarded the "2009 CALICO Access to Language Education Award", from CALICO, (Computer Assisted Language Instruction Consortium), Lernu.net and the Esperantic Studies Foundation, for an open access web site offering exceptional access to language learning resources.
(http://calico.org)

Français interactif received the National Endowment for the Humanities Edsitement Award for "Best of Humanities on the Web Award" in 2005 and both **Français interactif** and **Tex's French Grammar** received 5-star reviews on MERLOT (Multimedia Educational Resource for Learning and Online Teaching). The MERLOT reviews cite the 'intrinsically interesting and engaging content, clean design, and clear and intuitive navigation,' which provide 'access to a wealth of high-quality language materials for a truly worldwide audience.' (http://www.merlot.org/merlot/viewCompositeReview.htm?id=350514)

Glossary of Symbols
How to Use Français interactif

Vocabulary

The vocabulary, both online and printed, is a comprehensive list of the chapter's key vocabulary items arranged according to semantic fields, e.g., salutations, colors, days of the week, etc. Students listen to the native speaker pronunciation and may download the files in mp3 format. Students complete the vocabulary preparation using a template which guides them to identify salient associations, cognates, and word families. Students also categorize vocabulary in the "Chassez l'intrus" exercises.

Phonetics

The phonetics section introduces essential aspects of French pronunication. Each phonetics lesson focuses on the chapter's vocabulary (recycles previously learned vocabulary).

Preparation Exercises (to prepare at home in textbook)

Students prepare these exercises in the printed material before coming to class. During class instructors may use many different techniques to check responses: choral participation, pop quizzes, or pair and small group discussions.

Online Video Clip (to prepare at home)

Students watch videos and prepare the corresponding exercises before coming to class. Each chapter contains three different kinds of videos:

- **Introductory video**, a short video of a student on the study abroad program who presents the chapter's thematic and grammatical material. The introductions also include a preview of the communicative tasks that form the basis of the lesson.
- **Vocabulary presentation videos (vocabulaire en contexte)** which present vocabulary items in an authentic cultural context. The vocabulary video captures native speakers who use the new vocabulary in a context that provides important visual support. For example, a fruit vendor names each type of fruit on sale at the market that day. Students watch these short videos several times. First they try to recognize the vocabulary words in context. During subsequent listenings, students try to piece together what the speaker is saying. And finally, students are asked to perform a written activity based on the video.
- **Interviews** of four native French speakers (Franck, Virginie, Jean-Charles, and Stéphanie) and three American students learning French (Laila, Blake, and Karen). In these spontaneous interviews, speakers respond to questions that require them to employ the grammar and vocabulary featured in the chapter. Transcripts and English translations are available, but students are encouraged to watch the videos without this visual support.

Online Grammar (to prepare at home)

Students access the Tex's French Grammar website to study individual grammar points before coming to class. Grammar items are carefully explained in English, then exemplified in a dialogue, and finally tested in self-correcting, fill-in-the-blank exercises. Students print out their answers to these "Texercises" to turn in to their instructor. Instructors may also use these exercises as pop quizzes. Tex's French Grammar also includes a verb conjugator, a verb tutor, and an on-line French dictionary.

Pair Exercises

Students complete pair exercises in class with a partner. They ask each other questions and report their responses back to the class, read and categorize true/false or bizarre/normal sentences, fill in the blanks, etc.

Class or Group Exercises

Group exercise involve groups of three or four students, or the entire class.

Listening Comprehension Exercises

Listening exercises are led by the instructor and include listening discrimination exercises and dictations.

Homework/ Writing Exercises (to turn in)

Students write out homework assignments on a separate sheet of paper to turn in to their instructor. Homework includes the "Texercises" on the Tex's French Grammar website as well as several writing assignments in each chapter.

Cultural Notes

Students read information about cultural topics related to the chapter's content. Culture videos enhance the cultural notes in many chapters.

Grammaire interactive

Students complete inductive grammar exercises as homework.

Chansons exercises

Students listen to songs and perform accompanying activities.

Using the textbook with the website

Vocabulaire

·fiche d'identité
·questions personnelles
·la famille
·les amis
·mots interrogatifs
·l'heure
·l'heure officielle
·passe-temps et activités
·adverbes
·continents, pays, nationalités

Phonétique

·les symboles phonétiques
·l'élision
·la liaison

Grammaire

·2.1 avoir 'to have'
·2.2 -er verbs
·2.3 possessive determiners
·2.4 yes/no questions: est-ce que, n'est-ce pas
·2.5 basic negation: ne... pas
·2.6 introduction to adverbs
·2.7 interrogative and exclamative quel
·2.8 introduction to adjectives
·2.9 adjectives: formation and placement

·testez-vous!, chapitre deux
·verb conjugation reference
·verb practice

Vidéos

Vocabulaire en contexte

·Franck Guilloteau - me voici
·Franck Guilloteau - ma famille
·l'heure
·les passe-temps Audrey et Camille
·l'heure
·les continents
·les pays

Interviews

·questions personnelles
·ma famille

Culture

·la voiture de Franck

table des matières

introduction

Me voici!
In this chapter we will talk about ourselves, our families, our pastimes, and nationalities. We will also learn how to tell time.

liste de vocabulaire

preparation du vocabulaire
fiche d'identité
questions personnelles
la famille
les amis
mots interrogatifs
l'heure
l'heure officielle
passe-temps et activités
adverbes
continents, pays, nationalités

phonétique
les symboles phonétiques

grammaire
Tex's French Grammar
2.1 avoir 'to have'
2.2 -er verbs (regular) present tense
2.3 possessive determiners
2.4 yes/no questions: est-ce que, n'est-ce pas
2.5 basic negation: ne ... pas
2.6 introduction to adverbs
2.7 interrogative and exclamative quel
2.8 introduction to adjectives
2.9 adjectives: formation and placement
testez-vous!, chapitre 02
verb conjugation reference
verb practice

vidéos

vocabulaire en contexte
Franck Guilloteau - me voici
Franck Guilloteau - ma famille
les passe-temps Audrey et Camille
l'heure
les continents
les pays

interviews - les Français à Austin

questions personnelles	*Franck J-C*	*Stéphanie*	*Virginie*
ma famille	*Franck J-C*	*Stéphanie*	*Virginie*

interviews - les étudiants - UT Austin

questions personnelles	*Blake*	*Karen*	*Laila*
ma famille	*Blake*	*Karen*	*Laila*

culture
la voiture de Franck

@ activité internet
un correspondant français
activité, au cinéma

PDF: chapitre deux 2009
cahier_02.pdf
grammaire_interactive_02.pdf

- Purchase the Français interactif textbook in print-on-demand format (black and white or color)
- Download the pdf of each individual chapter and print it yourself!

00 · 01 · 02 · 03 · 04 · 05 · 06 · 07 · 08 · 09 · 10 · 11 · 12 · 13 · map · icons

liste de vocabulaire

table des matières

introduction

Me voici!
In this chapter we will talk about ourselves, our families, our pastimes, and nationalities. We will also learn how to tell time.

vidéos

vocabulaire en contexte
Franck Guilloteau - me voici
Franck Guilloteau - ma famille

liste de vocabulaire

preparation du voc
fiche d'identité
questions personnell
la famille
les amis
mots interrogatifs
l'heure
l'heure officielle
passe-temps et activ
adverbes
continents, pays, nat

mp3s: download archive
jump: - Select -

liste de vocabulaire

0:06 / 0:49

fiche d'identité	identification form
Nom (de famille)	*last name*
Prénom(s)	*first (and middle) name(s)*
Age	*age*
Nationalité	*nationality*
Résidence actuelle	*current address*
Profession	*profession*
Passe-temps préférés	*pastimes*

0:00 / 0:36

questions personnelles	personal questions
Comment vous appelez-vous?	*What is your name?*
Quel âge avez-vous?	*How old are you?*
Quelle est votre nationalité?	*What is your nationality?*
Vous êtes d'où?	*Where are you from?*
Où habitez-vous?	*Where do you live?*
Que faites-vous dans la vie?	*What do you do for a living?*
Quels sont vos passe-temps préférés?	*What are your favorite pastimes?*

Préparation du vocabulaire

Be sure to download the pdf vocabulary preparation template from the FI website to complete Exercises B, E, and F.

! Your instructor will collect this homework.

Tex's French Grammar
2.1 avoir 'to have'
2.2 -er verbs (regular) p
2.3 possessive determin
2.4 yes/no questions: es
ce pas
2.5 basic negation: ne ..
2.6 introduction to adve
2.7 interrogative and ex
2.8 introduction to adjec
2.9 adjectives: formatio
testez-vous!, Chapitre 02
verb conjugation referen
verb practice

The verb **avoir** is irregular in the present tense. Listen carefully to the pronunciation of the **-s** in the plural pronouns **nous, vous,** and **ils/elles.** This **-s** is pronounced as a **/z/** to link with the vowel sound in the plural forms of **avoir.** This **liaison,** or linking, is especially important in distinguishing **ilsont** (they have) from the third person plural of être **ilssont** (they are).

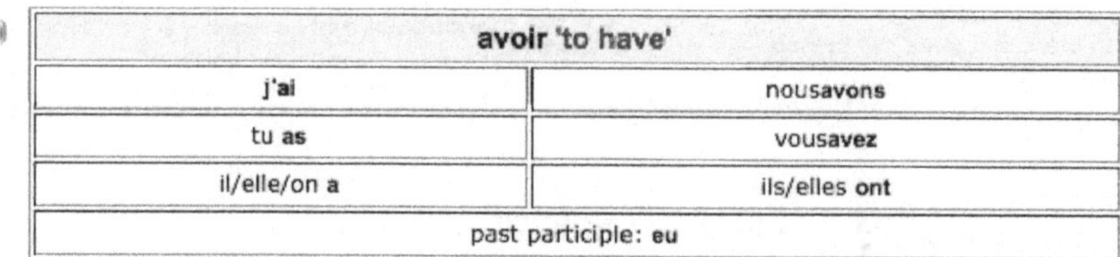

avoir 'to have'	
j'**ai**	nous**avons**
tu **as**	vous**avez**
il/elle/on **a**	ils/elles **ont**
past participle: **eu**	

Avoir is also used as an auxiliary in compound tenses (passé composé with avoir, plus-que-parfait, futur antérieur, etc.) Besides ownership, the verb **avoir** expresses age in French, unlike the English equivalent, which uses the verb 'to be.'

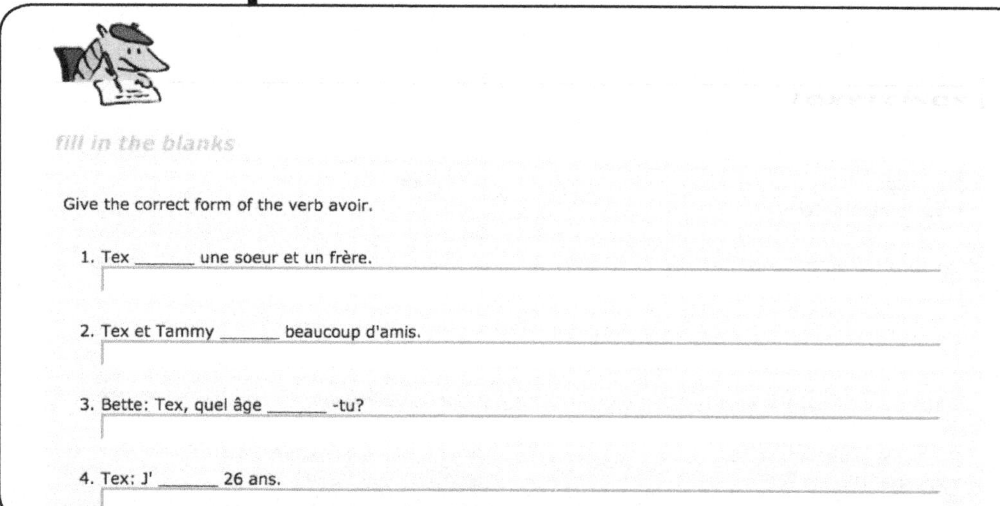

fill in the blanks

Give the correct form of the verb avoir.

1. Tex _______ une soeur et un frère.
2. Tex et Tammy _______ beaucoup d'amis.
3. Bette: Tex, quel âge _______ -tu?
4. Tex: J' _______ 26 ans.

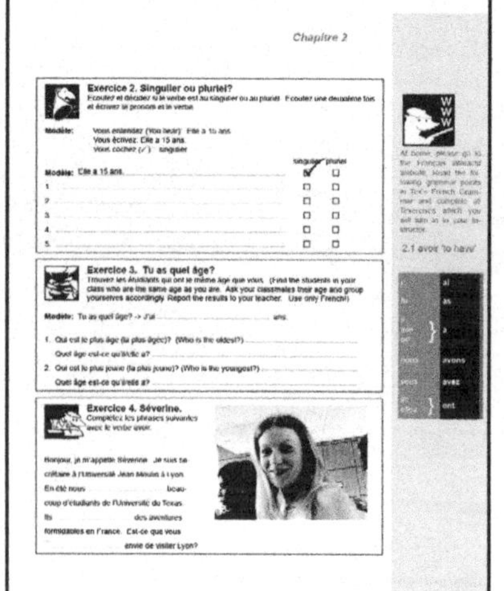

2.1 avoir 'to have'

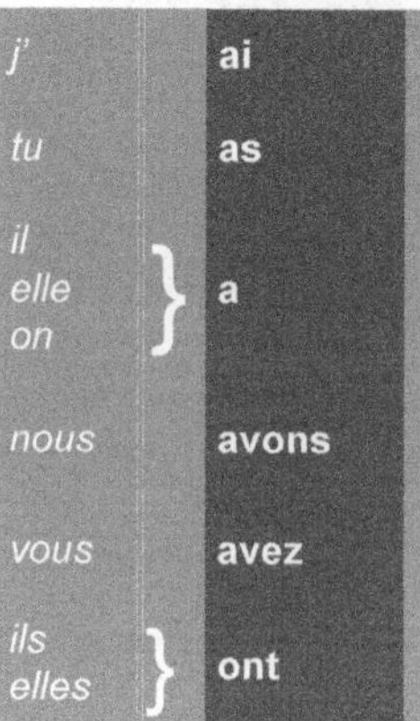

j'	ai
tu	as
il / *elle* / *on*	a
nous	avons
vous	avez
ils / *elles*	ont

Entering accented characters

Windows PC

Method 1: *Alt + key sequence*

Make sure the *Num Lock* key is down. Hold down the *Alt* key while entering a number sequence on the keypad. Release the *Alt* key: you should see the accented character.

Number sequences for specific characters are listed in the character table below.

Method 2: Windows *Character Map* tool

Use the Windows *Character Map* tool – a small pop-up accessory that allows you to copy and paste special characters into any application (such as a web browser). On your Windows PC, access

Start Menu > Programs > Accesories > System Tools > Character Map

Click on and copy the character you need from the *Character Map* tool. Then, click back in the browser form field and paste the character (ctrl-v or 'Paste' via browser menu selection).

Apple Macintosh

Method: *option + key* [+ *key*]

Hold down the *option* key while entering the first letter of a sequence (e.g., **option `** or **option e**).

Release the option key and enter the second character of the sequence (e.g., **a**, **e**, **i**, **n**, **o**, or **u**): you should see the accented character.

Exceptions: A few special characters (**ç**, **ß**, **¡**) are produced by simply entering *option + key*. The **¿** character is produced by simultaneously entering 'opt shift ?'

Character Table

character	Macintosh	PC	character	Macintosh	PC
à	*opt* ` + a	*alt* + 0224	**ñ**	*opt n* + n	*alt* + 0241
á	*opt e* + a	*alt* + 0225	**ò**	*opt* ` + o	*alt* + 0242
â	*opt i* + a	*alt* + 0226	**ó**	*opt* e + o	*alt* + 0243
ä	*opt u* + a	*alt* + 0228	**ô**	*opt i* + o	*alt* + 0244
ç	*opt c*	*alt* + 0231	**ö**	*opt u* + o	*alt* + 0245
è	*opt* ` + e	*alt* + 0232	**ß**	*opt* + s	*alt* + 0223
é	*opt e* + e	*alt* + 0233	**ù**	*opt* ` + u	*alt* + 0249
ê	*opt i* + e	*alt* + 0234	**ú**	*opt e* + u	*alt* + 0250
ë	*opt u* + e	*alt* + 0235	**û**	*opt i* + u	*alt* + 0251
ì	*opt* ` + i	*alt* + 0236	**ü**	*opt u* + u	*alt* + 0252
í	*opt e* + i	*alt* + 0237	**¡**	*opt 1*	*alt* + 0161
î	*opt i* + i	*alt* + 0238	**¿**	*opt shift ?*	*alt* + 0191

Vocabulaire

·je me présente
·les matières
·l'alphabet
·la grammaire de Tex: les animaux

Phonétique

·l'alphabet

Grammaire

·Tex's French Grammar overview
·Tex's characters

Vidéos

Vocabulaire en contexte

·les étudiants de l'Université du Texas

Culture

·impressions de la France

Bienvenue!

We will explore the French language and culture by following the lives of real students from the University of Texas who have participated in the UT Summer Program in Lyon, France. In addition to following the exploits of these UT students, we will also watch interviews of native French speakers, as well as scenes of day-to-day interactions in France.

Watch the introductory video to **Français Interactif**. Where are the UT students? As you can see from this video, **Français Interactif** will help you explore the French language and culture by following the lives of real UT students who participated in the UT Summer Program in Lyon, France. The UT students will introduce you to their French host families, their French university, and their lives in France. Keep in mind as you watch these students that they were in your position only a year ago--enrolled in beginning French! This program shows you that it IS possible to learn French well enough to communicate with native speakers.

In addition to following the exploits of these UT students, you will also watch videos of native French speakers as well as scenes of day-to-day interactions (e.g., vendors in the market, waiters at a café, children getting ready to go to school, etc.). A bilingual family in Austin will bridge the gap between UT and France and French-speaking critters will help you learn with **Tex's French Grammar**. Bienvenue! We hope you will enjoy studying French with **Français Interactif**.

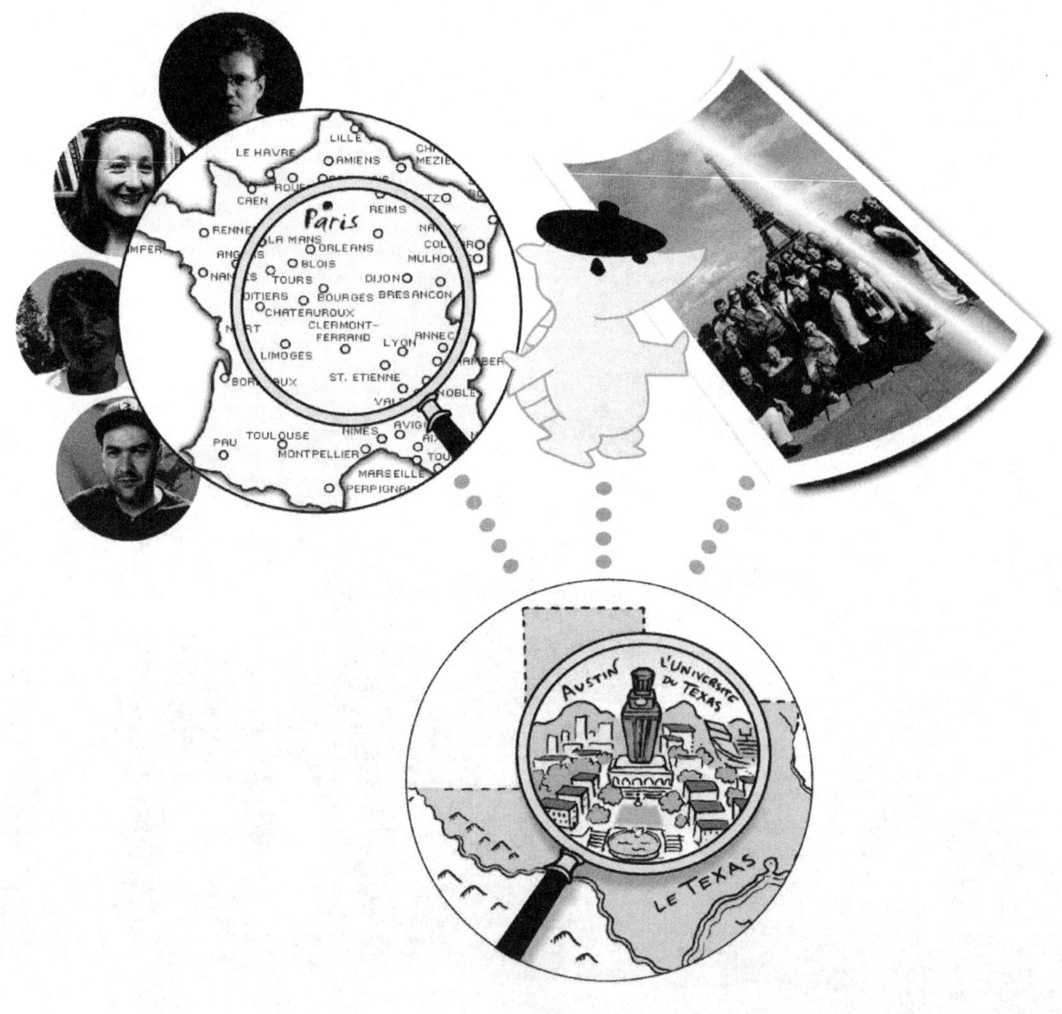

Vocabulaire

Je me présente.	Let me introduce myself.
Je m'appelle...	My name is ...
Je suis de ...	I am from ...
Je suis étudiant en... (français, maths, etc.)	I am a student (male) in...(French, math, etc.)
Je suis étudiante en...(français, maths, etc.)	I am a student (female) in...(French, math, etc.)
Il/Elle s'appelle...	His/Her name is...
Il/Elle est de...	He/She is from...
Il est étudiant en... (français, maths, etc.)	He is a student (m) in...(French, math, etc.)
Elle est étudiante en...(français, maths, etc.)	She is a student (f) in...(French, math, etc.)

Les matières	Subjects
le commerce	business
la comptabilité	accounting
les langues (f)	languages
l'anglais (m)	English
le français	French
l'espagnol (m)	Spanish
la littérature	literature
l'histoire (f)	history
la géographie	geography
les sciences politiques (f)	political science
les mathématiques/les maths (f)	math
les sciences (f)	sciences
la biologie	biology
la chimie	chemistry
l'informatique (f)	computer science
la musique	music
la philosophie	philosophy
la psychologie	psychology

Grammaire de Tex: Les animaux	Tex's French Grammar: Animals
le cafard	cockroach
le chat / la chatte / la minette	cat / female cat / kitty
l'écureuil (m)	squirrel
l'escargot (m)	snail
la fourmi	ant
le tatou	armadillo

Préparation du vocabulaire

Be sure to download the pdf vocabulary preparation template from the FI website to complete Exercises B, E, and F.

! Your instructor will collect this homework.

Phonétique

Go to the website for a complete explanation and practice exercises.

Exercice 1. Je me présente

A. Complete the following sentences.

Je me présente. Je m'appelle______________________________ .
Je suis de ______________________________ . (ville)
Je suis étudiant(e) en ______________________________ . (matière)

B. Introduce yourself to two of your classmates using the sentences above and listen as two of your classmates introduce themselves to you. Complete the following sentences according to the information they tell you.

Il/Elle s'appelle______________________________ .
Il/Elle est de______________________________ .
Il/Elle est étudiant(e) en______________________________ .

Il/Elle s'appelle______________________________ .
Il/Elle est de______________________________ .
Il/Elle est étudiant(e) en______________________________ .

C. Introduce one of your classmates to the class.

Modèle: Je vous présente Robert. Il est de Fort Worth. Il est étudiant en maths.

1 Bonjour!

In this chapter we will learn to introduce ourselves. We will also learn useful vocabulary and phrases pertaining to the classroom.

Vocabulaire

- salutations
- présentations
- la salle de classe
- en classe
- les nombres cardinaux 1-69
- la date

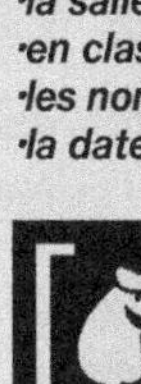

Phonétique

- les accents

Grammaire

- 1.1 subject pronouns
- 1.2 être 'to be'
- 1.3 introduction to nouns
- 1.4 determiners: definite articles
- 1.5 determiners: indefinite articles
- 1.6 gender: masculine, feminine
- 1.7 voilà vs. il y a

- testez-vous!, chapitre 01
- verb conjugation reference
- verb practice

Vidéos

Vocabulaire en contexte

- bienvenue à Lyon
- la salle de classe
- 1 à 10
- les jours de la semaine
- le calendrier
- les anniversaires

Interviews

- je me présente
- qui est-ce?

Culture

- je m'appelle

Vocabulaire

Préparation du vocabulaire

Be sure to download the pdf vocabulary preparation template from the FI website to complete Exercises B, E, and F.

! Your instructor will collect this homework.

Salutations	**Greetings**
Monsieur	Sir
Madame	Ma'am (Mrs.)
Mademoiselle	Miss
Bonjour, Monsieur	Good day (Hello), Sir
Bonsoir	Good evening
Au revoir	Goodbye
Salut!	Hi!
À tout à l'heure!	See you in a little while. (same day)
À ce soir.	See you this evening.
À demain.	See you tomorrow.
À bientôt.	See you soon. (probably not on the same day)
Comment vous appelez-vous?	What's your name? (formal)
Comment tu t'appelles?	What's your name? (informal)
(Comment t'appelles-tu?)	
Je m'appelle...	My name is...
Comment allez-vous?	How are you? (formal)
Comment vas-tu?	How are you? (informal)
Je vais très bien, merci.	I am very well, thank you.
Je vais bien, merci.	I am fine, thank you.
Pas mal, merci.	Not bad, thank you.
Bien, merci!	Great, thanks!
Comment ça va?	How are things going?
Ça va (bien)?	Are things going (well)?
Ça va bien.	Things are going well.
Et vous? Vous êtes d'où?	And you? Where are you from? (formal)
Et toi? Tu es d'où?	And you? Where are you from? (informal)

Présentations	**Introductions**
Monsieur, je vous présente...	Sir, I would like to introduce to you... (formal)
Je te présente...	I would like to introduce to you.... (informal)
Voici...	This is...
Qui est-ce?	Who is it?
C'est...	It's...
Ce sont...	They are...
Comment s'appelle-t-il/elle?	What's his/her name?
Il/Elle s'appelle...	His/Her name is...
Il/Elle est de...	He/She is from...
Comment s'appellent-ils/elles?	What are their names?
Ils/Elles s'appellent...	Their names are...

Vocabulaire

Qu'est-ce qu'il/elle fait?	What does he/she do?
Qu'est-ce qu'ils/elles font?	What do they do?
Il est... Elle est...	He/She is a/an...
acteur / actrice	actor / actress
architecte	architect
chanteur / chanteuse	singer
coiffeur / coiffeuse	hair dresser
dentiste	dentist
ingénieur	engineer
journaliste	journalist
médecin	doctor
professeur	teacher, professor
retraité / retraitée	retired man/woman
stagiaire	intern

La salle de classe	**The classroom**
Qu'est-ce que c'est?	What is it?
C'est...	It's...
C'est une salle de classe.	It's a classroom.
Dans la salle de classe, il y a...	In the classroom, there is...
une porte	door
une fenêtre	window
un tableau (noir)	blackboard
une télévision	television
une carte (du monde)	map (of the world)
une affiche	poster
une chaise	chair
un bureau	desk
Sur le bureau, il y a...	On the desk, there is...
une craie	chalk
un crayon	pencil
un stylo	pen
un cahier	notebook'
un livre	book
un dictionnaire	dictionary
un sac à dos	backpack
Au labo, il y a...	In the lab, there are...
des ordinateurs (m)	computers
Les étudiants travaillent!	The students work!
des devoirs (m)	homework
un exercice	exercise
un examen	test

Les nombres cardinaux 1-69

1	un, une
2	deux
3	trois
4	quatre
5	cinq
6	six
7	sept
8	huit
9	neuf
10	dix
11	onze
12	douze
13	treize
14	quatorze
15	quinze
16	seize
17	dix-sept
18	dix-huit
19	dix-neuf
20	vingt
21	vingt et un
22	vingt-deux
23	vingt-trois
24	vingt-quatre
25	vingt-cinq
26	vingt-six
27	vingt-sept
28	vingt-huit
29	vingt-neuf
30	trente
31	trente et un
32	trente-deux
39	trente-neuf
40	quarante
41	quarante et un
42	quarante-deux
49	quarante-neuf
50	cinquante
51	cinquante et un
52	cinquante-deux
59	cinquante-neuf
60	soixante
61	soixante et un
62	soixante-deux
69	soixante-neuf

Vocabulaire

En classe	**In class**
Écoutez.	Listen.
Écrivez.	Write.
Levez le doigt.	Raise your finger (hand).
Répétez.	Repeat.
Ouvrez vos livres.	Open your books.
Ouvrez le livre à la page...	Turn to page...
s'il vous plaît	please
Vous comprenez?	Do you understand?
Oui, je comprends.	Yes, I understand.
Non, je ne comprends pas.	No, I don't understand.
Que veut dire...?	What does... mean?
Comment dit-on ...?	How do you say...?
Voici...	Here is ... (here are...)
Voilà...	There is... (there are...)
Il y a...	There is, there are...
Il y a combien de...?	There are how many...?

! Note that days of the week are not capitalized in French!

La date	**The date**
le calendrier	calendar
le jour	day
Quels sont les jours de la semaine?	What are the days of the week?
lundi	Monday
mardi	Tuesday
mercredi	Wednesday
jeudi	Thursday
vendredi	Friday
samedi	Saturday
dimanche	Sunday
C'est quel jour?	What day is it?
C'est lundi.	It's Monday.
aujourd'hui	today
demain	tomorrow
la semaine	week
la semaine prochaine	next week
la semaine dernière	last week
Quelle est la date?	What's the date?
C'est le premier septembre.	It's September 1st.
C'est le deux octobre.	It's October 2nd.
C'est le 30 août.	It's August 30th.

Vocabulaire

le mois	month
Quels sont les mois de l'année?	What are the months of the year?
janvier (not capitalized in French)	January
février	February
mars	March
avril	April
mai	May
juin	June
juillet	July
août	August
septembre	September
octobre	October
novembre	November
décembre	December

! Note that months of the year are not capitalized in French!

Phonétique

Go to the website for a complete explanation and practice exercises.

Introduction

Regardons la video ensemble pour répondre aux questions suivantes: Qui présente le chapitre? Où est-il/elle? Quels sont les thèmes du chapitre?

NOTE CULTURELLE

'Tu' ou 'Vous'? Forms of address

When introducing oneself for the first time, does one use the informal French pronoun 'tu' or the formal 'vous'? In general, 'tu' is used with friends, family, and children. 'Vous' is used to express politeness, formality, and social distance. 'Vous' is the form of address used for all formal situations.

Exercice 1. Salutations polies

Using the dialogue suggestions below, greet three students formally. Tell them your name, ask about theirs and ask them how they are doing. Say good-bye.

Bonjour, (Monsieur, Madame, Mademoiselle)
Je m'appelle ________________________
Et vous, comment vous appelez-vous?

Moi, je m'appelle ____________________

Comment allez-vous?

Je vais très bien (bien / pas mal / mal), merci.

Et vous?

________________________________, merci.

Au revoir, (Monsieur/ Madame/ Mademoiselle)

Exercice 2. Salutations familières

Using the informal dialogue suggestions below, greet two students that you haven't talked to yet. Tell them your name, ask about theirs and ask them how they are doing. Tell them you will see them soon.

Salut, je m'appelle ____________________

Et toi, comment t'appelles-tu?

Moi, je m'appelle ______________________

Comment vas-tu? (Comment ça va?)

Je vais (très bien / pas mal / mal). Et toi?

Je vais (très bien / pas mal / mal), merci.

____

Exercice 3. Répondez!

Would you be prepared to greet your host family in Lyon? Give logical responses to the following greetings or farewells. Be prepared to go over these in class.

1. Bonjour, Mademoiselle. ____________________________________
2. Au revoir, Monsieur. ____________________________________
3. Comment allez-vous? ____________________________________
4. Salut. ____________________________________
5. Ça va? ____________________________________
6. A demain! ____________________________________

Exercice 4. Salut!

In this photo Toño is meeting his host family in Lyon for the first time. As homework, write a brief dialogue of 6 sentences to imagine the conversation. In class, your instructor will ask you to act out your dialogue with a partner.

(Use a blank sheet of paper)

Exercice 5. Ça s'écrit comment?

Introduce yourself to a classmate who will ask you to spell your last name. Write down each other's last names.

Modèle:

Salut, je m'appelle Laila Kiblawi.

Kiblawi, **ça s'écrit comment?**

K-I-B-L-A-W-I Et toi, comment tu t'appelles?

Je m'appelle Blake Dublin.

Dublin, **ça s'écrit comment?**

D-U-B-L-I-N

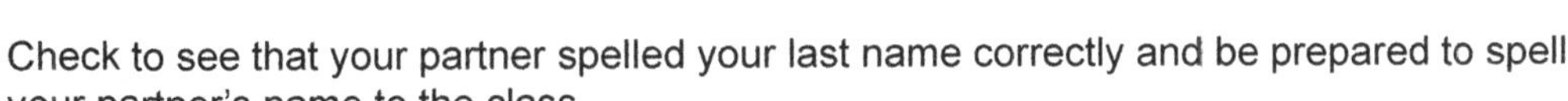

Check to see that your partner spelled your last name correctly and be prepared to spell your partner's name to the class.

Exercice 6. Grammaire interactive.

A. Do you remember how to spell the following subjects? Take turns asking your partner to spell the subjects below.

English:	l'____________________
Business:	le ____________________
History:	l'____________________
Languages:	les ____________________
Computer science:	l'____________________
Accounting:	la ____________________

B. **le**, **la**, **les** and l' are called definite articles.
What is the English equivalent? Do you use it before nouns referring to school subjects in English?

Give the gender of each noun in Exercice A.
Modèle: les maths = feminine
(If you don't remember a gender, refer back to the vocabulary list in Chapitre Préliminaire.)

Fill in the blanks:
Before a **plural** noun , the form of the definite article is: _____
Before a **singular** noun starting **with a vowel or a mute "h"**, the form of the definite article is: _____ (regardless of whether the noun is masculine or feminine)
Before a **singular masculine** noun starting with a **consonant**, the form of the definite article is: ___
Before a **singular feminine** noun starting with a **consonant**, the form of the definite article is: ____

NOTE CULTURELLE

Faire connaissance
Getting to know someone

In France, friends and family members exchange kisses on alternating cheeks to say hello and goodbye. This action is expressed by the French phrase 'faire la bise'. While the number of kisses exchanged varies by region, the most common practice is two kisses, one on each cheek, although it is not uncommon to exchange three or even four.

In an informal situation, young adults will most often 'faire la bise'. Older adults or men would normally shake hands. In a formal situtation, it is necessary to shake hands with everyone. A 'bise' is always given to children.

Contrary to the hug in the United States, kisses are exchanged with friends and family members that one sees everyday. In France, hugging is reserved for more intimate (romantic) relationships.

At home, please go to the Français interactif website. Read the following grammar points in Tex's French Grammar and complete all Texercises which you will turn in to your instructor.

1.1 subject pronouns

je	*nous*
tu	*vous*
il *elle* *on*	*ils* *elles*

1.2 être 'to be'

je	**suis**
tu	**es**
il *elle* *on* }	**est**
nous	**sommes**
vous	**êtes**
ils *elles* }	**sont**

Exercice 7. Singulier ou pluriel?

Listen and decide if the following sentences are singular or plural. Listen again and write the sentence.

	singulier	pluriel
Modèle: Ils sont étudiants. You check:	❑	√
1. ______________________	❑	❑
2. ______________________	❑	❑
3. ______________________	❑	❑
4. ______________________	❑	❑
5. ______________________	❑	❑
6. ______________________	❑	❑

Exercice 8. Vrai ou faux?

Are the following sentences true or false? In groups of three, one student will read the following statements, and the other two will react. Afterwards, your group will report your answers to the class.

	Vrai	Faux
1. Toi, tu es de Beaumont et toi, tu es de San Antonio.	❑	❑
2. Le professeur de français est de Paris.	❑	❑
3. Vous êtes à l'université du Texas.	❑	❑
4. Virginie est architecte.	❑	❑
5. Nous sommes étudiants.	❑	❑
6. Jean-Charles est ingénieur.	❑	❑
7. Stéphanie et Laila sont professeurs.	❑	❑
8. Toi, tu es chanteur (chanteuse) et toi, tu es acteur (actrice).	❑	❑

Exercice 9. Tu es d'où?

Find students in your class who are from the same city as you. Ask your classmates where they are from and group yourselves according to city. Use only French!

Modèle: Tu es d'où? -> Je suis de Dallas. Et toi? -> Moi aussi! Je suis de Dallas.

Il y a combien d'étudiants de chaque ville (each city)? Il y a combien d'étudiants du Texas? Ecrivez les résultats au tableau.

Exercice 10. Bonjour!

This photo was taken at a reception for UT students at the University of Lyon. Who are the people in the photograph? To find out, complete the following paragraph with the appropriate form of the verb être. You will go over this in class.

Bonjour! Je m'appelle Marylène et voici Carl et Marie-Christine. Nous ________________ professeurs. Je ________________ de Lyon et Marie-Christine ______________ de la Réunion. Et vous? Vous ____________ d'où?

Exercice 11. Présentations

Answer the following questions according to the photos below. If you aren't sure, ask a classmate (en français, bien sûr!). Write out the answer in a complete sentence.

Qui est-ce?	Il/elle est d'où? Ils/elles sont d'où?	Qu'est-ce qu'il/elle fait? Qu'est-ce qu'ils font?

Devoirs: Bring a photo of a famous person to class and be prepared to answer questions from your classmates about them (who they are, where they are from, what they do for a living).

! ... there is NO article in French in the sentences above with professions.

At home, please go to the Français interactif website. Read the following grammar points in Tex's French Grammar and complete all Texercises which you will turn in to your instructor.

1.3 gender: masculine, feminine

Joe Bob...	est étudiant.
Tammy...	est étudiante

1.4 introduction to nouns

1.5 determiners: definite articles: forms

masc. sing.:	le (l')
fem. sing.:	la (l')
pl.:	les

1.6 determiners: indefinite articles: forms

masc. sing.:	un
fem. sing.:	une
pl.:	des

Exercice 12. Masculin ou féminin ?

Listen and decide if the following words are masculine or feminine.

	masculin	féminin
Modèle: You hear: ***le livre.***	√	❑
1.	❑	❑
2.	❑	❑
3.	❑	❑
4.	❑	❑
5.	❑	❑
6.	❑	❑
7.	❑	❑
8.	❑	❑

Exercice 13. Singulier ou pluriel?

Listen and decide if the following words are singular or plural.

	singulier	pluriel
Modèle: You hear: ***la porte.***	√	❑
1.	❑	❑
2.	❑	❑
3.	❑	❑
4.	❑	❑
5.	❑	❑
6.	❑	❑
7.	❑	❑
8.	❑	❑

Exercice 14. La salle de classe de Mme Meunier.

Complete the following paragraph with the appropriate definite article: le, la, or les. Be prepared to go over these in class.

Voici ____ tableau dans ____ salle de classe de Mme Meunier , ____ professeur. Voilà ____ bureau et ____ chaise de Mme Meunier. Et voici ____ livres et ____ stylos de ses (her) étudiants.

Exercice 15. Grammaire interactive.

Look at the underlined element:

un bureau	**une** carte	**une** chaise
une affiche	**un** ordinateur	**un** tableau

How would you translate the underlined elements in English?
What do you think the difference between **"un"** and **"une"** is related to?

Fill in the blanks:
un is used when the noun is ______________________________
une is used when the noun is ______________________________

Look at the following pairs. What is the difference between the words in each pair?

un ordinateur / **des** ordinateurs	**une** affiche / **des** affiches
un cahier / **des** cahiers	**une** chaise / **des** chaises

Fill in the blanks:
des is used when the noun (masculine or feminine) is: ______________________________

Now, compare the two sentences:
Il y a des ordinateurs dans le bureau. / **There are computers** in the office.
What do you notice about the bolded sections in these two sentences?

Exercice 16. Masculin ou féminin ?

Listen and decide if the following words are masculine or feminine.

	masculin	féminin
Modèle: You hear: ***une porte.***	❑	√
1.	❑	❑
2.	❑	❑
3.	❑	❑
4.	❑	❑
5.	❑	❑
6.	❑	❑
7.	❑	❑
8.	❑	❑

Exercice 17. Singulier ou pluriel?

Listen and decide if the following words are singular or plural.

	singulier	pluriel
Modèle: You hear: ***des cahiers.***	❑	√
1.	❑	❑
2.	❑	❑
3.	❑	❑
4.	❑	❑
5.	❑	❑
6.	❑	❑
7.	❑	❑
8.	❑	❑

Exercice 18. Qu'est-ce que c'est?

Complete the following paragraph with the appropriate indefinite article: un, une, or des. Be prepared to go over these in class.

Ça, c'est ______ cahier et ça, c'est ______ stylo. Voici ______ livres et ______ crayons. Dans la salle de classe il y a ______ tableau noir, ______chaises et ______ télévision.

Exercice 19. Grammaire interactive.

In Exercice 18, look at "voici" and "il y a".
How would you translate these two phrases into English?

Exercice 20. Ouvrez vos livres, s'il vous plaît!

Listen as your teacher reads a dialogue between Mme Meunier at Lyon 3 and students in the Lyon program. Working in groups of two or three, reconstruct the text with as many details as possible.

Chut! ______________________________ vos livres
______________________________.
Quelle page, Madame?
Ah... ______________________________ bien, Léonard!
Et ______________________________.
A la page 12, le premier dialogue. ____________________ le dialogue?
______________________________ "stagiaire"?
"Stagiaire" ______________________________ "intern."

Exercice 21. En classe.

How would you say the following in French? Translate the following sentences.

1. What's your name? (asking a classmate) ____________________
2. How do you say 'armadillo'? ____________________
3. I don't understand. ____________________
4. Please repeat. ____________________
5. Here is a book. ____________________
6. There are how many computers? ____________________
7. What does 'chef d'entreprise' mean? ____________________
8. See you in a little while! (later today) ____________________

Exercice 22. Une salle de classe à Lyon!

A. Name at least six objects / people in the classroom at Lyon 3 below. Remember to add the appropriate indefinite article: un, une, or des.

Il y a ......

1. ______________________
2. ______________________
3. ______________________
4. ______________________
5. ______________________
6. ______________________

B. Compare the classroom above to your classroom. How many of the same objects/people are in your French classroom? Make a list of items in your classroom with a partner. Compare your lists with those of your classmates.

Exercice 23. Ecrivez en toutes lettres!

Write out the following numbers. Be prepared for a possible quiz.

47 ______________________

16 ______________________

25 ______________________

61 ______________________

52 ______________________

39 ______________________

12 ______________________

8 ______________________

Exercice 24. Calculez!

Write out the following arithmetic problems. Be prepared for a possible quiz.
+ plus / - moins / = égal

10 + 9 = ______________________

18 + 7 = ______________________

29 + 4 = ______________________

45 + 19 = ______________________

16 - 5 = ______________________

57 - 6 = ______________________

36 + 13 = ______________________

34 - 7 = ______________________

Exercice 25. Les numéros de téléphone.

Listen as your teacher gives the addresses and telephone numbers for the UT students in Lyon and complete the table below.

	Adresse	Numéro de téléphone
Laila	_____ quai Jean-Jacques Rousseau	__ __ __ __ __
Blake	_____ rue M. Dutarte	__ __ __ __ __
Karen	_____ rue Chambonnet	__ __ __ __ __

Exercice 26. Comment dit-on?

How would you say the following in French? Translate the following sentences. Be prepared to go over these in class.

1. Here's the classroom. ______________________
2. There are twenty-one students. ______________________
3. What is it? It's a poster. ______________________
4. Who is that? It's Mrs. Meunier. She's a professor. ______________________

____

Exercice 27. Quelle est la date?

Write out the dates of the following French holidays:

1. la Saint-Sylvestre (December 31): ____________________
2. la Saint-Valentin (February 14): ____________________
3. l'Assomption (August 15): ____________________
4. la Toussaint (November 1): ____________________

Exercice 28. Répondez!

Answer the following questions with a partner.

1. On est quel jour aujourd'hui? ____________________
2. Quelle est la date aujourd'hui? ____________________
3. Quelle est la date de l'examen? ____________________

Exercice 29. C'est quand ton anniversaire?

Find the students in your class who have birthdays in the same month as you. Ask your classmates their birthdays and group yourselves according to the month of your birth. How many students have birthdays in the same month? Does anyone have the same birthday? Report the results to your teacher. Use only French!

Modèle:
C'est quand, ton anniversaire?
C'est le 2 mai.

At home, please go to the Français interactif website. Read the following grammar points in Tex's French Grammar and complete all Texercises which you will turn in to your instructor.

1.7 Voila vs. il y a

Here is *Here are*	**Voila/** **Voici...**
There is *There are*	**Il y a..**

Exercice 30. Paris - Gare de Lyon.

Look at the group train ticket that the Lyon Program used to travel from Paris to Lyon and answer the following questions.

1. Comment s'appelle la gare (train station) à Paris? ______________________
2. Comment s'appelle la gare à Lyon? ______________________
3. Il y a combien de voyageurs? ______________________
4. Quelle est la date du départ? ______________________
5. Quel est le numéro du train? ______________________
   TGV = Train à Grande Vitesse (Bullet train)

2 Me voici!

Me voici! In this chapter we will talk about ourselves, our families, our pastimes, and nationalities. We will also learn how to tell time.

Vocabulaire

- fiche d'identité
- questions personnelles
- la famille
- les amis
- mots interrogatifs
- l'heure
- l'heure officielle
- passe-temps et activités
- adverbes
- continents, pays, nationalités

Phonétique

- les symboles phonétiques
- l'élision
- la liaison

Grammaire

- 2.1 avoir 'to have'
- 2.2 -er verbs
- 2.3 possessive determiners
- 2.4 yes/no questions: est-ce que, n'est-ce pas
- 2.5 basic negation: ne... pas
- 2.6 introduction to adverbs
- 2.7 interrogative and exclamative quel
- 2.8 introduction to adjectives
- 2.9 adjectives: formation and placement

- testez-vous!, chapitre 02
- verb conjugation reference
- verb practice

Vidéos

Vocabulaire en contexte

- Franck Guilloteau - me voici
- Franck Guilloteau - ma famille
- l'heure
- les passe-temps Audrey et Camille
- l'heure
- les continents
- les pays

Interviews

- questions personnelles
- ma famille

Culture

- la voiture de Franck

Vocabulaire

Préparation du vocabulaire

Be sure to download the pdf vocabulary preparation template from the FI website to complete Exercises B, E, and F.

! Your instructor will collect this homework.

Fiche d'identité	**Identification form**
Nom (de famille) (m)	last name
Prénom(s) (m)	first (and middle) name(s)
Age (m)	age
Nationalité (f)	nationality
Résidence actuelle (f)	current address
Profession (f)	profession
Passe-temps préférés (m)	pastimes

Questions personnelles	**Personal questions**
Comment vous appelez-vous?	What is your name?
Quel âge avez-vous?	How old are you?
Quelle est votre nationalité?	What is your nationality?
Vous êtes d'où?	Where are you from?
Où habitez-vous?	Where do you live?
Que faites-vous dans la vie?	What do you do for a living?
Quels sont vos passe-temps préférés?	What are your favorite pastimes?

La famille	**The family**
un homme	man
une femme	woman, wife
un mari	husband
un fiancé / une fiancée	fiancé / fiancée
des parents (m)	parents, relatives
un père	father
une mère	mother
un/une enfant	child
un fils	son
une fille	daughter
un fils unique	only child (male)
une fille unique	only child (female)
un frère	brother
une soeur	sister
des grands-parents (m)	grandparents
un grand-père	grandfather
une grand-mère	grandmother
un petit-enfant	grandchild
un oncle	uncle
une tante	aunt
un neveu	nephew
une nièce	niece

Vocabulaire

L'heure

Les amis	**Friends**
un ami / une amie	friend
un/une camarade	friend
un copain / une copine	friend; boyfriend / girlfriend

Mots interrogatifs	**Interrogative words**
où?	where?
quand?	when?
qui?	who?
comment?	how?
quel / quelle / quels / quelles	which?
pourquoi?	why?
parce que (+ clause)	because
à cause de (+ noun)	because of

L'heure	**Time**
l'heure (f)	the time
Quelle heure est-il?	What time is it?
Il est huit heures.	It's 8 o'clock.
Il est huit heures dix.	It's ten after 8.
Il est huit heures et quart.	It's quarter after 8.
Il est huit heures vingt-cinq.	It's twenty-five after 8.
Il est huit heures et demie.	It's eight-thirty.
Il est neuf heures moins vingt.	It's twenty to nine.
Il est neuf heures moins le quart.	It's quarter to nine.
Il est midi.	It's noon.
Il est midi et demi.	It's twelve-thirty.
Il est minuit.	It's midnight.
Il est trois heures...	It's three o'clock...
du matin	in the morning (3 a.m.)
de l'après-midi	in the afternoon (3 p.m.)
Il est sept heures....	It's seven o'clock..
du soir	in the evening (7 p.m.)

L'heure officielle	**Official time**
Il est 10h.	It's 10 a.m.
Il est 12h05.	It's 12:05 p.m.
Il est 13h15.	It's 1:15 p.m.
Il est 15h35.	It's 3:35 p.m.
Il est 18h45.	It's 6:45 p.m.
Il est 22h59.	It's 10:59 p.m.

Vocabulaire

! irregular verbs: Refer to Tex's French Grammar: 'lire, dire, écrire' for conjugation.

Chapitre 2

Passe-temps et activités	Pastimes and activities
avoir	to have
avoir besoin de...	to need
avoir envie de...	to feel like (to want to)
avoir l'intention de...	to intend (to)
chercher	to look for
trouver	to find
(Qui cherche, trouve!)	(Who looks for (searches), finds!)
tomber amoureux (de) /amoureuse (de)	to fall in love
embrasser	to kiss
écouter...	to listen to...
de la musique	music
la radio	the radio
chanter	to sing
danser	to dance
aimer	to like, to love
la musique classique / le jazz /	classical music / jazz /
le hip-hop / la techno /	hip-hop / techno /
le sport / le tennis / le football /	sports / tennis / soccer /
le basket / le golf / le footing	basketball / golf / running
préférer	to prefer
adorer	to adore
détester	to detest
habiter	to live
rester à la maison	to stay at home
étudier	to study
lire	to read
oublier	to forget
regarder la télévision	to watch television
téléphoner à	to telephone
parler	to speak
jouer...	to play...
à (+ a sport):	a sport:
au foot / au tennis / aux cartes (f)	soccer / tennis / cards
de (+ an instrument):	an instrument
de la guitare / du piano	guitar / piano
nager	to swim
rencontrer	to meet
rêver	to dream
travailler	to work
voyager	to travel

Vocabulaire

Adverbes	Adverbs
aussi	also
maintenant	now
plus tard	later
beaucoup	a lot
peu / un peu	little / a little
rarement	rarely
parfois	at times
quelquefois	sometimes
souvent	often
toujours	always
ne...jamais	never

Continents Pays / Nationalités	Continents Countries / Nationalities
un continent	continent
un pays	country
l'Afrique (f) / africain(e)	Africa / African
l'Algérie (f) / algérien(ne)	Algeria / Algerian
le Maroc / marocain(e)	Morocco / Moroccan
le Sénégal / sénégalais(e)	Senegal / Senegalese
la Tunisie / tunisien(ne)	Tunisia / Tunisian
l'Amérique du Nord (f)	North America
le Canada / canadien(ne)	Canada / Canadian
les Etats-Unis (m) / américain(e)	United States / American
le Mexique / mexicain(e)	Mexico / Mexican
l'Amérique du Sud (f)	South America
la Guyane française / guyanais(e)	French Guyana / Guyanese
l'Asie (f) / asiatique	Asia / Asian
la Chine / chinois(e)	China / Chinese
le Japon / japonais(e)	Japan / Japanese
le Vietnam / vietnamien(ne)	Vietnam / Vietnamese
l'Océanie (f)	Oceania (the South Sea Islands)
l'Australie (f) / australien(ne)	Australia / Australian
l'Europe (f) / européen(ne)	Europe / European
l'Allemagne (f) / allemand(e)	Germany / German
l'Angleterre (f) / anglais(e)	England / English
la Belgique / belge	Belgium / Belgian
l'Espagne (f) / espagnol(e)	Spain / Spanish
la France / français(e)	France / French
l'Italie (f) / italien(ne)	Italy / Italian
la Suisse / suisse	Switzerland / Swiss

! Refer to Tex's French Grammar: 'Negation – Alternate forms of negation' for correct formation and use of ne...jamais.

Phonétique

Go to the website for a complete explanation and practice exercises.

Introduction

Watch the introductory video to Chapitre 2 to answer the following questions: Qui présente le chapitre? Où est-il / elle? Quels sont les thèmes du chapitre?

NOTE CULTURELLE

La famille

En français, on utilise les mêmes mots pour parler des "in-laws" et des "step relatives". Par exemple, une belle-mère peut être une "stepmother" ou une "mother-in-law". C'est le contexte qui donne son sens (meaning) au mot. Comprenez-vous le sens de beau-père, belle-soeur ou beau-frère ?!

Exercice 1. La famille Simpson.

Voilà la famille Simpson. Complétez les phrases suivantes avec les mots qui conviennent.

Trademark & Copyright Notice: ™ and ©FOX and its related entities. http://www.fox.com

1. Marge est ______________________________ de Homer.
2. Homer est ______________________________ de Marge.
3. Marge et Homer sont ____________________ de Maggie, Lisa et Bart.
4. Maggie, Lisa et Bart sont ____________________ de Marge et Homer.
5. Lisa et Maggie sont ______________________________ de Bart.
6. Bart est ______________________________ de Maggie et Lisa.
7. Marge est ____________________ de Maggie, Lisa et Bart.
8. Homer est ____________________ de Maggie, Lisa et Bart.
9. Patty et Selma sont ______________ de Maggie, Lisa et Bart. (aunts)
10. Patty et Selma sont ______________________________ de Marge.
11. Patty est ______________________________ de Homer.
12. Abe est ____________________ de Maggie, Lisa et Bart.
13. Bart est ______________________________ de Selma et Patty.
14. Lisa est ______________________________ de Selma et Patty.
15. Maggie et Lisa sont ______________________________ d'Abe.
16. Maggie, Lisa et Bart sont ______________________________ d'Abe.

Exercice 2. Singulier ou pluriel?

Ecoutez et décidez si le verbe est au singulier ou au pluriel. Ecoutez une deuxième fois et écrivez le pronom et le verbe.

	singulier	pluriel
Modèle: Elle a quinze ans.	√	❑
1. ______________________	❑	❑
2. ______________________	❑	❑
3. ______________________	❑	❑
4. ______________________	❑	❑
5. ______________________	❑	❑
6. ______________________	❑	❑

At home, please go to the Français interactif website. Read the following grammar points in Tex's French Grammar and complete all Texercises which you will turn in to your instructor.

2.1 avoir 'to have'

j'	ai
tu	as
il elle on }	a
nous	avons
vous	avez
ils elles }	ont

Exercice 3. Tu as quel âge?

Trouvez les étudiants qui ont le même âge que vous. (Find the students in your class who are the same age as you are. Ask your classmates their age and group yourselves accordingly. Report the results to your teacher. Use only French!)

Modèle: Tu as quel âge? J'ai ______________ ans.

1. Qui est le plus âgé (la plus âgée)? (Who is the oldest?) ______________
   Quel âge est-ce qu'il/elle a? ______________
2. Qui est le plus jeune (la plus jeune)? (Who is the youngest?) ______________
   Quel âge est-ce qu'il/elle a? ______________

Exercice 4. Séverine.

Complétez les phrases suivantes avec le verbe avoir.

Bonjour, je m'appelle Séverine. Je suis secrétaire à l'Université Jean Moulin à Lyon. En été nous ______________ beaucoup d'étudiants de l'Université du Texas. Ils ______________ des aventures formidables en France. Est-ce que vous ______________ envie de visiter Lyon?

At home, please go to the Français interactif website. Read the following grammar points in Tex's French Grammar and complete all Texercises which you will turn in to your instructor.

2.2 –er verbs

danser 'to dance'

je	danse
tu	danses
il / *elle* / *on*	danse
nous	dansons
vous	dansez
ils / *elles*	dansent

Exercice 5. Qu'est-ce qu'ils font?

Trouvez la phrase correcte pour chaque image.

a. Ils regardent la télévision.
b. Ils voyagent.
c. Ils dansent.
d. Il joue du piano.
e. Ils étudient.
f. Ils jouent au tennis.
g. Il chante.
h. Il écoute de la musique.

Exercice 6. Singulier ou pluriel?

Ecoutez et décidez si le verbe est au singulier ou au pluriel. Ecoutez une deuxième fois et écrivez le pronom et le verbe.

	singulier	pluriel	impossible à distinguer
Modèle: Ils étudient le français.	❑	√	❑
1. ______________________	❑	❑	❑
2. ______________________	❑	❑	❑
3. ______________________	❑	❑	❑
4. ______________________	❑	❑	❑
5. ______________________	❑	❑	❑
6. ______________________	❑	❑	❑

Exercice 7. Les activités de la famille Simpson.

A. Pensez à la famille Simpson. Décidez si les phrases suivantes sont vraies ou fausses.

	Vrai	Faux
1. Homer adore jouer du piano.	❑	❑
2. Bart préfère lire.	❑	❑
3. Homer a toujours envie de manger.	❑	❑
4. Maggie adore jouer au tennis.	❑	❑
5. Marge aime rester à la maison.	❑	❑
6. Homer déteste Monsieur Burns.	❑	❑
7. Bart préfère la musique classique.	❑	❑
8. Lisa aime étudier.	❑	❑
9. Homer adore parler avec Monsieur Flanders.	❑	❑

B. Maintenant, complétez les phrases suivantes avec un des verbes de la liste. (Vous allez utiliser un des verbes deux fois.)

téléphoner jouer regarder embrasser travailler lire

1. Homer adore ______________________ Marge.
2. Bart aime ______________________ au football américain.
3. Homer déteste ______________________ .
4. Bart et Lisa aiment ______________________ à Moe.
5. Lisa adore ______________________ .
6. La famille Simpson ______________________ Itchy et Scratchy à la télé.
7. Lisa aime ______________________ du saxophone.

Exercice 8. Tes passe-temps

Posez des questions à vos camarades de classe.

Est-ce que tu...

1. ..téléphones souvent à tes parents? ______________________
2. ..tombes souvent amoureux/amoureuse? ______________________
3. ..joues au foot? ______________________
4. ..détestes la télévision? ______________________
5. ..aimes étudier? ______________________
6. ..voyages beaucoup? ______________________
7. ..joues du piano? ______________________
8. ..chantes? ______________________
9. .adores le hip-hop? ______________________
10. ..écoutes de la musique classique? ______________________

NOTE CULTURELLE

Les anglicismes préférés des Français

Le français, comme toutes les langues vivantes, emprunte à d'autres (borrows from others) des mots (words) et des expressions. Certains anglicismes (d'origine anglaise): le tunnel, le week-end, la baby-sitter, le parking, le hip-hop, le mail (l'email), bloguer, etc. ont enrichi le vocabulaire français. www.asapfrance.info

- Quels mots anglais sont d'origine française? (Give at least 5 English words of French origin.)
- Quelles villes américaines ont des noms français?
- Combien de personnes dans le monde parlent français? (Guess!)*
- See cultural note 'Le français' in this chapter for answer.

! Parlez uniquement en français! Si la réponse est "OUI",demandez la signature de cette apersonne. Changez de camarade pour chaque question. Ecoutez attentivement les questions qu'on vous pose. Ne répondez pas à des questions incomplètes.

Exercice 9. Quel verbe?

Complétez les phrases avec le verbe logique.

aimer étudier avoir jouer écouter habiter rencontrer voyager

1. Corey ______________________________ envie de rester à la maison.
2. Vous ______________________________ au tennis?
3. Tex et Tammy, ils ______________________________ de la musique.
4. Joe-Bob et Corey ______________________________ au Texas.
5. Nous ______________________________ nos amis au café le week-end.
6. Joe-Bob ____________________ rarement. Il n'est pas un étudiant sérieux.
7. Les étudiants ______________________________ à Lyon.
8. Est-ce que tu ______________________________ danser?.

Exercice 10. Le sport à Lyon.

If you participate in the Lyon program, you will be spending a good amount of time in France and might want to try new pastimes while you're there! This document is from the *Livret d'accueil* de l'étudiant of the Université Jean-Moulin, where you will study in Lyon. The *Livret d'accueil* gives information about the university to new or foreign students. This page describes the sports and activities offered by the university.

Before consulting the Livret d'acceuil, consider the following two questions. Be prepared to discuss these in class.

1. What kinds of sports and activities would you expect an American university to offer? What kinds of facilities might they have?
2. What kind of information would you expect to find on a document intended for new students?

Scan the information on the following page to find answers to the comprehension questions, and then give your answers to the opinion questions. Don't worry if you don't understand every word of the text! Just look for words that you already know and cognates (words that look similar to English or Spanish) to help you!

You may answer in English. We will discuss your responses in class.

Comprehension Questions

1. What outdoor sports/activities are offered? Give at least 2 options.

   ____

2. What individual sports/activities are offered? Give at least 2 options.

   ____

3. Does the University have facilities for sports and activities? Give one example.

   ____

4. What days and times is the Bureau du Service des Sports open? Where could you send an email if you had a question for them?

   ____

5. What off-campus sports and activities are offered through partnerships with other clubs?

   ____

Sport

Initiation - perfectionnement - entraînement - compétition - santé

Parce que l'épanouissement intellectuel passe aussi par une bonne condition physique, commencez l'entraînement dès la rentrée...

Plus de 35 activités sportives

Sportifs débutants ou confirmés, des cours vous seront proposés dans une multitude d'activités : sports aquatiques ou de combats, athlétisme, danses, muscu-fitness, sports de raquettes (tennis, tennis de table, badminton), sports collectifs, activités en plein-air (équitation, golf, escalade...). Vous pourrez également pratiquer ces activités en compétition.

Toute l'année, différentes manifestations vous sont proposées : des stages de danse (Bruno Vandelli, Gianin Loringett), des courses à pied (le marathon de Lyon, les 10 km sport et santé), des sorties de ski, des rando-raids...

Des activités spécifiques sont proposées aux étudiants handicapés : Contactez le Service des Sports

Des infrastructures modernes et de qualité au sein même de l'Université

- **Studio de danse** (modern'jazz, street jazz, danses sportives, gym d'entretien, aérobic, abdo-fessiers).
- **Espace cardio-training fitness** (3 salles entièrement modernisées).
- **Salle de combat** (karaté, judo, boxe française, taekwondo, aikido).
- **Salle de tir** (carabine, pistolet).

À proximité, d'autres installations vous permettront de choisir parmi une grande variété de sports collectifs et des activités comme l'escalade, l'escrime, la natation, le water-polo, le badminton et le tennis.

Grâce à nos partenariats avec des clubs extérieurs, vous pourrez également pratiquer d'autres activités :

- **Golf** (golf de Chassieu)
- **Équitation** (choix parmi 8 grands centres équestres lyonnais)
- **Plongée** (club universitaire « le glup »)
- **Aviron** (avec le club lyonnais l'AUNL)

Plus d'infos et inscriptions

Bureau du Service des Sports

- **Manufacture des Tabacs** Espace rue Sud
- **Horaires** du lundi au vendredi de 9h30 à 16h30
- 04 78 78 78 50
- **sport@univ-lyon3.fr**

Plein-air	**Open-air/ Out-door**
Des cours vous seront proposes	**Courses will be offered**
Au sein	**within**
Parte-nariat	**partner-ship**
Infra-structures	**facilities**
A prox-imité	**nearby**
Du... au...	**From..... to...**

Exercise 10. Discussion Questions

1. What similarities and/or differences do you see between sports and activities at the Université Jean-Moulin and at the University of Texas (or any typical American university)?
2. What sport(s) or activities would you choose to do while you're abroad in Lyon? Why? Please choose at least one pastime that is included on this document.
3. Do you see any benefits or disadvantages to participating in sports/activities when studying abroad? What are they?

Exercice 11. C'est moi.

Complétez les phrases suivantes.

1. **Mon** nom est ______________________ et **mes** prénoms sont ______________.
2. **Ma** nationalité est ____.
3. **Mon** adresse (f) est ____.
4. **Mes** passe-temps préférés sont ____.

Exercice 12. Grammaire interactive.

A. Reliez les équivalents.

Comment tu t'appelles?	• Quelle est ton adresse?
Où habites-tu?	• Quels sont tes prénoms?
Tu es d'où?	• Quelle est ta nationalité?
Tu as des passe-temps préférés?	• Quel est ton nom?
	• Quels sont tes passe-temps préférés?

B. Look at the questions in Exercice A. What does **quel** mean? How can you explain the difference between **quel – quelle – quels - quelles**?

	gender (m/f)	number (s/p)
Quel is used when the noun it refers to is		
Quelle is used when the noun it refers to is		
Quels is used when the noun it refers to is		
Quelles is used when the noun it refers to is		

Exercice 13. Et votre camarade?

Posez des questions à un camarade pour compléter les phrases suivantes.

1. **Son** nom est________________________ et **ses** prénoms sont _________.
2. **Sa** nationalité est ____.
3. **Son** adresse (f) est ____.
4. **Ses** passe-temps préférés sont ___________________________________.

Exercice 14. La famille de Madame Guilloteau.

La famille de Madame Guilloteau est grande. Dans les phrases suivantes elle décrit sa famille. Trouvez les corréspondances entre les deux colonnes.

_____1. Mes nièces étudient à l'université.	a. Elles dansent souvent.
_____2. Ma belle-soeur adore Paris.	b. Ils jouent au football américain.
_____3. Mes cousins aiment les concerts.	c. Elles téléphonent souvent à leurs amies.
_____4. Mes frères adorent le sport.	d. Elle voyage souvent en Europe.
_____5. Mes filles aiment le ballet.	e. Elles oublient leurs devoirs à la maison.
_____6. Mes tantes aiment parler.	f. Il regarde des films.
_____7. Mon mari adore James Bond.	g. Ils écoutent de la musique classique.
_____8. Mon grand-père rencontre rarement ses amis.	h. Il reste à la maison.

At home, please go to the Français interactif website. Read the following grammar points in Tex's French Grammar and complete all Texercises which you will turn in to your instructor.

2.3 possessive determiners

Masc. singular	**mon ton son notre votre leur**
Fem. singular	**ma ta sa notre votre leur**
Plural	**mes tes ses nos vos leurs**

Exercice 15. Votre famille.

Maintenant, pensez à votre famille. Qu'est-ce que les membres de votre famille font ("do")? Complétez les phrases suivantes, et si c'est possible, donnez plusieurs possibilités.

Modèle: Mon cousin étudie tout le temps.

1. Ma mère et mon père ______________________.
2. Mes grands-parents ______________________.
3. Mes amis ______________________.
4. Ma soeur / Mon frère ______________________.
5. Mon oncle ______________________.
6. Ma tante ______________________.

Exercice 16. Mon, ma, mes.

Donnez la forme correcte.

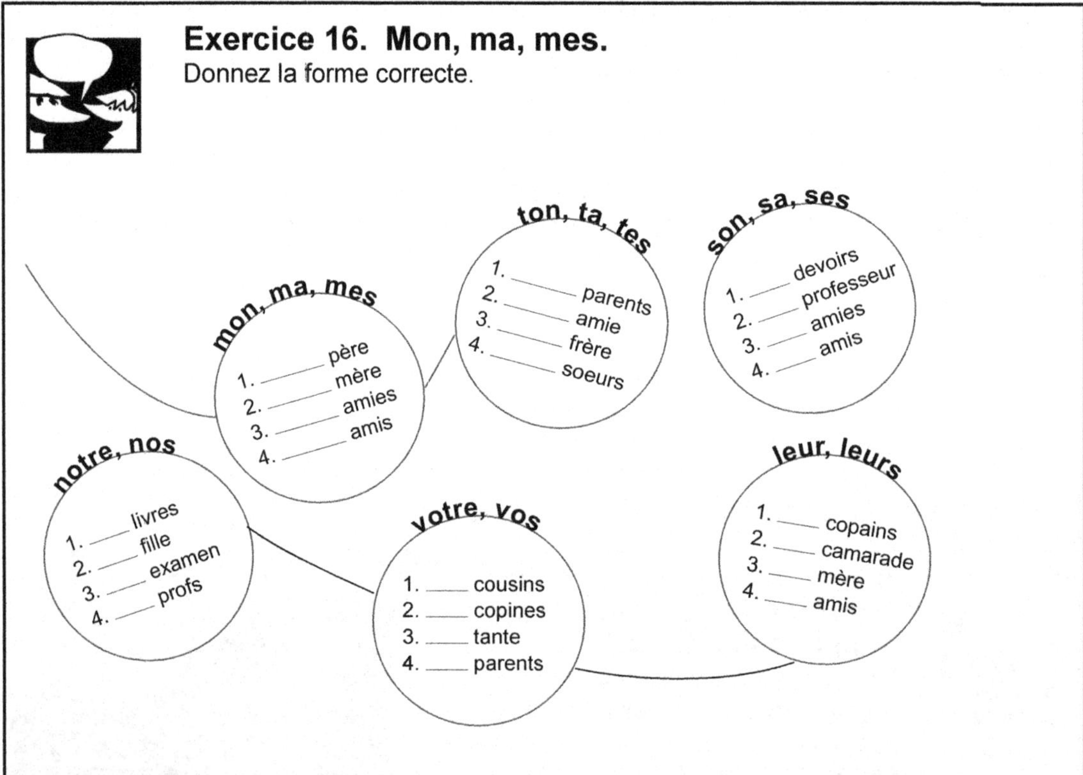

Exercice 17. Comment dit-on?

En bon français, s'il vous plaît....

1. **his** grandmother ______________________.
2. **your** son (tu) ______________________.
3. **their** parents ______________________.
4. **her** brother ______________________.
5. **our** cousins ______________________.
6. **my** aunt ______________________.
7. **his** sisters ______________________.
8. **your** children (vous) ______________________.

Exercice 18. Ma famille.

A. Préparez une description de votre famille.

B. En classe, présentez (oralement) votre famille à un/une partenaire. Après, votre partenaire va dessiner (draw) un arbre généalogique pour représenter votre famille selon votre description. Votre partenaire pose des questions pour verifier l'information, par exemple, "Anne, c'est ta soeur, n'est-ce pas (right?)?" ou "Tu as un frère et une soeur, n'est-ce pas (right?)?" Après, changez de role. Pour finir, vous et votre partenaire vérifiez les arbres généalogiques.

(Prepare a description of your family. Present your description orally to a partner. Your partner will draw a family tree to represent your family according to your description. Your partner will ask questions to verify the information, for example, "Anne is your sister, right?" or "You have one brother and one sister, right?" After, change roles. Finally, you and your partner will check each other's trees for accuracy.)

C. Maintenant, votre professeur va choisir deux ou trois volontaires pour donner leurs descriptions à la classe. Tous les étudiants vont dessiner des arbres généalogiques et posez des questions. Ensuite, les étudiants vont rendre leurs dessins au professeur à la fin de l'exercice.

(Now your professor will choose two or three volunteers to give their descriptions to the class. All students will draw the family trees and ask questions. Students will then turn in their drawings to the instructor at the end of the exercise.)

NOTE CULTURELLE

L'heure officielle

L'heure officielle des Français est l'heure militaire, comme disent les Américains ("military time"). La journée des Français a 24 heures, de minuit (00 am) à 23 heures (11pm). En France, les horaires sont à l'heure officielle dans les gares, les aéroports, les programmes de télévision ou de cinéma. Ainsi, il n'y a pas de confusion: 4 heures (4am) est différent de 16 heures (4pm).

Exercice 19. Quelle heure est-il?
Regardez les photos. Quelle heure est-il?

Il est ______________ Il est ______________ Il est ________________

Dictogloss 1.
Ecoutez et complétez les phrases suivantes. (Listen and take notes as your teacher
reads a dialogue. Working in groups, reconstruct the text with as many details as
possible.)

- Oh non! Pas possible...il est déjà ____________________________ ! Allez vite!
- Mais il est____ ton train?
- Euh...ah! Voilà! le________________ à Paris, il est à ________________pile.
- Mais ___________________, encore _______________. Pas de problème.
- ________________________________ Maman.
- ________________________________ chéri. Bon voyage.

Trains au départ

14:36	LILLE BRUXELLES MIDI TGV		9573
14:48	DIJON VILLE		5510 H
14:48	LYON PERRACHE	TER	17629 D
14:54	ANNECY	TER	5406 A
15:00	PARIS GARE DE LYON TGV		622 C
15:03	STRASBOURG		4378 G
15:06	NANTES		4506
15:07	ST ETIENNE CHATEAUCREUX TGV		685 E
15:11	GENEVE	TER	17612 A
15:15	ST ETIENNE CARNOT	TER	54375 D

Exercice 20. Le cinéma

Le film Amélie est à quelle heure? (Write out the times indicated in official time,twenty-four hour time.)

Voici le film 'Le Fabuleux Destin d'Amélie Poulain.' Il y a une séance (showing)

> **Modèle:**
> à 14h10: quatorze heures dix

à ________________________,

à ________________________,

à ________________________.

Le mercredi, le samedi et le dimanche, il y a aussi une séance

à ________________________.

Exercice 21. Il est quelle heure?

Quelle heure est-il (l'heure non-officielle)? (Give the non-official time for the following official times.)

1. 14h00 ________________________________
2. 15h55 ________________________________
3. 19h45 ________________________________
4. 21h45 ________________________________
5. 12h05 ________________________________

Exercice 22. A quelle heure?

Posez les questions suivantes à un camarade de classe et comparez vos réponses.

1. En général, à quelle heure est-ce que tu étudies?
2. A quelle heure est-ce que tu écoutes de la musique?
3. A quelle heure est-ce que tu regardes la télé?
4. Est-ce que tu travailles? A quelle heure?
5. A quelle heure est-ce que tu téléphones à tes parents?
6. A quelle heure est-ce que tu rencontres tes amis?

At home, please go to the Français interactif website. Read the following grammar points in Tex's French Grammar and complete all Texercises which you will turn in to your instructor.

2.4 yes/no questions

rising intonation	**Tex, tu aimes les films?**
est-ce que	**Tex, est-ce que tu aimes les films?**
n'est-ce pas	**Tex, tu aimes les films, n'est-ce pas?**

Exercice 23. Tu as raison!

A. Posez les questions suivantes à un camarade. (Find out how well you know a classmate by asking the following questions. Insert the information that you think is true.)

Tu t'appelles______________________________ , n'est-ce pas?

Tu es ______________________________ , n'est-ce pas? (nationalité)

Tu habites à ______________________________ , n'est-ce pas?

Est-ce que tu aimes ______________________________ ?

B. Votre camarade répond: (Your classmate will confirm or correct your information)

Modèle:
Oui, je m'appelle...
Mais non, je m'appelle...

At home, please go to the Français interactif website. Read the following grammar points in Tex's French Grammar and complete all Texercises which you will turn in to your instructor.

2.5 Basic negation

ne...pas

Joe-Bob ne travaille pas beaucoup.

ne > n'

Il n'est pas très intelligent.

un, une, des > de or d'

Joe-Bob n'a pas de frère.

(See 2.5 for more information.)

Exercice 24. Les étudiants d'Austin!

A. Connaissez-vous (do you know) les étudiants du programme de Lyon? Transformez les phrases suivantes en questions en employant l'intonation. (Make the following sentences into questions using intonation.)

Modèle:
C'est Laila.
C'est Laila?

B. Maintenant (now) transformez les phrases ci-dessous (below) en questions avec 'est-ce que'.

Modèle:
C'est Laila.
Est-ce que c'est Laila?

C. Ensuite (finally) transformez les phrases ci-dessous (below) en questions avec 'n'est-ce pas'.

Modèle:
C'est Laila.
C'est Laila, n'est-ce pas?

1. Laila est de Dallas.
2. Elle parle arabe.
3. Blake adore les sports.
4. Karen est de Mexico.
5. Elle aime le hip-hop.

Exercice 25. Mais non!

Joe-Bob n'est pas très intelligent. Mettez ses phrases au négatif.

Joe-Bob:	Vous:
Modèle: Tex est de Dallas.	Mais non, il n'est pas de Dallas.
1. Laila est ingénieur.	____________________
2. Karen déteste le hip-hop.	____________________
3. Nous sommes à Paris.	____________________
4. Blake étudie les sciences.	____________________
5. Il est 5 heures du matin.	____________________
6. Il y a un piano dans la salle de classe.	____________________
7. Franck a un fils.	____________________
8. Sa femme s'appelle Jane.	____________________

Exercice 26. Nous n'aimons pas!

A. Ecrivez cinq questions. (You are going to compare your pastimes and activities with your classmates to find the activities that you have in common. First think of the activities you like and dislike and formulate at least five questions. Consult the list of pastimes in the vocabulary list.)

Modèle:
Est-ce que tu aimes la musique française?
Est-ce que tu regardes la télévision?

1. ____
2. ____
3. ____
4. ____
5. ____

B. En groupes de trois, posez vos questions et comparez vos préférences et vos passe-temps avec vos camarades.

Modèle:

Moi, j'aime la musique française. Et toi?	... Oui, j'adore la musique française
Est-ce que tu aimes la musique française?	ou ... Non, je n'aime pas la musique française.

C. Be prepared to report to the class at least three activities that you all like and do and three that you do not like or do.

Modèle:

Nous aimons le jazz.	Nous n'aimons pas la techno.
Nous regardons la télévision.	Nous n'écoutons pas la radio.

1. ______________________ ______________________
2. ______________________ ______________________
3. ______________________ ______________________

Exercice 27. Tu es plutôt sérieux / sérieuse ou frivole?

A. Décidez si chaque activité est un loisir (a leisure activity) ou une obligation.

	un loisir	une obligation
1. voyager en France	❑	❑
2. écouter le professeur	❑	❑
3. travailler à Macdo	❑	❑
4. étudier le français	❑	❑
5. jouer aux cartes	❑	❑
6. rêver	❑	❑

B. Ecrivez quatre autres (other) activités. Est-ce que ces activités sont des loisirs ou des obligations?

	un loisir	un obligation
	❑	❑
1. ______________________	❑	❑
2. ______________________	❑	❑
3. ______________________	❑	❑
4. ______________________	❑	❑

C. Rapportez vos décisions à la classe. Est-ce que tout le monde est d'accord?

D. Comparez (écoutez et écrivez) vos activités avec un partenaire. (Tell him/ her how often you do these activities. Use adverbs to describe your activities. Are there any activities that you never do? Remember that adverbs follow the verb: beaucoup ...)

Rappel: –er verbs
parler
'to speak'

je	**parle**
tu	**parles**
il / *elle* / *on*	**parle**
nous	**parlons**
vous	**parlez**
ils / *elles*	**parlent**

2.6 Introduction to adverbs

In French most adverbs end in -ment.

Adverbs follow the verb:
beaucoup, parfois, un peu, rarement, quelquefois, souvent, toujours, ne ... jamais

Modèle: J'étudie beaucoup. Je ne joue jamais aux cartes.

E. Décidez si votre partenaire est plutôt sérieux ou plutôt frivole. (After comparing your activities, decide if your partner is more serious or more frivolous. Be prepared to explain your decision to the class with at least two sentences.)

Modèle: X est plutôt frivole, parce qu'il étudie rarement et il regarde beaucoup la télévision.

Devoirs: Est-ce que vous êtes d'accord avec votre partenaire? Ecrivez un paragraphe de six phrases.

Modèle:
Je suis d'accord avec X. (Je ne suis pas d'accord.) Je suis sérieux, parce que je travaille toujours...

At home, please go to the Français interactif website. Read the following grammar points in Tex's French Grammar and complete all Texercises which you will turn in to your instructor.

2.7 interrogative and exclamative quel

Masculine singular	**quel**
Masculine	**quels**
Feminine singular	**quelle**
Feminine plural	**quelles**

Exercice 28. Quelle question?

A. Quelle forme de 'quel'?

a. Quel...
b. Quelle...
c. Quels...
d. Quelles...

_____1. ... sont tes passe-temps préférés?
_____2. ... est ton nom?
_____3. ... est ton prénom?
_____4. ... est ta nationalité?
_____5. ... sport est-ce que tu préfères?
_____6. ... âge as-tu?
_____7. ... musiques est-ce que tu préfères?
_____8. ... est ta profession?
_____9. ... est ton lieu de naissance?
_____10. ...est ton adresse?

B. Posez des questions à une personne dans la classe avec qui vous n'avez jamais parlé et complétez la fiche. (Find someone you have not yet talked with!)

THE UNIVERSITY OF TEXAS AT AUSTIN

?

Nom de famille: ____________________
Prénom: ____________________
Age: ____________________
Nationalité (fém.): ____________________
Résidence actuelle: ____________________
Passe-temps: ____________________

NOTE CULTURELLE

Le français

Le français n'est pas seulement (only) la langue des Français: 160 millions de personnes de 49 pays différents sont francophones.

Le français est la langue maternelle de 70 millions d'Européens: Français, Belges Wallons, Suisses Romands, Luxembourgeois, Monégasques et Andorrans et de 6 millions de Canadiens principalement de la province du Québec.

Langue officielle de 31 pays d'Afrique, le français est couramment parlé au Maghreb (l'Algérie, la Tunisie, le Maroc) et au Liban. D'autres pays encore ont en commun la langue française notamment la Louisiane, Haïti, les Seychelles, Madagascar, l'Ile Maurice...

Le français est l'une des langues officielles des organismes internationaux (ONU, UNESCO, OCDE...) mais aussi la plus traduite (translated) dans le monde après l'anglais. Langue diplomatique du Vatican, avec l'italien, elle est aussi la langue officielle des jeux olympiques en hommage à Pierre de Coubertin, qui créa (created) les Olympiades modernes.
Enfin, l'Union postale universelle (169 pays membres) communique en français.

www.asapfrance.info/

Exercice 29. Quelle image?

Quelle phrase va avec chaque image? (Which caption goes with which picture? Note the use of quel in these exclamative expressions.)

a. Tammy: Quel beau tatou!
b. Joe-Bob: Quel tatou snob!
c. Joe-Bob: Quelle belle minette!
d. Vous: Ah, Quels animaux absurdes!

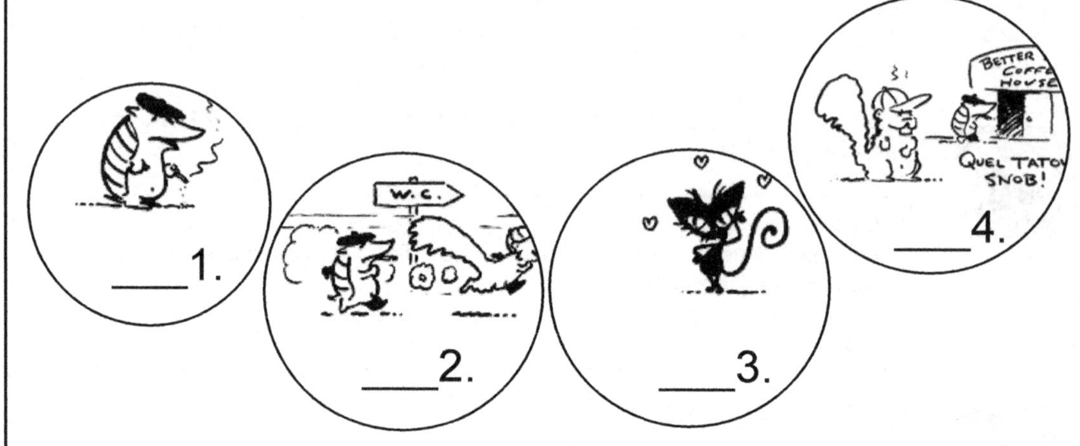

Exercice 30. Quel mot interrogatif?

Voici des réponses de Bette. Quelle est la question?
Utilisez **quel**, **quand**, **qui**, **comment**, **pourquoi**, **où**.

		Bette:
1.	______________________	Je m'appelle Bette.
2.	______________________	J'ai 22 ans.
3.	______________________	Je suis américaine.
4.	______________________	J'habite à Austin.
5.	______________________	J'aime parler français et voyager.
6.	______________________	Parce que j'adore les hommes français.

Exercice 31. Quel continent?

A. Ecrivez le pays que vous entendez et ensuite cochez ( ) l'adjectif qui correspond au continent convenable (appropriate).

	africain	européen	américain	asiatique
Modèle: la France, c'est un pays...	❑	√	❑	❑
1. ____________	❑	❑	❑	❑
2. ____________	❑	❑	❑	❑
3. ____________	❑	❑	❑	❑
4. ____________	❑	❑	❑	❑
5. ____________	❑	❑	❑	❑
6. ____________	❑	❑	❑	❑

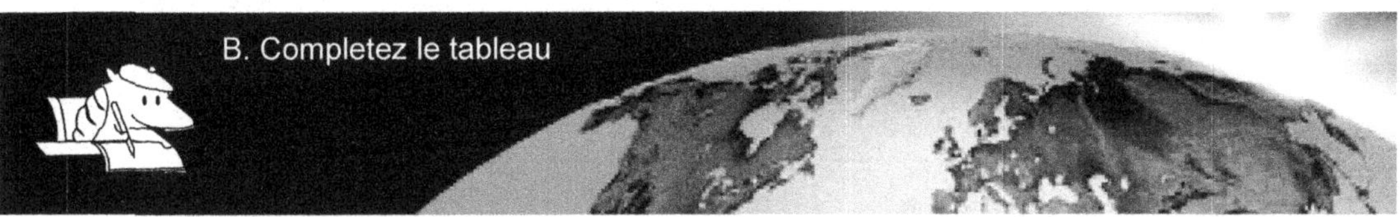

B. Completez le tableau

Pays	Continent	Nationalité (fém)	Langue(s)
Modèle: la France	**l'Europe**	**française**	**le français**
		sénégalaise	
	l'Afrique		
le Maroc			
		espagnole	
	l'Amérique du Nord		**l'anglais et le français**
			le chinois
		vénézuélienne	
	l'Asie		
			l'anglais (m.)
	l'Europe		
		suisse	
		belge	

At home, please go to the Français interactif website. Read the following grammar points in Tex's French Grammar and complete all Texercises which you will turn in to your instructor.

2.8 introduction to adjectives

2.9 adjectives: formation and placement (regular)

Masc. singular	**petit** **grand** **aimable** **français**
Fem. singular	**petite** **grande** **aimable** **française**
Masc. plural	**petits** **grands** **aimables** **français**
Fem. plural	**petites** **grandes** **aimables** **françaises**

! Adjectives typically follow the noun in French.

Exercice 32. Vous aimez la géographie?

A. Donnez le nom d'....

1. une ville algérienne: ______
2. une voiture allemande: ______
3. un prince anglais: ______
4. une ville espagnole: ______
5. un acteur français: ______
6. une femme italienne: ______
7. une ville japonaise: ______
8. un président mexicain: ______

B. Quelles sont leurs nationalités?

1. Céline Dion: Elle est ______
2. Edith Piaf: Elle est ______
3. Hillary Clinton: Elle est ______
4. George Clooney: Il est ______
5. Léopold Senghor: Il est ______
6. Nicholas Sarkozy: Il est ______
7. La reine Elizabeth: Elle est ______
8. Votre prof: Il/elle est ______

Dictogloss 2. La famille de Franck Guilloteau.

Ecoutez et complétez les phrases suivantes. (Dictogloss. Listen and take notes as your teacher reads a paragraph. Working in groups, reconstruct the text with as many details as possible.)

Voici la famille de Franck Guilloteau.

Sur la photo, il y a ______________________, Caroline et ____________________ Natasha. Elles habitent ____ . Il y a aussi ________________________ de Franck. Elle ____________________________ en Provence avec leur père . Ils sont ______________________________.

Sur la photo, il y a aussi ______________________de Franck et ______________________, Camille et Audrey. Les filles sont ____. Elles habitent ____________________________________mais elles _____________________ voyager en France en été pour être avec ____ et pour jouer avec _______________________________________.

3 Les vacances en France.

In this chapter we will talk about the weather, seasons, and geography. We will also plan vacation activities in France.

Vocabulaire

- *le temps*
- *les saisons*
- *la géographie*
- *les points cardinaux*
- *L'Hexagone*
- *les activités*
- *les transports*
- *verbes*
- *les nombres cardinaux 70-100*

Phonétique

- *l'accentuation*
- *l'intonation*

Grammaire

- *3.1 faire 'to do, to make'*
- *3.2 faire expressions*
- *3.3 -ir verbs (irregular) partir, sortir, and dormir*
- *3.4 -er verbs (stem changing) present tense*
- *3.5 aller 'to go'*
- *3.6 futur proche*
- *3.7 prepositions with places*

- *testez-vous!, chapitre 03*
- *verb conjugation reference*
- *verb practice*

Vidéos

Vocabulaire en contexte

- *L'Hexagone*
- *à la gare*
- *quel temps fait-il?*
- *au lac*
- *en ville*

Interviews

- *le temps*
- *le week-end*
- *le week-end prochain*
- *en vacances*

Culture

- *les Alpes*
- *la Provence*

Chapitre 3

Vocabulaire

Préparation du vocabulaire

Be sure to download the pdf vocabulary preparation template from the FI website to complete Exercises B, E, and F.

! Your instructor will collect this homework.

Le temps	**The weather**
Quel temps fait-il?	What's the weather?
Il fait beau.	It's nice.
Il fait chaud.	It's hot.
Il fait du soleil. / Il y a du soleil.	It's sunny.
Il fait frais.	It's cool.
Il fait mauvais.	It's bad.
Il fait froid.	It's cold.
Il fait du brouillard. / Il y a du brouillard.	It's foggy.
Il fait du vent. / Il y a du vent.	It's windy.
Il y a des nuages.	It's cloudy.
Il y a des orages.	There are storms.
Il pleut. (pleuvoir)	It's raining. (to rain)
Il neige. (neiger)	It's snowing. (to snow)

Les saisons (f)	**Seasons**
le printemps / au printemps	spring / in the spring
l'été (m) / en été	summer / in the summer
l'automne (m) / en automne	fall / in the fall
l'hiver (m) / en hiver	winter / in the winter

La géographie	**Geography**
la campagne	countryside
la ville	town, city
une province	province
une région	region
un lac	lake
un fleuve	major river (that flows to the sea)
la Loire	the Loire (river)
la Garonne	the Garonne (river)
le Rhône	the Rhône (river)
la Seine	the Seine (river)
la mer	sea
la mer Méditerranée	the Mediterranean Sea
l'océan (m)	ocean
l'océan Atlantique	the Atlantic Ocean
la Manche	the English Channel
la plage	beach
une forêt	forest
la montagne	mountain
les Alpes (f)	the Alps
le Jura	the Jura (mountains)
les Pyrénées (f)	the Pyrenees
le Massif Central	the Massif Central
les Vosges (f)	the Vosges

Vocabulaire

Les points cardinaux	Points of the compass
dans le nord, au nord	in the north
dans le sud / au sud	in the south
dans l'est / à l'est	in the east
dans l'ouest / à l'ouest	in the west
au centre	in the center
sur la côte	on the coast

L'Hexagone (m)	France
l'Alsace (f)	Alsace
la Bourgogne	Burgundy
la Bretagne	Brittany
la Côte d'Azur	the Riviera
la Corse	Corsica
l'Ile de France (f)	Ile de France
(la région parisienne)	(Parisian region)
la Lorraine	Lorraine
la Normandie	Normandy
la Provence	Provence
la Vallée de la Loire	the Loire Valley

Les activités	Activities
aller	to go
aller au cinéma	to go to the movies
aller en boîte	to go clubbing
aller au concert	to go to a concert
aller à l'université	to go to the university
aller au parc	to go to the park
faire de la bicyclette	to go bicycle riding
faire du bateau	to go boating
faire de la planche à voile	to go windsurfing
faire des randonnées	to go hiking
faire du ski	to go skiing
faire du vélo	to go cycling
faire de la voile	to go sailing
faire une promenade	to take a walk
passer les vacances (f pl)	spend a vacation
visiter... (un lieu, pas une personne)	to visit... (a place, not a person)
une cathédrale	a cathedral
un château	a castle
une exposition	an exhibition, show
un monument	a monument
un musée	a museum
voyager	to travel
à l'étranger	abroad

Les nombres cardinaux 70-100

70	soixante-dix
71	soixante et onze
72	soixante-douze
73	soixante-treize
74	soixante-quatorze
75	soixante-quinze
76	soixante-seize
77	soixante-dix-sept
78	soixante-dix-huit
79	soixante-dix-neuf

80	quatre-vingts
81	quatre-vingt-un
82	quatre-vingt-deux
83	quatre-vingt-trois
84	quatre-vingt-quatre
85	quatre-vingt-cinq
86	quatre-vingt-six
87	quatre-vingt-sept
88	quatre-vingt-huit
89	quatre-vingt-neuf

90	quatre-vingt-dix
91	quatre-vingt-onze
92	quatre-vingt-douze
93	quatre-vingt-treize
94	quatre-vingt-quatorze
95	quatre-vingt-quinze
96	quatre-vingt-seize
97	quatre-vingt-dix-sept
98	quatre-vingt-dix-huit
99	quatre-vingt-dix-neuf

100	cent
102	cent-deux
200	deux cents
1.000	mille
2.000	deux mille
1.000.000	un million

Vocabulaire

Les transports	Means of transport
Comment voyagez-vous?	How do you travel?
Je voyage...	I travel...
en avion / un avion	by plane / plane
en bateau / un bateau	by boat / boat
en train / un train	by train / train
en car / un car	by tour bus (from city to city) / tour bus
en voiture / une voiture	by car / car
Comment allez-vous... (à l'université, chez vos parents, au travail, etc.)?	How do you go... (to the university, to your parents' house, to work, etc.) ?
Je vais...	I go...
en métro / le métro	by subway / subway
en bus / un bus	by bus / bus
en taxi / un taxi	by taxi / taxi
à moto / une moto	by motorcycle / motorcycle
à vélo / un vélo	by bicycle / bicycle
à pied	on foot

Verbes	Verbs
acheter	to buy
amener	to bring somebody (along)
changer	to change
dormir	to sleep
emmener	to take somebody (along)
espérer	to hope
essayer	to try
manger	to eat
nager	to swim
partager	to share
partir	to leave
sortir	to go out

Phonétique

Go to the website for a complete explanation and practice exercises.

Introduction

Regardons la video ensemble pour répondre aux questions suivantes: Qui présente le chapitre? Où est-il/elle? Quels sont les thèmes du chapitre?

Exercice 1. La Géographie

Qu'est-ce que c'est?

C'est.../Ce sont...	un fleuve	des montagnes	une région	une ville
1. les Alpes	❑	❑	❑	❑
2. l'Alsace	❑	❑	❑	❑
3. la Normandie	❑	❑	❑	❑
4. Nice	❑	❑	❑	❑
5. la Loire	❑	❑	❑	❑
6. Strasbourg	❑	❑	❑	❑
7. la Provence	❑	❑	❑	❑
8. la Seine	❑	❑	❑	❑

NOTE CULTURELLE

L'Hexagone

La forme de la France ressemble à celle d'un hexagone. La superficie du pays est de 550 000 km2. La France est le plus grand des 27 pays qui forment l'Union européenne tandis que l'Allemagne est le plus peuplé. La capitale de la France est Paris.

http://www.asapfrance.info/france/hexagone-est-mon-nom/

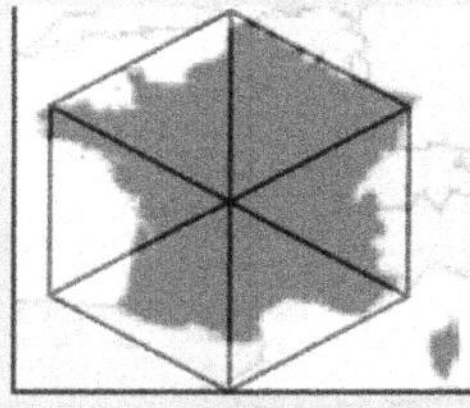

NOTE CULTURELLE

Les départements de France

La France métropolitaine est divisée en 96 départements. Chaque département a un numéro, deux chiffres qui se trouvent sur les plaques d'immatriculation (license plates) et dans les codes postaux (zip). Par exemple, le numéro du département du Rhône est 69 (Lyon est dans ce département). Sur la droite des plaques d'immatriculation françaises, il y a une bande bleue obligatoire avec le numéro du département du propriétaire de la voiture et le logo de la région du département.

Exercice 2. La géographie en chiffres.

Ecrivez les nombres en toutes lettres.

1. Lyon se trouve dans le département du Rhône (69)

   ____.

2. Il y a plusieurs départements dans la région parisienne: La Seine et Marne (77)

   ____.

   les Yvelines (78) , l'Essonne (91)________________________________

   et Paris (75)____

3. Les Vosges, ce sont des montagnes et c'est aussi un département (88)
4. La Loire est un grand fleuve français qui passe par plusieurs départements, par exemple, la

   Saône-et-Loire (71) ________________________________

   l'Indre et Loire (37) ________________________________et la

   Loire-Atlantique (44) ________________________________.

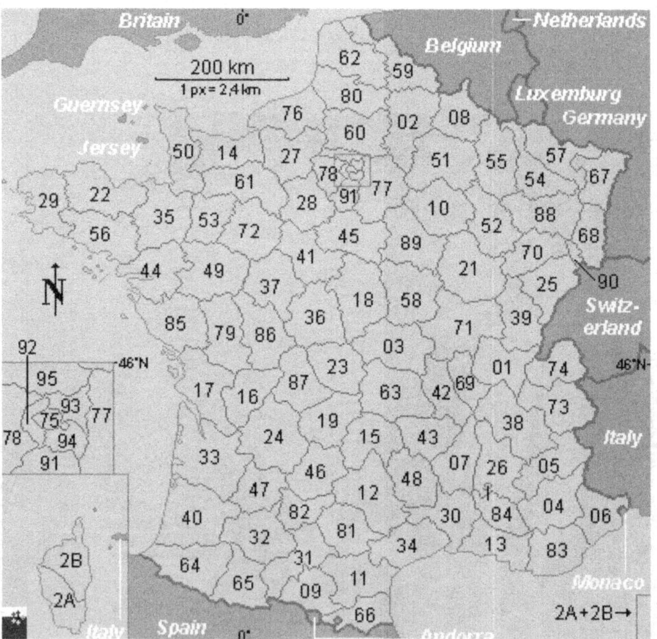

Exercice 3. Les fleuves français

Votre professeur va lire les longueurs des fleuves français. Ecoutez et complétez le tableau.

Fleuve	Longueur
la Garonne	km
la Loire	km
le Rhin	(184 km en France) km
le Rhône	km
la Seine	km

Exercice 4. Trains au départ

Ecoutez et complétez le tableau suivant. (Listen carefully as your teacher gives information about trains departing from the train station in Lyon. Fill in the relevant information in the chart below.)

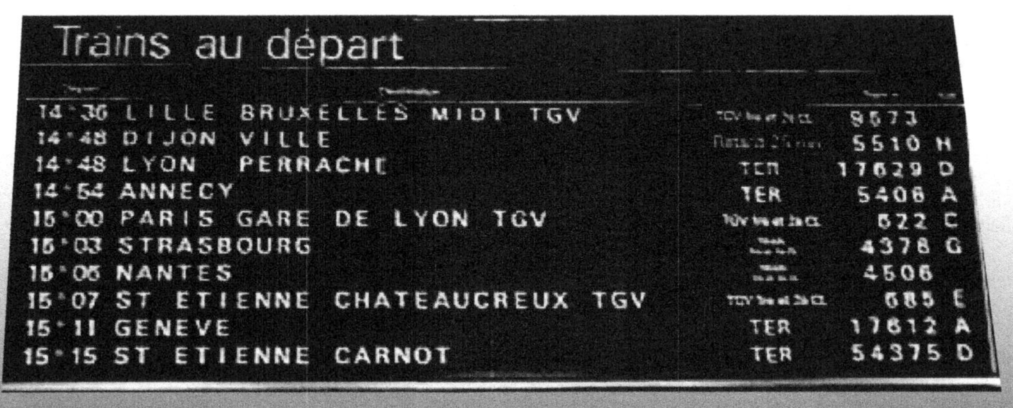

	Numéro de train	Destination	Heure de départ
Modèle:	# 9573	Lille, Bruxelles	14h36
1			
2			
3			
4			

Rhône-Alpes

La région Rhône-Alpes où se trouve Lyon est la deuxième région de France en superficie, en économie et en population. Cette région offre des paysages très divers: montagnes, vignobles et douces vallées, champs de lavande et d'oliviers. En Rhône-Alpes, l'eau se trouve sous toutes les formes: neige et glaciers, fleuves, rivières et lacs.

http://fr.wikipedia.org/wiki/Portail:Rhône-Alpes

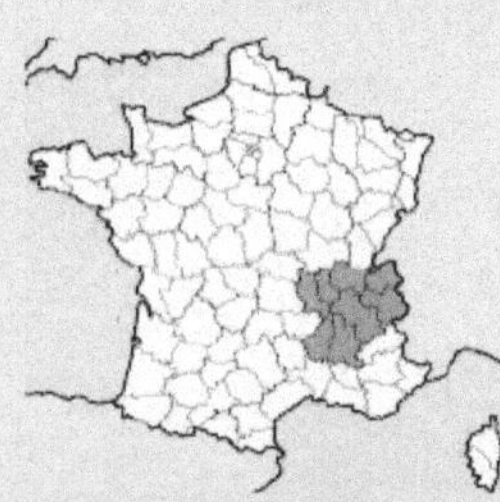

Exercice 5. Bizarre ou normal?

	bizarre	normal
1. Il neige dans les Alpes en hiver.	❑	❑
2. Il fait froid à Nice en été.	❑	❑
3. Il fait chaud à Dallas en automne.	❑	❑
4. Il fait du soleil au Maroc au printemps.	❑	❑
5. Il fait du vent à Chicago en mars.	❑	❑
6. Il y a des orages au Texas au printemps.	❑	❑
7. Il fait beau en Californie en automne.	❑	❑
8. Il n'y a jamais de nuages à Seattle.	❑	❑

Exercice 6. Quel temps fait-il?

Quand vous faites les activités suivantes, quel temps fait-il en général? Plusieurs (several) réponses sont possibles.

	Il fait beau.	Il fait froid.	Il pleut.	Il fait du vent.	Il neige.
aller au parc	❑	❑	❑	❑	❑
faire de la planche à voile	❑	❑	❑	❑	❑
faire des randonnées	❑	❑	❑	❑	❑
faire du ski	❑	❑	❑	❑	❑
aller au cinéma	❑	❑	❑	❑	❑
faire du vélo	❑	❑	❑	❑	❑
visiter un musée	❑	❑	❑	❑	❑

Exercice 7. Les villes?

Quel temps associez-vous avec ...

1. Boston?
2. San Francisco?
3. Anchorage?
4. Phoenix?
5. Miami?

Exercice 8. Les saisons

Quel temps fait-il au Texas...

1. en été?
2. en hiver?
3. au printemps?
4. en automne?

Exercice 9. Quel temps fait-il en France aujourd'hui?

http://fr.weather.yahoo.com

Regardez le site Yahoo et complétez le tableau suivant.

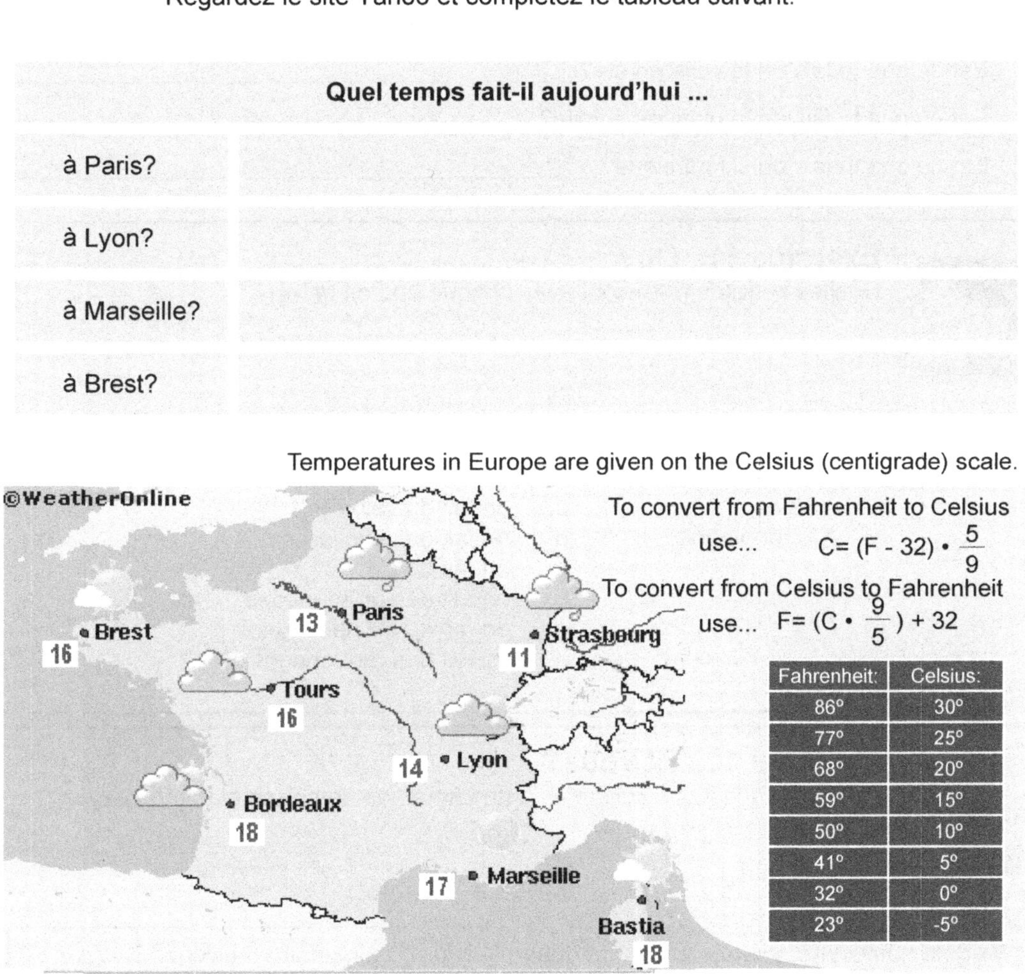

Quel temps fait-il aujourd'hui ...	
à Paris?	
à Lyon?	
à Marseille?	
à Brest?	

Temperatures in Europe are given on the Celsius (centigrade) scale.

To convert from Fahrenheit to Celsius use... $C = (F - 32) \cdot \frac{5}{9}$

To convert from Celsius to Fahrenheit use... $F = (C \cdot \frac{9}{5}) + 32$

Fahrenheit:	Celsius:
86°	30°
77°	25°
68°	20°
59°	15°
50°	10°
41°	5°
32°	0°
23°	-5°

At home, please go to the Français interactif website. Read the following grammar points in Tex's French Grammar and complete all Texercises which you will turn in to your instructor.

3.1 faire 'to do', 'to make"

je	**fais**
tu	**fais**
il / *elle* / *on*	**fait**
nous	**faisons**
vous	**faites**
ils / *elles*	**font**

3.2 faire expressions

Il fait...	**beau.** **mauvais.**
faire...	**du bateau** **une promenade**

! Parlez uniquement en français! Si la réponse est "OUI", demandez la signature de cette personne. Changez de pour camarade chaque question. Ecoutez attentivement les questions qu'on vous pose. Ne répondez pas à des questions incomplètes.

NOTE CULTURELLE

La Provence-Alpes-Côte d'Azur

La Provence-Alpes-Côte d'Azur est la première région de France pour l'accueil des touristes français et seconde pour les touristes étrangers. Située en bordure de la mer méditerranée, au sud -est de la France, la région est peuplée de 4,8 millions d'habitants, qui résident dans ses quatre grandes métropoles, Marseille, Nice, Toulon et Avignon.

http://fr.wikipedia.org/wiki/Provence-Alpes-Côte_d%27Azur

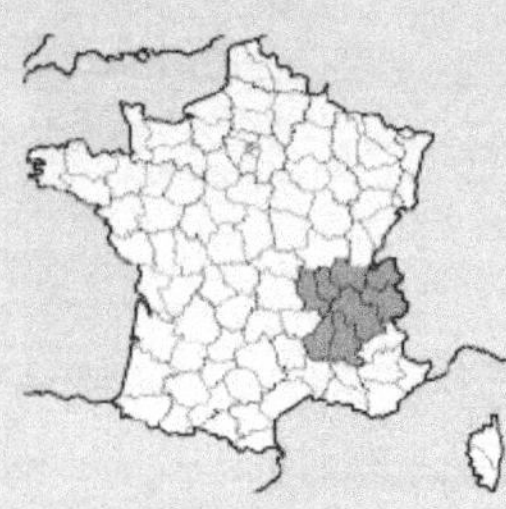

Exercice 10. Tu es sportif?

Posez les questions suivantes à vos camarades de classe.

1. Est-ce que tu fais du ski en hiver?____________________.
2. Est-ce que tu fais des randonnées à la montagne?____________________.
3. Est-ce que tu fais souvent du bateau?____________________.
4. Est-ce que tu fais du vélo le week-end?____________________.
5. Est-ce que tu fais une promenade tous les jours?____________________.
6. Est-ce que tu fais de la voile en été?____________________.
7. Est-ce que tu fais de la planche à voile?____________________.
8. Est-ce que tu fais du ski nautique?____________________.

Exercice 11. Où?

Quelles activités (a-h) vont avec chaque endroit (#1-4)?

_____1. A la campagne...	a. ... on fait du bateau.
_____2. A la mer...	b. ... on fait de la planche à voile.
_____3. Au lac...	c. ... on fait du vélo.
_____4. A la montagne...	d. ... on fait de la voile.
	e. ... on fait du ski.
	f. ... on fait des promenades.
	g. ... on fait du ski nautique.
	h. ... on fait des randonnées.

Exercice 12. Et vous?

Posez les questions suivantes à un camarade de classe et comparez vos réponses.

Modèle: Qu'est-ce que tu aimes faire quand il neige? J'aime faire du ski.

Qu'est-ce que tu aimes faire...

1. ... quand il fait beau?____________________.
2. ... quand il fait froid?____________________.
3. ... quand il pleut?____________________.
4. ... quand il fait chaud?____________________.

Exercice 13. Des activités.

Complétez avec la forme correcte du verbe faire.

1. Qu'est-ce que vous ________________________________ en été?
2. Tex ________________________________ du ski en hiver.
3. Nous ________________________________ une promenade au parc.
4. Je ________________________________ du vélo en été.
5. Tex et Tammy ________________________________ du bateau à la mer.
6. Nous ________________________________ des randonnées en automne.

Exercice 14. La Provence.

Répondez aux questions suivantes.

Voici l'itinéraire de l'excursion en Provence.

1. Quel monument est-ce que les étudiants visitent vendredi?
2. Qu'est-ce que les étudiants font vendredi après-midi aux Saintes Maries de la Mer?
3. Où dînent les étudiants vendredi soir?
4. Quelle ville est-ce que les étudiants visitent samedi?
5. Qu'est-ce que les étudiants font dimanche?
6. A quelle heure est-ce que les étudiants arrivent à Lyon dimanche soir?

VENDREDI

Départ en autocar vers 08h00.
Déjeuner en cours de route.
A 13.00 viste guidé du Palais des Papes, symbole de la puissance de la paupauté témoigne, par son architecture et son décor, de cette splendeur passée.
Arrivée en début d'après-midi aux Saintes Maries de la Mer.
Installation à l'hôtel : HOTEL CAMILLE, 13 ave de la plage
Après midi libre pour baignade à la plage.
Départ à pied pour le dîner flamenco à 20.00 h au restaurant : EL CAMPO , 13 rue Victor Hugo

SAMEDI

Départ après le petit déjeuner pour Arles.
Visite à 10h de la ville : les arènes, le théâtre, l'Espace Van Gogh, le marché.
Déjeuner libre
Retour sur les Saintes Maries de la Mer. Fin d'après-midi libre.

DIMANCHE

Petit déjeuner, Libération des chambres.
Départ pour le célèbre Pont Du Gard. La beauté de cet édifice romain est due à sa simplicité et à sa grandeur. La hauteur et l'exceptionnelle largeur de ses voûtes ont contribué à le rendre célèbre et lui confère cette allure de légèreté surprenante.
Pique-nique au Pont du Gard.
16h30 Retour direct sur Lyon en fin d'après midi
Arrivée prévue aux alentours de 19.00h/20.00h.

At home, please go to the Français interactif website. Read the following grammar points in Tex's French Grammar and complete all Texercises which you will turn in to your instructor.

3.3 Partir, sortir, dormir

***partir* 'to leave'**
***sortir* 'to go out'**
***dormir* 'to sleep'**

je	pars sors dors
tu	pars sors dors
il *elle* *on*	part sort dort
nous	partons sortons dormons
vous	partez sortez dormez
ils *elles*	partent sortent dorment

Exercice 15. Typique ou pas typique?

	typique	pas typique
1. Tu dors huit heures par jour.	❑	❑
2. Tu sors chaque soir.	❑	❑
3. Tu pars à cinq heures du matin pour aller en classe.	❑	❑
4. Tu pars pour la Louisiane en été.	❑	❑
5. Tu dors en cours.	❑	❑
6. Tu sors le lundi soir.	❑	❑

Exercice 16. Singulier ou pluriel?

Ecoutez chaque phrase et décidez si le verbe est au singulier ou au pluriel. Ecoutez une deuxième fois et écrivez la phrase.

	singulier	pluriel
Modèle: Ils sortent souvent au cinéma.	❑	√
1. ______________________________	❑	❑
2. ______________________________	❑	❑
3. ______________________________	❑	❑
4. ______________________________	❑	❑
5. ______________________________	❑	❑
6. ______________________________	❑	❑

Exercice 17. Le/la colocataire agréable. Avec un partenaire, regardez les phrases suivantes. Décidez si ces phrases décrivent **le/la colocataire agréable** ou **le/la colocataire désagréable**. Rapportez vos décisions à la classe.

	le/la colocataire agréable	**le/la colocataire désagréable**
Il/elle part le matin à 6h.		
Il/elle sort tout le temps.		
Il/elle dort jusqu'à midi.		
Il/elle fait la cuisine (cook).		

A. Ajoutez encore 2 phrases qui correspondent au colocataire agréable et désagréable. Utilisez une variété de verbes (acheter, partager, manger, etc.)

Le/la colocataire agréable ______________________________

______________________ et ______________________.

Le/la colocataire désagréable ______________________________

______________________ et ______________________.

B. Rapportez vos phrases à la classe. Est-ce que tout le monde est d'accord?

Décrivez les habitudes du/de la colocataire agréable et désagréable dans un paragraphe de 6 phrases.

> **Modèle:**
> Le/la colocataire agréable étudie tout le temps. Il ne sort pas pendant la semaine.
> Le/la colocataire désagréable ne partage pas et il dort tout le temps.

Dictogloss 1. Vendredi soir.

Formez des groupes de 3 ou 4 personnes. Ecoutez le texte lu par votre professeur. Complétez les phrases suivantes et donnez le plus de détails possibles.

C'est vendredi soir. Laila et Blake parlent au téléphone.

Laila:	______________________________
Blake:	Ben, non, je reste ici.
Laila:	Ah bon!!!!!______________________
Blake:	Oh, je ne sais pas. ______________
Laila:	______________ Un nouveau groupe va jouer ce soir.
Blake:	C'est quelle sorte de musique?
Laila:	______________________________
Blake:	Non, je suis fatigué, ______________
Laila:	Oh, tu deviens ennuyeux! (You're becoming boring!)

Exercice 18. Quelles vacances?

A. Choisissez un(e) étudiant(e) dans la classe que tout le monde connaît assez bien. Cette personne va s'asseoir dans le couloir pendant que les autres étudiants font cet exercice. (Choose a student that everyone knows well. This person will go sit in the corridor while the other students do this exercise.)

At home, please go to the Français interactif website. Read the following grammar points in Tex's French Grammar and complete all Texercises which you will turn in to your instructor.

3.4 -er verbs (stem-changing)

appeler 'to call'

je	appelle
tu	appelles
il / elle / on	appelle
nous	appelons
vous	appelez
ils / elles	appellent

préférer 'to prefer'

je	préfère
tu	préfères
il / elle / on	préfère
nous	préférons
vous	préférez
ils / elles	préfèrent

B. En groupes de 3 ou 4, écrivez le nom de cette personne dans le premier blanc. Puis, complétez chaque phrase.

_____________________ (l'étudiant[e])

1. préfère aller ______________________________ (quelle destination?)
2. préfère ______________________________ (quelle saison?)
3. préfère ______________________________ (quelles activités?)
4. achète beaucoup de ______________________________ (quelles choses?)
5. essaie toujours ______________________________ (de)+verb / noun
6. emmène ______________________________ (qui?)

C. Quel groupe connaît le mieux (knows best) l'étudiant(e)? Chaque groupe va annoncer ses résultats à la classe. Puis, l'étudiant(e) va donner les réponses correctes. Votre groupe a combien de réponses correctes? Quel groupe a gagné? Quel groupe connaît cette personne le mieux?

At home, please go to the Français interactif website. Read the following grammar points in Tex's French Grammar and complete all Texercises which you will turn in to your instructor.

3.5 aller 'to go'

je	**vais**
tu	**vas**
il / *elle* / *on*	**va**
nous	**allons**
vous	**allez**
ils / *elles*	**vont**

Exercice 19. Quelles sont vos activités en vacances?

Sondage (survey). Qu'est-ce que vous et vos camarades de classe font en vacances? En groupes de 4, décidez qui fait les activités suivantes en vacances.

Modèle:

Les noms des 4 membres du groupe:	**Tex**	**Tammy**	**Joe-Bob**	**Corey**
Qui préfère regarder la télévision?	❑	❑	√	√

Les noms des 4 membres de votre groupe:				
Qui préfère regarder la télévision?	❑	❑	❑	❑
Qui voyage souvent à l'étranger?	❑	❑	❑	❑
Qui emmène ses parents?	❑	❑	❑	❑
Qui nage dans la mer?	❑	❑	❑	❑
Qui mange des plats exotiques?	❑	❑	❑	❑
Qui préfère les hôtels de luxe?	❑	❑	❑	❑
Qui achète beaucoup de souvenirs?	❑	❑	❑	❑
Qui paie toujours son propre voyage? (Who always pays for his own trip?)	❑	❑	❑	❑
Qui essaie de parler une langue différente?	❑	❑	❑	❑

Maintenant, comparez les réponses de votre groupe avec les autres groupes dans la classe.

Modèle:
Joe Bob: Corey et moi, nous préférons regarder la télé, mais Tex et Tammy préfèrent sortir.

NOTE CULTURELLE

L'Île-de-France

L'Île-de-France, où on trouve Paris, compte 11 millions d'habitants. C'est avant tout la «région capitale», centre administratif, politique, économique et culturel de la France. Sa tour Eiffel, symbole de la France, est le premier monument visité au monde.

http://fr.wikipedia.org/wiki/Portail:Île-de-Francer

Exercice 20. Les transports

A. Bizarre ou normal?

	bizarre	normal
1. On va en Europe en car.	❑	❑
2. On va à Dallas en voiture.	❑	❑
3. On va à l'université en avion.	❑	❑
4. On va au concert en voiture.	❑	❑
5. On va au cinéma à pied.	❑	❑

Exercice 21. Et vous?

Posez les questions suivantes à un partenaire.

Comment est-ce que tu vas...

1. chez tes parents?____________________
2. à Houston?____________________
3. à New York? ____________________
4. à l'université?____________________
5. à Paris? ____________________

Exercice 22. Comment ça va?

Posez les questions suivantes à un partenaire.

1. Comment vas-tu?
2. Et tes cours, est-ce qu'ils vont bien?
   Pourquoi ou pourquoi pas?

Exercice 23. Le week-end

A. En général, où est-ce que votre prof va le week-end? En groupes de 3 ou 4, lisez les phrases et décidez si les phrases sont vraies ou fausses.

	oui	non
1. Le prof va au cinéma.	❑	❑
2. Le prof va à la mer.	❑	❑
3. Le prof va au parc.	❑	❑
4. Le prof va à l'université.	❑	❑
5. Le prof va au concert.	❑	❑
6. Le prof va au restaurant.	❑	❑
7. Le prof va en boîte.	❑	❑
8. Le prof va à Dallas.	❑	❑

Est-ce que vous avez raison? Posez des questions à votre professeur pour savoir.

Modèle: Est-ce que vous allez au cinéma?

B. Et vous? En général, où est-ce que vous allez le week-end?

	oui	non
1. Je vais au cinéma.	❑	❑
2. Je vais à la mer.	❑	❑
3. Je vais au parc.	❑	❑
4. Je vais à l'université.	❑	❑
5. Je vais au concert.	❑	❑
6. Je vais au restaurant.	❑	❑
7. Je vais en boîte.	❑	❑
8. Je vais à Dallas.	❑	❑

C. Comparez vos réponses avec celles (those) d'un partenaire. Où est-ce que votre partenaire va le week-end? Est-ce que vous allez aux mêmes endroits (same places) (aux mêmes restaurants, concerts, boites, parc, etc.)? Expliquez.

Modèle:
Mon partenaire et moi, nous allons à Jester pour manger.
Mais il/elle va souvent à Dallas et moi, je reste à Austin.

At home, please go to the Français interactif website. Read the following grammar points in Tex's French Grammar and complete all Texercises which you will turn in to your instructor.

3.6 Futur proche (the near future)

conjugated aller + infinitive	Je vais voyager.
je	vais voyager
tu	vas voyager
il / elle / on	va voyager
nous	allons voyager
vous	allez voyager
ils / elles	vont voyager

Exercice 24. Où est-ce que vous allez?

Posez les questions suivantes à un partenaire.

Où est-ce que tu vas pour…

Modèle:
1. rencontrer des amis?
Je vais au café pour rencontrer des amis.

2. faire une promenade?
3. faire du ski?
4. dormir?
5. faire du bateau?
6. visiter un musée?
7. nager?
8. faire du vélo?

Exercice 25. Grammaire interactive

A. Et qu'est-ce que votre professeur va faire le week-end prochain (next week-end)? En groupe de trois decidez si les phrases suivantes sont vraies ou fausses:

Le week-end prochain,
1. votre professeur va aller en France.
2. votre professeur ne va pas nager à Barton Springs.
3. votre professeur va écouter de la musique.
4. votre professeur ne va pas dormir.
5. votre professeur va danser en boîte.

B. Look at the following sentences:

Votre professeur **va** **aller** en France
Votre professeur ne **va** pas **dormir**

Do they refer to past, present or future situations?
What is the form of aller and dormir? Are the verbs conjugated or not?
Now try and fill in the following blanks.

To express the **future** *in French, you can use the conjugated form of the verb* ______________ *followed by an* ______________ *. Negation is placed around* ______________________________.

Exercice 26. Tous les jours ou le week-end prochain?

Ecoutez et décidez si les phrases sont au présent (tous les jours) ou au futur proche (le week-end prochain). Ecoutez une deuxième fois et écrivez la phrase.

	tous les jours	le week-end prochain
Modèle: Je vais visiter un musée.	❑	√
1. ______________________	❑	❑
2. ______________________	❑	❑
3. ______________________	❑	❑
4. ______________________	❑	❑
5. ______________________	❑	❑
6. ______________________	❑	❑
7. ______________________	❑	❑
8. ______________________	❑	❑

Exercice 27. Votre week-end.

Posez des questions à vos camarades de classe.

1. Est-ce que tu vas rencontrer des amis vendredi soir? ______________________
2. Est-ce que tu vas sortir au restaurant? ______________________
3. Est-ce que tu vas rentrer tard (late) samedi soir? ______________________
4. Est-ce que tu vas regarder la télé? ______________________
5. Est-ce que tu vas acheter des livres? ______________________
6. Est-ce que tu vas faire une promenade? ______________________
7. Est-ce que tu vas nager? ______________________
8. Est-ce que tu vas embrasser quelqu'un (anyone)? ______________________

! Parlez uniquement en français! Si la réponse est "OUI", demandez la signature de cette personne. Changez de camarade pour chaque question. Ecoutez attentivement les questions qu'on vous pose. Ne répondez pas à des questions incomplètes.

Dictogloss 2. Le week-end de Laila

Formez des groupes de trois ou quatre personnes. Ecoutez le texte lu par votre professeur. Complétez les phrases suivantes et donnez le plus de détails possibles.

Aujourd'hui c'est vendredi.

Ce soir, ______________________________

des amis au café.

Après, nous allons ______________________________

et ______________________________

Samedi matin, ______________________________

avec ma mère et nous allons visiter ______________________________

____

Samedi soir, mon copain et moi ______________________________

ou nous allons ______________________________

Dimanche je vais ______________________________

et ______________________________

Exercice 28. Ce week-end?

A. Quels sont les projets de vos camarades de classe pour ce week-end (this weekend)? Qu'est-ce qu'ils vont faire? Ecrivez trois questions.

Modèle:
Est-ce que tu vas sortir ce week-end?
Est-ce que tu vas faire du sport?

1. ______________________________
2. ______________________________
3. ______________________________

B. En groupes de quatre, posez vos questions à des camarades de classe et comparez leurs réponses. Qu'est-ce qu' ils vont faire ce week-end?

Devoirs: Ecrivez un paragraphe de six phrases pour décrire (describe) les activités de vos camarades de classe. Essayer de varier (vary) vos expressions et le vocabulaire.

Modèle:
X va faire des randonnées avec son frère. Y va aller à Dallas. Moi, je vais rester à Austin.

Exercice 29. Grammaire interactive

Look at the following sentences.

Votre professeur va **à** Dallas.	On va **au** Canada.
On va **en** France.	On va **aux** Etats-Unis.

What do the bolded prepositions in the sentences above mean?

Do you remember the gender of Canada and France?

Now fill in the blanks below.

To express **going to** a particular destination, ...

the preposition ______ is used before cities.

the preposition ______ is used before masculine singular countries.

the preposition ______ is used before feminine singular countries.

the preposition ______ is used before plural countries.

At home, please go to the Français interactif website. Read the following grammar points in Tex's French Grammar and complete all Texercises which you will turn in to your instructor.

3.7 prepositions with places

à (to/in)	*de (from)*
Feminine country/state	
en France	*de France*
Masculine country/state	
au Canada	*du Canada*
Masculine w./ vowel	
en Iran	*d' Iran*
Plural country	
aux Etats-Unis	*des* **Etats-Unis**
City	
à Paris	*de Paris*
Island	
à Tahiti	*de Tahiti*

Exercice 30. Tu es plutôt plage, montagne ou ville?

A. Où est-ce qu'on fait les activités suivantes: à la plage, à la montagne ou en ville?

	à la plage	à la montagne	en ville
1. faire du bateau	❑	❑	❑
2. faire du ski	❑	❑	❑
3. visiter un musée	❑	❑	❑
4. faire de la voile	❑	❑	❑
5. aller au concert	❑	❑	❑
6. faire une randonnée	❑	❑	❑

B. Qu'est-ce que vous aimez faire en vacances? Ecrivez quatre phrases pour décrire vos activités. Variez vos expressions.

Modèle: J' aime aller au cinéma.

1. ______________________________
2. ______________________________
3. ______________________________
4. ______________________________

C. Qu'est-ce que vous **ne** faites **JAMAIS** en vacances?

Modèle: Je ne fais jamais de voile.

1. ______________________________
2. ______________________________

D. Comparez vos activités avec un camarade. Ecoutez et prenez des notes.

Est-ce que votre camarade est plutôt montagne, plutôt plage ou plutôt ville? Ecrivez au moins (at least) 2 phrases pour justifier votre réponse.

Modèle:
X est plutôt montagne, parce qu'il adore faire du ski en hiver et il fait des randonnées en été. Il ne fait jamais de voile. Il n'aime pas la mer.

Devoirs pour demain: Est-ce que vous êtes d'accord avec la décision de votre partenaire? Ecrivez un paragraphe de 6 phrases (au moins 2 au négatif) pour décrire (to describe) vos activités.

Modèle:
Je suis d'accord avec X. /Je ne suis pas d'accord. (I agree with X./ I do not agree with X.)
Je suis plutôt ville, parce que j'adore aller au théâtre…

Feminine states (European origin):
la Californie
la Caroline du Nord
la Floride...

Masculine states (Native American origin):
le Colorado
l'Iowa
le Texas...

exceptions:
au Nouveau Mexique
dans l'état de New York...

Exercice 31. Quelle ville?

Quelle ville (a-h) va avec chaque pays (#1-8)?

_____1. On va en Italie...	a. ...pour visiter Tokyo.
_____2. On va en France...	b. ...pour visiter Dakar.
_____3. On va aux Etats-Unis...	c. ...pour visiter Rome.
	d. ...pour visiter Alger.
_____4. On va en Algérie...	e. ...pour visiter Montréal.
_____5. On va au Japon...	f. ....pour visiter Londres.
_____6. On va en Angleterre...	g. ...pour visiter Paris.
_____7. On va au Sénégal	h. ...pour visiter New York.
_____8. On va au Canada	

Exercice 32. Où est-ce que les étudiants vont?

Voici les villes et les provinces que les étudiants de UT vont visiter cet été. Donnez la préposition correcte pour chaque ville ou province.

Modèle: Ils vont en France.

Ils vont....

1. ______ Paris
2. ______ Lyon
3. ______ Texas
4. ______ Chamonix (une ville)
5. ______ Provence
6. ______ Avignon
7. ______ Bourgogne
8. ______ Etats-Unis

Exercice 33. Et vous?

Où est-ce que vous allez en vacances? Posez des questions à un partenaire pour comparer vos réponses.

Modèle:
Floride. Est-ce que tu vas en Floride?
Oui, je vais (souvent) en Floride. ou Non, je ne vais jamais en Floride.

Exercice 34. Grammaire interactive.

Look at the following sentences.

Le Prince William et Kate sont **de** Londres. Lance Armstrong est **d'**Austin.

Jean-Paul Sartre est **de** France.
Santa Anna est **du** Mexique.

Johann Sebastian Bach est **d'**Allemagne.
Tex est **des** Etats-Unis.

What do the bolded prepositions in the sentences above mean?

Fill in the blanks.

To express provenance **from** a particular destination, …

the preposition **de** is used before nouns referring to ___________ or ______________

the preposition **du** is used before ______nouns referring to ____________________

the preposition **des** is used before _______nouns referring to ____________________

de becomes **d'** in front of a ____

Exercice 35. Il/elle est d'où?

Quel pays va avec chaque personne?

_____1.	Oprah Winfrey est...	a. ...du Mexique.
_____2.	Jacques Cousteau est...	b. d'Algérie.
		c. du Mississippi.
_____3.	Albert Camus est...	d. du Canada.
_____4.	Salvador Dali est...	e. d'Espagne.
_____5.	Albert Einstein est...	f. de Londres.
_____6.	Santa Anna est...	g. d'Allemagne.
_____7.	Céline Dion est...	h. de France.
_____8.	La reine Elizabeth est..	

Exercice 36. Votre famille est d'où?

Posez les questions suivantes à un partenaire. Vos ancêtres sont d'où?

1. Tes parents sont d'où? ______________________________________
2. Tes grands-parents sont d'où? _________________________________
3. Tes arrière-grands-parents sont d'où?____________________________

Exercice 37. La géographie: un petit quizz.

Indiquez ces (these) fleuves, les montagnes, les villes, et les régions sur la carte:

Les fleuves	la Saône, le Rhône, la Seine, la Loire, la Garonne
Les villes	Paris, Lyon, Avignon
Les montagnes	le Jura, les Alpes, les Pyrénées, le Massif Central, les Vosges
Les régions	la Normandie, la Bretagne, le Beaujolais, l'Alsace, la Côte d'Azur, la Provence, la Vallée de la Loire, la Lorraine, l'Ile de France, la Bourgogne
Autres	la mer Méditerranée, la Manche, l'océan Atlantique, la Corse

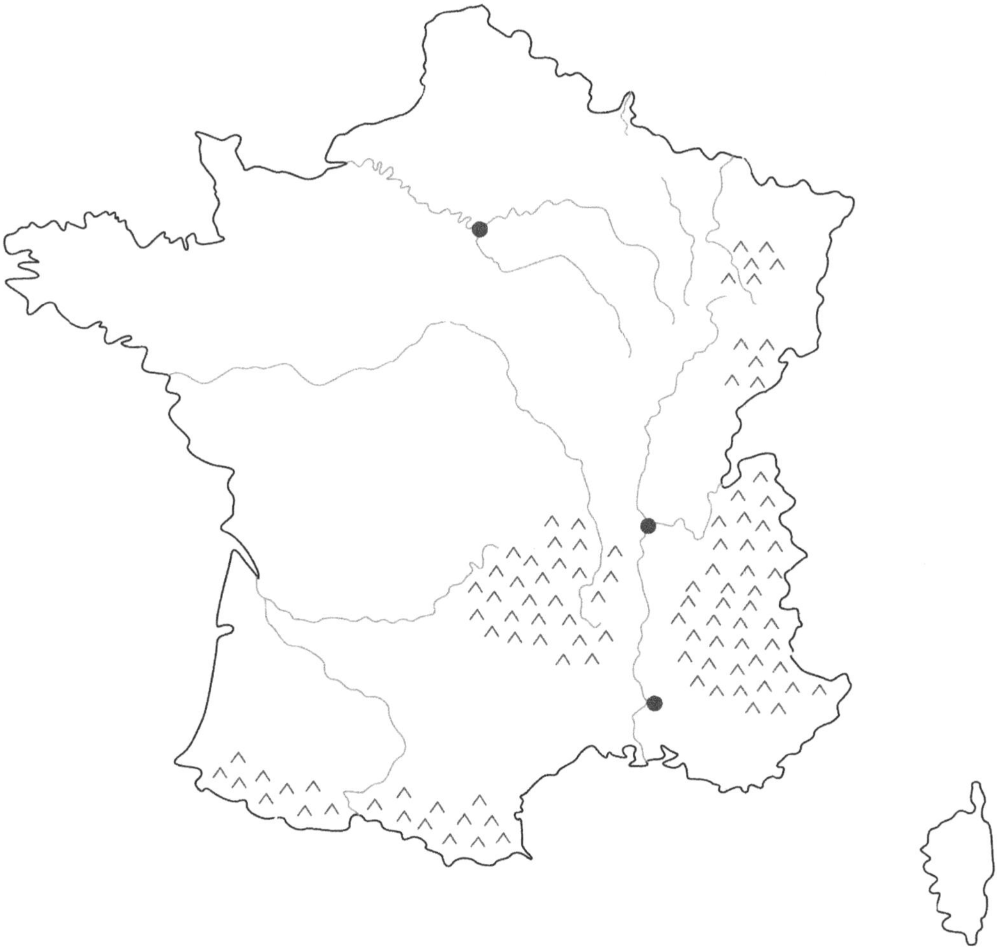

4 Les gens

In this chapter we will learn to describe people, their physical characteristics, and personalities. We will also talk about daily routines and stereotypes.

Vocabulaire

- *le visage*
- *les couleurs(f)*
- *le portrait physique*
- *le portrait moral (adjectifs)*
- *adjectifs qui précèdent le nom*
- *verbes pronominaux*

Phonétique

- *La consonne /R/*

Grammaire

- *4.1 definite articles with physical characteristics*
- *4.2 irregular adjectives*
- *4.3 adjectives that precede the noun*
- *4.4 c'est vs il/elle est*
- *4.5 pronominal verbs*
- *4.6 comparisons with adjectives*

- *testez-vous!, chapitre 04*
- *verb conjugation reference*
- *verb practice*

Vidéos

Vocabulaire en contexte

- *le visage*
- *les couleurs Audrey*
- *le portrait physique*
- *le portrait moral*
- *la routine*

Interviews

- *votre portrait*
- *votre célébrité favorite*
- *les stéréotypes*

Culture

- *les grenouilles*
- *les Français*
- *Aurélien - les Américains*
- *Clément - les Américains*

Chapitre 4

Vocabulaire

Préparation du vocabulaire

Be sure to download the pdf vocabulary preparation template from the FI website to complete Exercises B, E, and F.

! Your instructor will collect this homework.

Le visage	**The face**
la tête	head
les cheveux (m)	hair
le front	forehead
les sourcils (m)	eyebrows
les yeux (m) / l'oeil	eyes
le nez	nose
les joues (f)	cheeks
les oreilles (f)	ears
la bouche	mouth
les dents (f)	teeth
le menton	chin
le cou	neck

Les couleurs (f)	**Colors**
blanc / blanche	white
bleu / bleue	blue
gris / grise	gray
jaune	yellow
marron (invariable)	brown
noir / noire	black
orange (invariable)	orange
rouge	red
vert / verte	green
violet / violette	purple

Le portrait physique	**Physical description**
Quelle est votre taille (f)?	What's your height?
Je fais 1 m. 60.	I'm one meter 60.
de taille moyenne	of medium height
Je suis de taille moyenne.	I am of medium height.
Combien pesez-vous?	How much do you weigh?
Je fais 55 kilos.	I weigh 55 kilos.
maigre	thin, skinny
mince	thin, slender
De quelle couleur sont vos cheveux?	What color is your hair?
J'ai les cheveux blonds / bruns /	I have blond / brown /
châtains / roux.	light brown, chestnut / red hair.
Il est... Elle est...	He is... She is...
blond. blonde.	a blond.
brun. brune.	a brunette.
roux. rousse.	a red-head.
Comment est-il coiffé?	What is his hair like?
Il a les cheveux longs /	He has long /
courts / bouclés / raides.	short / curly / straight hair.
De quelle couleur sont vos yeux?	What color are your eyes?

J'ai les yeux marron.	I have brown eyes.
Quelle est la forme de son visage?	What's the shape of his face?
Il a le visage carré / long / rond.	He has a square / long / round face.
Il a le nez retroussé / pointu.	He has a snub / pointed nose.
Il a de grandes oreilles.	He has big ears.
Il/Elle a...	He/She has...
des lunettes (f)	glasses
une cicatrice	scar
un piercing	body piercing
un tatouage	tattoo

Le portrait moral (adjectifs)	**Psychological description**
actif / active	active
agréable	pleasant
ambitieux / ambitieuse	ambitious
amusant / amusante	funny
arrogant / arrogante	arrogant
calme	calm
compétitif / compétitive	competitive
créatif / créative	creative
curieux / curieuse	curious
débrouillard / débrouillarde	resourceful
désagréable	unpleasant
drôle	funny
égoïste	selfish
ennuyeux / ennuyeuse	boring
enthousiaste	enthusiastic
être de bonne humeur	to be in a good mood
être de mauvaise humeur	to be in a bad mood
fou / folle	crazy
franc / franche	frank
généreux / généreuse	generous
gentil / gentille	kind, nice
heureux / heureuse	happy
honnête	honest
hypocrite	hypocritical
idéaliste	idealistic
incapable	incapable, incompetent
indifférent / indifférente	indifferent
intelligent / intelligente	intelligent
intéressant / intéressante	interesting
malhonnête	dishonest
mignon / mignonne	cute
naïf / naïve	naive
nerveux / nerveuse	nervous
optimiste	optimistic

Vocabulaire

paresseux / paresseuse	lazy
patient / patiente	patient
pessimiste	pessimistic
prétentieux / prétentieuse	pretentious
réaliste	realistic
réservé / réservée	reserved
sensible	sensitive
sérieux / sérieuse	serious
sincère	sincere
sociable	sociable
sportif / sportive	athletic
têtu / têtue	stubborn
timide	shy, timid
tolérant / tolérante	tolerant
travailleur / travailleuse	hard-working

Adjectifs qui précèdent le nom	**Adjectives which precede the noun**
autre	other
beau / bel / belle	beautiful
bon / bonne	good
grand / grande	tall, big
gros / grosse	big, fat
jeune	young
joli / jolie	pretty
long / longue	long
mauvais / mauvaise	bad
nouveau / nouvel / nouvelle	new
petit / petite	little
vieux / vieil / vieille	old

Verbes pronominaux	**Pronominal verbs**
se réveiller	to wake up
se lever	to get up
se laver	to wash (oneself)
s'habiller	to dress (oneself)
se brosser les dents	to brush your teeth
se brosser les cheveux	to brush your hair
se maquiller	to put on make-up
se raser	to shave
se coucher	to go to bed
s'amuser	to have fun
s'ennuyer	to be bored
se dépêcher	to hurry
se promener	to take a walk
se reposer	to rest
se fâcher	to get angry

Phonétique

Go to the website for a complete explanation and practice exercises.

Introduction

Regardons la video ensemble pour répondre aux questions suivantes: Qui présente le chapitre? Où est-il/elle? Quels sont les thèmes du chapitre?

Exercice 1. Les athlètes

Complétez les phrases suivantes.

1. Quel athlète a le menton pointu?
   C'est___________________________
2. Quel athlète a de grandes dents?
   C'est___________________________
3. Quel athlète a de petites oreilles?
   C'est___________________________
4. Quel athlète a le nez retroussé?
   C'est___________________________
5. Quel athlète a un grand front?
   C'est___________________________

Yannick Noah — Tony Parker

Zinedine Zidane — Roger Federer

Caricatures reprinted with permission from www.magixl.com

Exercice 2. Grammaire interactive. Quel athlète?

A. Look at the following questions and underline the adjective in each one.

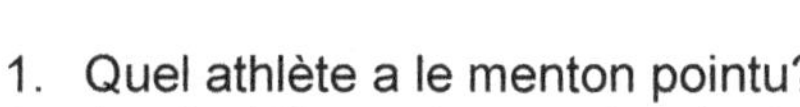

1. Quel athlète a le menton pointu?
2. Quel athlète a de grandes dents?
3. Quel athlète a de petites oreilles?
4. Quel athlète a le nez retroussé?
5. Quel athlète a un grand front?

B. Circle the word in parentheses to complete the sentences below. After each statement, write the number(s) of the question above which exemplify the statement.

1. The **definite article** is used when the adjective is **(before / after)** the noun. _______
2. The **indefinite article** is used when the adjective is **(singular / plural)** and **(before / after)** the noun. _______
3. **De** is used when the adjective is **(singular / plural)** and **(before / after)** the noun. ________

At home, please go to the Français interactif website. Read the following grammar points in Tex's French Grammar and complete all Texercises which you will turn in to your instructor.

4.1 definite articles with physical characteristics

! The definite article (le, la, l', les) is often used with parts of the body instead of a possessive determiner (mon, ma, mes, etc.).

Tammy a les yeux brillants, le nez pointu ....

! An indefinite article (un, une, des) is used, however, if an adjective comes before the part of the body.

Tammy a une belle bouche et de petites oreilles!

! **Rappel:** If this adjective is plural, des changes to de (de is the correct form!)

Exercice 3. Les actrices

Complétez les phrases suivantes.

1. Quelle actrice a un long cou?
   C'est________________________
2. Quelle actrice a une jolie bouche?
   C'est________________________
3. Quelle actrice a le nez pointu?
   C'est________________________
4. Quelle actrice a les joues rondes?
   C'est________________________
5. Quelle actrice a le menton carré?
   C'est________________________

Brigitte Bardot

Juliette Binoche

Audrey Tautou

Catherine Deneuve

Caricatures reprinted with permission from www.magixl.com

Exercice 4. C'est qui?

A. Comment est-elle coiffée?

1. Elle a les cheveux longs.
   C'est________________________
2. Elle a les cheveux courts.
   C'est________________________
3. Elle a les cheveux bouclés.
   C'est________________________
4. Elle a les cheveux raides.
   C'est________________________

Céline Dion

Edith Piaf

Josephine Baker

Caricatures reprinted with permission from www.magixl.com

B. Quelle est la forme de son visage?

1. Il a le visage rond.
   C'est__________________________
2. Il a le visage long.
   C'est__________________________
3. Il a le visage carré.
   C'est__________________________

François Mitterrand

Charles De Gaulle

Napoléon Bonaparte

Caricatures reprinted with permission from www.magixl.com

Exercice 5. Allez Lance!
Posez les questions suivantes à un partenaire.

US POSTAL SERVICE
1 - ARMSTRONG
Lance (Etats-Unis)
Né le 18/09/1971
Taille : 1,77 m
Poids : 75,0 kg

Quel âge a-t-il?	Il a ________________________
Quelle est sa taille?	Il fait ________________________
Combien est-ce qu'il pèse?	Il pèse ________________________
De quelle couleur sont ses yeux?	Il a les yeux ____________________
De quelle couleur sont ses cheveux?	Il a les cheveux __________________
Comment est-il coiffé?	Il a les cheveux __________________
Quelle est la forme de son visage?	Il a le visage____________________

! Tour de France winners:

2010	Alberto Cantador
2009	Alberto Cantador
2008	Carlos Sastre
2007	Alberto Cantador
2006	Oscar Pereiro Sio
2005	Lance Armstrong
2004	Lance Armstrong
2003	Lance Armstrong
2002	Lance Armstrong
2001	Lance Armstrong
2000	Lance Armstrong
1999	Lance Armstrong
1998	Marco Pantani
1997	Jan Ullrich
1996	Bjarne Riis

Exercice 6. Le portrait physique

A. Dessinez un visage. Ecrivez 5 ou 6 bonnes phrases à propos du visage. Faites attention aux accords des adjectifs.

Modèle:
Vous écrivez: Voilà Tammy. Elle a de petits yeux noirs et un grand nez pointu. Elle a les cheveux raides et blonds...

votre dessin

____

____

____

____

____

____

____

____

B. Travaillez avec un partenaire. Ne montrez pas votre dessin à votre partenaire. Lisez vos phrases à votre partenaire. Votre partenaire va dessiner le visage selon vos phrases. Comparez vos dessins pour vérifier vos descriptions.

le dessin de votre partenaire

Exercice 7. Karen

A. Trouvez la bonne réponse pour chaque question.

______1.	Quel âge as-tu?	a. J'ai les yeux marron.
______2.	Quelle est ta taille?	b. Je fais 1 m.60.
______3.	Combien est-ce que tu pèses?	c. J'ai les cheveux châtains.
______4.	De quelle couleur sont tes yeux?	d. Je fais 58 kilos.
______5.	Quelle est la forme de ton visage?	e. J'ai 20 ans.
______6.	De quelle couleur sont tes cheveux?	f. J'ai le visage rond.

B. Posez des questions à un partenaire pour compléter sa fiche signalétique!

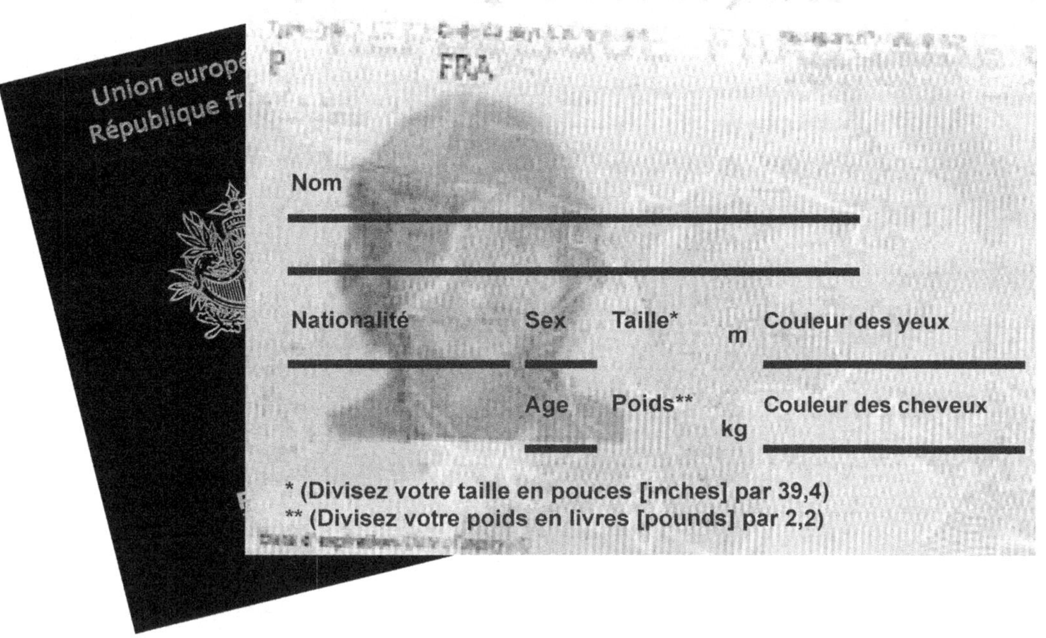

Exercice 8. Ils sont comment?

Choisissez l'adjectif convenable pour chaque personnage.

Charles de Gaulle

Marie Curie

Jacques Cousteau

Jean-Paul Sartre

1. Charles de Gaulle est.... ...franc / hypocrite.
2. Marie Curie est............. ...incapable / travailleuse.
3. Napoléon est................ ...prétentieux / modeste.
4. Marie Antoinette est....... ...naïve / débrouillarde.
5. Jacques Cousteau est... ...indifférent / curieux.
6. Brigitte Bardot est.......... ...idéaliste / folle.
7. Albert Camus est........... ...pessimiste / optimiste.
8. Jean-Paul Sartre est...... ...drôle / sérieux.

Caricatures reprinted with permission from www.magixl.com

At home, please go to the Français interactif website. Read the following grammar points in Tex's French Grammar and complete all Texercises which you will turn in to your instructor.

4.2 irregular adjectives

Masc.	*Fem.*
faux	**fausse**
favori	**favorite**
long	**longue**

-il	*-ille*
-on	*-onne*
-s	*-sse*
-en	*-enne*
-eux	*-euse*
-eur	*-euse*
-f	*-ve*
-c	*-che*
-ou	*-olle*

! Add –s to make adjectlives plural except
- un tatou curieux
- des tatous curieux
- un tatou international
- des tatous internationaux

Some adjectives have only one form regardless of number and gender
- Elle a les yeux marron

Exercice 9. Jay ou Oprah?

Ecoutez les adjectifs suivants. Est-ce que l'adjectif décrit Jay Leno (forme masculine) ou Oprah Winfrey (forme féminine) ou est-ce que c'est impossible à distinguer?

	Jay	Oprah	impossible à distinguer
Modèle: Vous entendez: **généreuse**	❑	√	❑
1. ________________	❑	❑	❑
2. ________________	❑	❑	❑
3. ________________	❑	❑	❑
4. ________________	❑	❑	❑
5. ________________	❑	❑	❑
6. ________________	❑	❑	❑
7. ________________	❑	❑	❑
8. ________________	❑	❑	❑

Caricatures reprinted with permission from www.magixl.com

Exercice 10. Quelle est votre réaction?

Lisez les phrases suivantes qui décrivent Tex et ses amis. Lisez chaque phrase avec un partenaire. Est-ce que chaque phrase vous décrit ou pas? Cochez la colonne appropriée.

	MOI		MON PARTENAIRE	
	moi aussi!	**pas moi!**	**lui / elle aussi**	**pas lui / elle!**
1. Tammy a le nez pointu.				
2. Tex est souvent têtu.				
3. Rita a des amis sérieux et débrouillards.				
4. Tammy est optimiste.				
5. Tammy a les cheveux bouclés.				
6. Joe-Bob a un colocataire paresseux.				
7. Tammy a des parents tolérants et généreux.				
8. Corey est franc.				
9. Tammy est enthousiaste en classe.				
10. Bette déteste les professeurs indifférents.				

Exercice 11. Morphopsychologie.

Lisez les phrases suivantes.

Samuel L. Jackson — Sandra Bullock — Arnold Schwarzenegger

- Un grand front signifie que la personne est intelligente.
- Un petit front signifie que la personne est sociable.
- De grands sourcils signifient que la personne est têtue.
- De petits sourcils signifient que la personne est naïve.
- De longs sourcils signifient que la personne est réaliste.
- Des sourcils courts signifient que la personne est paresseuse.
- De grands yeux signifient que la personne est franche mais égoiste.
- De petits yeux signifient que la personne est active.
- Une grande bouche et de grosses joues signifient que la personne est débrouillarde et de bonne humeur.
- Une petite bouche et des joues minces signifient que la personne est pessimiste, réservée et timide.

Caricatures reprinted with permission from www.magixl.com

1. Décrivez le visage de votre partenaire. D'après la morphopsychologie, quelle est sa personnalité?

> **Modèle:** Mon partenaire a un grand front et de gros sourcils.
> Donc il est intelligent et têtu!

2. Etes-vous d'accord avec le portrait de votre partenaire. Pourquoi ou pourquoi pas?

Devoirs: Quel est votre portrait moral? Comparez votre personnalité avec celle de votre partenaire. Ecrivez un paragraphe de 6 phrases.

Exercice 12. L'Amour, l'amour, toujours l'amour

A. Regardez les adjectifs suivants. Décidez si les adjectifs décrivent le copain de rêve / la copine de rêve ou le copain horrible / la copine horrible. Rapportez votre décision à la classe.

	le copain la copine ...de rêve	le copain la copine ...horrible
1. amusant(e)	❑	❑
2. difficile	❑	❑
3. sérieux(se)	❑	❑
4. intelligent(e)	❑	❑
5. pessimiste	❑	❑
6. sympathique	❑	❑
7. français(e)	❑	❑

NOTE CULTURELLE

Quel ques stéréotypes sur la France et les Français

Voici quelques stéréotypes américains les plus courants sur la France et les Français:

- Les Français sont petits, maigres, ont un long nez et les cheveux noirs. Les hommes ont une moustache et portent un béret.
- Les Français sont un peuple intellectuel.
- Les Français sont des gourmets, experts en vins et en haute cuisine.
- Les Français sont romantiques. Les hommes ont tous des maîtresses.
- La France est le pays du charme, de l'élégance, du style..
- Les femmes françaises sont très chics, très sophistiqués et 'sexy.'
- La France produit surtout des objets de luxe: parfums, haute-couture, bijoux, vins fins, etc.
- Les Français sont arrogants.

B. Ajoutez encore 2 adjectifs qui correspondent au copain / à la copine de rêve et au copain / à la copine horrible:

Le copain / la copine de rêve est ________________ et ________________ .

Le copain / la copine horrible est ________________ et ________________ .

C. Ecrivez 2 phrases: une phrase qui décrit le copain / la copine de rêve et l'autre phrase qui décrit le copain / la copine horrible.

Modèle:
Le copain de rêve est amusant, sympathique et intelligent....
Le copain horrible est..

D. Rapportez vos phrases à la classe. Est-ce que tout le monde est d'accord?

E. Devoirs. Décrivez votre copain / copine de rêve dans un paragraphe de 6 phrases. Comparez avec votre copain/copine actuel(le).

Modèle:
Le copain de rêve est amusant, sympathique et très intelligent. En réalité, mon copain n'est pas très intelligent, mais il est sympathique.

Exercice 13. C'est qui?

Avec un partenaire nommez:

1. un acteur amusant: ________________ / un bon acteur: ________________
2. une actrice agréable: ________________ / une mauvaise actrice: ________________
3. un vieil homme: ________________ / un nouvel acteur: ________________
4. une chanteuse réservée: ________________ / une jeune chanteuse: ________________
5. une femme ennuyeuse: ________________ / une belle femme: ________________
6. un film intéressant: ________________ / un beau film: ________________
7. un grand pays: ________________ / un petit pays: ________________
8. une voiture française: ________________ / une grosse voiture: ________________

Exercice 14. Grammaire interactive. Les adjectifs.

In the following table, indicate whether each adjective refers to beauty, age, a number, goodness, size or none of these.

	Beauty	Age	Number	Goodness	Size	Other
un **grand** pays	❑	❑	❑	❑	√	❑
un acteur **amusant**	❑	❑	❑	❑	❑	√
un **vieil** homme	❑	❑	❑	❑	❑	❑
une femme **ennuyeuse**	❑	❑	❑	❑	❑	❑
un **bon** acteur	❑	❑	❑	❑	❑	❑
une **grosse** voiture	❑	❑	❑	❑	❑	❑
un film **intéressant**	❑	❑	❑	❑	❑	❑
une **belle** femme	❑	❑	❑	❑	❑	❑
un **premier** homme sur la	❑	❑	❑	❑	❑	❑
lune	❑	❑	❑	❑	❑	❑
Une actrice **réservée**	❑	❑	❑	❑	❑	❑

What can you say about the placement of all the adjectives that refer to beauty,age, number, goodness or size (BANGS) ?

Exercice 15. C'est quoi? / C'est qui?

Identifiez les endroits et les personnes suivants. Utilisez c'est ou ce sont avec l'adjectif entre les parenthèses. Faites attention à la forme et la position des adjectifs dans vos phrases.

Modèle:
La Loire et le Rhône (fleuve / long) Ce sont de longs fleuves.

1. New York (ville/grand):
____
2. Jennifer Aniston et Courteney Cox (actrices/beau):
____
3. N. Sarkozy et J. Chirac (présidents/français):
____
4. Macgyver et Jack Bauer (hommes/débrouillard):
____
5. Les étudiants de 506 (étudiants/bon):
____
6. Notre Dame (cathédrale/vieux):
____
7. Camille et Audrey (filles/mignon):
____
8. Amy Winehouse (chanteuse/fou):
____
9. Mia Hamm et Venus Williams (femmes/sportif):
____
10. P. Picasso et S. Dali (peintres/créatif):
____

At home, please go to the Français interactif website. Read the following grammar points in Tex's French Grammar and complete all Texercises which you will turn in to your instructor.

4.3 adjectives that precede the noun

! Remember that adjectives in French are normally placed after the noun:

un tatou intelligent

The following adjectives are exceptions and usually precede the noun.
To remember them, think of the mnemonic 'BANGS' (Beauty, Age, Numbers, Goodness & Size)

autre
beau (bel, belle)
bon (bonne)
grand (grande)
gros (grosse)
jeune
joli (jolie)
mauvais (mauvaise)
nouveau (nouvel, nouvelle)
petit (petite)
vieux (vieil, vieille)

ordinal numbers:	premier (première), deuxième, troisième, etc.

Exercice 16. C'est toi, Tex!

Donnez la forme correcte de l'adjectif entre parenthèses.

Tex et Tammy regardent le ______________________ album de famille de Rita. (new)

Tammy:	Qui est cette __________________________________ femme? (beautiful)
Rita:	C'est notre mère.
Tammy:	Et qui sont ces __________________________________ personnes? (other)
Rita:	Le ______________ homme, c'est Paw-Paw Louis. Et puis, à côté, c'est moi. (old)
Tammy:	Et ce ________________________ bébé, qui est-ce? (little) Comme il est laid!
Rita:	C'est toi, Tex. C'est la ____________________________ photo de toi. (first)

Exercice 17. Qui est-ce?

Avec un partenaire nommez:

1. C'est une femme. Elle est italienne. Elle est brune et belle. C'est la femme de Nicolas Sarkozy. Qui est-ce? C'est ____
2. C'est un garçon. Il est amusant et débrouillard. Il n'est pas discipliné. C'est un personnage de la télévision. Son père s'appelle Homer. Qui est-ce? C'est ____________
3. C'est une femme. C'est une chanteuse canadienne. Elle a les cheveux châtains. Elle est riche et célèbre. Qui est-ce? C'est ______________________________________
4. C'est un homme. C'est un golfeur américain. Il est de Californie. Il est grand, noir, et beau. Qui est-ce? C'est ____

Exercice 18. Grammaire interactive.

How would you translate?

C'est un garcon. ____

Il est amusant . ____

How is "he is" translated in French?
Look at Exercice 17 and decide for each phrase if c'est or il/elle est was used.

	C'est	Il /elle est
1. un garçon	√	❑
2. amusant	❑	√
3. une chanteuse canadienne	❑	❑
4. riche et célèbre	❑	❑
5. de Californie	❑	❑

What part of speech (noun, verb, preposition, adjective, etc.) is **de**?
What part of speech is **riche**, **célèbre**?

Fill in the blanks with c'est or il/elle est:

Before a noun (with an article), we use ____________

Before an adjective, we use ____________

Before a preposition, we use ____________

Exercice 19. Une célébrité

Est-ce que vous connaissez bien les célébrités internationales? Pensez à deux personnes et décrivez-les en complétant les phrases suivantes.

Woody Allen   Sigmund Freud (autrichien)

Par exemple: Sigmund Freud, Bill Gates, Albert Einstein, Céline Dion, Claude Monet, etc.

1. C'est un(e)____________________(profession).
   Il/elle est ____________________(nationalité).
   Il/elle est ____________________ et ________________(deux adjectifs).
2. C'est un(e)____________________(profession).
   Il/elle est ____________________(nationalité).
   Il/elle est ____________________ et ________________ (deux adjectifs).

Caricatures reprinted with permission from www.magixl.com

At home, please go to the Français interactif website. Read the following grammar points in Tex's French Grammar and complete all Texercises which you will turn in to your instructor.

4.4 c'est vs il/elle est
C'est/Ce sont

+ *noun*	Tex et Tammy? Ce sont des tatous.
+ *proper noun*	Qui est-ce? C'est Bette.
+ *disjunct. pronoun*	C'est moi!
+ *dates*	C'est le quatorze juillet.
+ *infinitive*	Vivre, c'est parler français!
+ *adj. for non-specific referents*	C'est formidable! C'est bien!

Il/Elle est...
Ils/Elles sont

+ *adjective alone*	Tex? Il est arrogant!
+ *nationality occupation religion*	Il est... poète. améric-ain.

Exercice 20. C'est qui?

Complétez les phrases suivantes avec c'est, il/elle est, ce sont, ou ils/elles sont et devinez (guess) qui sont ces personnes.

1. ______________________ un homme.
   ______________________ de taille moyenne.
   ______________________ français.
   ______________________ prétentieux et ambitieux.
   ______________________ franc.
   ______________________ le président de la République française.
2. ______________________ une femme.
   ______________________ brune et jolie.
   ______________________ actrice.
   ______________________ une bonne actrice.
   ______________________ française.
   ______________________ dans les films Amélie, Da Vinci Code, et Priceless.

Exercice 21. C'est vs il/elle est

Complétez les phrases suivantes avec c'est, il/elle est, ce sont, ou ils/elles sont.

1. UT, ______________________ une grande université.
2. Fiona, __________ une fourmi intelligente. __________ sincère et gentille.
3. Bette et Tammy, ______________________ des Américaines.
4. Edouard, __________ un serveur (waiter). __________ prétentieux et snob.
5. Joe-Bob et Edouard, ______________________ les amis de Tex.
6. ______________________ amusants, mais un peu bizarres.

Exercice 22. Quel verbe?

Quels verbes pronominaux associez-vous avec…

1. les vacances ____________________
2. le matin ____________________
3. le soir ____________________
4. les amis ____________________
5. le stress ____________________

Exercice 23. Logique ou illogique?

	logique	illogique
1. Les étudiants paresseux se réveillent tôt le matin.	❑	❑
2. Les dentistes se brossent les dents une fois par semaine.	❑	❑
3. Les hommes se maquillent tous les jours.	❑	❑
4. Les petits enfants se couchent à 8 heures du soir.	❑	❑
5. Les étudiants s'amusent en classe.	❑	❑

Exercice 24. La journée typique de votre prof…

A. Avec un partenaire, regardez les phrases suivantes et devinez l'ordre chronologique des habitudes de votre prof (#1-8).
B. Ensuite écoutez le récit de votre professeur et comparez.

_____a. Je me maquille / me rase devant le miroir.

_____b. Je me lève en général à 7 heures et demie.

_____c. Je m'habille lentement.

_____d. Je me réveille avec difficulté.

_____e. Je me lave.

_____f. Je ne me couche jamais avant minuit.

_____g. Je me brosse les dents avec soin (with care).

_____h. Je me coiffe en 2 minutes.

C. Et vous? Comparez ces phrases avec un partenaire. Quelles phrases sont vraies pour vous? Pourquoi ou pourquoi pas?

At home, please go to the Français interactif website. Read the following grammar points in Tex's French Grammar and complete all Texercises which you will turn in to your instructor.

4.5 verbes pronominaux

se raser
'to shave oneself'

je	**me rase**
tu	**te rases**
il / elle / on	**se rase**
nous	**nous rasons**
vous	**vous rasez**
ils / elles	**se rasent**

! Les femmes sont plus propres que les hommes !

88% des femmes se lavent les mains après être allées aux toilettes, contre seulement 66% des hommes. C'est en tous cas ce que montrent les résultats d'une étude américaine menée par la Société américaine de microbiologie (ASM) et l'Association américaine des produits d'hygiène (SDA).

www.plurielles.fr/sante-forme/sante/femmes-plus-propres-que-hommes-3549983-402.html

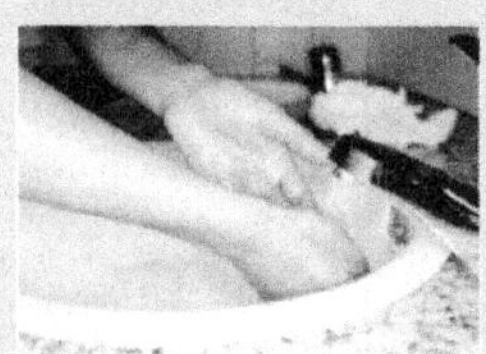

Exercice 25. Votre hygiène?

Est-ce que vous avez une bonne hygiène? Assez bonne? Pas bonne? Posez les questions suivantes à votre partenaire.

	oui	non
1. Tu te laves toujours les mains avant de manger?	❑	❑
2. Tu te laves les cheveux tous les jours?	❑	❑
3. Tu te brosses les dents après chaque repas?	❑	❑
4. Tu te brosses les cheveux trois ou quatre fois pendant la journée?	❑	❑
5. Tu te maquilles ou tu te rases tous les jours?	❑	❑

Marquez un point pour les réponses "oui", zéro pour les réponses "non". Additionnez les points.
En classe: Calculez les points. Est-ce que votre partenaire a une bonne hygiène? Assez bonne? Pas bonne?

5 points	3 ou 4 points	Moins de 3 points
Vous vous intéressez peut-être un peu trop à votre hygiène. Pensez un peu aux choses plus sérieuses. Est-ce que vous aimez lire un bon livre de temps en temps?	C'est bien. Vous faites attention à votre hygiène, mais pas trop.	**Attention!** Vous risquez de vous négliger

Exercice 26. Votre journée

Décrivez votre journée typique. Ecrivez au moins 10 phrases. Utilisez au moins 5 verbes pronominaux, mais variez vos verbes.

Exercice 27. Les amoureux

Regardez l'image et cochez la phrase qui est vraie.

1.	Ils se disputent.	❑	Ils ne se disputent pas.	❑
2.	Ils se fâchent.	❑	Ils ne se fâchent pas.	❑
3.	Ils s'amusent.	❑	Ils ne s'amusent pas.	❑
4.	Ils s'embrassent.	❑	Ils ne s'embrassent pas.	❑
5.	Ils se parlent.	❑	Ils ne se parlent pas.	❑
6.	Ils se regardent.	❑	Ils ne se regardent pas.	❑
7.	Ils se marient.	❑	Ils ne se marient pas.	❑

Exercice 28. Tes habitudes.

Posez ces questions à vos camarades.

1. Est-ce que tu t'amuses en classe? ________________________________ .
2. Est-ce que tu te disputes souvent avec tes copains? ____________________ .
3. Est-ce que tu t'ennuies pendant les vacances?__________________________ .
4. Est-ce que tu te reposes le week-end? ______________________________ .
5. Est-ce que tu te couches toujours avant minuit?_________________________ .

! Parlez uniquement en français! Si la réponse est "OUI", demandez la signature de cette personne. Changez de camarade pour chaque question. Ecoutez attentivement les questions qu'on vous pose. Ne répondez pas à des questions incomplètes.

Exercice 29. Vous êtes perfectionniste ou fumiste?

A. Avec un partenaire, décidez si les activités suivantes caractérisent quelqu'un qui est perfectionniste ou fumiste.

	Perfectionniste	Fumiste
1. Il/Elle s'amuse tout le temps avec des amis.	❑	❑
2. Il/Elle se dépêche tout le temps.	❑	❑
3. Il/Elle se réveille à six heures du matin.	❑	❑
4. Il/Elle se lève à midi.	❑	❑
5. Il/Elle écoute de la musique quand il/elle fait des devoirs.	❑	❑
6. Il/Elle ne s'ennuie pas dans un cours de finance.	❑	❑
7. Il/Elle étudie tout le temps.	❑	❑
8. Il/Elle se couche à quatre heures du matin parce que les bars sont fermés (closed).	❑	❑
9. Il/Elle ne se repose jamais!	❑	❑
10. Il/Elle se couche à quatre heures du matin parce qu' il/elle fait des devoirs "extra-credit".	❑	❑

Perfectionniste

Quelqu'un qui est travailleur et ambitieux, très actif et sérieux, assez compétitif.

Fumiste

Quelqu'un qui est sociable, amusant, pas très sérieux et quelquefois un peu paresseux

B. Avec votre partenaire, ajoutez quatre activités qui caractérisent les gens qui sont perfectionniste ou fumiste. Utilisez au moins deux verbes pronominaux. Donnez deux activités pour chaque type de personnalité.

	perfectionniste	fumiste
Modèle: Il/Elle se fâche rarement.	❑	√
1. ________________________________	❑	❑
2. ________________________________	❑	❑
3. ________________________________	❑	❑
4. ________________________________	❑	❑

C. Décidez si votre partenaire est plutôt perfectionniste ou fumiste. Pour chaque activité, posez une question en phrase complète.

Modèle:
Tu t'amuses tout le temps avec tes amis?

Devoirs:
Votre partenaire a quel type de personalité? Pourquoi?

Modèle:
Mon partenaire est perfectionniste parce qu'il se réveille à six heures du matin, il se dépêche tout le temps....

Selon (according to) votre partenaire, est-ce que vous êtes plutôt perfectionniste ou fumiste? Etes-vous d'accord? Pourquoi? Pourquoi pas?
Dans un autre paragraphe, indiquez si vous êtes d'accord avec votre partenaire, et expliquez pourquoi.

Modèle:
Je suis d'accord avec mon partenaire. Je suis plutôt fumiste, parce que je ne me réveille jamais à six heures du matin...

Exercice 30. Vrai ou faux?

Avec un partenaire, décidez si les phrases suivantes sont vraies ou fausses.

	vrai	faux
1. Tony Parker est plus grand que Brad Pitt.	❑	❑
2. Johnny Depp est plus beau que George Clooney.	❑	❑
3. Nelson Mandela est moins tolérant que Rush Limbaugh.	❑	❑
4. Albert Einstein est aussi intelligent que Marie Curie.	❑	❑
5. Andy Roddick est plus sportif que Lance Armstrong.	❑	❑
6. Oprah est aussi ambitieuse que Sandra Bullock.	❑	❑
7. Le président américain est moins arrogant que le président français.	❑	❑
8. Tiger Woods est aussi hypocrite que Jesse James.	❑	❑

Exercice 31. Et vous?

A. Complétez les phrases suivantes avec les célébrités de votre choix.

1. ________________________ est un bon acteur, mais _____________ est meilleur.
2. __________________ est une mauvaise chanteuse, mais _____________ est pire.
3. ______________________ est une bonne actrice, mais _____________ meilleure.
4. ____________________ est un mauvais journaliste, mais _____________ est pire.
5. _____________ et _____________ sont de bon(ne)s étudiant(e)s, mais _____________ sont meilleur(e)s.

B. Et vous? Comparez vos phrases avec un partenaire. Est-ce que vous êtes d'accord?

NOTE CULTURELLE

Les stéréotypes français sur l'Amérique

(des jeunes de 14-15 ans dans la ville d'Orléans)

- Les garçons sont blonds aux yeux bleus, c'est-à-dire en deux mots très mignons.
- Ils ont de très bonnes musiques.
- Ils sont sportifs, grands, blonds, les yeux bleus. Ils sont aventureux, accueillants (welcoming), serviables (accomodating).
- Ils sont gros. Ils mangent mal.
- Ils sont très riches et ils ont tous des révolvers. Ils sont violents.
- Ils nous imposent des mots. Exemple: parking, tee-shirt, un stop ou des magazines portant comme nom Girl.
- Ils portent un tee-shirt d'université et un short.
- Ils sont nationalistes et impérialistes

Adapté de Les Français by Laurence Wylie (2nd ed, Prentice-Hall, 1995)

At home, please go to the Français interactif website. Read the following grammar points in Tex's French Grammar and complete all Texercises which you will turn in to your instructor.

4.6 comparisons with adjectives

Plus ... que	more... than
Moins ... que	less than
Aussi ... que	as ... as

Exercice 32. Et vous?

A. Complétez les phrases suivantes.

Modèle:
Je suis aussi intelligent que Johnny Depp!

1. Je suis aussi ________________________________ que ...
2. Je suis moins ________________________________ que...
3. Mais je suis plus ________________________________ que..

B. Comparez vos descriptions avec les autres étudiants dans la classe.

Exercice 33. Quelques comparaisons.

Comparez les choses et les personnes suivantes. Utilisez plus que, moins que, et aussi que.

Modèle:
le sport / la musqique   La musique est plus agréable que le sport.

1. la télévision / l'internet (intéressant)
2. la ville / la campagne (calme)
3. les chats / les chiens (affectueux)
4. les hommes / les femmes (travailleur)
5. Et vous? Ecrivez une phrase avec une bonne comparaison.

Exercice 34. A votre avis.

Avec un partenaire, complétez les phrases suivantes.

1. ________________________________ sont aussi patients que les parents.
2. ________________________________ sont plus débrouillards que les enfants.
3. ________________________________ sont moins indépendants que les chats.

Exercice 35. Meilleur.
Comparez d'après vos préférences.

Modèle:
l'hiver et l'été   L'hiver est bon, mais l'été est meilleur.

1. les sciences et les langues
2. la famille et les amis
3. le bus et le métro
4. Et vous? Faites une phrase personnelle.

5 Bon appétit!

In this chapter we will talk about French food, what the French like to eat, where they buy it, and how to prepare typical French dishes.

Vocabulaire

- *à table*
- *au marché, au supermarché*
- *à la boucherie*
- *à la charcuterie*
- *à la poissonnerie*
- *à l'épicerie*
- *à la boulangerie-pâtisserie*
- *au café*
- *au restaurant*
- *des plats typiquement français*
- *expressions de quantité*
- *adjectifs*
- *verbes*

Phonétique

- *les syllables*

Grammaire

- *5.1 partitive articles*
- *5.2 expressions of quantity*
- *5.3 -ir verbs (regular)*
- *5.4 -re verbs (irregular)*
- *5.5 boire, croire, voir*
- *5.6 interrogative words: où, quand, comment ...*
- *5.7 questions with subject/verb inversion*

- *testez-vous!, chapitre 05*
- *verb conjugation reference*
- *verb practice*

Vidéos

Vocabulaire en contexte

- *au marché, les fruits*
- *au marché, les légumes*
- *une poissonnerie*
- *une épicerie*
- *une boulangerie-pâtisserie*
- *au restaurant, en entrée*
- *au restaurant, en plat principal*
- *au restaurant, en dessert*

Interviews

- *les repas*
- *la cuisine*
- *la cuisine française*

Culture

- *impressions of French food*
- *une cave dans le Beaujolais*
- *la fondue*
- *les galettes de Pérouges*

Chapitre 5

Vocabulaire

Préparation du vocabulaire

Be sure to download the pdf vocabulary preparation template from the FI website to complete Exercises B, E, and F.

! Your instructor will collect this homework.

! Note: These can be used as expressions of quantity by adding 'de'; un verre de = a glass of

A table	**At the table**
un verre	glass
une tasse	cup
un bol	bowl
une assiette	plate
un couteau	knife
une fourchette	fork
une cuillère	spoon
la cuisine	kitchen, cooking
un repas	meal
le petit déjeuner	breakfast
le déjeuner	lunch
le goûter	snack
le dîner	dinner, supper

Au marché / Au supermarché	**At the market / At the supermarket**
des fruits (m)	**fruits**
des bananes (f)	bananas
des cerises (f)	cherries
des citrons (m)	lemons
des fraises (f)	strawberries
des framboises (f)	raspberries
des oranges (f)	oranges
des pamplemousses (m)	grapefruit
des pêches (f)	peaches
des poires (f)	pears
des pommes (f)	apples
du raisin	grapes

des légumes (m)	**vegetables**
de l'ail (m)	garlic
des asperges (f)	asparagus
des aubergines (f)	eggplants
des carottes (f)	carrots
des champignons (m)	mushrooms
des choux (m)	cabbage
des concombres (m)	cucumbers
des courgettes (f)	zucchini
des épinards (m)	spinach
des haricots verts (m)	green beans
une/de la laitue	lettuce
des oignons (m)	onions
des petits pois (m)	peas
des poireaux (m)	leeks
des poivrons verts (m)	green peppers
des pommes de terre (f)	potatoes

de la salade	salad, lettuce
des tomates (f)	tomatoes

A la boucherie	**At the butcher shop**
Chez le boucher, on achète...	At the butcher's, you buy...
de la viande	meat
du boeuf	beef
du porc	pork
du veau	veal
du canard	duck
de la dinde	turkey
du poulet	chicken

A la charcuterie	**At the pork butcher shop/delicatessen**
Chez le charcutier, on achète...	At the pork butcher's, you buy...
du jambon	ham
du pâté	pâté
des saucisses (f)	sausages
du saucisson	hard sausage (salami)

A la poissonnerie	**At the seafood shop**
Chez le poissonnier, on achète...	At the fish merchant's, you buy...
du poisson	fish
du saumon	salmon
de la sole	sole
du thon	tuna

A l'épicerie	**At the grocery store**
Chez l'épicier, on trouve...	At the grocer's, you find...
des céréales (m)	cereal
un oeuf, des oeufs	eggs
des noix (f)	walnuts
des produits laitiers (m)	dairy products
du beurre	butter
du lait	milk
du fromage	cheese
du yaourt	yogurt
de la glace	ice cream
des épices (f)	spices
du sel	salt
du poivre	pepper

de l'huile (f)	oil
du vinaigre	vinegar
de la mayonnaise	mayonnaise
de la moutarde	mustard

A la boulangerie-pâtisserie	**At the bakery-pastry shop**
Chez le boulanger, on trouve...	At the baker's, you find...
du pain	bread
une baguette	baguette
une brioche	brioche
un croissant	croissant
un petit pain	roll
Chez le pâtissier, on trouve...	At the pastry chef's, you find...
des pâtisseries (f)	pastries
un gâteau	cake
un gâteau au chocolat	chocolate cake
une tarte	tart
une tarte aux pommes	apple tart
une tarte au citron	lemon tart
une tarte à la fraise	strawberry tart

Au café	**At the café**
Au café, on commande...	At the café, you order...
des boissons non-alcoolisées (f)	non-alcoholic beverages
du café	coffee
du thé (chaud, glacé)	tea (hot, iced)
du coca-cola	cola
de l'eau (f)	water
de l'eau minérale	mineral water
du jus de fruit	fruit juice
des boissons alcoolisées (f)	alcoholic beverages
de la bière	beer
du champagne	champagne
du vin	wine
du vin blanc (du blanc)	white wine
du vin rosé (du rosé)	rosé wine
du vin rouge (du rouge)	red wine
un sandwich jambon beurre	sandwich with ham and butter
un croque-monsieur	toasted cheese sandwich with ham
un croque-madame	croque-monsieur with a fried egg
une quiche (lorraine, au saumon, etc.)	quiche (lorraine, salmon, etc.)
une omelette (aux fines herbes, au fromage)	omelette (with herbs, cheese)

Au restaurant	**At the restaurant**
Au restaurant, on commande...	At the restaurant, you order...
un apéritif	before dinner drink
une entrée	appetizer / first course
un plat principal	main course
un dessert	dessert
une boisson	drink, beverage

Des plats typiquement français	**Typical French dishes**
Des entrées	**appetizers**
des crudités (f)	raw vegetables plus vinaigrette
une salade (avec des lardons, des noix, etc.)	salad (with bacon, nuts, etc.)
de la soupe à l'oignon	onion soup
Des plats principaux	**main courses**
du boeuf bourguignon	beef stewed in red wine
du coq au vin	chicken (rooster) stewed in red wine
un steak-frites	steak and French fries
Des desserts	**desserts**
de la mousse au chocolat	chocolate mousse
de la crème caramel	caramel custard
de la crème brûlée	crème brûlée
du fondant au chocolat	rich chocolate flourless cake

Expressions de quantité	**Expressions of quantity**
un peu de	a little
assez de	enough
beaucoup de	a lot
trop de	too much (too many)
une cuillère de	a spoonful of
une bouteille de	a bottle of
un pichet de	a pitcher of
un litre de	a liter of
50 grammes de	50 grams of
un kilo de	a kilo of
un morceau de	a piece of
une tranche de	a slice of
une boîte de	a can of
un rôti de boeuf	a beef roast
une côtelette de porc	a pork chop
une douzaine d'oeufs	a dozen eggs

Chapitre 5

Vocabulaire

Adjectifs	**Adjectives**
délicieux / délicieuse	delicious
frais / fraîche	fresh
épicé(e)	spicy
grillé(e)	grilled
hâché(e)	chopped
salé(e)	salty
sucré(e)	sweet

Verbes	**Verbs**
avoir faim / avoir soif	to be hungry / to be thirsty
boire	to drink
déjeuner	to have lunch
dîner	to have dinner
faire le marché	to go grocery shopping
faire la cuisine	to cook
prendre un repas	to have a meal
faire la vaisselle	to do the dishes
grossir	to gain weight
faire un régime	to be on a diet
maigrir	to lose weight
choisir	to choose
finir	to finish
grandir	to grow up
obéir à	to obey
réfléchir à	to reflect (on)
réussir à	to succeed
croire	to believe
prendre	to take
apprendre	to learn
(apprendre à quelqu'un)	(to teach someone)
comprendre	to understand
surprendre	to surprise

Phonétique

Go to the website for a complete explanation and practice exercises.

Introduction

Regardons la video ensemble pour répondre aux questions suivantes: Qui présente le chapitre? Où est-il/elle? Quels sont les thèmes du chapitre?

! **Rappel:** Use a definite article (le, la, les) with verbs of preference.

Exercice 1. Quels sont vos goûts (tastes)?

A. Complétez les phrases suivantes.

1. Comme légume, j'aime __________ et je déteste __________
2. Comme fruit, j'aime __________ et je déteste __________
3. Comme viande, j'aime __________ et je déteste __________
4. Comme poisson, j'aime __________ et je déteste __________
5. Comme charcuterie, j'aime __________ et je déteste __________
6. Comme boisson, j'aime __________ et je déteste __________

B. Ensuite, en classe, vous allez comparer vos goûts avec les goûts d'un partenaire. Ecoutez ses phrases et puis, complétez les phrases suivantes.

1. Comme légume, il/elle aime__________ et il/elle déteste __________
2. Comme fruit, il/elle aime __________ et il/elle déteste __________
3. Comme viande, il/elle aime __________ et il/elle déteste __________
4. Comme poisson, il/elle aime __________ et il/elle déteste __________
5. Comme charcuterie,il/elle aime __________ et il/elle déteste __________
6. Comme boisson, il/elle aime __________ et il/elle déteste __________

C. Est-ce que vous avez les mêmes goûts que votre partenaire? Pourquoi ou pourquoi pas?

> **Modèle:**
> J'adore les escargots mais mon partenaire préfère la truite.

Dictogloss 1. Faire une omelette.

Formez des groupes de 3 ou 4 personnes. Ecoutez le texte lu par votre professeur.
Complétez les phrases suivantes et donnez le plus de détails possibles.

Aujourd'hui nous allons preparer une omelette au jambon et aux champignons.

Dans une omelette au jambon, il y a ______________ , ________________,

________________ , ____

et ________________ .

Casser ____________________ et mélanger. J'adore _______________ !

Découper ____________ et verser les morceaux de _______ dans le bol.

Ajouter ____ .

Verser ___________________________________ dans le bol. Pas trop!

Verser une __________________________ d' ________ dans la poêle,

Verser les morceaux de __________________________ dans la poêle.

C'est prêt! Hmmm c'est délicieux!

Exercice 2. Grammaire interactive. La recette.

How do you translate the following sentence into English?

Il y a **des** oeufs, **du** jambon, **des** champignons **du** fromage, **de la** crème et **de l**'huile.

When you translated the sentence above, did you use articles before the nouns?
- **du**, **de la**, **de l'** are called partitive articles.

The partitive article _______ is used before a noun starting with a vowel or a mute "h".

The partitive article _______ is used before a masculine noun starting with a consonant.

The partitive article _______ is used before a feminine noun starting with a consonant.

Countable vs Uncountable

Countable *nouns refer to items that can be counted:*
- She eats an apple every day.
  Elle mange une pomme chaque jour.

Uncountable nouns refer to items that cannot be counted:
- She's eating bread.
  Elle mange du pain.
- Do you have some water?
  Tu as de l'eau?

Some nouns can be either **countable or uncountable**
- We'll have some coffee, please.
  On va prendre du café, s'il vous plaît.
- We'll have two coffees, please.
  On va prendre deux cafés, s'il vous plaît.

Can you think of a context for the two last sentences?

For each of the following items decide if they are countable or uncountable

	countable	uncountable
1. oeufs	❑	❑
2. jambon	❑	❑
3. champignons	❑	❑
4. fromage	❑	❑
5. crème	❑	❑
6. huile	❑	❑

Look at the following sentence
Il y a **des** oeufs, **du** jambon, **des** champignons **du** fromage, **de la** crème et **de l**'huile.

Countable or uncountable? Fill in the blank.

The partitive article **du – de la – de l**' is used with ________________________ nouns.

Definite article vs partitive

The definite article designates something in its totality, or as a whole:

- Bread is good.
  Le pain est bon.
- I love apples!
  J'adore les pommes.

The partitive article designates a part of the whole.

- She's eating bread.
  Elle mange du pain.
- She's eating apples.
  Elle mange des pommes.

Look at the following sentences and decide whether they refer to something as a whole or a part of the whole.

1. Il y a des oeufs.
2. Il y a du jambon.
3. Je déteste le lait.
4. J'adore les oeufs!
5. Elle mange de la salade.

NOTE CULTURELLE

Le petit-déjeuner

D'habitude au petit-déjeuner on prend un croissant (ou du pain avec du beurre et de la confiture) avec du café au lait ou du chocolat chaud. Les Français ne mangent jamais d'oeufs ou de jambon le matin. On boit aussi du jus de fruit. Certains gens préfèrent les céréales.
En général, les Français aiment les repas structurés, en famille ou avec des amis, qui durent assez longtemps. Il n'est pas rare de passer trois ou quatre heures à table le dimanche après-midi. Pour manger correctement, il est nécessaire de prendre son temps et de diversifier sa nourriture.

Le repas de midi

Le repas de midi est traditionnellement le repas le plus important de la journée. Souvent, les magasins, les banques, et les bureaux de poste sont fermés entre midi et deux heures. A quatorze heures, les restaurants ferment et le service recommence vers vingt heures. D'habitude, les Français ne prennent pas le dîner avant vingt heures.

Exercice 3. Quelle photo va avec chaque mot?

a

b c

d e

f g h

i j k

l m n o

p q r s t

_____1. un oeuf
_____2. une tarte
_____3. du jus d'orange
_____4. de l'eau
_____5. une fraise
_____6. du lait
_____7. des champignons
_____8. du fromage
_____9. du pain
_____10. de la dinde
_____11. des carottes
_____12. du raisin
_____13. un croissant
_____14. des cerises
_____15. un poivron
_____16. un gâteau
_____17. des poires
_____18. de la glace
_____19. une pomme
_____20. de la salade

Exercice 4. Les repas.

Décidez avec un partenaire quand les Français prennent les aliments suivants.

	au petit déjeuner	au déjeuner
1. On prend de la salade...	❑	❑
2. On prend des céréales...	❑	❑
3. On boit du thé...	❑	❑
4. On boit du café au lait...	❑	❑
5. On mange du boeuf ou du veau...	❑	❑
6. On prend du beurre et de la confiture...	❑	❑
7. On mange des oeufs...	❑	❑
8. On prend du pain.	❑	❑
9. On boit du jus d'orange...	❑	❑
10. On prend une tarte aux pommes...	❑	❑
11. On mange des croissants...	❑	❑
12. On boit de l'eau minérale...	❑	❑

Exercice 5. Quel magasin?

On vend...

______1.	du saucisson et du pâté	a.	à la boucherie
______2.	des gâteaux et des tartes	b.	à la boulangerie-pâtisserie
______3.	du fromage et des céréales	c.	à la charcuterie
______4.	une baguette et des croissants	d.	à l'épicerie
______5.	des oignons et des tomates	e.	au marché
______6.	de la sole et du thon	f.	à la poissonnerie
______7.	des bananes et des cerises		
______8.	du poulet et du veau		

At home, please go to the Français interactif website. Read the following grammar points in Tex's French Grammar and complete all Texercises which you will turn in to your instructor.

5.1 determiners: partitive articles

masc.	**du (pain)**
fem.	**de la (viande)**
masc. or fem. before vowel.	**de l'ail (m.) de l'eau (f.)**

Partitive articles are used before mass nouns. They express quantities that are indivisible or cannot be counted.

Exercice 6. Qu'est-ce que tu manges?

Posez ces questions à vos camarades.

1. Est-ce que tu manges du pâté? ____________________
2. Est-ce que tu prends de la salade tous les jours? ____________________
3. Est-ce que tu bois de l'eau minérale? ____________________
4. Est-ce que tu manges des escargots? ____________________
5. Est-ce que tu prends souvent du poisson? ____________________
6. Est-ce que tu manges du yaourt? ____________________
7. Est-ce que tu bois du jus d'orange au petit déjeuner? ____________________
8. Est-ce que tu prends le dessert avant le dîner? ____________________
9. Est-ce que tu manges souvent de la viande? ____________________
10. Est-ce que tu aimes manger des plats épicés? ____________________ .

! Parlez uniquement en français! Si la réponse est "OUI", demandez la signature de cette personne. Changez de camarade pour chaque question. Ecoutez attentivement les questions qu'on vous pose. Ne répondez pas à des questions incomplètes.

prendre is used to say what you 'have' at a meal. See 5.4 for conjugation of prendre.

! **Remember:** After the negative, indefinite articles (un, une, des) and partitive artices (du, de la, de l') change to de or d' in a negative sentence : Il n'y a pas de chocolat dans une quiche.

Exercice 7. Bizarre ou normal?

	bizarre	normal
1. Dans une quiche, il y a des oeufs, du jambon et du sucre.	❑	❑
2. Dans un hamburger, il y a du boeuf, de la laitue et du ketchup.	❑	❑
3. Dans une fondue, il y a du fromage, du vin blanc et du pain.	❑	❑
4. Dans un gâteau au chocolat, il y a du chocolat, du sucre et du poivre.	❑	❑
5. Dans une vinaigrette, il y a de l'huile, du sel et de la moutarde.	❑	❑
6. Dans une tarte aux pommes, il y a du fromage, des pommes et du sucre.	❑	❑

Exercice 8. Les habitudes alimentaires de Tex.

Trouvez la bonne association pour chaque phrase.

Tex ...	Il ...
______1. ...va à la boucherie.	a. ne mange pas de marrons.
______2. ...va à la charcuterie.	b. va manger une tarte aux pommes.
______3. ...mange des céréales.	c. achète du jambon.
______4. ...est allergique aux noix.	d. va manger du gâteau au chocolat.
______5. ...aime les pommes.	e. achète de la viande.
______6. ...aime les desserts sucrés.	f. prend le petit déjeuner.

Exercice 9. Vous et votre régime

Qu'est-ce que vos préférences gastronomiques indiquent sur votre personnalité? Pour savoir (to know, to find out), faites ce petit test.

1. Au petit déjeuner, vous prenez en général:
   a. rien du tout (nothing at all)
   b. des oeufs et des toasts
   c. du yaourt avec des céréales
   d. un croissant ou un pain au chocolat

2. A midi, en général, vous prenez:
   a. une pizza
   b. un bifteck hâché avec des frites
   c. une salade d'épinards
   d. un plat chinois

3. Pour votre goûter de quatre heures en général:
   a. une tablette de chocolat
   b. un taco
   c. une pomme (ou un autre fruit)
   d. du thé avec une brioche

4. Si c'est vous qui préparez le dîner, vous faites en général:
   a. des spaghettis à la sauce tomate
   b. de la pizza
   c. une soupe de légumes
   d. un canard à l'orange

Une majorité d' A	Une majorité de B	Une majorité de C	Une majorité de D
Vous êtes plus pressé(e) que réellement intéressé(e) par la cuisine. Apprenez à prendre le temps de bien manger.	Vous mangez comme un(e) vrai(e) Américain(e). C'est bien, mais vous avez besoin d'essayer de nouveaux plats!	Est-ce que vous êtes végétarien(ne)? C'est très bon pour la santé, mais n'oubliez pas de manger des protéines (du tofu, des céréales complets, des haricots, etc.)	Vous êtes un(e) vrai(e) gourmet avec des goûts variés!

Adapté du livre ENCORE!

Exercice 10. Qu'est-ce qu'ils mangent?

Qu'est-ce qu'ils mangent? Qu'est-ce qu'ils ne mangent pas?

Modèle:
les végétariens: Les végétariens mangent des oranges, des carottes et de la salade. Ils mangent peut-être du poisson, mais ils ne mangent jamais de boeuf.

1. les athlètes (Lance Armstrong, par exemple)
2. les personnes qui font un régime
3. les enfants

Dictogloss 2. Les goûts alimentaires de votre prof

Formez des groupes de 3 ou 4 personnes. Ecoutez le texte lu par votre professeur. Complétez les phrases suivantes et donnez le plus de détails possibles.

Tous les jours je bois ______________________________________

au petit déjeuner et je mange __________________________________.

Je ne mange pas ____________________________________.

Pour le déjeuner, je prends souvent ____________________ avec de la viande ou

__________________________________. J'aime beaucoup________________

ou ______________________. Je mange toujours ______________________

et ____ et en dessert je prends

______________________________ ou ___________________________.

Pour le dîner, j'aime prendre ___________________ et du pain. Comme___________

j'aime ________________________ mais ______________________________

le vin rouge. Je bois toujorus. __________________________________

____

Exercice 11. Madame Guilloteau fait la cuisine.

Madame Guilloteau va préparer le déjeuner. Complétez les phrases suivantes avec un article défini, indéfini ou partitif:

Madame Guilloteau adore _________ cuisine française. Pour le déjeuner, elle va préparer _________ quiche lorraine en entrée et _________ coq au vin en plat principal. Pour le dessert, elle va faire _________ mousse au chocolat.

Madame Guilloteau va acheter _________ farine, _________ beurre, _________ lait, _________ jambon et _________ fromage pour faire la quiche. Elle achète aussi _________ poulet, _________ vin rouge, _________ carottes et _________ oignons pour le plat principal. Pour _________ mousse au chocolat elle va prendre _________ chocolat, _________ sucre et _________ oeufs.

Elle achète aussi _________ eau minérale et _________ café. Elle n'achète pas _________ coca, parce que sa famille n'aime pas _________ coca.

Exercice 12. Vos goûts -- Qu'est-ce que vous prenez?

A. Posez les questions suivantes à un partenaire. Donnez 3 choses pour chaque question.

1. Qu'est-ce que tu prends au petit-déjeuner d'habitude? ______________________________ .
2. Qu'est-ce que tu prends au déjeuner d'habitude? ______________________________ .
3. Qu'est-ce que tu prends au goûter d'habitude? ______________________________ .
4. Qu'est-ce que tu prends au dîner d'habitude? ______________________________ .

B. Partagez vos réponses avec la classe

Exercice 13. Au supermarché

Donnez un produit logique pour chaque quantité.

1. une bouteille de ______________________________ .
2. un litre de ______________________________ .
3. un kilo de ______________________________ .
4. un morceau de ______________________________ .
5. 500 grammes de ______________________________ .

At home, please go to the Français interactif website. Read the following grammar points in Tex's French Grammar and complete all Texercises which you will turn in to your instructor.

5.2 determiners: expressions of quantity

Expressions of quantity are always followed by
- de: beaucoup de pain
- d' if the noun begins with a vowel sound: une bouteille d'eau

Exercice 14. Trop, beaucoup, un peu, ou pas du tout?

Posez les questions suivantes à un camarade et notez ses réponses.

Modèle:
Tu manges du pain?

Oui, je mange	❑ trop ❑ beaucoup ❑ un peu	...de pain.
ou		
Non, je ne mange	❑ pas	...de pain.

	Je mange…	
1. Tu manges de la viande rouge?	❑ trop de ❑ beaucoup de ❑ un peu de ❑ ne…pas	...viande rouge.
2. Tu manges de la salade?	❑ trop de ❑ beaucoup de ❑ un peu de ❑ ne…pas	...salade.
3. Tu manges du beurre?	❑ trop de ❑ beaucoup de ❑ un peu de ❑ ne…pas	...beurre.
4. Tu manges des pâtisseries?	❑ trop de ❑ beaucoup de ❑ un peu de ❑ ne…pas	...pâtisseries.
5. Tu manges des fruits?	❑ trop de ❑ beaucoup de ❑ un peu de ❑ ne…pas	...fruits.

6. Tu manges des légumes?

Je mange…
- ❑ trop de
- ❑ beaucoup de
- ❑ un peu de
- ❑ ne…pas

…légumes.

7. Tu manges du chocolat?

Je mange…
- ❑ trop de
- ❑ beaucoup de
- ❑ un peu de
- ❑ ne…pas

…chocolat.

8. Tu manges du poisson?

Je mange…
- ❑ trop de
- ❑ beaucoup de
- ❑ un peu de
- ❑ ne…pas

…poisson.

Est-ce que votre partenaire mange bien? Pourquoi ou pourquoi pas?

Exercice 15. Des recettes de Madame Guilloteau

Voici des recettes de Madame Guilloteau. Décidez quelle recette va avec chaque photo.

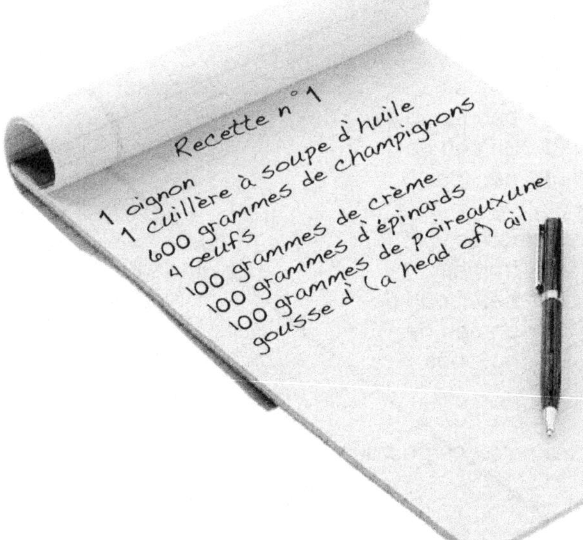

Recette n°2 _____
- *50 grammes de sucre*
- *2 oeufs*
- *20 grammes de beurre*
- *100 grammes de chocolat*

Recette n°3 _____
- *50 grammes de farine (flour)*
- *1 cuillère à café de cognac*
- *1 bouteille de vin rouge*
- *2 cuillères à soupe de cognac*
- *1,5 kilo de coq*
- *100 grammes de petits oignons*
- *100 grammes de carottes*
- *une gousse d' (a head of) ail*
- *250 grammes de champignons*

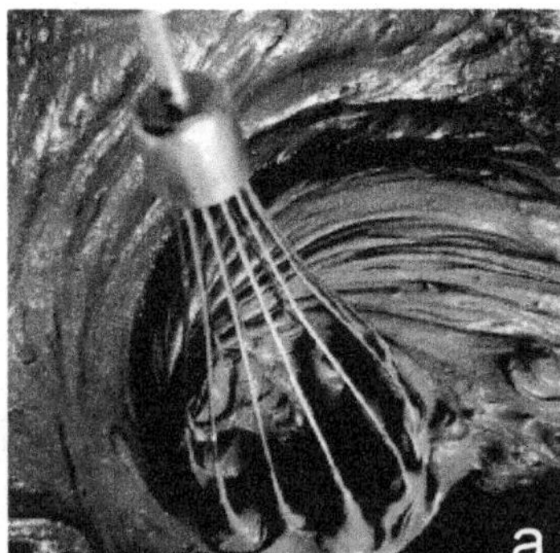

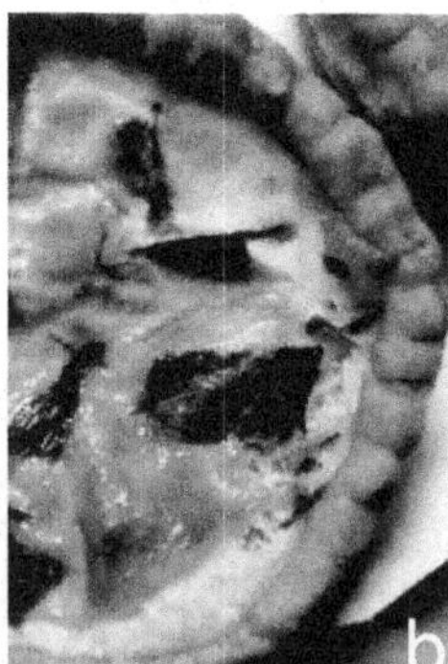

Recette n°4 _____
- *200 grammes de lardons (bacon)*
- *4 tranches de pain*
- *4 oeufs*
- *300 grammes de laitue*
- *2 cuillères à soupe d'huile*
- *1 cuillère à soupe de vinaigre*
- *sel et poivre*

Quelles recettes sont pour l'entrée? Et pour le plat principal? Et pour le dessert?

Exercice 16. Quelle recette préférez-vous?

A. Votre professeur va lire deux recettes. Ecoutez et complétez le tableau suivant.

	le pho	le fattouche
1. Quel pays d'origine:		
2. Quelle sorte de plat:		
3. Pour quel repas:		
4. Les légumes et les fruits dans la recette:		
5. Les épices:		
6. La viande:		

B. Maintenant, trouvez un partenaire. Comparez vos réponses pour chaque recette. Parlez uniquement en français.

C. Quel plat est-ce que vous aimez le plus? Et votre partenaire? Expliquez pourquoi. Rapportez votre discussion à la classe.

Exercice 17. Dans votre frigo

A. Qu'est-ce que vous avez dans votre frigo? Dessinez les fruits, les légumes, les boissons et les autres choses que vous avez dans votre frigo. Dessinez au moins (at least) six choses et écrivez les noms aussi.

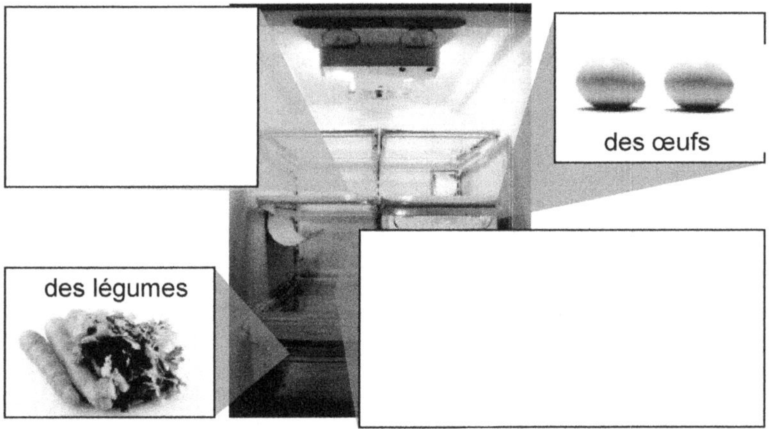

B. Maintenant, comparez votre dessin avec le dessin d'un partenaire. Est-ce que vous avez les mêmes choses dans vos frigos? Chez vous, est-ce que vous avez des choses différentes de votre partenaire? Qu'est-ce que vous avez dans votre frigo que votre partenaire n'a pas? Est-ce que votre partenaire a assez de provisions dans son frigo pour préparer un bon dîner? Expliquez pourquoi ou pourquoi pas.

C. Discutez vos résultants avec la classe.

At home, please go to the Français interactif website. Read the following grammar points in Tex's French Grammar and complete all Texercises which you will turn in to your instructor.

5.3 –ir verbs (regular)

finir 'to finish'

je	**finis**
tu	**finis**
il *elle* *on* }	**finit**
nous	**finissons**
vous	**finissez**
ils *elles* }	**finissent**

grossir
maigrir
choisir
grandir
obéir à
réfléchir à
réussir à

! **Rappel:** Sortir, partir, dormir are irregular -ir verbs. Review their conjugations in 3.3.

Exercice 18. Quel verbe en -ir?

Quels verbes associez-vous avec…

1. les enfants ______
2. les parents ______
3. les gourmands ______
4. les amis ______
5. les étudiants ______
6. les sportifs ______

Exercice 19. Singulier ou pluriel?

Ecoutez et decidez si le verbe est au singulier ou au pluriel. Ecoutez une deuxième fois et écrivez la phrase.

	singulier	pluriel
Modèle: Ils réussissent leurs examens.	❑	√
1. ______	❑	❑
2. ______	❑	❑
3. ______	❑	❑
4. ______	❑	❑
5. ______	❑	❑
6. ______	❑	❑
7. ______	❑	❑
8. ______	❑	❑

Exercice 20. Vrai ou faux?

Décidez si les phrases suivantes sont vraies ou fausses.

	vrai	faux
1. Les mauvais étudiants finissent toujours leurs devoirs	❑	❑
2. Les bons étudiants réussissent souvent leurs examens.	❑	❑
3. Les mauvais étudiants choisissent des cours difficiles.	❑	❑
4. Les mauvais étudiants obéissent aux règles. (rules).	❑	❑
5. Les bons étudiants réfléchissent avant de répondre.	❑	❑

Exercice 21. Et toi?

Posez les questions suivantes à un camarade et comparez vos réponses.

Modèle:
Tu finis toujours tes devoirs?
-Oui, je finis toujours mes devoirs. / Non, je ne finis pas mes devoirs.
Et toi, est-ce que tu finis tes devoirs?
-Oui, moi aussi, je finis toujours mes devoirs./ Non, moi non plus (me neither), je ne finis pas mes devoirs.

	oui	non
1. Tu finis toujours tes devoirs?	❑	❑
2. Tu réussis souvent tes examens?	❑	❑
3. Tu choisis des cours difficiles?	❑	❑
4. Tu accomplis beaucoup?	❑	❑
5. Tu obéis aux règles?	❑	❑
6. Tu réfléchis avant de répondre?	❑	❑

Modèle:
Nous sommes de bon(ne)s étudiant(e)s parce que nous finissons toujours nos devoirs....

Exercice 22. Les choix

Quand vous allez au restaurant, qu'est-ce que vous choisissez en général? Posez les questions suivantes à un partenaire et notez ses réponses. Est-ce que vous choisissez les mêmes choses?

Quand tu vas au restaurant, est-ce que tu choisis.....

1. …en entrée: une salade ou de la soupe ou ____________________________ ?
2. …comme plat principal: du poulet, du boeuf, un plat végétarien ou ________________ ?
3. …comme boisson: un coca, de l'eau, du thé ou ____________________________ ?
4. …en dessert: de la glace à la vanille, au chocolat, à la fraise ou ________________ ?

At home, please go to the Français interactif website. Read the following grammar points in Tex's French Grammar and complete all Texercises which you will turn in to your instructor.

5.4 –re verbs (irregular) like prendre

prendre to take'

je	**prends**
tu	**prends**
il / *elle* / *on*	**prend**
nous	**prenons**
vous	**prenez**
ils / *elles*	**prennent**

apprendre
comprendre
surprendre

Exercice 23. Singulier ou pluriel?

Ecoutez chaque phrase et décidez si le verbe est au singulier ou au pluriel. Ecoutez une deuxième fois et écrivez la phrase.

	singulier	pluriel
Modèle: Il prend un taxi.	√	❑
1. ______________________	❑	❑
2. ______________________	❑	❑
3. ______________________	❑	❑
4. ______________________	❑	❑
5. ______________________	❑	❑

Exercice 24. Un camarade de classe

A. Choisissez un étudiant que tout le monde connaît bien. Cette personne va s'éloigner de la classe.

B. Ecrivez le prénom de l'étudiant choisi. Puis en groupes de 3 ou 4 complétez chaque phrase d'après les intuitions de votre groupe.

l'étudiant[e]: ____________________

1. prend ______________________(le bus, son vélo, sa voiture, un taxi...) pour aller à l'université.
2. apprend ______________________ (l'espagnol, l'italien, l'allemand)
3. comprend ______________________ .(les maths, les sciences, la philosophie)

Par contre, ____________(l'étudiant[e])

4. ne prend pas ________________
5. n'apprend pas ________________.
6. ne comprend pas ______________.

C. Chaque groupe va rendre ses phrases complètes au professeur. Puis le professeur va lire toutes les phrases. Si l'étudiant(e) choisi(e) dit "Oui, c'est vrai" alors le groupe reçoit un point. Quel est le groupe qui connaît le mieux l'étudiant(e) (who knows the student the best)?

Exercice 25. A quelle heure?

Posez les questions suivantes à un partenaire.

A quelle heure est-ce que tu prends le petit déjeuner? le déjeuner? et le dîner?

Est-ce que vous avez les mêmes habitudes que votre partenaire? Discutez avec la classe.

Exercice 26. Singulier, pluriel ou impossible à distinguer?

Ecoutez chaque phrase et décidez si le verbe est au singulier, au pluriel ou s'il est impossible à distinguer. Ecoutez une deuxième fois et écrivez la phrase.

	singulier	pluriel	impossible à distinguer
Modèle: Il boit du thé.	√	❑	❑
1. ______________________	❑	❑	❑
2. ______________________	❑	❑	❑
3. ______________________	❑	❑	❑
4. ______________________	❑	❑	❑
5. ______________________	❑	❑	❑

Exercice 27. Qu'est-ce qu'ils boivent?

Completez les phrases suivantes.

1. Les sportifs boivent ______________________.
2. Les Anglais boivent ______________________.
3. Pendant les examens, les étudiants boivent ______________________.
4. Les Allemands boivent______________________.
5. Les enfants boivent ______________________.
6. Les Américains ______________________.
7. Les Français. ______________________

Exercice 28. Qu'est-ce qu'on boit?

Vous allez au restaurant avec trois amis. Ils vous demandent de choisir les boissons. Un de ces amis ne boit pas d'alcool, donc trouvez au moins (at least) 2 boissons possibles.

1. Est-ce que vous prenez un apéritif? Si oui, on boit ______________________ ou ______________________.
2. Comme entrée, vous prenez du saumon avec du beurre sur des morceaux de pain. Donc on ______________________ boit ou ______________________.
3. Comme plat principal vous prenez du boeuf. Donc on boit ______________________ ou ______________________.
4. Après le dessert, on prend ______________________.

At home, please go to the Français interactif website. Read the following grammar points in Tex's French Grammar and complete all Texercises which you will turn in to your instructor.

5.5 boire, croire, voir

boire 'to drink'
croire 'to believe'
voir 'to see'

je	bois crois vois
tu	bois crois vois
il *elle* *on* }	boit croit voit
nous	buvons croy-ons voyons
vous	buvez croyez voyez
ils *elles* }	boivent croient voient

NOTE CULTURELLE

Les repas français

Les repas français sont bien variés et équilibrés. On mange un peu de tout...des légumes, de la viande, de la salade, du pain, et du fromage. Après le fromage, on prend un fruit, un yaourt, ou bien un dessert. Et n'oubliez pas...on ne boit pas le café avec le dessert, mais après!

Exercice 29. Est-ce que vous aimez les mêmes boissons?

Comparez vos boissons habituelles avec un partenaire. Est-ce que vous buvez les mêmes boissons?

Est-ce que vous avez les mêmes habitudes?

Modèle: Au petit déjeuner, qu'est-ce que tu bois? Je bois du café.

Qu'est-ce que tu bois...
1. au dîner?
2. quand il fait chaud?
3. quand tu regardes la télé?
4. avec des plats salés?
5. avec des plats sucrés?

Exercice 30. Vous êtes sceptique?

A. En groupes de 3 ou 4, répondez aux questions suivantes. Est-ce que vous...

	oui	non
	❑	❑
1. croyez aux fantômes?	❑	❑
2. croyez aux extra-terrestres?	❑	❑
3. croyez aux OVNIs (objets volants non-identifiés)?	❑	❑
4. croyez au Père Noël?	❑	❑

B. Comparez vos réponses avec celles de la classe. Quel groupe est le plus sceptique?

Exercice 31. Qu'est-ce que tu vois?

Complétez les phases suivantes.

1. Dans la salle de classe, on voit ______________________________
2. Dans un restaurant français, on voit ______________________________
3. A McDo, on voit ______________________________
4. De la fenêtre, on voit ______________________________

Exercice 32. Vos habitudes.

A. Avec un partenaire, décidez si les aliments suivants sont bons ou mauvais pour la santé.

	bon	mauvais
1. le pain	❑	❑
2. le poulet	❑	❑
3. le coca-cola	❑	❑
4. la salade	❑	❑
5. le fromage	❑	❑
6. la pizza	❑	❑
7. les légumes	❑	❑
8. le poisson	❑	❑
9. le lait	❑	❑
10. la bière	❑	❑
11. la viande rouge	❑	❑
12. la glace	❑	❑

Est-ce que la classe est d'accord avec vous?

B. Ajoutez cinq aliments ou boissons que votre partenaire mange et boit régulièrement. Est-ce qu'ils sont bons ou mauvais pour la santé?

Modèle:	**Vous demandez:**	**Votre partenaire répond:**
	Qu'est-ce que tu manges régulièrement?	Je mange des céréales.
	Qu'est-ce que tu bois régulièrement?	Je bois de la bière

	bon	mauvais
Modèle: des céréales	√	❑
Modèle: des céréales	❑	√
1. ______________________	❑	❑
2. ______________________	❑	❑
3. ______________________	❑	❑
4. ______________________	❑	❑
5. ______________________	❑	❑

NOTE CULTURELLE

Déroulement d'un repas français

On prend l'apéritif avant le dîner pour ouvrir l'appétit. On mange souvent des olives, du saucisson, des chips, et des cacahuettes (peanuts). On prend ou bien des boissons non-alcoolisées comme des jus de fruits ou du coca, ou bien des boissons alcoolisées comme du muscat (a sweet wine from Provence), du pastis (licorice flavored liqueur mixed with water), un kir (white wine with cassis syrup) ou du porto (port). Avec le dîner on boit du vin ou de l'eau. Après le dessert, on prend un café et peut-être un digestif (an alcoholic after-dinner drink, such as a brandy or other liqueur).

At home, please go to the Français interactif website. Read the following grammar points in Tex's French Grammar and complete all Texercises which you will turn in to your instructor.

5.6 interrogative words: où, quand, comment...

Interrogative words (où, quand, comment, pourquoi, combien, combien de) are used with either

• *est-ce que:*

Où est-ce qu'elles sont?

or

• *subject/verb inversion:*

Tammy et Bette, où sont-elles? (See 5.7)

*Note that the question word always goes before est-ce que

C. Qu'est-ce que vous pensez des habitudes alimentaires de votre partenaire?

Modèle: Les habitudes de mon/ma partenaire, ___________, sont (très bonnes, bonnes, normales, mauvaises ou très mauvaises), parce qu'il/qu'elle mange beaucoup de ....., et boit souvent de.... A mon avis il/elle ne mange pas assez de___________.

Devoirs: Etes-vous d'accord avec votre partenaire? Expliquez et décrivez vos habitudes alimentaires dans un paragraphe de 8 phrases.

Exercice 33. Vendredi soir!

A. Choisissez un étudiant que tout le monde connaît bien. Cette personne va s'éloigner du groupe.
B. Ecrivez le prénom de l'étudiants choisi. Puis complétez chaque phrase d'après les intuitions de votre groupe.

l'étudiant[e]: ___________________________

1. Où est-ce qu'il/elle va vendredi soir? Il/Elle va ___________________________
(au cinéma, à la bibliothèque, au restaurant, ...)
2. Avec qui est-ce qu'il/elle va? Il/Elle va avec ___________________________
(ses parents, ses amis, sa copine/son copain, ...)
3. Comment est-ce qu'ils vont à cet endroit (that place)? Ils vont à cet endroit ________
(en voiture, à pied, en bus, ...)
4. Quand est-ce qu'ils vont à cet endroit? Ils vont à cet endroit ___________________
(à quelle heure?)
5. Pourquoi est-ce qu'ils vont à cet endroit? Ils vont à cet endroit parce que (+ sujet + verbe) / pour ___________________________
(+ infinitif) ___________________________

Exercice 34. Les grandes vacances?

A. Transformez les questions suivantes en utilisant l'inversion.

1. Où est-ce que vous allez passer les grandes vacances? ______________________
____
2. Est-ce que vous aimez aller à l'étranger? ______________________________
____
3. Qu'est-ce que vous faites en vacances? ________________________________
____
4. Avec qui est-ce que vous voyagez? ____________________________________
____
5. Est-ce qu'il(s)/elle(s) font les mêmes activités que vous? ______________
____

B. Ensuite posez ces questions à votre professeur.

Exercice 35. Encore des questions!

A. Quelles sont les questions à poser à un camarade de classe pour connaître (know)

1. son nom ______________________
2. sa nationalité ______________________
3. son âge ______________________
4. ses passe-temps préférés ______________________

B. Quelles sont les questions avec "est-ce que" pour savoir:

1. pourquoi il étudie le français

____

2. ce qu'il/elle boit le matin

____

3. si il/elle sort souvent

____

4. si il/elle a une page sur Facebook

____

5. quand il/elle prend le petit déjeuner

____

6. où il/elle habite

____

C. En classe, posez les questions de la section B à votre partenaire.

D. Devoirs: Ecrivez un dialogue basé sur votre conversation avec au moins 4 questions et 4 réponses complètes.

At home, please go to the Français interactif website. Read the following grammar points in Tex's French Grammar and complete all Texercises which you will turn in to your instructor.

5.7 questions with subject/verb inversion

Inversion is sometimes used to ask formal questions:

• formed by reversing subject pronoun/verb order.

Avez-vous faim? Préférez-vous le vin blanc ou le vin rouge?

Exercice 36. Paul Bocuse.

Connaissez-vous Paul Bocuse, le grand chef cuisinier français? Chevalier de la Légion d'honneur et désigné "Cuisinier du Siècle" par Gault-Millau en 1989, il a trois étoiles au Guide Michelin depuis 1965! Voici le menu classique de l'Auberge du Pont de Colonges, son restaurant près de Lyon.

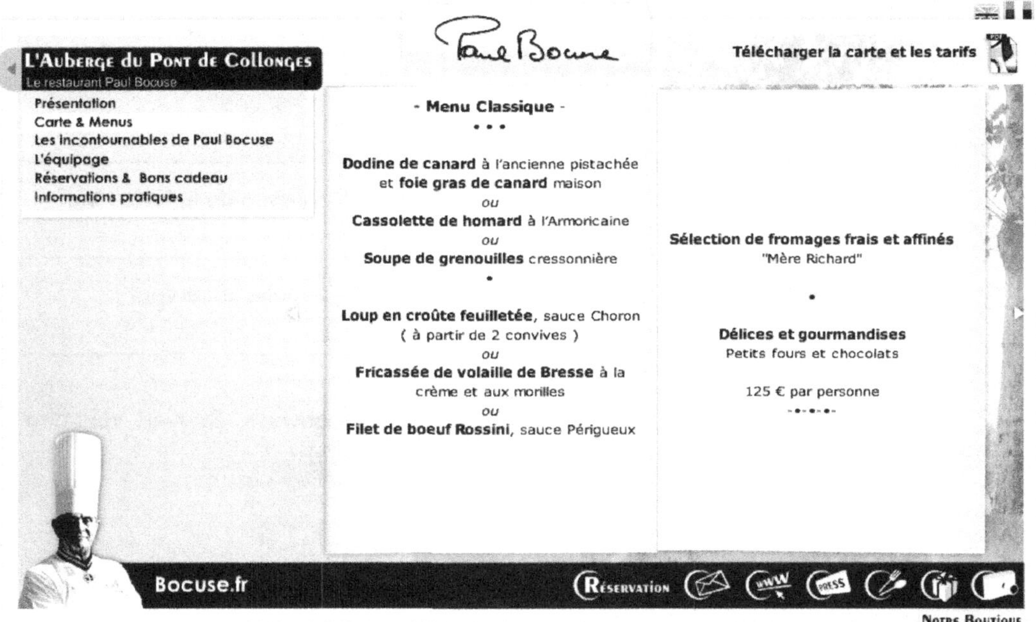

Regardez le menu avec un partenaire.

1. Quel est le prix de ce menu fixe?

   Quels sont les quatre plats (courses)?

   ____

   ____

   ____

   ____

2. Quelle entrée préférez-vous? Pourquoi?

   ____

   ____

3. Quel plat principal préférez-vous?

   Pourquoi?

   ____

   ____

Exercice 37. Les brasseries de Bocuse.

Heureusement Paul Bocuse a aussi cinq brasseries à Lyon. Ses brasseries sont beaucoup moins chères que son restaurant.

Voici l'addition d'une de ses brasseries. Regardez l'addition avec un partenaire et répondez aux questions suivantes.

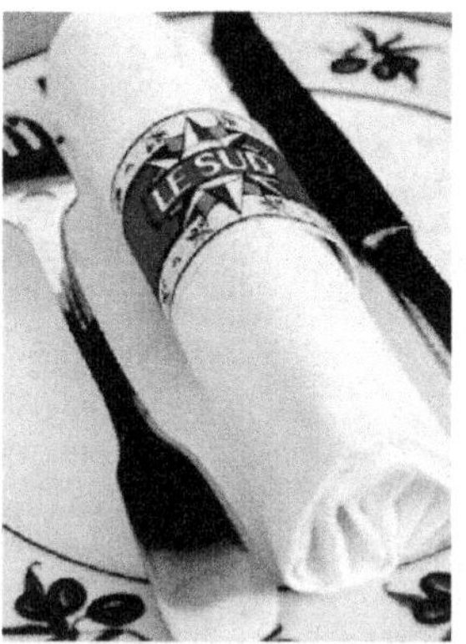

LE SUD - 11, PLACE ANTONIN-PONCET - 69002 LYON - TÉL. 04 72 77 80 00 - FAX 04 72 77 80 01
S.A.R.L. CAPITAL 160 000 € • RCS B 400 778 742 - SIRET 400 778 742 00017 - N° TVA intracommunautaire FR 92 400 778 742

Serveur: Serge 2

Table: 203 — 2 Couvert(s)
Facture: 0434 01 RS — Le 08/07/09

2 KIR	9.60
1 BOURGOGNE RGE	22.00
2 MENU ENTREE PLAT	39.20
2 DESSERT	4.40
1 EXPRESSO	2.20
1 DECAFEINE	2.20
TOTAL EN EURO	79.60

TVA 19.60% :
26.42 * 19.60% 5.18
TVA 5.5% :
45.50 * 5.50% 2.50

L'ÉTABLISSEMENT N'ACCEPTE PLUS LES RÈGLEMENTS PAR CHÈQUE BANCAIRE.
PRIX NET INCLUANT : TVA 19,6 % ET SERVICE 12 %
CETTE FACTURE NE DOIT COMPORTER AUCUNE RECTIFICATION MANUSCRITE.

1. C'est quelle brasserie?

 ____

2. Quelle est l'adresse de la brasserie?

 ____

3. Comment s'appelle le serveur?

 ____

4. Il y a deux couverts. 'Couvert' veut dire:
   a. place setting
   b. spoon
   c. blanket
   d. person

5. Qu'est-ce que les clients prennent comme apéritif?

 ____

6. Qu'est-ce qu'ils boivent avec le dîner?
   a. de l'eau
   b. du vin rouge
   c. du vin blanc
   d. du café

7. Qu'est-ce qu'ils boivent après le dessert?
   a. de l'eau
   b. du vin rouge
   c. du vin blanc
   d. du café

8. Ils prennent quels plats (courses)?
   a. une entrée + un plat principal
   b. un plat principal
   c. une entrée + un plat principal + un fromage
   d. une entrée + un plat principal + un dessert

Vocabulaire

- *la ville*
- *les petits commerces*
- *s'orienter*
- *les nombres ordinaux*
- *verbes qui prennent être au passé composé*
- *autres verbes*
- *participes passés irréguliers*

Phonétique

- *Les voyelles /i/ /y/ /u/*

Grammaire

- *6.1 -re verbs (regular)*
- *6.2 contractions of à and de with definite article*
- *6.3 demonstrative determiners*
- *6.4 passé composé with avoir*
- *6.5 passé composé with être*

- *testez-vous!, chapitre 06*
- *verb conjugation reference*
- *verb practice*

Vidéos
Vocabulaire en contexte

- *à l'aéroport Roissy Charles de Gaulle*
- *la ville de Lyon*
- *Chamonix*

Interviews

- *le week-end dernier*
- *votre vie*

Culture

- *les monuments de Paris*
- *le Louvre*
-

6 *La ville*

In this chapter we will learn vocabulary to describe places in a French city and how to give directions. We will also learn to talk about the past.

Chapitre 6

Vocabulaire

Préparation du vocabulaire

Be sure to download the pdf vocabulary preparation template from the FI website to complete Exercises B, E, and F.

! Your instructor will collect this homework.

La ville	The city
une place	public square
une rue	street
un boulevard	boulevard
une avenue	avenue
un quartier	neighborhood
l'arrondissement (m)	administrative district in a large city (e.g. Paris)
le centre-ville	downtown
la banlieue	suburbs
un bâtiment	building
un bureau	office
un immeuble	apartment building
une maison	house
un hôtel	hotel
une boutique	boutique
un magasin (de musique, de vidéo, etc.)	store (music, video, etc.)
un centre commercial	shopping center, mall
un supermarché	supermarket
un café	café
un restaurant	restaurant
un musée	museum
un cinéma	movie theater
une boîte de nuit / une discothèque	a nightclub, dance club
un théâtre	theater
un stade	stadium
un parking	parking lot
un parc	park
un jardin public	park, large garden
un fleuve	river
un pont	bridge
une banque	bank
un bureau de poste	post office
une boîte aux lettres	**mailbox**
une cabine téléphonique	phone booth
une laverie	laundromat
l'hôtel de ville (m)	city hall, mayor's office
la mairie	city hall, mayor's office
l'office du tourisme (m)	tourist information office
un hôpital	hospital

Vocabulaire

un aéroport	airport
une gare	train station
une école (6 ans à 11 ans)	school
un collège (11 ans à 15 ans)	junior high, middle school
un lycée (15 ans à 18 ans)	high school
une université	university
une bibliothèque	library
une église	church
une cathédrale	cathedral
une mosquée	mosque
une synagogue	synagogue
un temple (protestant)	temple
Les petits commerces	Small businesses
une épicerie	grocery store
une boucherie	butcher shop
une charcuterie	pork butcher's shop, deli
un traiteur	deli, catering shop
une boulangerie	bakery
une pâtisserie	pastry shop
un bureau de tabac	tobacco shop
une librairie	bookstore
une papeterie	paper/stationery store
une pharmacie	pharmacy
S'orienter	**Getting your bearings**
Où se trouve... ?	Where is... ?
(Où se trouve la poste?)	(Where is the post office?)
à côté (de)	beside, next to
à deux pas (de)	just a step from
à droite (de)	on the right
à gauche (de)	on the left
au bout (de)	at the far end of
au carrefour (de)	at the intersection of
au centre	in the center
au coin (de)	at the corner of
chez	at someone's house
derrière	behind
devant	in front of
en face (de)	facing, opposite
en ville	in the city
loin (de)	far

Les nombres ordinaux

1st	premier, première
2nd	deuxième
3rd	troisième
4th	quatrième
5th	cinquième
6th	sixième
7th	septième
8th	huitième
9th	neuvième
10th	dixième

11th	onzième
12th	douzième
13th	treizième
14th	quatorzième
15th	quinzième
16th	seizième
17th	dix-septième
18th	dix-huitième
19th	dix-neuvième
20th	vingtième

Vocabulaire

avoir	**j'ai eu...**
être	**j'ai été..**
faire	**j'ai fait ..**
prendre	**j'ai pris..**
mettre	**j'ai mis..**
boire	**j'ai bu ..**
croire	**j'ai cru..**
voir	**j'ai vu..**

mourir	**il est mort elle est morte**
naître	**il est né elle est née**

près (de)	near, close
sous	under
sur	on
sur votre droite/gauche	on your right/left
tout droit	straight ahead
tout près	nearby

Verbes qui prennent être au passé composé	**Verbs which take être in the passé composé**
aller	to go
sortir	to go out
partir	to leave
rentrer	to go home, to go back
retourner	to return
arriver	to arrive
entrer	to enter
rester	to stay
monter	to go up, to go upstairs, to climb
descendre	to go down, to go downstairs
tomber	to fall
passer	to pass, to go by (intransitive)
naître	to be born
mourir	to die

Autres verbes	**Other verbs**
se déplacer (en ville)	to get around (town)
prendre le métro, un taxi, etc.	to take the metro, a taxi, etc.
aller à pied	to go on foot
marcher	to walk
tourner	to turn
traverser	to cross
continuer	to continue
demander	to ask (for)
se trouver	to be found, to be located
attendre	to wait for
entendre	to hear
perdre	to lose
rendre	to hand in, give back
rendre visite à quelqu'un	to visit someone
répondre	to answer
vendre	to sell

Phonétique

Go to the website for a complete explanation and practice exercises.

Introduction

Regardons la video ensemble pour répondre aux questions suivantes: Qui présente le chapitre? Où est-il / elle? Quels sont les thèmes du chapitre?

Exercice 1. Vous connaissez Paris?

Est-ce que les phrases suivantes sont vraies ou fausses?

	vrai	faux
1. Les Champs-Elysées c'est une avenue.	❑	❑
2. La Sorbonne est un lycée.	❑	❑
3. CDG est une gare.	❑	❑
4. La Comédie Française est un théatre.	❑	❑
5. Le Ritz est un hôtel.	❑	❑
6. La cathédrale de Notre Dame se trouve dans la banlieue.	❑	❑
7. Il y a vingt arrondissements à Paris.	❑	❑
8. Le fleuve qui traverse Paris s'appelle la Loire.	❑	❑
9. Le Louvre est un grand musée.	❑	❑
10. La Tour d'Argent est un restaurant élégant.	❑	❑

Exercice 2. Où?

Où est-ce qu'on va....

Modèle: Où est-ce qu'on va ... pour poster une lettre? — On va ... au bureau de poste.

_____1. pour voir un match de foot?
_____2. quand on a envie de voyager en train?
_____3. pour trouver des informations sur des sites touristiques?
_____4. pour un rendez-vous romantique?
_____5. pour chercher un livre?
_____6. quand on a besoin de calme et de nature?
_____7. pour boire un café?
_____8. pour visiter une exposition?
_____9. pour prendre l'avion?
_____10. pour aller à la messe?

a. au parc
b. à l'église
c. au café
d. à l'aéroport
e. au pont
f. à l'office du tourisme
g. à la gare
h. à la bibliothèque
i. au stade
j. au musée

NOTE CULTURELLE

Paris

Paris est la plus grande ville de France et la capitale. La ville de Paris est divisée en 20 arrondissements. La Seine court au coeur de Paris et divise la ville en 2 parties, la rive gauche et la rive droite. Les deux rives sont reliées par 37 ponts qui traversent la Seine. Le pont le plus célèbre et le plus ancien s'appelle le Pont Neuf. Il y a aussi beaucoup de monuments à Paris. La Tour Eiffel est le site touristique le plus visité du monde.

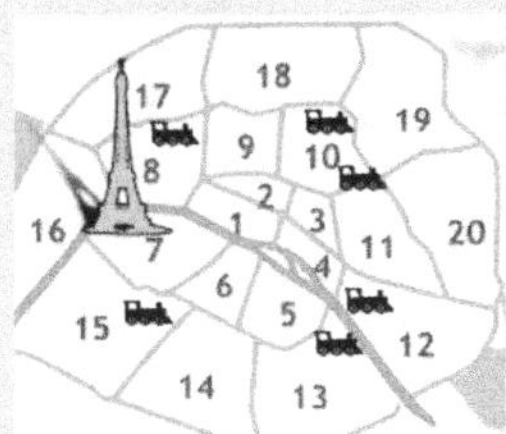

www.asapfrance.info/france/36-000-villes-et-villages/paris-la-capitale

At home, please go to the Français interactif website. Read the following grammar points in Tex's French Grammar and complete all Texercises which you will turn in to your instructor.

6.1 –re verbs (regular)

vendre 'to sell'

je	**vends**
tu	**vends**
il / *elle* / *on*	**vend**
nous	**vendons**
vous	**vendez**
ils / *elles*	**vendent**

Exercice 3. Quel verbe en -re?

A. Quel verbe en -re associez-vous avec...

1. le téléphone ____________________
2. le bus ____________________
3. un magasin ____________________
4. la patience ____________________
5. la musique ____________________
6. les devoirs ____________________
7. une surprise ____________________
8. mes parents ____________________

B. Quel verbe en -re est le contraire de..

1. trouver ____________________
2. acheter ____________________
3. poser une question ____________________
4. monter ____________________

Exercice 4. Grammaire interactive. L'année dernière à Paris.

Qu'est-ce qu'ils ont fait à Paris l'année dernière? (last year) Complétez les phrases suivantes.

Modèle:
A Austin, Karen n'achète pas de viennoiserie mais l'année dernière à Paris elle a acheté ... *des croissants*

1. A Austin, Blake mange des hamburgers mais l'année dernière à Paris, il a mangé ____________________
2. A Austin, Leila et Karen ne visitent pas de monuments, mais l'année dernière à Paris, elles ont visité ____________________
3. A Austin, Toño ne prend pas le bus, mais l'année dernière à Paris, il a pris ____________________
4. A Austin, Blake ne va pas au musée, mais l'année dernière à Paris, il est allé ____________________
5. A Austin, Leila ne boit pas d'alcool, mais l'année dernière à Paris, elle a bu ____________________
6. A Austin Toño fait du sport, mais l'année dernière à Paris, il n'a pas fait de ____________________
7. A Austin, Leila et Karen ne sortent pas, mais l'année dernière à Paris, elles sont sorties ____________________

Exercice 5. Grammaire interactive.

Look at the following sentences

À Austin Blake mange des hamburgers mais l'année dernière à Paris, il a mangé des escargots.
À Austin Blake ne va pas au musée, mais l'année dernière à Paris, il est allé au Louvre.

1. Does il a mangé / il est allé refer to the past, present, or future?
How would you translate the sentences above?

2. Look at the boldfaced elements below.
Il **a** mangé / il **est** allé

What are the infinitives of these verbs? __________________ and ________________

These two verbs are used in the passé composé as auxiliary verbs.

mangé and **sorti** are **past participles**.

3. Fill in the blanks
To express the past, we use the conjugated forms of the auxiliary __________ or ____________

with the ________________________________of the verb.

4. Look at the sentences in Exercise 4 and fill in the following table.

INFINITIVE	Avoir	Etre	Past Participle
acheter	√		acheté
1. manger			
2. visiter			
3. prendre			
4. aller			
5. boire			
6. faire			
7. sortir			

5. Look at the following sentence:
Il n'a pas fait de vélo.

Choose the correct words in parentheses to complete the sentence:

Negation is placed around the (auxiliary / past participle).

6. Look at the following pairs of sentences.

Il a visité la Tour Eiffel / Elle a visité la Tour Eiffel
Ills ont mangé un hamburger / Elles ont mangé un hamburger
Il est allé au Louvre / Elle est allée au Louvre
Ils sont sortis en boite / Elles sont sorties en boite

What do you notice about the past participle in these sentences?

NOTE CULTURELLE

l'aéroport Roissy Charles de Gaulle à Paris

Quand on arrive à l'aéroport CDG, pour aller au centre ville, on prend un taxi, un bus, ou le RER jusqu'au métro. Du Terminale 2, on va à la gare et on prend la ligne du RER. Le RER (RéseauxExpress Régional) sert les alentours (surrounding areas) de Paris. Les lignes du RER sont indiquées par des lettres. Par contre, le métro est pour se déplacer en ville. Les lignes du métro sont indiquées par des numéros. Voici un ticket pour le RER de Paris à Versailles. N'oubliez pas de composter (punch) votre ticket!

! Parlez uniquement en français! Si la réponse est "OUI", demandez la signature de cette personne. Changez de camarade pour chaque question. Ecoutez attentivement les questions qu'on vous pose. Ne répondez pas à des questions incomplètes.

Exercice 6. Singulier ou pluriel?

Ecoutez et décidez si le verbe est au singulier ou au pluriel. Ensuite écrivez la phrase.

	singulier	pluriel
Modèle: Il répond au professeur.	√	❑
1. ______	❑	❑
2. ______	❑	❑
3. ______	❑	❑
4. ______	❑	❑
5. ______	❑	❑
6. ______	❑	❑
7. ______	❑	❑
8. ______	❑	❑

Exercice 7. Oui ou non?

A. L'étudiant typique...

	oui	non
1. attend l'autobus tout le temps.	❑	❑
2. perd souvent ses affaires (ses livres, ses cahiers, etc.)	❑	❑
3. répond toujours aux emails (de ses amis, de ses parents).	❑	❑
4. vend ses livres à la fin du semestre.	❑	❑
5. rend visite à ses parents tous les week-ends.	❑	❑

B. Vous êtes typique? Pourquoi ou pourquoi pas?

Exercice 8. Qu'est-ce que tu fais?

Posez ces questions à vos camarades.

1. Est-ce que tu attends les vacances impatiemment? ______
2. Est-ce que tu apprends l'espagnol? ______
3. Est-ce que tu réponds souvent en classe? ______
4. Est-ce que tu perds souvent ton temps? ______
5. Est-ce que tu vas vendre tes livres? (à la fin du semestre) ______
6. Est-ce que tu vas rendre visite à tes parents ce week-end? ______
7. Est-ce que tu comprends la politique? ______
8. Est-ce que tu prends le bus régulièrement? ______

Exercice 9. Sérieux (sérieuse) ou paresseux (paresseuse)

A. Quel type d'étudiant êtes-vous? Lisez les activités suivantes et indiquez la fréquence de chacune dans votre vie.

Short adverbs are placed directly after the verb.

	toujours	souvent	rarement	ne...jamais
1. Je perds les devoirs.	❑	❑	❑	❑
2. Je réponds aux questions du prof.	❑	❑	❑	❑
3. J'apprends beaucoup.	❑	❑	❑	❑
4. Je comprends la leçon.	❑	❑	❑	❑
5. J'attends la veille (the night before) de l'examen pour réviser.	❑	❑	❑	❑
6. Je rends les devoirs au prof.	❑	❑	❑	❑

B. Comparez vos réponses avec un partenaire. Indiquez la fréquence de chaque activité; utilisez des adverbes. Remplissez le tableau avec les réponses de votre partenaire.

Modèle:
Je perds **toujours** les devoirs. Et toi?
Moi aussi, je perds toujours les devoirs ou Pas moi, je ne perds jamais les devoirs.

	toujours	souvent	rarement	jamais
1. Il/Elle perd les devoirs.	❑	❑	❑	❑
2. Il/Elle répond aux questions du prof.	❑	❑	❑	❑
3. Il/Elle apprend beaucoup.	❑	❑	❑	❑
4. Il/Elle comprend la leçon.	❑	❑	❑	❑
5. Il/Elle attend la veille de l'examen pour réviser. Il/Elle rend les devoirs au prof.	❑	❑	❑	❑
6. Je rends les devoirs au prof.	❑	❑	❑	❑

C. Décidez si votre partenaire est plutôt sérieux(se) ou plutôt paresseux(se). Ecrivez au moins 2 phrases pour justifier votre réponse.

Modèle:
X est plutôt paresseux parce qu'il répond rarement aux questions du prof et il attend toujours la veille de l'examen pour réviser.

D. Devoirs pour demain: Est-ce que vous êtes d'accord avec la décision de votre partenaire? Ecrivez un paragraphe de 8 phrases pour justifier votre opinion.

Modèle:
Je suis d'accord avec X. (Je ne suis pas d'accord.) Je suis sérieux parce que j'apprends beaucoup...

Exercice 10. Quel verbe?

1. Les étudiants __________ toujours aux questions du professeur. (attendre, répondre)
2. Quand nous allons au café, nous ___________ du thé à la menthe. (prendre, vendre)
3. Chez le pâtissier, on ________________________des croissants. (descendre, vendre)
4. Vous__________________ vos devoirs à votre professeur _______________ régulièrement, n'est-ce pas ? (perdre, rendre)
5. Est-ce que tu ______________tes clefs (keys) de temps en temps? (descendre, perdre)
6. A chaque heure, nous _______________ la cloche (bell) sonner. (entendre, répondre)
7. Je suis un étudiant sérieux. Je ne/n' ________________ pas la veille de l'examen pour réviser. (attendre, rendre)
8. Quand je vais en France, je ____________________le RER jusqu'à Paris. (prendre, entendre)

Exercice 11. Les petits commerces

Trouvez la bonne correspondance.

Où est-ce qu'on vend...

_____1. du saucisson et du pâté?	a. à la boucherie.
_____2. des gâteaux et des tartes?	b. à la boulangerie.
_____3. des fruits et du lait?	c. à la charcuterie.
_____4. des cahiers et des stylos?	d. à l'épicerie.
_____5. une baguette et des croissants?	e. au bureau de tabac.
_____6. du poulet et du boeuf?	f. à la pharmacie.
_____7. des timbres et des cigarettes?	g. à la librairie-papeterie.
_____8. de l'aspirine et des vitamines?	h. à la pâtisserie.

Exercice 12. On fait des courses

Choisissez 3 activités de la liste en bas. Annoncez ce que vous allez faire. Votre partenaire va confirmer vos activités en utilisant du vocabulaire de "La Ville" et de "Les Petits Commerces". Cochez (√) les activités complétées. Puis changez de rôle.

Modèle:

- ❑ acheter des timbres
- ❑ voir un film
- ❑ rendre visite à mon prêtre

Partenaire 1: Je vais acheter des timbres, voir un film et rendre visite à mon prêtre.
Partenaire 2: Alors, tu vas aller au bureau de tabac, au cinéma et à l'église, n'est-ce pas?

A FAIRE:

- ❑ acheter des oranges
- ❑ faire du jogging
- ❑ voir un nouveau film
- ❑ prendre un verre de vin
- ❑ envoyer une lettre
- ❑ Je rends les devoirs au prof.
- ❑ téléphoner à ma mère
- ❑ demander des brochures touristiques
- ❑ acheter des médicaments
- ❑ voir une exposition de Manet
- ❑ chercher un livre de philosophie
- ❑ écouter un nouveau disque de rap
- ❑ acheter du pâté

At home, please go to the Français interactif website. Read the following grammar points in Tex's French Grammar and complete all Texercises which you will turn in to your instructor.

6.2 contractions with à and de

de + le	**du**
de + les	**des**
à + le	**au**
à + les	**aux**

NOTE CULTURELLE

Les Halles de Lyon

La ville de Lyon est la capitale de la gastronomie. Les Halles de Lyon sont bien connues (well known) chez les Lyonnais et les gourmands partout. C'est un marché couvert qui existe depuis 1859. On y trouve des traiteurs, des charcutiers, des fromagers, des boulangers-patissiers, des cavistes, des poissonniers, des bouchers, et même des restaurateurs célèbres. En tout, il y a 56 commerçants et artisans qui vendent leurs produits de la meilleure qualité.

Exercice 13. C'est où?

Regardez les photos et complétez les phrases avec une préposition logique.

Modèle: Le casino est sur la place.

1. Les gens sont__________ le musée.

2. Le café se trouve ___________ la rue.

3. Le fleuve est_____________le pont.

4. Les étudiants sont ________________ les Guilloteau.

5. La basilique est _________ les filles.

Exercice 14. Traductions.

Traduisez les phrases suivantes en français.

1. The train station is to the right of the post office.
___
2. The high school is behind the hospital.
___
3. The stadium is close to the university.
___
4. The bank is at the end of the street.
___
5. The tourist information office is on Place Bellecour.
___
6. The pharmacy is just a step away from the catering shop.
___
7. The school is across from (faces) the bakery.
___
8. The shopping center is far from downtown.
___

Exercice 15. Vous connaissez les capitales du monde?

Faites correspondre la capitale avec le pays. Utilisez la forme correcte de: **de + article défini**.

Modèle:
Madrid est la capitale de l'Espagne.

_____1. Ottawa	a. la France
_____2. Niamey	b. le Maroc
_____3. Paris	c. les Antilles Néerlandaises
_____4. Camberra	d. le Canada
_____5. Washington D.C.	e. le Niger
_____6. Willemstad	f. l'Australie
_____7. Londres	g. le Japon
_____8. Tokyo	h. l'Angleterre
_____9. Berne	i. la Suisse
_____10. Rabat	j. les Etats-Unis

NOTE CULTURELLE

Le Louvre et le Musée d'Orsay

Bien sûr il y a beaucoup de musées à Paris. Mais les deux musées les plus connus sont le Louvre et le Musée d'Orsay. Le Louvre, l'ancienne forteresse des rois de France, et un des plus grands musées du monde. On y trouve des sculptures, des objets d'art, des peintures, et des antiquités. Le musée d'Orsay est dans l'ancienne (former) gare d'Orsay. On y trouve beaucoup de sculptures et des oeuvres (works) de Monet, Degas, Manet, Gaugin, Van Gogh, et autres.

At home, please go to the Français interactif website. Read the following grammar points in Tex's French Grammar and complete all Texercises which you will turn in to your instructor.

6.3 demonstrative determiners

ce
cet
cette
ces

Exercice 16. Les activités de Karen.

Complétez les phrases suivantes avec l'article approprié.(au, à la, du, de la,...)

Karen aime l'art et la musique. Le week-end elle va souvent ______ musée et ______ concert. Elle adore la mer. Elle aime faire ______ bateau, et elle fait ______ planche à voile. Elle va souvent ______ campagne ou ______ parc pour faire ______ vélo, mais elle ne fait pas de moto. Les motos sont dangereuses.

Exercice 17. Cette université

Est-ce que les phrases suivantes sont vraies ou fausses?

	vrai	faux
1. Cette université est grande.	❑	❑
2. Ce cours de français commence à midi.	❑	❑
3. Ces étudiants sont travailleurs.	❑	❑
4. Ce professeur est blond.	❑	❑
5. Cet exercice est difficile.	❑	❑
6. Ces étudiantes sont intelligentes.	❑	❑
7. Cet après-midi il va faire beau.	❑	❑
8. Ce vendredi il y a un examen.	❑	❑

Exercice 18. Tu préfères...?

Indiquez ce que vous préférez.

Modèle:
this bank > cette banque

1. this airport > ______
2. that cathedral > ______
3. that restaurant > ______
4. those stores > ______
5. this bakery > ______
6. that café > ______
7. those hotels > ______
8. that train station > ______

Exercice 19. Déjà ou pas encore?

Imaginez…Est-ce que votre professeur a déjà (already) fait ces activités ou est-ce qu'il/elle n'a pas encore (not yet) fait ces activités **aujourd'hui**?

	déjà	pas encore
Modèle: Il/Elle a bu du vin. (Mais non, il/elle n'a pas encore bu de vin.)	❑	√
1. Il/Elle a répondu aux emails.	❑	❑
2. Il/Elle a dit bonjour aux étudiants.	❑	❑
3. Il/Elle a pris le déjeuner.	❑	❑
4. Il/Elle a regardé la télé.	❑	❑
5. Il/Elle a fait du sport.	❑	❑
6. Il/Elle a parlé au téléphone.	❑	❑

At home, please go to the Français interactif website. Read the following grammar points in Tex's French Grammar and complete all Texercises which you will turn in to your instructor.

6.4 passé composé with avoir

je	ai mangé
tu	as mangé
il / *elle* / *on*	a mangé
nous	avons mangé
vous	avez mangé
ils / *elles*	ont mangé

To negate a sentence in passé composé, place ne…pas around auxiliary avoir.

Irregular past participles:

avoir	**j'ai eu...**
être	**j'ai été..**
faire	**j'ai fait ..**
prendre	**j'ai pris..**
mettre	**j'ai mis..**
boire	**j'ai bu ..**
croire	**j'ai cru..**
voir	**j'ai vu..**

Exercice 20. Qu'est-ce qu'elles ont fait?

Trouvez la phrase correcte pour décrire chaque image.

_____a. Elle a chanté.

_____b. Elle a cherché sa soeur.

_____c. Elle a trouvé des cadeaux.

_____d. Elle a parlé au téléphone.

_____e. Elle a choisi les Teletubbies.

_____f. Elle a dansé.

Exercice 21. Tout le temps ou hier?

Ecoutez les phrases suivantes et décidez si les phrases décrivent les activités habituelles de Tex (tout le temps) ou ses activités au passé (hier). Ensuite écrivez la phrase.

	tout le temps	hier
Modèle: Il boit du café au lait.	√	❑
1. ______________________________	❑	❑
2. ______________________________	❑	❑
3. ______________________________	❑	❑
4. ______________________________	❑	❑
5. ______________________________	❑	❑
6. ______________________________	❑	❑
7. ______________________________	❑	❑
8. ______________________________	❑	❑

Exercice 22. Est-ce que vous connaissez (know) bien votre professeur?

En groupes de 3 ou 4 devinez (guess) ce que votre professeur a fait hier.

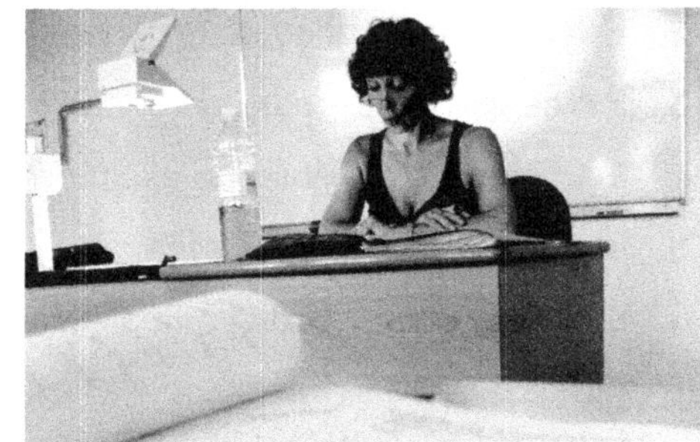

1. Le professeur a dîné…
   a. au restaurant indien.
   b. au restaurant tex-mex.
   c. au restaurant français.
   d. à la maison

2. Le professeur a écouté…
   a. de la musique classique.
   b. du jazz.
   c. du hip-hop.
   d. les informations à la radio

3. Le professeur a fait…
   a. une promenade.
   b. du vélo.
   c. la cuisine.
   d. des corrections.

4. Au supermarché, le professeur a choisi une bouteille…
   a. de coca-cola.
   b. de vin rouge.
   c. de vin rosé.
   d. de lait.

5. Le professeur a rendu visite…
   a. à des amis.
   b. à sa mère.
   c. à son copain/ sa copine.
   d. à un collègue.

6. Le professeur a regardé…
   a. un film français.
   b. la télé.
   c. un match de foot.
   d. un concert.

Quel groupe connaît le prof le mieux?

Exercice 23. Les fêtes!

Lisez les activités de Tammy et décidez pour quelle fête elle a fait chaque activité.

_____1. Tammy a mangé de la dinde avec sa famille.
_____2. Tammy a porté un t-shirt vert.
_____3. Tammy a bu du champagne.
_____4. Tammy a acheté des cadeaux (gifts) pour toute sa famille.
_____5. Tammy a donné des chocolats à Tex.

a. la St-Sylvestre (le 31 décembre)
b. Noël
c. la St-Patrick
d. Thanksgiving
e. la St-Valentin

! Parlez uniquement en français! Si la réponse est "OUI", demandez la signature de cette personne. Changez de camarade pour chaque question. Ecoutez attentivement les questions qu'on vous pose. Ne répondez pas à des questions incomplètes.

Exercice 24. Qu'est-ce que tu as fait la semaine dernière?

Posez ces questions à vos camarades.

1. Est-ce que tu as rencontré tes amis au cinéma?____________________
2. Est-ce que tu as dîné au restaurant?____________________
3. Est-ce que tu as étudié le français?____________________
4. Est-ce que tu as réussi un examen? ____________________
5. Est-ce que tu as fini tes devoirs?____________________
6. Est-ce que tu as rendu visite à tes parents? ____________________
7. Est-ce que tu as pris l'autobus?____________________
8. Est-ce que tu as répondu en classe?____________________

Exercice 25. Et pendant les vacances?

A. Regardez les activités suivantes et complétez les phrases pour parler de vos vacances.

1. J'ai écouté ____________________(du rap, du rock, autre)
2. J'ai été ____________________ (actif/active, paresseux/paresseuse, autre)
3. J'ai rendu visite à ____________________ (mes parents, mes amis, autre)
4. J'ai voyagé ____________________ (à Houston, en France, autre)
5. J'ai regardé ____________________ (la télévision, un film,autre)
6. J'ai joué ____________________ (au basket, aux cartes,autre)

B. Ensuite, en classe, vous allez comparer vos activités avec celles d'un partenaire.

Modèle:
Qu'est-ce que tu as écouté pendant les vacances?
Moi, j'ai écouté du rock. Et toi? J'ai écouté de la musique classique.

C. Est-ce que vous avez fait les mêmes activités pendant les vacances?

Modèle:
Oui et non.
Tous les deux, nous avons voyagé à Dallas. Mais j'ai aussi voyagé à New York.

Exercice 26. Vous connaissez (do you know) les Etats-Unis?

A. Regardez les activités suivantes et indiquez si vous avez déjà fait ces activités ou jamais.

Activités:	Oui, déjà	Non, jamais
1. J'ai mangé de la pizza à Chicago.	❑	❑
2. J'ai pris un taxi à Los Angeles.	❑	❑
3. J'ai fait du bateau en Floride.	❑	❑
4. J'ai visité Alcatraz.	❑	❑
5. J'ai bu du café à Seattle.	❑	❑
6. J'ai fait du ski dans le Colorado.	❑	❑
7. J'ai vu une pièce de théâtre à Broadway.	❑	❑
8. J'ai dansé dans un club à la Nouvelle Orléans.	❑	❑
9. J'ai rencontré des amis au Nouveau Mexique.	❑	❑

B. Comparez vos réponses en A avec un partenaire. Remplissez le tableau avec les réponses de votre partenaire.

Modèle: J'ai déjà mangé de la pizza à Chicago. Et toi?
Moi aussi, j'ai déjà mangé de la pizza à Chicago.
or
Pas moi, je n'ai pas encore mangé de pizza à Chicago.

Activités:	Oui, déjà	Non, pas encore
1. Il/Elle a mangé de la pizza à Chicago.	❑	❑
2. Il/Elle a pris un taxi à Los Angeles.	❑	❑
3. Il/Elle a fait du bateau en Floride.	❑	❑
4. Il/Elle a visité Alcatraz.	❑	❑
5. Il/Elle a bu du café à Seattle.	❑	❑
6. Il/Elle a fait du ski dans le Colorado.	❑	❑
7. Il/Elle a vu une pièce de théâtre à Broadway.	❑	❑
8. Il/Elle a dansé dans un club à la Nouvelle Orléans.	❑	❑
9. Il/Elle a rencontré des amis au Nouveau Mexique.	❑	❑

C. Posez les questions suivantes à votre partenaire. Qu'est-ce qu' il/elle a vu d'autre aux Etats-Unis?

	moi	mon partenaire
Tu as visité quelles villes?	____________	____________
Tu as vu quels monuments?	____________	____________
Tu as fait quelles activités?	____________	____________
____________ ....?	____________	____________

D. Devoirs. Est-ce que votre partenaire connaît les Etats-Unis mieux ou moins bien que vous? Justifiez votre réponse avec des exemples. Ecrivez un bon paragraphe de 8 phrases.

Modèle:
Mon/Ma partenaire, X, connaît mieux les Etats-Unis que moi (connaît moins bien les Etats-Unis que moi), parce qu'il/elle a déjà vu une pièce de théatre à Broadway et il/elle a fait du ski dans le Colorado.

Exercice 27. Qu'est-ce que M et Mme Guilloteau ont fait ce week-end?

Complétez les phrases suivantes avec le verbe qui convient, conjugué au passé composé. Utilisez chaque verbe une fois.

jouer dîner faire regarder boire oublier visiter rendre écouter

Ce week-end M et Mme Guilloteau ____________ beaucoup de choses! Vendredi soir, ils ______________________________ au restaurant et ils ______________________________du très bon vin. Samedi matin, elle ______________________________ au tennis avec son mari. Ensuite ils ______________________________ leur musée préféré. Samedi soir, ils ______________ du jazz dans un club. Dimanche matin, ils ______________________________ un peu la télévision et ensuite, ils ______________________________visite à des amis.

Exercice 28. Et vous?

Posez les questions suivantes à un partenaire.

1. Qu'est-ce que tu as mangé hier soir?
2. Quand est-ce que tu as fait tes devoirs?
3. Quel(s) film(s) est-ce que tu as vu récemment?
4. Avec qui est-ce que tu as parlé en classe aujourd'hui?
5. A qui est-ce que tu as rendu visite le week-end dernier?
6. Qu'est-ce que tu as bu avec ton dîner hier soir?

Partagez vos réponses avec la classe. Est-ce que vous avez les mêmes habitudes ou quelques habitudes en commun?

At home, please go to the Français interactif website. Read the following grammar points in Tex's French Grammar and complete all Texercises which you will turn in to your instructor.

6.5 passé compos with être

je	**suis allé(e)**
tu	**es allé(e)**
il / *elle* / *on*	**est allé** / **est allée**
nous	**sommes allé(e)s**
vous	**êtes allé(e)(s)**
ils / *elles*	**sont allées**

To negate a sentence in passé composé, place ne...pas around auxiliary être

Irregular past participles:

mourir	**il est mort elle est morte**
naître	**il est né elle est née**

Exercice 29. Qu'est-ce que Laila a fait hier soir?

Laila s'est bien amusée (had a lot of fun) hier soir. Elle téléphone à un ami pour lui dire ce qu'elle a fait. Mettez ses phrases en ordre chronologique. (#1-9).

_____a. J'ai regardé la télé jusqu'à une heure du matin.

_____b. J'ai écouté de la musique et j'ai dansé avec mes amis.

_____c. J'ai mangé un sandwich avant de partir.

_____d. J'ai rencontré mes amis au bar.

_____e. J'ai fini mes devoirs à 20h30.

_____f. J'ai téléphoné à mes amis à 20h10. On a décidé d'aller à un concert à 21h.

_____g. Après le concert, nous sommes allés au café.

_____h. J'ai pris un taxi pour rentrer.

_____i. Je suis arrivée chez moi à minuit.

Exercice 30. Avoir ou être?

Ecoutez les phrases et décidez si l'auxiliaire de chaque phrase au passé composé est avoir ou être. Ensuite écrivez la phrase.

	avoir	être
Modèle: Elle a fait ses devoirs.	√	❑
1. ______________________________	❑	❑
2. ______________________________	❑	❑
3. ______________________________	❑	❑
4. ______________________________	❑	❑
5. ______________________________	❑	❑
6. ______________________________	❑	❑
7. ______________________________	❑	❑
8. ______________________________	❑	❑

Exercice 31. Qu'est-ce que tu as fait hier?

Posez ces questions à vos camarades.

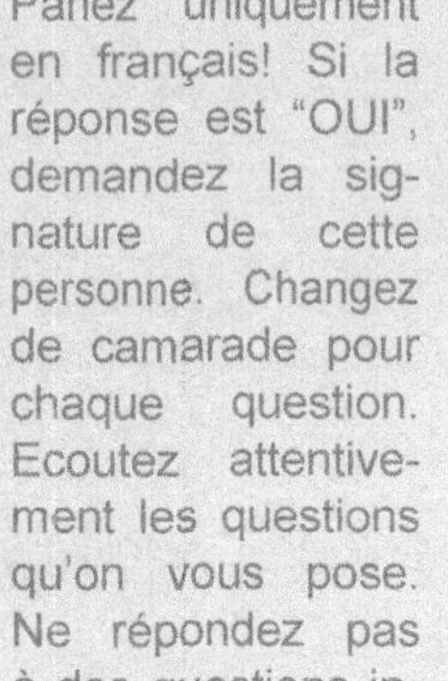

Parlez uniquement en français! Si la réponse est "OUI", demandez la signature de cette personne. Changez de camarade pour chaque question. Ecoutez attentivement les questions qu'on vous pose. Ne répondez pas à des questions incomplètes.

1. Est-ce que tu es sorti(e)? ______________________________
2. Est-ce que tu es allé(e) à la bibliothèque? ______________________________
3. Est-ce que tu es arrivé(e) en retard (late) pour la classe? ______________________________
4. Est-ce que tu es resté(e) à la maison hier soir? ______________________________
5. Est-ce que tu es rentré(e) avant minuit? ______________________________
6. Est-ce que tu es déjà tombé(e) amoureux/amoureuse? ______________________________
7. (Pas hier!) Est-ce que tu es né(e) à Austin? ______________________________

Exercice 32. Au restaurant

A. Parlez de la dernière fois que vous avez mangé au restaurant.

1. Je suis sorti(e) avec ______________________________ (avec qui?)
2. Je suis parti(e) de la maison à ______________________________(à quelle heure?)
3. Nous sommes allé(e)s à ______________________________ (à quel restaurant?)
4. Nous sommes arrivé(e)s au restaurant ______________________________(à quelle heure?)
5. Nous sommes resté(e)s ____________ (combien de temps, une heure, deux heures?)
6. Après, nous sommes allé(e)s à ______________________________ (où?)
7. Je suis rentré(e) ______________________________(à quelle heure?)
8. Le lendemain (the next day) je suis resté(e) au lit jusqu'à (until) ______ (quelle heure?)

B. Ensuite, en classe, vous allez comparer votre soirée avec la soirée d'un partenaire. Complétez les phrases suivantes.

1. Il/Elle est sorti(e) avec ______________________________(avec qui?)
2. Il/Elle est parti(e) de la maison à ______________________________ (à quelle heure?)
3. Ils/Elles sont allé(e)s à______________________________ (à quel restaurant?)
4. Ils/Elles sont arrivé(e)s au restaurant ______________________________ (à quelle heure?)
5. Ils/Elles sont restés(e)s ______________________________(combien de temps?)
6. Après, ils/elles sont allé(e)s à ______________________________ (où?)
7. Il/Elle est rentré(e) ______________________________ (à quelle heure?)
8. Le lendemain il/elle est resté(e) au lit jusqu'à ______________________________(quelle heure?)

C. Qui a eu la meilleure (best) soirée, vous ou votre partenaire? Pourquoi? Rapportez votre décision à la classe. Justifiez votre réponse.

Exercice 33. Les grandes vacances.

A. Choisissez un(e) étudiant(e) dans la classe que tout le monde connaît assez bien. Cette personne va s'asseoir dans le couloir pendant que les autres étudiants font cet exercice.
B. En groupes de 3 ou 4, écrivez le nom de cette personne dans le premier blanc. Puis, complétez chaque phrase.

l'étudiant[e]: ______________________________

1. est allé(e) ____ (quelle destination?)
2. est parti(e) ____ (quelle saison?)
3. a écouté ______________________ (quelle sorte de musique?/quel groupe musical?)
4. a rencontré ____ (quelqu'un de célèbre)
5. est sorti(e) ____________________________________ (avec quelqu'un?/quand?/où?)
6. n'a pas aimé ____ (?)
7. est resté(e) ____ (avec qui?/où?)
8. est rentré(e) ____ (quand?)

C. Quel groupe connaît le mieux (knows best) l'étudiant(e)? Chaque groupe va annoncer ses résultats à la classe. Puis, l'étudiant(e) va donner les réponses correctes. Votre groupe a combien de réponses correctes? Quel groupe a gagné? Quel groupe connaît cette personne le mieux?

Exercice 34. Qu'est-ce qu'ils ont fait?

Indiquez quelle photo correspond avec chaque phrase.

1. Elles sont parties.
2. Ils sont restés à la maison.
3. Il est arrivé.
4. Ils sont sortis.
5. Il est allé à l'Alamo.
6. Ils sont morts.

_____a. _____b. _____c.

_____d. _____e. _____f.

Dictogloss 1. Le week-end du professeur

Formez des groupes de 3 ou 4 personnes. Ecoutez le texte lu par votre professeur. Complétez les phrases suivantes et donnez le plus de détails possibles.

Samedi ____

____

____

____

____

____

____

Dimanche ____

____

____

____

____

____

____

Exercice 35. La journée de Tammy

Complétez les phrases suivantes avec la forme correcte du verbe au passé composé.

Tex: 1. Qu'est-ce que tu ______________________________ (faire) hier?

2. Je/J' ______________________________(téléphoner) toute la journée

3. et je/j' ______________________________(attendre) ton coup de téléphone.

Tammy: 4. Je me suis réveillée à huit heures du matin, et je/j'______________________________(prendre) le petit déjeuner avec mes parents.

5. Puis ma mère et moi ______________________________(faire) des courses.

6. Nous ______________________________(aller) à la pharmacie.

7. Puis nous ______________________________(acheter) une tarte à la pâtisserie,

8. et nous ______________________________(rendre) visite à ma tante.

9. Nous ______________________________(déjeuner) chez ma tante.

10. Ensuite ma mère et ma tante ______________________________(boire) du thé,

11. et je/j' ______________________________(regarder) une vidéo avec ma cousine.

12. Plus tard, ma mère ______________________________ (retourner) à la maison.

13. A sept heures du soir, je/j' ______________________________ (sortir) avec mon amie Sophie.

14. Tex, tu ______________________________(rencontrer) Sophie la semaine passée.

15. Sophie et moi ______________________________(dîner) dans un nouveau restaurant italien,

16. et puis nous ______________________________(voir) un film au cinéma.

17. Après le film, nous ______________________________(aller) au café, et

18. je/j'______________________________(choisir) un café au lait.

19. Je/j' ______________________________ (rentrer) chez moi à une heure du matin.

Tex: 20. Quelle histoire! Est-ce que tu ______________________________ (finir)?

7 Les fêtes

In this chapter we will talk about French holidays and traditions and how to describe childhood memories.

Vocabulaire

- *les fêtes*
- *expressions*
- *rites et coutumes*
- *verbes*

Phonétique

- *les semi-voyelles*

Grammaire

- *7.1 -ir verbs (irregular)*
- *7.2 direct object pronouns*
- *7.3 indirect object pronouns*
- *7.4 imparfait: formation*
- *7.5 imparfait: states of being, habitual actions*
- *7.6 imparfait: idiomatic uses*

- *testez-vous!, chapitre 07*
- *verb conjugation reference*
- *verb practice*

Vidéos

Vocabulaire en contexte

- *les noces*
- *l'anniversaire de Camille et d'Audrey*
- *Laetitia: ma fête favorite*
- *Noël et la Saint-Sylvestre*

Interviews

- *les fêtes*
- *quand vous étiez petit*
- *à 15 ans*

Culture

- *le Reveillon de Noël*

Vocabulaire

Préparation du vocabulaire

Be sure to download the pdf vocabulary preparation template from the FI website to complete Exercises B, E, and F.

! Your instructor will collect this homework.

! The French often take an extra day off from work when a holiday falls on Tuesday or Thursday. If the holiday falls on Tuesday, they take Monday off, and if the holiday falls on Thursday, they take Friday off thus "making a bridge" between the holiday and the weekend. The expression used for this is "faire le pont".

Les fêtes	**Holidays**
les jours fériés	national holidays (indicated below by *)
*le Jour de l'An, le premier janvier	New Year's Day
la Chandeleur, le 2 février	Candlemas (Crêpe Day, a Catholic feast day)
la Saint-Valentin, le 14 février	Valentine's Day
le Carnaval (Mardi Gras)	Mardi Gras, Carnival
La pâque juive / Pessach	Passover
*Pâques	Easter
le Premier Avril	April Fool's Day
*la fête du Travail, le 1er mai	Labor Day
*le 8 mai, la fête de la Victoire	VE Day (Victory in Europe)
*l'Ascension (f)	Ascension Day
la fête des mères	Mother's Day
la fête des pères	Father's Day
la Pentecôte (*lundi de Pentecôte)	Pentecost
*la fête nationale, le 14 juillet	Bastille Day, French National Day
*le 15 août, l'Assomption (f)	the feast of the Assumption
Halloween	Halloween
Yom Kippour	Yom Kippur
Rosh Hashana	Rosh Hashana
*la Toussaint, le 1er novembre	All Saints' Day
*l'Armistice (m), le 11 novembre	Armistice Day
le Ramadan	Ramadan
Hanouka	Hannukah
*Noël (m), le 25 décembre	Christmas
la Saint-Sylvestre, le 31 décembre	New Year's Eve

Expressions	**Expressions**
Bonne Année!	Happy New Year!
Bonne fête!	Happy Saint's Day!
Bon (Joyeux) anniversaire!	Happy Birthday!
Meilleurs Voeux!	Best wishes!
Poisson d'avril!	April Fool!
Joyeuses Pâques!	Happy Easter!
Joyeux Noël!	Merry Christmas!

Vocabulaire

Rites et coutumes	Rituals and customs
le réveillon	Christmas Eve or New Year's Eve party
des feux d'artifice (m)	fireworks
un défilé (militaire)	(military) parade
une fête	saint's day, celebration, party
un anniversaire	birthday, anniversary
un gâteau	cake
une bougie	candle
un cadeau	gift
les noces (f pl)	wedding
un anniversaire de mariage	wedding anniversary
une cérémonie	ceremony
le champagne	champagne
le muguet	lily of the valley
des blagues (f)	jokes
des costumes (m)	costumes
des crêpes (f)	crepes
un pique-nique	picnic
la bûche de Noël	Yule log (also a cake in the shape of a Yule log)
une carte de voeux	greeting card
le gui	mistletoe
le Père Noël	Santa Claus
le sapin de Noël	Christmas tree
la crèche	nativity
la messe	mass
le sabbat / le shabbat	sabbath

Verbes	Verbs
célébrer	to celebrate
faire la fête	to party
fêter	to celebrate
réveillonner	to celebrate Christmas or New Year's Eve
inviter	to invite
offrir	to give
donner	to give
recevoir	to receive
ouvrir	to open
souffler	to blow out (candles)
plaisanter	to joke
faire un poisson d'avril	to play a joke (on someone) on April Fool's Day
faire le pont	*literally 'to make a bridge'

verb: recevoir

recevoir 'to receive'

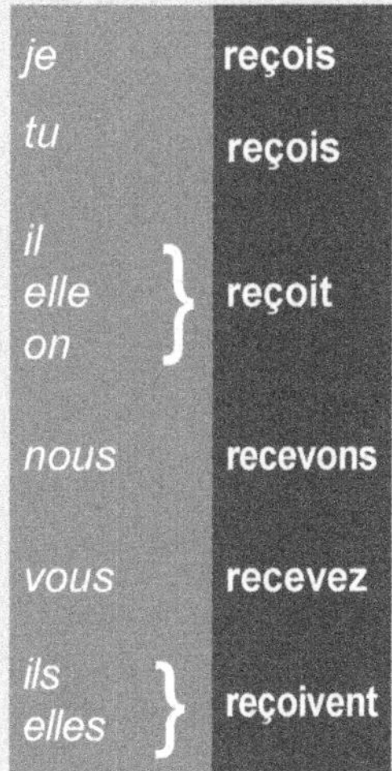

je	**reçois**
tu	**reçois**
il / *elle* / *on*	**reçoit**
nous	**recevons**
vous	**recevez**
ils / *elles*	**reçoivent**

Phonétique

Go to the website for a complete explanation and practice exercises.

NOTE CULTURELLE

La fête nationale

Le 14 juillet est la fête en souvenir de la Révolution de 1789 et la prise de la Bastille. Côté officiel, il y a de nombreux défilés militaires sur les Champs Elysées à Paris et dans toutes les villes. Côté populaire, c'est la fête avec des feux d'artifice, des concerts et des bals sur les places publiques qui commencent le 13 juillet.

Les jours fériés de mai

(un jour férié = un jour où on ne travaille pas) Pendant le mois de mai en France, les Français ne travaillent pas beaucoup.
D'abord, il y a la fête du Travail, le 1er mai. Après, on a la fête de la Victoire, le 8 mai. L'Ascension et la Pentecôte tombent aussi au mois de mai. On ne travaillent jamais le lundi après la Pentecôte.
On fait le pont souvent au mois de mai, ce qui permet à beaucoup de gens de ne pas travailler que (only) pendant deux semaines. De plus, les Français ont cinq semaines de congés payés chaque année, et d'autres fêtes comme Noël, Paques, etc. Les Français sont les champions de vacances dans le monde avec 37 jours par an.

Introduction

Watch the introductory video to Chapitre 2 to answer the following questions: Qui présente le chapitre? Où est-il / elle? Quels sont les thèmes du chapitre?

Exercice 1. Quelle est votre fête préférée?

A. Regardez les activités suivantes et faites une liste des fêtes où…

1. on offre des cadeaux à notre famille.______________________
2. on passe du temps avec notre famille. ______________________
3. on célèbre un événement religieux.______________________
4. on invite des amis chez nous. ______________________
5. on offre des fleurs. ______________________
6. on regarde des feux d'artifice. ______________________
7. on mange du gâteau.______________________

B. Comparez vos réponses avec celles d'un partenaire.

C. Maintentant, discutez votre fête préférée. Quelle est votre fête préférée et pourquoi? Faites une liste d'activités que vous associez avec cette fête.

Modèle:
Je préfère mon anniversaire parce que… OU Ma fête préférée est mon anniversaire parce que…

D. Comparez votre réponse avec la réponse de votre partenaire. Est-ce que vous avez choisi la même fête? Quelle fête préfère votre partenaire? Pourquoi? (2 raisons)

Devoirs: Pour demain, écrivez un paragraphe de 8 phrases pour faire une comparaison entre vous et votre partenaire. Quelles sont vos fêtes préférées et pourquoi?

Modèle:
Ma fête préférée est X parce que… Mon/ma partenaire préfère X parce que…

Exercice 2. Quel verbe?

Quels verbes associez-vous avec...

ouvrir **couvrir** **découvrir** **offrir** **rendre** **souffrir**

1. les cadeaux ________________
2. une bouteille de champagne ________________
3. une fenêtre ________________
4. Jacques Cartier (un explorateur français) ________________
5. une migraine ________________

Exercice 3. Qu'est-ce que tu fais?

1. Est-ce que tu sors en costume pour fêter Halloween? ________________
2. Est-ce que tu manges de la dinde à Thanksgiving? ________________
3. Est-ce que tu célèbres Noël avec un sapin et une crèche? ________________
4. Est-ce que tu bois du champagne pour la Saint-Sylvestre? ________________
5. Est-ce que tu fais la fête souvent le week-end? ________________
6. Est-ce que tu regardes des feux d'artifices le 4 juillet? ________________
7. Est-ce que tu rends visite à ta mère pour la fête des mères? ________________
8. Est-ce que tu fêtes ton anniversaire avec un défilé? ________________

! Parlez uniquement en français! Si la réponse est "OUI", demandez la signature de cette personne. Changez de camarade pour chaque question. Ecoutez attentivement les questions qu'on vous pose. Ne répondez pas à des questions incomplètes.

Exercice 4. Grammaire interactive. Les fêtes.

Look at the following sentences

Le Jour de l'An,	les Américains **le** fêtent.
La Toussaint,	les Américains ne **la** fêtent pas.
Halloween	les Américains **l'**adorent.
Les jours fériés,	les Français **les** adorent.
Thanksgiving,	les Français ne **le** fêtent pas.

1. How would you translate the sentences above?
2. What part of speech are the words in bold?
3. Fill in the blanks:

a. The direct object pronoun ____ is used to refer to a **masculine** noun before a **consonant**.
b. The direct object pronoun ____ is used to refer to a **feminine** noun before a **consonant**.
c. The direct object pronoun ____ is used to refer to a **singular** noun before a **vowel or mute "h"**.
d. The direct object pronoun ____ is used to refer to a **plural** noun.

4. What do you notice about the position of the direct object pronouns in the sentences below?

Le Jour de l'An, les Américains le fêtent.
La Toussaint, les Américains ne la fêtent.pas.

The direct object pronoun is placed ______________ the verb.
In the negative, the direct object pronoun is placed ______________ the verb.

Exercice 5. Le faire part du mariage des Guilloteau.

Répondez aux questions suivantes.

Madame Clarke
a l'honneur de vous faire part
du mariage de sa fille
Nancy
avec
Monsieur Franck Guilloteau
fils de
Monsieur et Madame Guilloteau
le samedi quinze juillet
mil neuf cent quatre-vingt-quinze
à dix heures et demie
à l'église Our Lady of Mercy
Bâton Rouge, Louisiane

Réception immédiatement après
1185 Colonial Drive

1. Quelle est la date de leur anniversaire de mariage? ______

   ____

2. En quelle année était la cérémonie? (en chiffres)?

   ____

   ____

3. A quelle heure était la cérémonie?

   ____

   ____

4. Où était la cérémonie?

   ____

   ____

5. Quel est le nom de jeune fille de Nancy?

   ____

   ____

Exercice 6. L'almanach.

Consultons le site web http://www.almanach.free.fr.
Répondons aux questions suivantes.
L'almanach (= calendar with the name of the saints and the fête)

janvier -juin
1. Quels sont les jours fériés?
2. Quel saint fête-t-on le 14 février?
3. Quelle est la date:
- du mardi gras?
- de la fête des mères?
- de la fête des pères?

juillet-décembre
1. Quelles sont les jours fériés?
2. Quel saint fête-t-on le 31 décembre?

Consultez le même site web. Quel saint fête-t-on le jour de votre anniversaire?

Exercice 7. Les cartes de vœux.

Associez chaque (each) carte avec sa fête. Ensuite, associez chaque (each) carte au message qui convient (A -I). Notez vos réponses dans le tableau ci-dessous (below).

Fête	Message
Modèle: la fête des mères	E

un anniversaire
le nouvel an
la Saint-Valentin
la fête des grands-mères
la fête du travail
la fête des mères
la fête des pères
la fête nationale
Noël

Les messages:

A.
Je t'offre cette carte et un brin de muguet pour te porter bonheur !
Profite bien de cette journée !
Amitiés,

Jean-Charles

PS-Est-ce que tu fais le pont ?

B.
Mais non, tu ne vieillis pas !
Tu es toujours jeune, beau et dynamique!
Je te souhaite un très bon anniversaire !
Amuse-toi bien en cette journée,
Bisous,

Virginie

C.
Je vous souhaite mes meilleurs voeux pour cette nouvelle année,
Cordialement,

Franck Guilloteau

D.
Je t'aime à la folie ! Tu es l'amour de ma vie !

Franck

E.
Bonne fête à la plus jolie des mamans,
Je t'aime,

Audrey

F.
Bonne fête Mamy !
Gros bisous,

Camille

G.
Je te souhaite un Joyeux Noël et un excellent réveillon en famille !
Affectueusement,

Stéphanie

H.
As-tu envie d'aller voir les feux d'artifice avec nous ce soir?
Appelle-nous !

Jean-Charles

I.
Bonne fête au meilleur papa du monde !
Bisous,

Camille et Audrey

Réussite, bonheur
Amour, argent, succès,
santé, travail
et aussi de gros bisous

Cette carte
est pleine de bons voeux
pour la
Nouvelle Année

NOTE CULTURELLE

Noel et la Saint-Sylvestre

Noël est une fête religieuse pour certains, pour d'autres un événement du calendrier avec des cadeaux. Le menu familial se compose traditionnellement de foie gras, d'huîtres (oysters), de dinde ou d'oie farcie (stuffed goose), et d'une bûche de Noël (gâteau roulé et décoré qui ressemble au morceau de bois (wood) que l'on brûlait dans la cheminée).

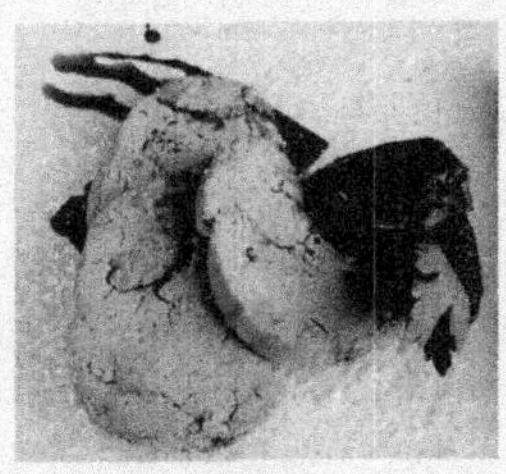

La Saint-Sylvestre est le 31 décembre et les Français préparent le réveillon. Ce repas de fête dure une partie de la nuit pour saluer l'année nouvelle entre amis, à la maison ou au restaurant. On dit que souhaiter (to wish) « bonne année » sous une boule de gui (mistletoe) porte chance (brings luck).

Exercice 8. Meilleurs vœux!

A. Regardez la carte de vœux à la page précédente (previous page) et trouvez les équivalents.

good wishes ______________________

love ______________________

success ______________________

happiness ______________________

work______________________

health ______________________

money ______________________

Est-ce qu'on envoie des cartes de vœux pour la Nouvelle Année aux Etats-Unis?

B. Consultez les messages et les expressions des Exercices 6 et 7. Ecrivez une carte de vœux.

Exercice 9. Qui a fait ça?

Connaissez-vous ces célébrités historiques? Qu'est-ce qu'ils ont fait?

_____1.	Hillary Clinton...	a. ont découvert le radium
_____2.	Rosa Parks...	b. a offert un message de paix (peace) au monde
_____3.	Mahatma Gandhi...	c. a couvert les fautes de son mari
_____4.	Pierre et Marie Curie...	d. ont souffert d'alcoolisme
_____5.	Van Gogh et Baudelaire...	e. a ouvert la porte aux droits des citoyens d'origine africaine aux Etats-Unis

Caricatures reprinted with permission from www.magixl.com

Exercice 10. En ce qui concerne...

Avec un partenaire, complétez les phrases suivantes avec la réponse qui est vraie pour vous.

En ce qui concerne...	Oui ou Non?
...le petit déjeuner	❑ Oui, je le prends toujours. ❑ Non, je ne le prends pas souvent.
...les devoirs	❑ Oui, je les fais toujours. ❑ Non, je ne les fais pas toujours.
...la télé	❑ Oui, je la regarde tout le temps. ❑ Non, je ne la regarde pas trop.
...la radio	❑ Oui, je l'écoute de temps en temps. ❑ Non, je ne l'écoute jamais.
...l'espagnol	❑ Oui, je le parle de temps en temps. ❑ Non, je ne le parle jamais.
...le président des Etats-Unis	❑ Oui, je l'admire beaucoup. ❑ Non, je ne l'admire pas vraiment.
...la leçon de français	❑ Oui, je la comprends. ❑ Non, je ne la comprends pas.
...les sciences	❑ Oui, je les étudie. ❑ Non, je ne les étudie pas.
...les musées	❑ Oui, je les visite souvent. ❑ Non, je ne les visite pas souvent.

Exercice 11. Qui ?

Complétez les phrases suivantes.

1. ______________________________ m'adorent.
2. ______________________________ me déteste.
3. ______________________________ m'écoutent.
4. ______________________________ me comprend.
5. ______________________________ m'invite chez lui.

Ensuite vous allez comparer vos réponses avec celles d'un/d'une camarade. Avez-vous les mêmes réponses?

Modèle: Qui **t'**adore? Ma mère **m'**adore.

At home, please go to the Français interactif website. Read the following grammar points in Tex's French Grammar and complete all Texercises which you will turn in to your instructor.

7.1 -ir verbs (irregular)

ouvrir 'to open'

je	**ouvre**
tu	**ouvres**
il / *elle* / *on*	**ouvre**
nous	**ouvrons**
vous	**ouvrez**
ils / *elles*	**ouvrent**

NOTE CULTURELLE

Le jour des Rois Mages ou l'Epiphanie

Le 6 janvier c'est une fête pour les chrétiens, le jour des Rois Mages, ou l'Epiphanie. La «galette des rois» est le gâteau préféré de tous au mois de janvier. Si la recette change selon la région, partout on y cache (hide) une petite figurine: «une fève» (charm). Si tu la découvres dans ta part (portion), tu vas être le roi ou la reine du jour et tu vas recevoir une couronne (crown) en papier doré (golden).

Exercice 12. Sondage: Réciprocité?

A. Cochez la colonne (√) appropriée.

	oui	non
1. Mes amis m'admirent...	❑	❑
...et je les admire.	❑	❑
2. Mes parents me comprennent...	❑	❑
...et je les comprends.	❑	❑
3. Les profs me respectent...	❑	❑
...et je les respecte.	❑	❑
4. Mon médecin m'écoute...	❑	❑
...et je l'écoute.	❑	❑
5. Mon patron (boss) m'apprécie...	❑	❑
...et je l'apprécie.	❑	❑
6. Mon copain / ma copine m'adore...	❑	❑
...et je l'adore.	❑	❑

B. Pour la classe entière, quels sont les résultats ?

Exercice 13. Devinettes

Trouvez les réponses possibles aux devinettes suivantes. Faites attention à la forme du pronom.

Modèle: On l'attend le matin pour aller en classe. le = bus

1. On **le** parle avec le professeur. le = ______________
2. On **la** fête le 1er novembre. la = ______________
3. On **la** fait souvent pendant le week-end. la = ______________
4. On **l'**étudie tous les soirs. l' = ______________
5. On **l'**écoute dans la voiture. l' = ______________
6. On **les** regarde le 4 juillet. les = ______________
7. On **les** souffle pour fêter son anniversaire. les = ______________

Exercice 14. Vous et votre partenaire: semblables (similar) ou non?

Posez les questions suivantes à un partenaire.

Modèle:
Est-ce que tu détestes les haricots verts.
Oui, je les déteste. ou Non, je ne les déteste pas. Et toi?

1. Est-ce que tu regardes la télé?
2. Est-ce que tu invites tes amis pour ton anniversaire?
3. Est-ce que tu finis toujours tes devoirs?
4. Est-ce que tu respectes ton professeur de français?
5. Est-ce que tu aimes le champagne?
6. Est-ce que tu fêtes la Saint-Valentin?

Exercice 15. Grammaire interactive. Tu es sociable?

Look at the following sentences

Ma grand-mère,	je **lui** rends visite de temps en temps.
Mes amis,	je ne **leur** téléphone pas, je **leur** envoie des textos.
Mes camarades de classe,	ils **me** parlent.
Le professeur,	il ne **nous** donne pas de cadeaux.

1. How would you translate the sentences above?
2. What part of speech are the words in bold?

Circle all that apply

3. The indirect object pronoun **lui** means ________ and is used for masculine/feminine and singular/plural
4. The indirect object pronoun **leur** means_______ and is used for masculine/feminine and singular/plural
5. The indirect object pronoun **me** means________ and is used for masculine/feminine and singular/plural
6. The indirect object pronoun **nous** means______ and is used for masculine/feminine and singular/plural

7. What do you notice about the position of the indirect object pronouns in the sentences below?

Ma grand-mère, je **lui** rends visite de temps en temps.

Le professeur, il ne **nous** donnent pas de cadeaux.

The indirect object pronoun is placed ______________ the verb.

In the negative, the indirect object pronoun is placed _______________ the verb.

Exercice 16. Conséquences?

Tex et Tammy font la fête et ils invitent tous leurs amis. Quelles sont les conséquences des faits suivants?

______1.	Les invités arrivent.	a. Les autres souffrent d'ennui (boredom).
______2.	Il fait du soleil.	b. On ne lui offre pas de viande.
______3.	Bette est végétarienne.	c. Tammy leur ouvre la porte.
______4.	Edouard parle trop.	d. Il découvre que les toilettes sont occupées.
______5.	Joe-Bob a bu trop de bière.	e. Rita couvre la tête de ses enfants.

Exercice 17. Généreux ou pas, créatif ou pas?

A. Complétez les phrases suivantes.

Pour la fête des mères j'offre ________________________________ à ma mère.

Pour la fête des mères j'offre ______________________________ à ma grand-mère.

Pour la fête des pères j'offre ________________________________ à mon père.

Pour la fête des pères j'offre ______________________________ à mon grand-père.

A l'occasion de mon anniversaire ...

mon copain/ma copine m'offre ____

mes parents m'offrent ____

mes amis m'offrent ____

B. En classe comparez vos réponses avec celles d'un partenaire. Qui est plus généreux/généreuse, vous ou votre partenaire? Qui est plus créatif/ créative?

Est-ce que le copain/la copine de votre partenaire est généreux/généreuse? Et ses parents? Expliquez vos réponses.

Modèle:
Mon partenaire est moins généreux que moi parce qu'il offre des cartes de voeux à tout le monde, mais il est plus créatif que moi parce qu'il fait les cartes lui-même!.

Dictogloss 1. Une soirée chez les Guilloteau

Formez des groupes de trois ou quatre personnes. Ecoutez le texte lu par votre professeur. Complétez les phrases suivantes et donnez le plus de détails possibles.

Les Guilloteau ont envie de ____

avec leur famille. Franck réfléchit .

Il imagine la soirée...

______________________________ la porte et mes oncles, mes tantes, et ________

___________________________________ et leurs enfants ____________________

dans la maison. Ils ___________________________________ de petits cadeaux,

des fleurs et des chocolats. Nancy ______________________________ un bon dîner.

Nous____________________ tous les plats mais nous ______________________

___________________________!

Je __________________________ un peu de musique et tous les enfants

_____________. On ____.

At home, please go to the Français interactif website. Read the following grammar points in Tex's French Grammar and complete all Texercises which you will turn in to your instructor.

7.2 direct object pronouns

me	*m'*
te	*t'*
le *la*	*l'*
nous	
vous	
les	

Exercice 18. Tu es sociable ou non?

Cochez les réponses appropriées aux situations suivantes.

En ce qui concerne...	Oui ou Non?
...vos camarades de classe	❑ Oui, je leur parle souvent. ❑ Non, je ne leur parle pas souvent.
...votre copain/votre copine	❑ Oui, je lui offre des fleurs. ❑ Non, je ne lui offre pas de fleurs.
...vos amis de lycée (high school)	❑ Oui, je leur envoie des emails quelquefois. ❑ Non, je ne leur envoie pas beaucoup d'e-mails.
..votre grand-mère	❑ Oui, je lui demande de l'argent. ❑ Non, je ne lui demande pas d'argent.
...vos amis à Austin	❑ Oui, je leur téléphone de temps en temps. ❑ Non, je ne leur téléphone pas souvent.
...votre professeur de français	❑ Oui, je lui rends visite dans son bureau. ❑ Non, je ne lui rends pas visite dans son bureau.
...vos parents	❑ Oui, je leur obéis sans question. ❑ Non, je ne leur obéis pas tout le temps.

Exercice 19. Tu es quel genre d'ami?

A. Répondez aux questions selon les adverbes suivants:

Ton/ta meilleur(e) ami(e):	jamais	de temps en temps	souvent
1. Tu **lui** téléphones.	❑	❑	❑
2. Tu **lui** offres des cadeaux pour son anniversaire.	❑	❑	❑
3. Tu **lui** envoies de longues lettres et des cartes de vœux.	❑	❑	❑
4. Tu **lui** prêtes (lend) de l'argent (si elle/il a besoin d'argent).	❑	❑	❑
5. Tu **lui** rends son argent (quand il/elle te prête de l'argent).	❑	❑	❑
6. Tu **lui** parles tous les jours.	❑	❑	❑
7. Tu **lui** rends visite quand il/elle est malade.	❑	❑	❑
8. Tu **lui** pardonnes s'il n'est pas sympa.	❑	❑	❑

Majorité de réponses 'souvent'	Majorité de réponses 'de temps en temps'	Majorité de réponses 'jamais'
Génial! Tu es l'ami(e) idéal(e)! Ne change pas!	Pas mal, mais tu peux faire mieux... (you could do better!)	Ça craint! (that sucks!) Tu es vraiment minable comme ami!

B. En classe: Calculez vos points et ensuite comparez vos réponses avec un/une partenaire. Quel genre d'ami est votre partenaire?

Exercice 20. Devinettes

Trouvez les réponses possibles aux devinettes suivantes. Ecrivez toute la phrase.

Modèle: Les étudiants lui parlent dans la salle de classe. lui = Les étudiants parlent au prof.

1. On **lui** offre des cadeaux d'anniversaire. lui = ____________________
2. On **lui** téléphone quand on a des problèmes. lui = ____________________
3. Les enfants **leur** obéissent. leur = ____________________
4. On **leur** demande de l'argent. leur = ____________________
5. On **leur** envoie des cartes de vœux. leur = ____________________

Exercice 21. Les profs

A. Dans les phrases suivantes, décidez si le pronom « nous» est direct ou indirect.

B. Etes-vous d'accord avec les phrases suivantes? Indiquez vos réponses.

Les professeurs de l'université...

	non, pas du tout	non	pas d'opinion	oui	oui, tout à fait
1. ils nous aident.	❑	❑	❑	❑	❑
2. ils nous donnent trop de devoirs.	❑	❑	❑	❑	❑
3. ils nous amusent.	❑	❑	❑	❑	❑
4. ils nous écoutent.	❑	❑	❑	❑	❑
5. ils aiment nous parler.	❑	❑	❑	❑	❑
6. ils nous offrent des chocolats	❑	❑	❑	❑	❑
en classe.	❑	❑	❑	❑	❑

NOTE CULTURELLE

La fête du 1er novembre

La fête du 1er novembre est en l'honneur de tous les saints. On place des fleurs sur les tombeaux dans les cimetières. Le 11 novembre est la date de l'anniversaire de la fin de la première guerre mondiale. Il y a des cérémonies pour rendre hommage aux soldats.

C. En classe, vous allez comparer vos réponses en groupe de 2 ou 3 personnes. Est-ce que votre groupe a une attitude positive, négative ou mitigée (mixed) envers les profs de l'université? Expliquez votre opinion.

Modèle:
Nous avons une attitude positive, parce que nous pensons que les profs nous aident beaucoup...

At home, please go to the Français interactif website. Read the following grammar points in Tex's French Grammar and complete all Texercises which you will turn in to your instructor.

7.3 indirect object pronouns

me	*m'*
te	*t'*
lui	
nous	
vous	
leur	

Exercice 22. Votre camarade de classe est sociable ou non?

A. Choisissez un étudiant(e) parmi vos camarades de classe. En groupes de 3 ou 4, vous allez répondre aux questions suivantes pour décider si **Etudiant X** est sociable ou non. (**Etudiant X** va noter les réponses correctes lui-même.)

l'étudiant[e]: ______________________________

Modèle: X parle souvent à ses camarades de classes?
Oui, il/elle leur parle souvent. ou Non, il/elle ne leur parle pas souvent.

Activités sociales...	oui	non
1. Il/Elle parle souvent à ses camarades de classe.	❑	❑
2. Il/Elle offre des fleurs à son copain/à sa copine.	❑	❑
3. Il/Elle envoie quelquefois des emails à ses amis de lycée.	❑	❑
4. Il/Elle rend souvent visite à sa grand-mère.	❑	❑
5. Il/Elle téléphone à ses amis à Austin.	❑	❑
6. Il/Elle répond toujours au professeur de français.	❑	❑
7. Il/Elle obéit à ses parents.	❑	❑

B. Quel groupe connaît le mieux (knows best) Etudiant X?
Chaque groupe va annoncer ses résultats à la classe. Le professeur va compter (count) les réponses "oui" et "non". Puis, Etudiant X va donner les réponses correctes. Votre groupe a combien de réponses correctes? Quel groupe a gagné? Alors, votre camarade est sociable ou non?

Exercice 23. Grammaire interactive.

Look at the following sentences

1. What difference do you notice between the objects in the two sentences below?
   Est ce que tu appelles **tes camarades de classes**? Oui, je **les** appelle. ____________
   Est-ce que tu téléphones **à tes amis**? Oui je **leur** téléphone.
2. Complete the following statement.
   An object introduced by the preposition _______ is an indirect object.
3. Can you think of verbs which take à and would thus be followed by an indirect object?
4. What do you notice about the following sentences?
   Je donne les fleurs à ma mère.
   Il offre les chocolats aux invités.

You will not be responsible for using two object pronouns in the same sentence in this course!

Exercice 24. Logique!

A. Qu'est-ce que ca remplace? Choisissez la réponse logique. Ensuite décidez si le pronom remplace un objet direct ou indirect.

	objet direct	objet indirect
1. On les trouve dans la salle de classe. a. les musées b. les étudiants c. les épinards	❑	❑
2. On leur obeit. a. aux parents b. au prof c. aux chiens	❑	❑
3. Quand il pose des questions aux étudiants, on lui répond. a. aux parents b. au prof c. au chat	❑	❑
4. On l'écoute. a. les chansons b. le film c. la musique	❑	❑
5. On les regarde au cinéma. a. les films b. les amis c. les livres	❑	❑
6. On leur rend visite. a. à ses amis b. aux monuments c. à sa famille	❑	❑
7. On leur ressemble. a. à sa soeur b. à son frère c. à ses parents	❑	❑
8. On l'achète le premier mai. a. le gui b. le muguet c. la crèche	❑	❑

B. En classe avec un partenaire, faites une liste des verbes dans cet exercice qui sont suivis (followed by) un objet indirect :

Exercice 25. Qu'est-ce qu'ils faisaient?

Bette est triste. Ses amis ne pouvaient pas la voir hier soir. Pourquoi? Qu'est-ce que ses amis faisaient?

Les excuses...

1. Corey: Qu'est-ce qu'il faisait?
   - Il étudiait.
   - Il regardait la télé.
   - Il buvait du thé.

2. Tammy: Qu'est-ce qu'elle faisait?
   - Elle faisait du jogging.
   - Elle faisait la cuisine.
   - Elle prenait des photos

TAMMY EST UNE BONNE CUISINIÈRE

3. Joe-Bob: Qu'est-ce qu'il faisait?
   - Il parlait au téléphone.
   - Il finissait ses devoirs.
   - Il mangeait un hamburger.

4. Paw-Paw: Qu'est-ce qu'il faisait?
   - Il faisait les courses.
   - Il dansait.
   - Il nageait.

5. Tex: Où était-il?
   - Il était dans sa voiture.
   - Il était au parc.
   - Il était chez lui.

6. Rita: Qu'est-ce qu'elle faisait?
   - Elle prenait un taxi.
   - Elle quittait son mari.
   - Elle dormait.

At home, please go to the Français interactif website. Read the following grammar points in Tex's French Grammar and complete all Texercises which you will turn in to your instructor.

7.4 imparfait: formation

danser 'to dance' *(-er/-re verb)*

je	**dansais**
tu	**dansais**
il / elle / on	**dansait**
nous	**dansions**
vous	**dansiez**
ils / elles	**dansaient**

finir 'to finish' *(-ir verb)*

je	**finissais**
tu	**finissais**
il / elle / on	**finissait**
nous	**finissions**
vous	**finissiez**
ils / elles	**finissaient**

The imparfait stem is regular for all verbs except être: nous sommes > ét-

Exercice 26. Maintenant ou autrefois?

Ecoutez les phrases et décidez si les phrases décrivent les activités que votre professeur fait **maintenant** (au présent) ou les activités qu'il/elle faisait **autrefois** (à l'imparfait). Ensuite écrivez la phrase.

	maintenant	autrefois
Modèle: Je passais mes vacances chez ma grand-mère.	❑	√
1. ______________________	❑	❑
2. ______________________	❑	❑
3. ______________________	❑	❑
4. ______________________	❑	❑
5. ______________________	❑	❑
6. ______________________	❑	❑
7. ______________________	❑	❑
8. ______________________	❑	❑

Exercice 27. Edouard

Faites correspondre les phrases de la colonne A avec les phrases de la colonne B.

Au lycée Edouard...

______1. célébrait Noël
______2. avait besoin d'argent
______3. aimait les congés et les longs week-ends
______4. aimait faire de l'exercice
______5. faisait la fête tous les soirs
______6. adorait regarder Facebook
______7. avait beaucoup d'amis
______8. étudiait beaucoup

donc il...

a. achetait des cadeaux
b. organisait beaucoup de soirées
c. travaillait dans un restaurant
d. faisait souvent le pont
e. se couchait très tard
f. était fatigué
g. faisait de l'aérobique
h. passait beaucoup de temps sur son ordinateur

At home, please go to the Français interactif website. Read the following grammar points in Tex's French Grammar and complete all Texercises which you will turn in to your instructor.

7.5 imparfait: states of being, habitual actions

The imperfect tense (l'imparfait) has two primary uses:
- to describe ongoing actions and states of being in the past, and
- to state habitual actions in the past.

Parlez uniquement en français! Si la réponse est "OUI", demandez la signature de cette personne. Changez de camarade pour chaque question. Ecoutez attentivement les questions qu'on vous pose. Ne répondez pas à des questions incomplètes.

Exercice 28. Quand tu étais jeune...

Posez ces questions à vos camarades de classe.

1. Est-ce que tu invitais beaucoup d'amis à tes fêtes d'anniversaire?________________
2. Est-ce que tu fumais? ________________
3. Est-ce que tu allais à l'école à pied? ________________
4. Est-ce que tu écoutais du hip-hop? ________________
5. Est-ce que tu rêvais d'aller à l'Université du Texas un jour? ________________
6. Est-ce que tu faisais du sport?________________
7. Est-ce que tu buvais du café? ________________
8. Est-ce que tu croyais au lapin de Pâques? ________________

Exercice 29. Pâques

Complétez les phrases suivantes avec l'imparfait du verbe entre parenthèses.

Quand j' ________________ (être) petit, nous __________ (aller) toujours chez ma grand-mère pour fêter Pâques. C'________________ (être) vraiment sympa. Le matin, on ________________ (aller) à la messe. Puis, on (rentrer) pour prendre un grand repas en famille, après quoi, Mamy nous ________________ (donner) des oeufs au chocolat! Les grandes personnes ________________ (rester) longtemps à table et les enfants________________ (jouer) dans le jardin.

Le soir, on ________________ (retourner) chez nous et mes parents nous ________________ (offrir) quelques petits cadeaux. Pâques, c'________________ (être) toujours ma fête préférée quand j' ________________ (être) petit.

NOTE CULTURELLE

Pâques

Pâques est une fête chrétienne, où les cloches des églises sonnent à toute volée (church bells peal). Les enfants adorent chercher les oeufs au chocolat qui sont cachés (hidden) dans le jardin. On dit que c'est les cloches de l'église qui déposent les chocolats, comme il n'y a pas de lapin de Pâques (Easter Bunny) en France!

Exercice 30. A l'âge de 15 ans.

A. Tammy rêve de son enfance. Lisez les phrases suivantes qui décrivent sa vie à 15 ans. Décidez si les phrases suivantes décrivent vos activités habituelles à l'âge de 15 ans.

Tammy:	Moi aussi	Pas moi
1. Je me réveillais tard le samedi.		
2. Je mangeais beaucoup de fast food.		
3. Je faisais du sport.		
4. Je regardais la télé tous les jours.		
5. Je finissais toujours mes devoirs.		
6. Je dormais peu.		
7. En été, je voyageais en Europe.		
8. J'étudiais beaucoup.		
9. J'avais un copain (une copine [fem.]).		
10. Je m'amusais beaucoup.		

B. Ajoutez quatre autres activités que vous faisiez à l'âge de 15 ans.

1. ______
2. ______
3. ______
4. ______

C. Comparez vos activités avec un partenaire. Est-ce que vous faisiez les mêmes choses? Pourquoi ou pourquoi pas? Quelle sorte d'adolescent était votre partenaire? (travailleur, sociable, sportif, compétitif, etc.)

D. **Devoirs pour demain:** Ecrivez un paragraphe de 8 phrases pour décrire votre personnalité et la personnalité de votre partenaire à l'âge de 15 ans. Comparez vos activités habituelles à l'âge de 15 ans.

Exercice 31. Les meilleures vacances.

A. En classe posez les questions suivantes à un partenaire.

1. Où est-ce que tu as passé vos meilleures vacances ? ______
2. Tu avais quel âge?______
3. Avec qui est-ce que tu es parti(e) ?______

B. Ecrivez cinq questions sur la journée typique de votre partenaire pendant (during) ses meilleures vacances.

1. ______
2. ______
3. ______
4. ______
5. ______

C. Posez vos questions à votre partenaire et écrivez ses réponses.

1. ______________________________
2. ______________________________
3. ______________________________
4. ______________________________
5. ______________________________

D. **Devoirs.** Dans un paragraphe de 8 phrases décrivez les meilleures vacances de votre partenaire.

8 La maison

In this chapter we will talk about where we live, our house or apartment, its rooms, and its furniture.

Vocabulaire

- *à la maison*
- *les pièces*
- *dans la chambre il y a...*
- *dans la salle de bains il y a ...*
- *dans la salle de séjour il y a ...*
- *dans la salle à manger il y a ...*
- *dans la cuisine il y a ...*
- *dans la buanderie il y a ...*
- *les tâches domestiques*
- *adjectifs*
- *verbes*
- *verbes réfléchis*
- *verbes réciproques*

Phonétique

- *Les voyelles moyennes*

Grammaire

- *8.1 passé composé of pronominal verbs*
- *8.2 pronoun y*
- *8.3 pronoun en*
- *8.4 imperative mood*
- *8.5 venir 'to come'*

- *testez-vous!, chapitre 08*
- *verb conjugation reference*
- *verb practice*

Vidéos

Vocabulaire en contexte

- *le salon*
- *la salle à manger, la cuisine et la lingerie*
- *la salle de douche et le couloir*
- *la chambre de Mme DeLeusse*
- *la chambre de la fille de Mme DeLeusse*

Interviews

- *chez vous*
- *les tâches domestiques*

Culture

- *La maison en Provence*
- *Versailles*

Chapitre 8

Vocabulaire

Préparation du vocabulaire

Be sure to download the pdf vocabulary preparation template from the FI website to complete Exercises B, E, and F.

! Your instructor will collect this homework.

A la maison	**At home**
une maison	house
un appartement	apartment
une résidence universitaire	university dorm
une pièce	a room (general term)
une fenêtre	window
un meuble / des meubles	a piece of furniture / furniture
le rez-de-chaussée	ground floor, first floor
un escalier	staircase, stairs
un balcon	balcony
une terrasse	terrace
un jardin	garden, yard

Les pièces	**Rooms**
une entrée	entranceway
un hall d'entrée	foyer
un séjour / un living / un salon / une salle de séjour	living room
une salle à manger	dining room
une cuisine	kitchen
un couloir	hallway
une chambre	bedroom
une salle de bains	bathroom
des toilettes (f pl) / des W.C. (m pl)	toilet
une buanderie	laundry room
un grenier	attic
une cave	cellar, wine cellar
un garage	garage

Dans la chambre il y a...	**In the bedroom...**
un lit	bed
une table de nuit	nightstand
une armoire	armoire
une commode	chest of drawers
un bureau	desk
une étagère	bookcase
une lampe	lamp
un placard	closet
de la moquette	carpet (wall to wall)
un lecteur DVD / MP3	DVD / MP3 player
un ordinateur	computer
un téléphone	telephone

Vocabulaire

Dans la salle de bains il y a...	In the bathroom...
une baignoire	bathtub
une douche	shower
un lavabo	sink
un miroir	mirror

Dans la salle de séjour il y a...	In the living room...
un canapé / un sofa	couch
un fauteuil	armchair
une table basse	coffee table
une télévision	television
un tableau/des tableaux	painting/paintings
un tapis	area rug or carpet

Dans la salle à manger il y a...	In the dining room...
une table	table
une chaise	chair
un buffet	hutch, buffet

Dans la cuisine il y a...	In the kitchen...
un réfrigérateur / un frigo	refrigerator / fridge
un congélateur	freezer
une cuisinière	stove
un four	oven
un four à micro-ondes	microwave
un lave-vaisselle	dishwasher
un évier	sink
un placard	cabinet
une poubelle	trash can

Dans la buanderie il y a...	In the laundry room...
un lave-linge	washing machine
un sèche-linge	dryer

Les tâches domestiques	Household chores
faire des achats (m pl)	to go shopping
faire le marché	to do the grocery shopping
faire des courses (f pl)	to do errands
faire le ménage	to do housework
faire la cuisine	to cook
faire la vaisselle	to do the dishes
ranger	to straighten up
faire le lit	to make the bed

Vocabulaire

passer l'aspirateur (m)	to pass the vacuum cleaner
faire la lessive	to do laundry
repasser	to iron
bricoler	to make home repairs or improvements
Adjectifs	**Adjectives**
ancien(ne)	old
moderne	modern
sombre	dark
clair(e)	bright, full of light
en désordre	messy
en ordre	straightened up
propre	clean
sale	dirty
pratique	practical
confortable	comfortable
Verbes	**Verbs**
déménager	to move (change residences)
Verbes réfléchis	**Reflexive verbs**
s'amuser	to have fun
s'ennuyer	to be bored
se dépêcher	to hurry
s'inquiéter	to worry
se fâcher	to get angry
Verbes réciproques	**Reciprocal verbs**
se disputer	to argue (with one another)
s'entendre	to get along (with one another)
se parler	to talk to (one another)

Phonétique

Go to the website for a complete explanation and practice exercises.

Introduction

Regardons la video ensemble pour répondre aux questions suivantes: Qui présente le chapitre? Où est-il/elle? Quels sont les thèmes du chapitre?

Exercice 1. La maison de votre prof.

Décidez si la maison de votre professeur est normale ou bizarre.

_____1. Dans la chambre du professeur, il y a sept lits.
_____2. Il y a un chat dans la douche.
_____3. Il y a un téléphone sur le bureau.
_____4. Il y a des fleurs dans le congélateur.
_____5. Il y a un lave-vaisselle dans la cuisine.
_____6. Il y a un lit dans la salle à manger.
_____7. Il y a un canapé dans le salon.
_____8. Il y a une baignoire dans la salle de bains.
_____9. Il y a un four à micro-ondes dans la chambre.
_____10. Il y a de la moquette dans les WC.

Exercice 2. Les meubles indispensables.

A votre avis, quels meubles sont indispensables (**absolutely necessary**) pour le confort d'un étudiant à l'université? Mettez-les en ordre d'importance de 1 (le plus important) à 14 (le moins important).

_____ un lit	_____ une télévision	_____ un fauteuil
_____ des chaises	_____ un bureau	_____ une commode
_____ une table basse	_____ un placard	_____ une table
_____ un frigo	_____ un lave-vaisselle	_____ un canapé
_____ une table de nuit	_____ une étagère	

Comparez votre liste de meubles indispensables avec la liste d'un camarade. Est-ce que vous êtes d'accord? Est-ce qu'il y a des meubles indispensables que vous ne trouvez pas sur la liste?

Exercice 3. Quelle pièce?

A. Quelles pièces associez-vous aux activités suivantes? Discutez les activités suivantes avec votre partenaire.

Modèle: bricoler: le garage

1. manger
2. parler avec des amis
3. s'ennuyer
4. se coucher
5. regarder la télé
6. lire
7. chanter
8. faire les devoirs

B. Dans quelles pièces se trouvent les meubles suivants?

Modèle: le buffet ➔ On le trouve dans la cuisine.

1. l'évier
2. le buffet
3. le canapé
4. le four à micro-ondes
5. les fauteuils
6. la télévision
7. le lave-linge
8. la baignoire

Exercice 4. Vive la différence!

Votre professeur va vous donner une image d'une maison. Regardez votre image (A ou B), mais ne regardez pas l'image de votre partenaire. Décrivez votre maison à votre partenaire pour découvrir les sept différences entre vos maisons.

Modèle : Dans la maison A il y a deux lits, mais dans la maison B il y a sept lits!

1. ______________________________
2. ______________________________
3. ______________________________
4. ______________________________
5. ______________________________
6. ______________________________
7. ______________________________

Exercice 5. Votre colocataire (ou camarade de chambre)

A. As-tu un(e) bon(ne) colocataire (ou camarade de chambre)? Posez les questions suivantes à un partenaire. Répondez avec les phrases complètes.

1. Est-ce que ton/ta co-locataire fait souvent le ménage?
   Oui, il/elle le fait souvent. Non, il/elle ne le fait pas souvent.
2. Est ce que ton/ta colocataire a déjà fait la cuisine pour toi?
   Oui, il/elle l'a déjà faite. Non, il/elle ne l'a jamais faite.
3. Est-ce que ton colocataire te parle souvent?
   Oui, il/elle me parle souvent. Non, il/elle ne me parle pas souvent.
4. Est-ce que ton/ta colocataire va souvent à l'université avec toi?
   Oui, il/elle y va souvent avec moi. Non, il/elle n'y va pas souvent avec moi.
5. Est-ce que ton/ta colocataire reste toujours dans sa chambre?
   Oui, il/elle y reste toujours. Non, il/elle n'y reste pas toujours.
6. Est-ce que ton/ta colocataire achète souvent de la bière?
   Oui, il/elle en achète souvent. Non, il/elle n'en achète jamais.
7. Est-ce que ton/ta colocataire t'offre des cadeaux?
   Oui, il/elle m'en offre. Non, il/elle ne m'en offre pas.
8. Est-ce que ton/ta colocataire fait beaucoup de bruit (**noise**)?
   Oui, il/elle en fait beaucoup. Non, il/elle n'en fait pas beaucoup.

B. D'après ses réponses, décidez si votre partenaire a un(e) bon(nne) colocataire (ou camarade de chambre).

> **Modèle:** Mon / ma partenaire a un(e) bon(ne) colocataire parce qu'il/elle lui offre beaucoup de cadeaux et ne reste pas toujours dans sa chambre.

C. Répondez aux questions suivantes et discutez avec la classe.

The pronoun y

What does the pronoun **y** refer to in item #4 above? ____________________

What does the pronoun **y** refer to in item #5 above ____________________

What does the pronoun **y** refer to in general?

____

The pronoun en

What does the pronoun **en** refer to in item #6 above? ____________________

What does the pronoun **en** refer to in item #7 above? ____________________

What does the pronoun **en** refer to in item #8 above? ____________________

What do the phrases replaced by the pronoun **en** all have in common? ____________________

____

NOTE CULTURELLE

La maison française et la vie privée

La propriété privée et la vie privée (privacy) sont un droit (a right) en France depuis la Révolution de 1789. La maison protège (protect) la vie privée.

Une clôture (enclosure) ferme la propriété : une haie (hedge), un mur (wall), du grillage (wire fencing), du bois (wood fencing), du fer forgé (wrought iron)... On entre dans la propriété par un portail (gate).

On ne voit pas dans la maison : le jour il y a des rideaux (curtains) ou des voilages (sheer curtains). La nuit, il y a des volets (shutters). Les volets protègent aussi la maison l'été, quand il fait chaud.

Dictogloss 1. Chez Madame de Leusse

Formez des groupes de 3 ou 4 personnes. Ecoutez le texte lu par (**read by**) votre professeur. Complétez les phrases suivantes et donnez le plus de détails possibles.

Pour commencer, Laila nous a présenté Madame Véronique de Leusse. Madame de Leusse a ______________________________ à Lyon. D'abord, elle nous a montré ________________________ et ______________________________, deux belles pièces très claires. Ensuite, on a vu ______________________. Elle était _________________ et bien équipée. Puis, nous avons visité ____________________, _________________________ et _________________ qui étaient dans _________________ pièce à côté. Après, nous sommes montés pour visiter __________________. Dans _________________, on a vu un ordinateur. Nous sommes entrés dans _____________________de Madame de Leusse. Elle avait ______________ confortable, ______________ de nuit, et de _________________________. Pour finir, on a quitté ___________________ pour visiter ___________________de sa fille.

Parlez uniquement en français! Si la réponse est "OUI", demandez la signature de cette personne. Changez de camarade pour chaque question. Ecoutez attentivement les questions qu'on vous pose. Ne répondez pas à des questions incomplètes.

Exercice 6. Est-ce que tu as passé une bonne journée hier?

1. Est-ce que tu es allé(e) au cinéma? ______________________________
2. Est-ce que tu t'es levé(e) avant midi? ______________________________
3. Est-ce que tu t'es brossé les dents? ______________________________
4. Est-ce que tu es sorti(e)? ______________________________
5. Est-ce que tu t'es disputé(e) avec quelqu'un? ______________________________
6. Est-ce que tu as fait le ménage? ______________________________
7. Est-ce que tu t'es amusé(e)? ______________________________
8. Est-ce que tu as rangé tes affaires? ______________________________

Exercice 7. La journée de Karen.

A. Mettez les phrases dans un ordre logique.

_____ Karen a pris le petit déjeûner.

_____ Karen est allée en cours

_____ Karen s'est lavé les cheveux

_____ Karen s'est lavée.

_____ Karen a vu la maison en désordre

_____ Karen s'est brossé les dents

_____ Karen s'est réveillée

_____ Karen est rentrée chez elle

_____ Karen et sa colocataire se sont disputées.

_____ Karen s'est couchée.

B. Comparez avec un partenaire. Avez-vous les mêmes réponses?

Exercice 8. Dominique, femme ou homme?

A. D'abord, dans chaque phrase, décidez si Dominique est une femme ou un homme, ou si il est impossible à distinguer.

	Femme	Homme	Impossible
1. Dominique est allée au cinema hier soir.	❑	❑	❑
2. Dominique s'est reveillée à 7h.	❑	❑	❑
3. Dominique ne s'est pas lavé ce matin.	❑	❑	❑
4. Dominique s'est brossé les dents ce matin.	❑	❑	❑
5. Dominique s'est amusée pendant les vacances.	❑	❑	❑
6. Dominique et sa mère se sont disputés la semaine dernière.	❑	❑	❑
7. Dominique et son meilleur ami se sont parlé hier soir.	❑	❑	❑
8. Dominique? Ses amis l'ont appelé hier soir.	❑	❑	❑
9. Dominique? Ses parents l'ont invitée au restaurant pour son anniversaire.	❑	❑	❑
10. Dominique? Ses parents lui ont offert une voiture pour son anniversaire	❑	❑	❑

B. Puis, avec un partenaire, lisez quelques phrases et réagissez!

Modèle: - Dominique est allée au cinéma hier soir
- Moi non, je ne suis pas allé(e) au cinéma hier soir. Et toi?

Exercice 9. Le week-end dernier...

A. Décidez si les phrases suivantes décrivent votre week-end dernier.

	Oui	Non
1. Il a fait beau.	❑	❑
2. J'ai fait de l'exercice.	❑	❑
3. Je suis resté(e) chez moi.	❑	❑
4. Je me suis ennuyé(e).	❑	❑
5. Je me suis fâché(e) avec mes parents.	❑	❑
6. Je suis sorti(e) avec des amis.	❑	❑
7. J'ai étudié tout le week-end.	❑	❑
8. Je me suis amusé(e).	❑	❑

B. Quelles autres activités est-ce que vous avez faites? (au moins 3 activités)

1. ______________________
2. ______________________
3. ______________________

At home, please go to the Français interactif website. Read the following grammar points in Tex's French Grammar and complete all Texercises which you will turn in to your instructor.

8.1 Passé composé of pronominal verbs

reflexive pronoun
+
present of être
+
past participle

s'amuser 'to have fun'

je	me suis amusé(e)
tu	t'es amusé(e)
il / *elle* / *on*	s'est amusé(e)
nous	nous sommes amusé(e)s
vous	vous êtes amusé(e)(s)
ils / *elles*	se sont amusé(e)s

To negate, place ne before the reflexive pronoun and pas after être: Elle <u>ne</u> s'est <u>pas</u> amusée.

C. En classe, comparez votre week-end avec le week-end de votre partenaire. Quelles activités avez-vous faites en commun? Qui a passé le meilleur week-end? Expliquez.

Exercice 10. La journée d'Audrey.

Racontez la journée d'Audrey en mettant les phrases au passé composé. (Attention! Not all verbs are reflexive verbs!)

Modèle: Audrey se lève. Audrey s'est levée.

1. Audrey se brosse les dents. ____________________
2. Audrey s'habille. ____________________
3. Audrey va au parc. ____________________
4. Audrey rencontre un petit chien. ____________________
5. Audrey écoute des musiciens avec papa. ____________________
6. Audrey dort dans la voiture. ____________________
7. Audrey mange des cerises. ____________________
8. Audrey regarde les fleurs dans le jardin. ____________________
9. Audrey prend le goûter. ____________________
10. Audrey se couche. ____________________

Devoirs: Racontez votre journée au passé composé. Utilisez beaucoup de verbes différents avec un minimum de **5 verbes pronominaux**. **Ecrivez un paragraphe de 8 phrases**.

Exercice 11. Typique ou pas typique?

		typique	pas typique
1.	Les étudiants n'ont pas beaucoup de meubles.	❑	❑
2.	Il y a une commode dans la salle de bains.	❑	❑
3.	On dort sur le canapé dans l'après-midi.	❑	❑
4.	On fait la cuisine dans la chambre.	❑	❑
5.	On range les vêtements (clothes) dans le placard.	❑	❑
6.	Il y a des fauteuils confortables dans le stade.	❑	❑
7.	Les étudiants font le ménage le weekend.	❑	❑
8.	Il y a une étagère dans la salle à manger.	❑	❑

Exercice 12. Les tâches domestiques

A. Chez vous, qu'est-ce que vous aimez ou détestez faire? Cochez (√) votre préférence pour chaque tâche domestique.

		J'aime…	Je déteste…
1.	faire les courses	❑	❑
2.	faire la cuisine	❑	❑
3.	faire la lessive	❑	❑
4.	faire le lit	❑	❑
5.	faire le ménage	❑	❑
6.	faire la vaisselle	❑	❑
7.	ranger la maison	❑	❑
8.	passer l'aspirateur	❑	❑
9.	repasser	❑	❑
10.	bricoler	❑	❑

B. Indiquez la fréquence de ces tâches domestiques chez vous. Ecrivez 4 phrases. Adverbes utiles: **toujours**, **souvent, parfois, tout le temps, rarement, ne…jamais, de temps en temps, une fois par semaine, etc.**

Modèle: Je fais souvent les courses, mais je fais rarement la cuisine.

____

____

____

____

C. Posez des questions à votre partenaire et comparez vos réponses.

Modèle: Est-ce que tu aimes faire des courses? Est-ce que tu fais souvent des courses?

D. Imaginez que vous êtes des camarades de chambre ou des colocataires. Est-ce que vous êtes des camarades de chambre ou colocataires compatibles? Pourquoi ou pourquoi pas? Rapportez votre discussion à la classe et expliquez.

Rappel!

Note that with pronominal verbs, the past participle agrees with the subject except when:

• the pronominal verb is followed by an object:

Modèle:
Karen s'est lavée. BUT Karen s'est lavé les cheveux.

• the verb has an indirect object.

Modèle:
Karen a parlé à son amie. → Elles se sont parlé.

At home, please go to the Français interactif website. Read the following grammar points in Tex's French Grammar and complete all Texercises which you will turn in to your instructor.

8.2 Le pronom y

y replaces a prepositional phrase of location:
- **à la maison**
- **chez moi**
- **en classe**

8.3 Le pronom en

en replaces <u>de</u> + a noun, including nouns with partitive or indefinite determiners:
- **du lait**
- **un rôti**
- **des éclairs**

Exercice 13. Qu'est-ce qu'on y achète?

Faites les correspondances entre la première et la deuxième colonne.

Qu'est-ce qu'on achète…

_____1.	à la boulangerie?	a. on y achète des éclairs
_____2.	au tabac?	b. on y achète du pain
_____3.	à la gare?	c. on y achète du saucisson
_____4.	à la librairie?	d. on y achète du lait
_____5.	à la charcuterie?	e. on y achète un rôti
_____6.	à la pâtisserie?	f. on y achète un billet de train
_____7.	à la boucherie?	g. on y achète des livres
_____8.	à l'épicerie?	h. on y achète des cigarettes

Exercice 14. Devinettes.

Modèle: On y prend un café. → On prend un café.
<u>chez ses amis</u> / <u>à Austin Java</u> / <u>sur la terasse</u>, etc.

1. On y voit la Tour Eiffel.
2. On y étudie.
3. On y achète les livres pour les cours.
4. On y travaille sur l'ordinateur.
5. On s'y repose.
6. On y passe l'aspirateur.
7. On y va quand on est malade.
8. On y fait la vaisselle.

Exercice 15. Qu'est-ce qu'on y fait?

Modèle: Qu'est-ce qu'on achète à la librairie? ➔ On y achète des livres.

1. Qu'est-ce qu'on mange au restaurant français? ______________________
2. Qu'est-ce qu'on achète au supermarché? ______________________
3. Qu'est-ce qu'on fait au centre ville? ______________________
4. Qu'est-ce qu'on fait au parc? ______________________
5. Qu'est-ce qu'on fait à la plage? ______________________
6. Qu'est-ce qu'on boit dans les bars? ______________________

Exercice 16. Test des connaissances géographiques.

Répondez aux questions suivantes selon vos connaissances en géographie.

Modèle: Qu'est-ce qu'on trouve à Londres? ➔ On y trouve Big Ben.

1. Qu'est-ce qu'on visite à Paris? ______________________
2. Qu'est-ce qu'on fait en Suisse? ______________________
3. Qu'est-ce qu'on trouve à New York (la ville)? ______________________
4. Qu'est-ce qu'on boit à Bordeaux? ______________________
5. Qu'est-ce qu'on mange en Italie? ______________________

Exercice 17. Au supermarché

Quelles sont les phrases équivalentes?

______1.	J'en ai acheté.	a. J'avais besoin de piles (**batteries**)
______2.	J'en ai acheté un.	b. J'ai acheté un aspirateur.
______3.	J'en ai acheté une.	c. J'avais besoin d'un nouvel ordinateur.
______4.	J'en avais besoin.	d. J'ai acheté du pain.
______5.	J'en avais besoin d'un.	e. J'ai acheté une poubelle.
______6.	Il y en avait beaucoup.	f. Il y avait beaucoup de monde.
______7.	Il y en avait peu.	g. Il y avait peu de soldes (**sales**).

Exercice 18. Devinettes.

Modèle:
On en prend au petit déjeuner. ➔ On prend du lait / du thé / du café au petit déjeuner.

1. Il y en a un dans la salle de classe.
2. On en mange chez Ben & Jerry's.
3. Les étudiants en ont besoin.
4. Le professeur de français en a une.
5. Les étudiants en offrent au professeur à la fin du semestre!!!
6. Les étudiants en font tous les jours.
7. Votre université en a beaucoup.
8. Vous en avez un.

Exercice 19. Votre semestre.

1. Tu as combien de cours ce semestre? J'en ai ______________________
2. Tu as acheté combien de livres? J'en ai acheté ______________________
3. Il y a combien d'étudiants dans la classe de français? Il y en a ______________
4. Tu as combien d'examens cette semaine? ______________________

Exercice 20. Qu'est-ce qu'il y a dans votre chambre?

Posez les questions suivantes à un partenaire. Votre partenaire va remplacer le nom avec le pronom **en** dans ses réponses.

Modèle: Est-ce qu'il y a un canapé? ➔ Non, il n'y en a pas.

1. Est-ce qu'il y a des photos sexy?
2. Est-ce qu'il y a un grand lit pour deux personnes?
3. Est-ce qu'il y a une vieille armoire?
4. Est-ce qu'il y a un miroir?
5. Est-ce qu'il y a des affiches?
6. Est-ce qu'il y a un frigo?
7. Est-ce qu'il y a une télévision?
8. Est-ce qu'il y a une commode?

Exercice 21. Avant le dîner.

Imaginez que votre colocataire et vous faites les préparatifs pour une soirée dîner chez vous. Faites correspondre le pronom souligné à la réponse logique dans la deuxième colonne.

Modèle: Pour faire une quiche on en a besoin. **du fromage**

_____1. Malheureusement (**unfortunately**), on ne l'a pas faite hier soir.	a. mes devoirs
_____2. Je vais lui demander d'apporter du vin.	b. à nos camarades de classe
_____3. Mon coloc et moi, nous y faisons les courses.	c. de la glace
_____4. Chez moi, il y en a dans le congélateur.	d. chez HEB
_____5. Je les ai finis hier soir, avant de faire les préparatifs.	e. la vaisselle
_____6. Mon coloc et moi allons leur demander leurs numéros de téléphone.	f. à mon/ma meilleur(e) ami(e)

Exercice 22. On se prépare.

Laila, Karen et Blake préparent une soirée américaine pour leurs amis français à Lyon.

A. Lisez le dialogue. D'après vous (**according to you**), quels sont les pronoms manquants (**missing**)?

1. Laila : Blake, est-ce qu'on va toujours (**still**) au restaurant?

2. Blake : Oui, on ________ va toujours avec Braxton et Hélène.

3. Laila : Tu ______ as téléphoné pour confirmer ?

4. Blake : Oui, je _____ ai appelés. Et toi, tu as acheté des fleurs pour Hélène?

5. Laila : Oui, j'____ ai acheté.

6. Blake : Super ! On _____ va ?

B. En classe écoutez votre professeur pour vérifier.

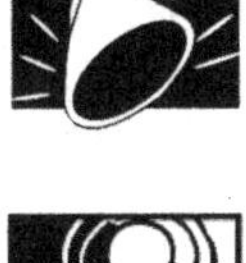

C. Répondez aux questions suivantes.

1. In Line 3, Laila uses the pronoun **leur.** Which people does this pronoun refer to? Why does Laila use **leur** with the verb **téléphoner**? ______________________________
2. Why does Blake use the pronoun **les** in Line 4 to refer to the same people?
____
3. In Line 2, why is the pronoun **y** used? ______________________________
4. In Line 4, why is the past participle of the verb **appeler** written with an *s*? __________
____
5. In Line 5, what does the pronoun **en** refer to? ______________________________
6. Give the equivalent of the expression **on y va** in English. Be careful! Don't translate the expression word for word! ______________________________

NOTE CULTURELLE

La Conversion

En France, après la Révolution de 1789, on utilise le système métrique (base 10 metrical system)

1 centimètre (cm)
1 mètre (1m = 100 cm)
1 kilomètre (1km = 1000 m)
etc…

Aux Etats-Unis, au Liberia et en Birmanie il n'y a pas le système métrique.
Aux USA, on a différentes unités. Par exemple, pour la superficie (area) d'une maison, ce sont les pieds (feet) :

1 Ft2 = 0.093 m2

une maison de 1500 pieds carrés (square feet) est une maison de 140 mètres carrés.

Un pouce (inch) = 2.54 cm
Un pied (foot) = 0.305 m
Un yard = 0.914 m
Un mile = 1.609 km

La distance de Austin à Houston est de 165 miles ou 265 kms

Exercice 23. Chez toi.

Répondez aux questions en utilisant un pronom d'objet (**direct, indirect, y** ou **en)** pour remplacer la partie soulignée.

Modèle: Est-ce que tu regardes la télévision ? <u>Oui, je la regarde souvent</u>.

1. Est-ce que tu étudies <u>dans ta chambre</u>?
2. Est-ce que tes amis <u>te</u> rendent souvent visite?
3. Dans ta chambre, est-ce qu'il y a <u>un ordinateur</u>?
4. Est-ce que tu as <u>des étagères</u>?
5. Est-ce que tu as fait <u>la lessive</u> cette semaine?
6. Est-ce que tu vas téléphoner <u>à tes parents</u> ce week-end?
7. Est-ce que tu es resté(e) <u>à Austin</u> le week-end passé?
8. Est-ce que tu as fini <u>tes devoirs</u> hier soir?

Exercice 24. Qui vous donne les ordres suivants?

		Mon professeur	Mes parents
1.	Range ta chambre!	❑	√
2.	Ouvre ton livre!	❑	❑
3.	Lave ta voiture!	❑	❑
4.	Fais tes exercices de grammaire!	❑	❑
5.	Sois attentif!	❑	❑
6.	Ne te dispute pas avec ta sœur!	❑	❑
7.	Lave-toi les mains!	❑	❑
8.	Révise pour l'examen!	❑	❑
9.	Aie de la patience avec ton petit frère!	❑	❑
10.	Réveille-toi tôt le matin!	❑	❑

Exercice 25. Votre prof, alors!

Votre professeur de français a souffert d'une crise d'amnésie et ne sait plus comment faire. Donnez-lui des conseils en employant une expression de la colonne B pour chaque situation de la colonne A.

Colonne A

______1. Votre prof prend son dîner dans la baignoire.
______2. Votre prof n'a pas de lit dans sa chambre.
______3. Votre prof dort dans le jardin.
______4. Votre prof a des affaires partout.
______5. Votre prof porte des vêtements sales.
______6. La moquette du salon de votre prof est très sale.
______7. Votre prof a besoin de se laver.
______8. Votre prof ne se couche pas avant 3 heures du matin.

Colonne B

a. Lavez-vous.
b. Dormez dans la maison.
c. Achetez un lit pour votre chambre.
d. Couchez-vous plus tôt.
e. Mangez dans la salle à manger.
f. Rangez vos affaires.
g. Passez l'aspirateur.
h. Faites la lessive.

Exercice 26. Vous êtes la baby-sitter de Camille et d'Audrey.

Lisez les situations suivantes et donnez des ordres à Camille et Audrey.

Modèle: La chambre des filles est en désordre. Rangez votre chambre!

1. Elles n'ont pas encore fait leurs devoirs. ________________ vos devoirs!
2. Elles ont faim. ___________________ un goûter.
3. Elles ont soif. ____________________ de l'eau.
4. Elles ont sommeil. _________________ au lit!

Exercice 27. Votre colocataire!

Votre colocataire vous demande des conseils tout le temps. Donnez-lui des conseils en employant l'impératif.

Modèle: Il/elle vous dit: J'ai faim.
Vous répondez: Fais la cuisine!

1. Je suis fatigué(e).
2. Je ne trouve pas de copain/copine.
3. Je suis toujours en retard pour mon cours de 10h.
4. J'ai faim mais je n'ai pas assez d'argent pour aller au restaurant.
5. J'ai envie d'aller au cinéma mais ma copine/ mon copain a envie de rester à la maison.
6. Je vais à une fête ce soir mais je n'ai pas de voiture.
7. J'ai besoin de livres pour mes cours.
8. Il fait trop chaud dans ma chambre.

At home, please go to the Français interactif website. Read the following grammar points in Tex's French Grammar and complete all Texercises which you will turn in to your instructor.

8.4 Imperative mood

-er verbs	**Regarde** **Regardons** **Regardez**
-ir verbs	**Finis** **Finissons** **Finissez**
-re verbs	**Attends** **Attendons** **Attendez**

Être	Avoir
Sois	**Aie**
Soyons	**Ayons**
Soyez	**Ayez**

Pronominal verbs
Amuse

Amuse-toi

Amusons-nous!

Amusez-vous!

Exercice 28. Discrimination auditive.

Ecoutez et décidez si le verbe est au singulier ou au pluriel.

	singulier	pluriel
Modèle: Elle vient en classe tous les jours.	√	❑
1. ______________________	❑	❑
2. ______________________	❑	❑
3. ______________________	❑	❑
4. ______________________	❑	❑
5. ______________________	❑	❑
6. ______________________	❑	❑

Exercice 29. Vrai ou faux?

	Vrai	Faux
1. Le professeur ne vient pas toujours en classe.	❑	❑
2. Mes parents viennent souvent à Austin.	❑	❑
3. Les étudiants viennent rarement en classe.	❑	❑
4. Les étudiants viennent toujours à l'heure en classe.	❑	❑
5. Le français devient de plus en plus facile.	❑	❑
6. Mon coloc revient de France.	❑	❑
7. Les hommes tiennent toujours la porte pour les femmes.	❑	❑
8. Je retiens le vocabulaire facilement.	❑	❑

Exercice 30. D'où est-ce qu'on vient?

A. Complétez les phrases avec la bonne réponse.

1. Céline Dion vient du ______________________.
2. Johnny Depp vient des ______________________.
3. Pierre et Marie Curie viennent de ______________________.
4. Le professeur vient de (ville) ______________________.

B. Et vous? Discutez les questions suivantes avec un partenaire.

1. D'où est-ce que tu viens?
2. D'où vient ton/ta meilleur(e) ami(e)?
3. D'où est-ce que tes ancêtres viennent?

At home, please go to the Français interactif website. Read the following grammar points in Tex's French Grammar and complete all Texercises which you will turn in to your instructor.

8.5 venir 'to come' and verbs conjugated like 'venir': devenir, revenir, tenir

je	**viens**
tu	**viens**
il / elle / on	**vient**
nous	**venons**
vous	**venez**
ils / elles	**viennent**

Pour aller plus loin

- in affirmative commands, object pronouns follow the verb (e.g., Parle-moi! 'Talk to me!')
- in negative commands, the object pronoun precedes the verb and ne... pas placed around object pronoun and imperative form (eg. Ne me parle pas! 'Don't talk to me!')

Exercice 31. Trouver un appartement.

A. D'abord, reliez les équivalents dans le tableau suivant.

______1.	Est-ce que l'appartement est toujours à louer?	a.	What floor is it on?
______2.	Quand est-il disponible?	b.	Is the apartment still for rent?
______3.	A quel étage est-ce qu'il se trouve?	c.	How much is the deposit?
______4.	Quelle est la station de métro la plus proche?	d.	How much is the rent, including utilities?
______5.	Quel est le montant du loyer, charges comprises?	e.	Is it an electric or gas-powered heater?
______6.	Est-ce que le chauffage est électrique ou au gaz?	f.	What is the closest metro station?
______7.	Est-ce qu'internet est inclus dans les charges?	g.	When is it available?
______8.	Quel est le montant de la caution?	h.	Is internet service included in the utilities?

B. Ensuite, écrivez des questions plus spécifiques sur la déscription de l'appartement.

Déscription de l'appartement (Employez des adjectifs.):

Modèle: Est-ce qu'il est grand?

1. ______________________________
2. ______________________________
3. ______________________________

La cuisine:

Modèle: Est-ce qu'il y a un frigo?

1. ______________________________
2. ______________________________
3. ______________________________

Les meubles:

Modèle: Est-ce qu'il y a une table dans le salon?

1. ______________________________
2. ______________________________
3. ______________________________

C. Votre professeur va vous donner soit (**either**) un Tableau A ou soit (**or**) un Tableau B. Posez les questions que vous avez écrites là-dessus (**above**) à votre partenaire pour compléter le tableau suivant.

Disponibilité	
Etage	
Métro	
Déscription	
Loyer + Charges	
Caution	
Cuisine	
Chambre	
Salon	
Divers (miscellaneous)	

D. Maintenant comparez les deux appartements. Quels sont les avantages et les inconvénients de chaque appartement?

9 Médias et communications

In this chapter we will talk about media: television and newspapers, movies, and the Internet.

Vocabulaire

- *la télévision, le cinéma*
- *la presse*
- *la radio*
- *l'internet*
- *le téléphone*
- *au téléphone*
- *adjectifs*
- *verbes*

Phonétique

- *La tension musculaire des voyelles françaises /i/ et /o/*

Grammaire

- *9.1 relative pronouns: qui and que*
- *9.2 alternate forms (1) ne ... jamais, rien, personne, etc.*
- *9.3 one-word negative sentences si, jamais, etc.*
- *9.4 dire, lire, écrire present tense*
- *9.5 modal verbs vouloir, pouvoir, devoir*
- *9.6 narration: passé composé vs. imparfait*
- *testez-vous!, chapitre 09*
- *verb conjugation reference*
- *verb practice*

Vidéos

Vocabulaire en contexte

- *Gérard - kiosquier*
- *Mme De Leusse et sa fille*

Interviews

- *les médias*

Culture

- *publicité Boursin*
- *publicité Minute Maid*
- *publicité Fiat*
- *publicité Brokeback Mountain*
- *publicité Le Parisien*
- *publicité Renault*

Vocabulaire

Préparation du vocabulaire

Be sure to download the pdf vocabulary preparation template from the FI website to complete Exercises B, E, and F.

! Your instructor will collect this homework.

La télévision / Le cinéma	Television / Cinema
la télé	TV
la télécommande	remote control
une chaîne	channel
un programme	television schedule
un feuilleton	series / soap opera
une série	series
une émission	show
un dessin animé	cartoon
un documentaire	documentary
une émission de variétés	variety show
un jeu télévisé	game show
la télé-réalité	reality television
un magazine d'actualités (à la télévision)	news show
les informations / les infos (f pl) / le journal	news
l'actualité (f)	current events
la météo	weather report
un reporter / un journaliste	reporter / journalist
une interview	interview
une publicité / une pub	commercial
un concert	concert
un film	movie
un film d'amour	romantic movie
un film de science-fiction	science-fiction movie
un film d'horreur	horror movie
un film d'action / un film d'aventures	action film / adventure film
un film policier	detective / police movie
un drame	drama
une comédie	comedy (movie, play)
un (film) musical	musical
un comédie musical	musical comedy
un western	western
en VO / en VF	original version / French version
avec / sans sous-titres	with / without subtitles
un acteur / une actrice	actor / actress
une célébrité	celebrity
une star / une vedette	star (refers to men or women)
une personnalité (de la télévision, du cinéma, de la radio…)	celebrity
le méchant	the bad guy

Vocabulaire

LE PETIT ROBERT

La presse	The press
un kiosque (à journaux)	news stand
un journal (national, régional)	newspaper (national, regional)
une bande-dessinée	comic strip
une petite annonce	classified ad
un magazine	magazine
un livre	book
un roman	novel

La radio	The radio
une station	radio station
une chanson	song
un chanteur / une chanteuse	singer
un groupe	a band

L'internet	The internet
un ordinateur	computer
un portable	laptop
le web	the web
un site	website
une page d'accueil	homepage
un forum	bulletin board, newsgroup
un moteur de recherche	search engine
un mot de passe	password
un email / courriel	e-mail
en ligne	online
un lien	link

Le téléphone	The telephone
un (téléphone) portable	cell phone
un répondeur / une boîte vocale	voicemail
un texto	text message

Au téléphone	On the phone
Allô...	Hello...
T'es où?	Where are you at / what are you doing?
Est-ce que je peux parler à...	May I speak to...
Je voudrais un renseignement.	I would like some information.
Un instant s'il vous plaît.	Please hold. / One moment please.
Ne quittez pas.	Stay on the line.
Je vous le / la passe.	I'm putting you through to him/her. / I'm connecting you to him/her.
Quel est votre numéro de téléphone?	What is your phone number?

Vocabulaire

Est-ce que vous voulez laisser un message?	Do you want to leave a message?
Pouvez-vous rappeler à 15h?	Could you call back at 3 p.m.?
Qui est à l'appareil?	Who's on the phone?

Adjectives	**Adjectifs**
célèbre	famous
amusant(e) / comique / marrant(e) / drôle	funny
doublé(e)	dubbed
effrayant(e)	frightening
ennuyeux / ennuyeuse	boring
étranger / étrangère	foreign
gratuit(e)	free
optimiste	optimistic/hopeful
pessimiste	pessimistic
réaliste	realistic
satirique	satirical
tragique	tragic
triste	sad
violent(e)	violent

Verbes	**Verbs**
surfer / aller (sur internet)	to surf (the web)
cliquer	to click
télécharger	to download
conduire	to drive
décrire	to describe
dire	to say
écrire	to write
durer	to last
lire	to read
montrer	to show
passer (du temps)	to spend (time)

Phonétique

Go to the website for a complete explanation and practice exercises.

Introduction

Regardons la video ensemble pour répondre aux questions suivantes: Qui présente le chapitre? Où est-il/elle? Quels sont les thèmes du chapitre?

Exercice 1. Les films.

A. Avec un partenaire, donnez 2 films pour chaque genre suivant:

1. des films d'horreur: ______________________
2. des films de science-fiction: ______________________
3. des films d'aventure: ______________________
4. des dessins animés: ______________________
5. des comédies: ______________________
6. des drames: ______________________

B. Quel genre de film?

_____1.	West Side Story	a. un drame
_____2.	L'arme fatale	b. un film de science-fiction
_____3.	Vendredi 13	c. un film d'amour
_____4.	Indiana Jones	d. un dessin animé
_____5.	2001, L'odysée de l'espace	e. un film policier/d'action
_____6.	La vie est belle	f. un musical
_____7.	Aladin	g. un film d'aventures
_____8.	Casablanca	h. un film d'horreur

C. Devinez les titres anglais de ces films:

1. Le Roi Lion ______________________
2. Quatre mariages et un enterrement ______________________
3. Le silence des agneaux ______________________
4. Sept ans au Tibet ______________________
5. Le magicien d'Oz ______________________
6. La guerre des étoiles ______________________
7. Trois hommes et un couffin ______________________
8. Minuit dans le jardin du bien et du mal ______________________
9. Retour vers le futur ______________________
10. Chantons sous la pluie ______________________

D. Discutez les questions suivantes avec un partenaire:

Quel est le dernier film que vous avez vu?
Est-ce que vous l'avez aimé? Pourquoi ou pourquoi pas?
Est-ce que vous avez vu des films français? Si oui, quels films?

NOTE CULTURELLE

Les journaux

En France les journaux ont une orientation politique. A gauche, il y a l'Humanité et Libération. Au centre il y a le Monde et à droite il y a le Figaro. Pour le sport il y a l'Equipe. Il y a aussi beaucoup de journaux régionaux, comme Le Progrès à Lyon.

Tous les journaux sont sur internet.

Vocabulaire supplémentaire:

l'histoire - story
l'intrigue - plot

Exercice 2. La communication.

Posez ces questions à vos camarades.

1. Est-ce que tu achètes des billets d'avion en ligne? ____________________
2. Est-ce que tu vas souvent sur internet? ____________________
3. Est-ce que tu reçois beaucoup de spam? ____________________
4. Est-ce que tu as un téléphone portable? ____________________
5. Est-ce que tu écoutes la radio en ligne? ____________________
6. Est-ce que tu regardes les informations en ligne? ____________________
7. Est-ce que tu télécharges des chansons illégalement? ____________________
8. Est-ce que tu envoies des textos pendant la classe? ____________________

! Utilisez uniquement le français! Si la réponse est "OUI", demandez la signature de cette personne. Changez de camarade pour chaque question. Ecoutez attentivement les questions qu'on vous pose. Ne répondez pas à des questions incomplètes.

Exercice 3. Devinettes.

A. A quoi correspondent les descriptions suivantes?

Modèle:
C'est quelque chose qui a la forme d'un rectangle et que vous utilisez pour changer de chaînes → C'est une télécommande.

1. C'est quelque chose qui a la forme d'un rectangle et que vous aimez lire pour vous détendre.
2. C'est quelque chose qui est généralement petit et que vous utilisez pour envoyer des textos.
3. C'est quelqu'un qui chante et que vous écoutez à la radio.
4. C'est quelqu'un qui est très célèbre et que vous voyez souvent à la télé et dans les magazines.

B. Répondez aux questions suivantes.

1. Translate the following sentence into English:

   C'est quelque chose qui est généralement petit et que vous utilisez pour envoyer des textos

   . ____________________

2. How did you translate **qui** and **que** in English? ____________________

3. Look at the following phrases and fill in the blanks with **subject** or **object**:

... qui a la forme d'un rectangle	... que vous vous aimez lire pour vous détendre.
... qui est très célèbre qui is the __________ of the verb.	... que vous voyez souvent à la télé que is the __________ of the verb.

Exercice 4. La télé

A. Donner un exemple pour chaque catégorie:

Modèle:
Une chaîne: ABC

1. une chaîne d'informations: __________
2. une émission d'actualité: __________
3. un jeu télévisé: __________
4. une série: __________
5. un feuilleton: __________
6. une émission de télé-réalité: __________
7. un dessin-animé: __________
8. une émission satirique: __________

B. Sondage

En groupes de trois, comparez ce que vous regardez à la télé. Complétez le tableau avec: **souvent – quelquefois – jamais**

Modèle: Est-ce que tu regardes des séries?
Partenaire 1:
Oui, je regarde souvent des séries → Ecrivez **souvent** dans la case (**box**) séries / Partenaire 1.
Partenaire 2:
Non je ne regarde jamais de séries → Ecrivez **jamais** dans la case séries / Partenaire 2.

	Partenaire 1	Partenaire 2	Partenaire 3
Les séries			
Les jeux télévisés			
Les feuilletons			
Les émissions de télé-réalité			
Le journal			
Les dessins-animés			
Les émissions comiques			
Les documentaires			

Quel type d'émission est-ce que votre groupe regarde le plus souvent? Le moins souvent?

Exercice 5. Le langage SMS.

Avec un partenaire, écrivez les textos suivants en français correct.

1. Keske tu fÉ? __________
2. Tu vi1 2m1 pr l'anniv' de Pierre? __________
3. Je V bi1, et twa? __________
4. G vu Amélie, CT super, GT mdr :))! __________

NOTE CULTURELLE

La télévision.

En France, il y a des chaines publiques et des chaines privées.
TF1, une chaine privée et France 2, France 3, France 4 (des chaînes publiques) ont des programmes généraux pour tous les publics (films, jeux télévisés, informations). La 5 et surtout Arte, deux autres chaînes publiques, ont des programmes plus culturels et plus spécialisés (documentaires sur l'art, la musique, le cinéma européen).
En plus des chaînes nationales, il y a aussi le câble, comme aux USA, avec une grande variété de chaînes de France et du monde entier.
En France, il n'y a jamais de publicités pendant les émissions.

Sur internet : TF1.fr, france2.fr, france3.fr, france4.fr, france5.fr, arte.tv

Note:
mdr = lol (mort de rire)

At home, please go to the Français interactif website. Read the following grammar points in Tex's French Grammar and complete all Texercises which you will turn in to your instructor.

9.1 Pronoms relatifs – qui et que

QUI	QUE
+ verbe	+ sujet + verbe

Exercice 6. Quiz culturel.

A. Avec un partenaire complétez les phrases suivantes.

1. Donnez le nom d'une émission télé qui parle de l'actualité:____________________
2. Donnez le nom d'un film qui est effrayant et drôle: ____________________
3. Donnez le nom d'un acteur/actrice célèbre qui joue souvent le rôle du méchant: __________
4. Donnez le nom d'une série qui se passe en Californie et qui est ennuyeuse:__________
5. Donnez le nom d'un film que vous regardez souvent à Noël: ____________________
6. Donnez le nom d'une émission de télé-réalité que les étudiants aiment:____________
7. Donnez le nom d'un livre que les enfants adorent lire: ____________________
8. Donnez le nom d'un chanteur/chanteuse que les adolescents adorent et que les paparazzi prennent souvent en photo: ______________________________

B. A votre tour! Complétez la phrase et demandez la réponse à un autre étudiant:

9. Donnez le nom d'un film qui______________________________
10. Donnez le nom d'un film que ______________________________
11. Donnez le nom d'une émission qui ____________________________
12. Donnez le nom d'une émission que____________________________

Exercice 7. Qu'est-ce que Laila regarde à la télé?

Remplissez les blancs avec **qui** ou **que**.

1. Laila préfère les émissions __________________ sont intéressantes et sérieuses.
2. Quelquefois, elle regarde aussi des séries ___________ elle télécharge sur internet.
3. La colocataire de Laila est une étudiante ___________________ n'étudie jamais et __________________________________ passe des heures à surfer sur internet.
4. Laila adore les films étrangers ______________ elle regarde souvent avec ses amis.
5. Mais elle déteste les chaînes _____________________ montrent toujours du sport.
6. Laila a déjà vu des émissions de télé-réalité __________ elle n'a pas aimées et des jeux télévisés ____ étaient ennuyeux.

  University of Texas at Austin

Exercice 8. Vos préférences.

Complétez toutes les phrases ci-dessous avec qui ou que.
Puis, entourez les phrases qui s'appliquent à vous.

1. Je préfère les films étrangers…
_____ sont drôles et intéressants.
_____ se passent en Europe.
_____ je peux regarder en V.O.

2. J'aime les acteurs…
_____ jouent dans des films d'action.
_____ les Français admirent.
_____ ont gagné un Oscar .

3. J'ai déjà vu des épisodes de 20/20…
_____ étaient passionnants.
_____ j'ai détestés.
_____ j'ai aimés.

4. Pour moi, une star est quelqu'un…
_____ travaille tout le temps.
_____ est très intelligent et amusant.
_____ les gens admirent.

5. Une cabine téléphonique, c'est quelque chose…
_____ je n'utilise jamais.
_____ je trouve utile.
_____ est difficile à trouver.

Exercice 9. Vos goûts culturels.

A. Préparez une liste de questions à poser à votre partenaire:

Modèle:
Quel est le genre de livre qui t'intéresse le plus?
Quel est le livre que tu as lu (**read**) le plus récemment?

1. Quel est le genre de films qui ____?
2. Quel est le film que ____?
3. Est-ce que tu aimes les films qui ____?
4. Quel est le livre que ____?
5. Est-ce que tu aimes les livres qui ____?
6. Quelle est l'émission télé que ____?
7. Est-ce que tu aimes les acteurs qui ____?
8. Quel est l'acteur/l'actrice que ____?

Rappel!
Agreement

Although qui and que are invariable, they assume the gender and number of the antecedent. Que functions as a direct object preceding the verb. Therefore, when the verb of the subordinate clause is in the passé composé, or any other compound tense, the past participle agrees in number and gender with que. The past participle also agrees in number and gender with qui if the verb forms its passé composé with 'être'

At home, please go to the Français interactif website. Read the following grammar points in Tex's French Grammar and complete all Texercises which you will turn in to your instructor.

9.2 négation: alternate forms (1) (ne...jamais, ne... rien, personne, etc.)

ne ... jamais	never, not ever
ne ... pas encore	not yet
ne ... rien	nothing, not anything
ne ... personne	nobody, no one, not anybody
ne ... plus	no more, not any longer
ne ... pas du tout	not at all

Personne ne ...	Nobody, No one Personne n'aime cette émission.
Rien ne ...	Nothing Rien n'est simple.

Note:

encore= still
toujours = always/ still

B. En classe, posez les questions à votre partenaire. Avez-vous les mêmes goûts culturels?

> **Modèle:**
> Nous n'avons pas les mêmes goûts culturels parce que mon/ma partenaire aime les films qui finissent bien et je préfère les films qui sont plutôt tristes.

C. Devoirs: Dans un paragraphe de 8 bonnes phrases comparez vos goûts culturels avec les goûts de votre partenaire.

Exercice 10. Vrai ou faux?

	Vrai	Faux
1. On n'a rien fait de marrant dans le cours de français hier.	❑	❑
2. Le professeur ne regarde plus de dessins animés.	❑	❑
3. Il n'y a personne dans notre salle de classe le vendredi soir.	❑	❑
4. Les étudiants n'ont pas encore pris le déjeuner.	❑	❑
5. Pendant les vacances, les étudiants n'ont plus besoin d'étudier.	❑	❑
6. Le professeur ne répond jamais à ses emails.	❑	❑
7. Le professeur de français ne parle à personne!	❑	❑
8. Les étudiants ne conduisent pas du tout le week-end.	❑	❑

Exercice 11. Le contraire!

A. Quelle phrase de la deuxième colonne veut dire le contraire pour chaque phrase dans la première colonne?

Quand j'avais 17 ans, ...

______1. je regardais déjà des films d'horreur.	a. je ne regardais jamais de films d'horreur
______2. je regardais encore des films d'horreur.	b. je ne regardais plus de films d'horreur
______3. je regardais toujours (encore) des films d'horreur.	c. je ne regardais pas encore de films d'horreur.
______4. je regardais toujours (tout le temps) des films d'horreur.	d. je ne regardais plus de films d'horreur.

B. Quelle(s) phrase(s) du tableau est (sont) vraie(s) pour vous?

Exercice 12. Menteur-menteur.

Quelle est la vérité? Ecrivez le contraire pour la trouver.

1. Joe-Bob est déjà venu à Austin. ______________________
2. Il aime beaucoup l'Université du Texas. ______________________
3. Il y va souvent! ______________________
4. Il étudie toujours! ______________________
5. Il est allé à Trudy's et il a dit bonjour à tout le monde. ______________________
6. C'était bon et il a tout mangé. ______________________

Exercice 13. Vos expériences audiovisuelles.

Posez les questions suivantes à un partenaire et notez ses réponses. Répondez avec une phrase complète.

Poster from the movie "A Bout de Souffle"
Director: Jean-Luc Godard

1. As tu déjà vu un film de Godard?
   ____
2. Est-ce que tu regardes toujours Sesame Street?
   ____
3. Est-ce que tu regardes souvent la télévision française sur internet?
   ____
4. Est-ce que tu aimes regarder des films étrangers en VO sans sous-titres?
   ____
5. As-tu déjà regardé toutes les vidéos du chapitre 13?
   ____

At home, please go to the Français interactif website. Read the following grammar points in Tex's French Grammar and complete all Texercises which you will turn in to your instructor.

9.3 one-word negative sentences si, jamais, etc.

Oui	**--'yes' answer to an affirmative question**
Si	**--'yes' to a negative question**
Non	**--negative answer to a yes / no question**
Pas	**--by itself negates part of a sentence**
Rien	**(nothing), personne (no one), and jamais (never)**
Personne	**(no one)**
Jamais	**(never)**

Rappel!

On utilise "SI" pour répondre affirmativement à une question négative.

! Utilisez uniquement le français! Si la réponse est "SI", demandez la signature de cette personne. Changez de camarade pour chaque question. Ecoutez attentivement les questions qu'on vous pose. Ne répondez pas à des questions incomplètes.

Exercice 14. Corey, le cafard dépressif!

Traduisez les phrases suivantes.

1. I don't love anybody!
2. I don't do anything!
3. I haven't seen a movie that I like yet!
4. I've never watched funny movies!
5. I don't watch TV anymore.
6. I don't listen to the radio at all!

Exercice 15. Si!

Posez les questions suivantes à vos camarades.

1. Tu n'as jamais écouté la radio sur internet? ____________________
2. Tu n'as rien regardé à la télé ce matin? ____________________
3. Tu n'as pas bien dormi hier soir? ____________________
4. Tu ne parles à personne quand tu te réveilles? ____________________
5. Tu n'aimes pas lire le journal? ____________________

Exercice 16. Tu cherches un colocataire: est-ce que vous avez les mêmes habitudes?

Posez les questions suivantes à un partenaire et il/elle répond avec un des mots suivants: si, rien, personne, ou jamais.

1. Moi, je me couche tôt. Est-ce que tu regardes souvent les informations à 3 heures du matin?
2. Je suis plutôt un(e) étudiant(e) sérieux/se et je lis beaucoup le weekend. Et toi, avec qui est-ce que tu étudies le samedi soir?
3. Tu n'as pas d'ordinateur?
4. Je suis fatigué(e). Qu'est-ce que tu écoutes comme musique à 4 heures du matin?
5. Tu ne regardes jamais tes emails?!?
6. Avec qui est-ce que tu partages ton mot de passe?

Exercice 17. Vrai ou faux?

	Vrai	Faux
1. Je lis beaucoup de magazines.	❑	❑
2. J'ai écrit des emails ce matin.	❑	❑
3. Les étudiants de français ont dit 'bonjour' au professeur aujourd'hui.	❑	❑
4. J'écris les mots de vocabulaire pour pratiquer.	❑	❑
5. Les étudiants de UT lisent The Daily Texan.	❑	❑
6. Le professeur conduit une Smart.	❑	❑
7. Les étudiants décrivent souvent leurs activités en classe.	❑	❑
8. Hier, j'ai lu le Daily Texan.	❑	❑

Exercice 18. Discrimination auditive avec lire, dire, écrire (et conduire).

A. Ecoutez et décidez si le verbe est au singulier ou au pluriel. Ensuite écrivez la phrase.

	singulier	pluriel
Modèle: Elle lit le journal tous les jours.	√	❑
1. ______________________	❑	❑
2. ______________________	❑	❑
3. ______________________	❑	❑
4. ______________________	❑	❑
5. ______________________	❑	❑
6. ______________________	❑	❑

Exercice 19. Qu'est-ce qu'on dit?

Avec un partenaire, trouvez la bonne expression en français pour les exemples suivants.

Qu'est-ce qu'on dit en français...

1. avant de se coucher? ______________________
2. quand quelqu'un part en voyage? ______________________
3. quand quelqu'un a un anniversaire? ______________________
4. avant le week-end? ______________________
5. avant un examen? ______________________
6. le matin? ______________________
7. le soir? ______________________
8. avant de manger? ______________________

Exercice 20. Etes-vous romantique?

A. Posez les questions suivantes à votre partenaire:

1. Est-ce que tu dis "je t'aime" tous les jours à ton copain/ta copine, e?
2. Quand tu lis une histoire d'amour triste, est-ce que tu pleures (**cry**)?
3. Est-ce que tu écris souvent des messages d'amour pour un copain/une copine?
4. Quand tu étais enfant, est-ce que tu disais souvent "je t'aime" pour la Saint-Valentin?
5. Quand tu étais adolescent, est-ce que tu lisais souvent des romans d'amour?
6. Quand tu étais jeune, est-ce que tu écrivais des poèmes d'amour?
7. Est-ce que tu as déjà dit "tu as de beaux yeux" à un copain/une copine?
8. Est-ce que tu as déjà lu Roméo et Juliette plusieurs fois (**several times**)?
9. Est-ce que tu as déjà écrit une lettre d'amour?

At home, please go to the Français interactif website. Read the following grammar points in Tex's French Grammar and complete all Texercises which you will turn in to your instructor.

9.4 lire, dire, écrire (conduire, décrire)

Lire 'to read'
Dire 'to say'
Ecrire 'to write'

j'(e)	**lis** **dis** **écris**
tu	**lis** **dis** **écris**
il / elle / on	**lit** **dit** **écrit**
nous	**lisons** **disons** **écrivons**
vous	**lisez** **dites** **écrivez**
ils / elles	**lisent** **disent** **écrivent**
Past participle:	**lu** **dit** **écrit**

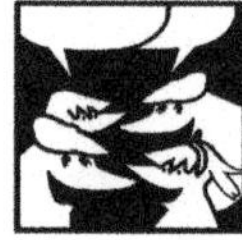

B. Pour chaque “oui” comptez un point et décidez si votre partenaire est romantique. Rapportez votre décision à la classe.

> **Modèle:** Mon/ma partenaire est romantique parce qu'il/elle dit “je t'aime” à sa copine/à son copain tous les jours et parce que quand il/elle était jeune, il/elle écrivait des poèmes d'amour…

C. Qui est le/la plus romantique? Vous ou votre partenaire? Expliquez.

Exercice 21. Marion Cotillard aux Oscars

A. Ecoutez le texte lu par votre professeur et mettez les phrases dans l'ordre chronologique:

_____ Elle est allée à son hôtel.
_____ Elle est arrivée à l'aéroport.
_____ Elle s'est couchée très tôt.
_____ Elle a pris son petit déjeuner.
_____ Elle s'est levée à 8 heures.
_____ Elle a eu des interviews jusqu'à 13 heures.
_____ Elle a attendu
_____ Il a ouvert l'enveloppe.
_____ Il a lu le nom des nominées.
_____ Il a dit son nom.

B. Votre professeur va vous montrer deux textes. Regardez-les et répondez aux questions suivantes.

1. Look at Text A and B. What is the difference between these two texts? Which text makes it more difficult to put the information in chronological order?
2. Does Text A give foreground or background information?
3. Does Text B give foreground or background information?
4. Look at the tense of the verbs in Text A and Text B and fill in the blanks with the appropriate tense:

In narration,

For background information, we use ______________________________

For foreground information, we use ______________________________

At home, please go to the Français interactif website. Read the following grammar points in Tex's French Grammar and complete all Texercises which you will turn in to your instructor.

9.5 modal verbs: vouloir, pouvoir, devoir

Vouloir, pouvoir and devoir act as auxiliary verbs when followed by an infinitive.

Vouloir 'to want'
Pouvoir 'to be able'
Devoir 'to have to, to owe'

j'(e)	**veux** **peux** **dois**
tu	**veux** **peux** **dois**
il *elle* } *on*	**veut** **peut** **doit**
nous	**voulons** **pouvons** **devons**
vous	**voulez** **pouvez** **devez**
ils *elles* }	**veulent** **peuvent** **doivent**
Past participle:	**voulu** **pu** **dû**

Exercice 22. Discrimination auditive avec vouloir, pouvoir, et devoir.

A. Ecoutez et décidez si le verbe est au singulier ou au pluriel.

	singulier	pluriel
Modèle: Elles doivent rentrer avant minuit.	❑	√
1. ______________________	❑	❑
2. ______________________	❑	❑
3. ______________________	❑	❑
4. ______________________	❑	❑
5. ______________________	❑	❑
6. ______________________	❑	❑

Exercice 23. Vrai ou faux?

Avec un partenaire, décidez si les phrases suivantes sont vraies ou fausses.

Au présent...	Vrai	Faux
1. Les étudiants veulent avoir un A à tous les examens de français.	❑	❑
2. Les Français ne peuvent pas regarder de séries américaines à la télé en France.	❑	❑
3. Les étudiants doivent étudier tout le temps.	❑	❑
4. Les Américains doivent beaucoup d'argent à la Chine.	❑	❑

Au passé...	Vrai	Faux
5. A l'âge de 12 ans, les étudiants ne pouvaient pas conduire.	❑	❑
6. Le professeur ne voulait pas venir en classe aujourd'hui.	❑	❑
7. Dans les années quatre-vingt, on pouvait fumer dans les restaurants à Austin.	❑	❑
8. Les étudiants ont dû parler italien en classe hier.	❑	❑

Exercice 24. Pourquoi?

Avec votre partenaire, faites correspondre les phrases à gauche aux phrases à droite.

_____1. Helen ne peut pas aller en classe.	a. Elle a acheté un nouvel ordinateur.
_____2. Helen veut acheter un nouvel ordinateur	b. Elle est très malade.
_____3. Helen veut sortir samedi soir.	c. Elle n'a pas d'argent.
_____4. Helen ne peut pas aller en vacances.	d. Elle passe des heures à surfer le web.
_____5. Helen doit beaucoup d'argent à VISA.	e. Elle aime s'amuser sur la sixième rue.

NOTE CULTURELLE

La radio.

Comme pour la télévision, il y a des radios publiques et des radios privées. Les radios publiques sont France Inter, France Musique, France Culture, France Info (Groupe Radio France, sur internet : radiofrance.fr). Les programmes de Radio France sont de bonne qualité.

Il y a beaucoup de radios privées. Des radios d'informations (RTL, Europe 1, RFM, RMC, BFM, LCI), des radios de musique (NRJ, Chérie FM, Nostalgie, Skyrock), des radios pour la jeunesse (Voltage, Fun Radio, Radio FG), des radios spécialisées (Radios Chrétiennes Francophones, Radio Courtoisie, Beur FM)

On peut écouter les radios sur internet.

At home, please go to the Français interactif website. Read the following grammar points in Tex's French Grammar and complete all Texercises which you will turn in to your instructor.

9.6 narration: passé composé vs imparfait

Narrating a story entails both recounting a plot or a series of events, actions, changes of feelings or thoughts and describing a setting (habitual actions, atmosphere, places and people).

•Passé composé

--for required plot line events of the story in their chronological order

•Imparfait

--for background supporting details and description, not strictly ordered (scene setting, on-going actions, habitual actions)

Exercice 25. Ce week-end.

Complétez les phrases.

1. Je veux ________________________________ ce week-end, mais je ne peux pas.
2. Je dois ________________________________ ce week-end, mais je ne veux pas.
3. Je peux ________________________________ ce week-end, mais je ne dois pas.

Exercice 26. Vive internet !

En groupe, faites une liste des activités que vous pouvez faire et que vous ne pouvez pas faire sur internet. Décidez quelle(s) activité(s) vous aimez faire sur internet. Après, discutez vos réponses avec la classe.

télécharger la musique illégalement
écouter de la musique
acheter des livres
payer les factures (**bills**)
faire les devoirs
acheter une voiture
regarder du sport
regarder des films
regarder des émissions télévisées
trouver l'amour
organiser un voyage
avoir un mot de passe difficile
avoir un virus
partager (**share**) son mot de passe
? ?

Modèle:

On peut commander (**order**) une pizza. . .

1. On peut ________________________________
2. On ne peut pas ________________________________
3. On doit ________________________________
4. On ne doit pas ________________________________

Exercice 27. Au téléphone.

Faites correspondre les phrases suivantes de manière logique.

_____1. Allô, est-ce que je peux parler à Mme de Leusse?
_____2. Ne quittez pas, s'il vous plaît…
_____3. Est-ce que vous voulez laisser un message?
_____4. Allô, qui est à l'appareil?
_____5. Quel est votre numéro de téléphone?
_____6. Est-ce que Laila est là?

a. Très bien, merci, j'attends…
b. C'est Blake! Comment ça va?
c. Non, elle est sortie. Elle rentre à 20 heures.
d. C'est le 01 45 67 34 87.
e. Non merci, je vais rappeler plus tard.
f. Oui, un instant, je vous la passe…

Exercice 28. On n'arrête pas le progrès!

Complétez les phrases suivantes avec devoir, pouvoir ou vouloir, à l'imparfait ou au présent. Soyez logiques!

1. Au Moyen-Age, les Français ______________________ travailler 70 heures par semaine. Maintenant, ils ______________________ seulement (**only**) travailler 35 heures par semaine.
2. Au XVIIème siècle, on ______________________ traverser l'océan Atlantique en bateau, maintenant, on ______________________ le traverser en avion ou en bateau.
3. Au XVIIIème siècle, on ne ____________ pas marcher sur la lune, maintenant on ______________________ le faire.
4. Au XXème, nous ne ______________________ pas consulter ______________________ internet sur les téléphones portables, maintenant nous ________ le faire, si nous ______________________.

Dictogloss 1. Au téléphone.

Formez des groupes de 3 ou 4 personnes. Ecoutez le texte lu par votre professeur. Complétez les phrases suivantes et donnez le plus de détails possibles.

Il est 14h. Blake est dans la rue et il a envie d'appeler Laila. Mme DeLeusse répond au téléphone.

Blake:	Allô!
Mme DeLeusse:	______________________ .
Blake:	Oui, bonjour, Mme DeLeusse. Comment allez-vous, aujourd'hui?
Mme DeLeusse:	Bonjour, Blake, Je vais très bien, merci. Et toi?
Blake:	Pas mal. Est-ce que Laila est là?
Mme DeLeusse:	Non, elle n'est pas encore rentrée de la fac. Tu veux ______________________?
Blake:	Non, je peux ______________________ . A quelle heure est-ce qu'elle va rentrer?
Mme DeLeusse:	Probablement d'ici 30 minutes…
Blake:	Très bien, alors ______________________ que j'ai appelé et que ______________________ .
Mme DeLeusse:	Pas de problème, ______________ . A plus tard, Blake.
Blake:	Merci et au revoir Mme DeLeusse.

Exercice 29. Une conversation téléphonique.

Avec un partenaire, imaginez et écrivez une conversation téléphonique en utilisant le vocabulaire et les expressions du chapitre.

Exercice 30. Tex au cinéma.

A. Remettez les phrases suivantes dans l'ordre chronologique.

_____ Ils ont vu le film.
_____ Ils sont entrés dans la salle.
_____ Ils sont allés au cinéma.
_____ Pour son anniversaire, sa mère lui a offert une place de cinéma.
_____ Ils ont regardé les bandes-annonces.
_____ Ils ont acheté du pop-corn et du coca.
_____ Tex a adoré!
_____ Il y avait beaucoup de gens.
_____ C'était super!
_____ Tex était heureux!
_____ Quand il avait 7 ans, Tex rêvait d'aller au cinéma.

B. Comparez l'ordre de vos phrases avec un partenaire. Avez-vous le même ordre?

C. Maintenant, supprimez (**get rid of**) les phrases à l'imparfait. Avez-vous le même ordre?

Exercice 31. Noël et la Saint-Sylvestre chez les Guilloteau.

En classe, regardez la vidéo qui se trouve au Chapitre 7.
A. Indiquez si les verbes sont à l'imparfait ou au passé composé.
B. Discutez pourquoi Franck a choisi l'imparfait ou bien le passé composé.

	IMP	PC
1. Aujourd'hui je vais vous parler de Noël chez nous. Regardez. C'est Audrey. Elle (avoir) un an.	❑	❑
2. Ici, elle (décorer) le sapin de Noël avec sa maman.	❑	❑
3. Ici, ce (être) la veille de Noël.	❑	❑
4. On (attendre) la famille.	❑	❑
5. Regardez: Voilà Virginie, son mari, et ma mère. Même ma sœur Barbara (venir) d'Afrique.	❑	❑
6. Avant le dîner, on (prendre) l'apéritif.	❑	❑
7. Mes parents (apporter) du muscat de France.	❑	❑
8. Tout le monde (attendre) le dîner avec impatience.	❑	❑
9. Ici, Audrey (admirer) le sapin avec sa grand-mère.	❑	❑
10. Regardez la belle table. C'est ma femme Nancy qui (préparer) la table.	❑	❑
11. Il y (avoir) un petit cadeau dans chaque assiette.	❑	❑
12. Il y (avoir) aussi des bougies et du gui.	❑	❑
13. Quand tout le monde (être) à table,	❑	❑
14. ..on (ouvrir) les petits cadeaux...	❑	❑
15. ..et on (plaisanter) beaucoup.	❑	❑
16. Après le dîner qui (durer) trois heures,...	❑	❑
17. ..il (être) temps d'ouvrir les cadeaux..	❑	❑
18. A minuit, nous (aller) à la messe.	❑	❑
19. Le matin, nous (être) fatigués...	❑	❑
20. ..mais Audrey (ouvrir) les cadeaux du Père Noël.	❑	❑
21. Pour la Saint-Sylvestre, on (faire) un autre repas en famille à la maison.	❑	❑
22. A minuit, on (boire) du champagne, ...	❑	❑
23. ..et tout le monde (danser)..même Audrey.	❑	❑

Exercice 32. Cadavre exquis.

A. Avec un partenaire, décidez si vous voulez être partenaire A ou B.

B. Puis lisez les directions pour votre rôle, A ou B et écrivez vos phrases comme devoirs.

Partenaire A: Passé composé
Ecrivez 5 phrases au passé composé pour décrire le week-end dernier du professeur (les grandes actions de son week-end, i.e. foreground information).

1. ______________________________
2. ______________________________
3. ______________________________
4. ______________________________
5. ______________________________

Partenaire B: Imparfait
Ecrivez 5 phrases à l'imparfait pour décrire le week-end dernier du professeur (le temps, le lieu, les émotions, etc., i.e. background information).

1. ______________________________
2. ______________________________
3. ______________________________
4. ______________________________
5. ______________________________

C. En classe créez une histoire complète avec vos phrases et les phrases de votre partenaire au passé composé et à l'imparfait.

D. Quel groupe de la classe a l'histoire la plus cohérente?

Rappel!

Pour pratiquer la narration, n'oubliez pas de faire les activités – publicités qui se trouvent sur le site de Français interactif.

Vocabulaire

- la mode
- les passe-temps
- la forme et la santé
- le corps
- adjectifs
- verbes
- expressions interrogatives
- expressions impersonnelles

Phonétique

- les voyelles nasales /ã/, /ɛ̃/, /õ/ et /œ/

Grammaire

- *10.1 -re verbs (irregular) like mettre*
- *10.2 interrogative pronouns*
- *10.3 impersonal verbs & expressions: il faut, il est important ...*
- *10.4 disjunctive pronouns*

- testez-vous!, chapitre 10
- verb conjugation reference
- verb practice

Vidéos

Vocabulaire en contexte

- les passe-temps

Interviews

- la forme et la santé
- les passe-temps
- votre look

Culture

- les Alpes
- le musée d'Orsay

10 Mode, forme et santé

In this chapter we will talk about health, fitness, and fashion.

Vocabulaire

Préparation du vocabulaire

Be sure to download the pdf vocabulary preparation template from the FI website to complete Exercises B, E, and F.

! Your instructor will collect this homework.

La mode	**Fashion**
un défilé de mode	fashion show
une marque	brand
un chapeau	hat
une casquette	cap
des vêtements (m)	clothes
un sur-vêtement/un jogging	tracksuit
des sous-vêtements	underwear
... un soutien-gorge	.... bra
un slip	briefs
une culotte	panties
... un caleçon / boxer	.... boxers
une chemise	man's shirt
un chemisier	blouse
un polo	polo shirt
un tee-shirt	T-shirt
un pull	sweater
un pantalon	(a pair of) pants
un jean (sing.)	jeans
un short (sing.)	(shorter) shorts
un bermuda	(longer) shorts
une ceinture	belt
des chaussettes (f pl)	socks
des chaussures (f pl)	shoes
des baskets (f pl)	basketball shoes/sneakers
des bottes (f pl)	boots
des sandales (f pl)	sandals
des tennis (f pl)	tennis shoes
des tongs	flip-flops
des talons (m) / des chaussures à talons	high-heels
une robe	dress
une jupe	skirt
un tailleur	woman's suit
un costume	man's suit
une cravate	tie
des lunettes (f) de soleil	sunglasses
un maillot de bain	swimsuit

un blouson	short jacket, leather jacket
une veste	jacket
un manteau	coat
un anorak	parka
un imperméable	raincoat
une écharpe	scarf
des gants (m)	gloves

Les passe-temps	**Pastimes**
la course à pied / faire de la course à pied	running
le footing / faire du footing	running
le roller / faire du roller	roller blading
le cyclisme / faire du cyclisme	cycling
l'escalade (f) / faire de l'escalade	rock-climbing
la musculation / faire de la musculation	weight training
la natation / faire de la natation	swimming
le canoë / faire du canoë	canoeing
le kayak / faire du kayak	kayaking
la peinture / faire de la peinture	painting
les échecs (m) / jouer aux échecs	chess
le yoga / faire du yoga	yoga
le surf / faire du surf	surfing
le cheval / faire du cheval	horseback riding

La forme et la santé	**Fitness and health**
une allergie	allergy
la grippe	the flu
une migraine	migraine headache
un rhume	a cold
des médicaments (m)	medicine
des vitamines (f)	vitamins
un somnifère	sleeping pill

Le corps	**The body**
la gorge	throat
le bras	arm
le coude	elbow
le poignet	wrist
la main	hand
le doigt	finger
la poitrine	chest
le ventre	stomach
le dos	back
le derrière	rear, behind

Vocabulaire

les fesses (f)	buttocks
la jambe	leg
le genou / les genoux	knee / knees
la cheville	ankle
le pied	foot
les orteils (m)	toes

Adjectifs	**Adjectives**
à la mode / branché(e)	in fashion
démodé(e)	out of style
décontracté(e)	casual
habillé(e)	dressy
discipliné(e)	disciplined
sportif / sportive	athletic
stressé(e)	stressed
malade	sick

Verbes	**Verbs**
s'habiller	to get dressed
mettre	to put (on)
porter	to wear
aller bien / aller mal	to fit well/poorly
grossir	to gain weight
être au régime / faire un régime	to be on a diet
faire du sport	to exercise
mincir	to lose weight
être en forme	to be in shape
tomber malade	to get sick
tousser	to cough
avoir mal à…	to hurt (body part)
(avoir mal à la tête, au dos, aux pieds, etc)	(to have a headache, a backache, sore feet, etc)
se reposer	to rest
se détendre	to relax
fumer	to smoke
être en bonne santé	to be in good health

Expressions interrogatives	**Interrogative expressions**
Qu'est-ce qui se passe?	What is going on?
Qu'est-ce qui t'intéresse?	What interests you?

Vocabulaire

Qu'est-ce qui t'énerve?	What bothers you?
Qu'est-ce qui te fait peur?	What scares you?
Qu'est-ce qui te fait plaisir?	What pleases you?
Qu'est-ce qui t'amuse?	What amuses you?

Expressions impersonnelles	**Impersonal expressions**
Il faut + infinitive	It is necessary (to)
Il vaut mieux + infinitive	It is advisable (to), It is better (to)
Il est important de + infinitive	It is important (to)
Il est nécessaire de + infinitive	It is necessary (to)
Il est essentiel de + infinitive	It is essential (to)
Il est indispensable de + infinitive	It is essential (to)
Il est + **adjectif** + de + infinitive	
Il est amusant de...	It is fun (to)...
Il est difficile de...	It is difficult (to)...
Il est facile de...	It is easy (to)...
Il est fatiguant de...	It is tiring/annoying (to)...

Phonétique

Go to the website for a complete explanation and practice exercises.

NOTE CULTURELLE

La forme

Pour rester en forme, les Français font toutes sortes d'activités et de sports. Cependant, ils ne sont pas accros (addicted) aux salles de gym comme les Américains. Les Français aiment simplement marcher en ville et se déplacer à pied. Leurs habitudes alimentaires aussi sont différentes des Américains.

Révisez le vocabulaire des passe-temps dans le chapitre 3

Introduction

Regardons la video ensemble pour répondre aux questions suivantes: Qui présente le chapitre? Où est-il / elle? Quels sont les thèmes du chapitre?

Exercice 1. Est-ce que vous êtes en forme?

A. Voici quelques questions que vous allez poser à un partenaire demain en classe. Ecrivez 3 questions de plus pour savoir si votre partenaire est en forme:

1. Combien de fois par semaine est-ce que tu fais du sport?
2. Est-ce que tu as déjà fait de l'escalade?
3. Est-ce que tu préfères lire ou faire du footing?
4. Est-ce que tu manges beaucoup de fast food?
5. Est-ce que tu as besoin de mincir?
6. ______________________________
7. ______________________________
8. ______________________________

B. Posez les questions à votre partenaire et décidez si votre partenaire est en forme ou non. Répondez avec des phrases complètes! Rapportez votre décision à la classe.

Modèle:
Mon/ma partenaire est en forme parce qu'il/elle fait du sport 3 fois par semaine et parce qu'il/elle mange bien.

C. Devoirs: Est-ce que vous et votre partenaire êtes en forme? Ecrivez un paragraphe de 10 phrases.

Exercice 2. Le corps humain: vrai ou faux?

	Vrai	Faux
Les doigts sont une partie des pieds.	❑	❑
Le genou est une partie de la jambe.	❑	❑
Le coude est une partie du bras.	❑	❑
Le cou est sur le bras.	❑	❑
Les dents sont dans la bouche.	❑	❑
Le ventre est sous la poitrine.	❑	❑
Le poignet est une partie du visage.	❑	❑
Les chevilles sont une partie des fesses.	❑	❑

Exercice 3. Quelle partie du corps?

Quelle(s) partie(s) du corps associez-vous avec les marques suivantes?

1. Evian
2. Bic
3. Chanel nº 5
4. Adidas
5. Lancôme
6. Lacoste
7. Kleenex
8. Rayban

Exercice 4. Associations

Modèle:
Qu'est-ce qu'on utilise pour parler?
La bouche, la langue, etc.

1. Qu'est-ce qu'on utilise pour faire de la natation?
2. Qu'est-ce qu'on utilise pour faire de l'escalade?
3. Qu'est-ce qu'on utilise pour écouter la radio?
4. Qu'est-ce qu'on utilise pour regarder la télé?
5. Qu'est-ce qu'on utilise pour jouer aux échecs?
6. Qu'est-ce qu'on utilise pour faire de la peinture?
7. Qu'est-ce qu'on utilise pour envoyer un email?
8. Qu'est-ce qu'on utilise pour parler français?

Rappel!

Révisez le vocabulaire du visage dans le Chapitre 4

Exercice 5. Aïe! Qu'est-ce que j'ai mal!

Expliquez où on a mal selon la situation indiquée.

Modèle:
Quand on fait trop de planche à voile…➔ On a mal aux bras, au dos…

1. Quand on mange trop de chocolat…
2. Quand on fait trop de musculation…
3. Quand on fait de la course à pied en portant des sandales…
4. Quand on étudie trop…
5. Quand on boit trop…
6. Quand on fait du cheval (**horseback riding**)...
7. Quand on chante beaucoup...
8. Quand on fait du roller…

NOTE CULTURELLE

La santé.

Les Français vont régulièrement chez le docteur, le dentiste ou l'ophtalmologue. Une visite médicale coûte environ 23 euros. Les gens qui travaillent donnent chaque mois une partie de leur salaire pour la santé de tout le monde et pour les retraités. La santé et la retraite sont donc offertes à tous. C'est la Sécurité Sociale, la Sécu comme disent les Français. Bien sûr, le système n'est pas économiquement parfait mais il respecte les valeurs démocratiques et républicaines de la France.

Dictogloss 1. Une consultation chez le médecin.

Laila est tombée malade en France. Elle est allée consulter le Docteur Dupont, médecin généraliste.

Docteur Dupont:	Bonjour Mademoiselle. ______________________________?
Laila:	Pas très bien docteur. J'ai mal partout______________________ ____.
Docteur Dupont:	Est-ce que vous avez de la fièvre?
Laila:	Oui, docteur. J'ai pris ma température ce matin et j'avais ________ de fièvre.
Docteur Dupont:	Est-ce que vous toussez beaucoup?
Laila:	Oui docteur.
Docteur Dupont:	Très bien, mademoiselle. Vous avez les symptômes d' _________ ______________. Vous devez ______________________________ pendant une semaine. ____ ____ .
Laila:	Merci, docteur. ______________________________?
Docteur Dupont:	______________________________ , Mademoiselle!

Exercice 6. Vous parlez de votre forme et de votre espérance de vie (life expectancy)

A. Répondez aux questions avec un des adverbes.
B. En classe, posez les questions à un(e) partenaire.

	souvent	quelquefois	jamais
1. Est-ce que vous prenez des vitamines?	❑	❑	❑
2. Est-ce que vous faites du sport?	❑	❑	❑
3. Est-ce que vous dormez assez?	❑	❑	❑
4. Prenez-vous le temps de vous détendre?	❑	❑	❑
5. Allez-vous chez le médecin ou le dentiste?	❑	❑	❑
6. Est-ce que vous buvez de l'eau minérale?	❑	❑	❑
7. Est-ce que vous faites attention à votre alimentation?	❑	❑	❑
8. Est-ce que vous consommez beaucoup d'alcool?	❑	❑	❑
9. Est-ce que vous fumez des cigarettes, des cigares, la pipe?	❑	❑	❑
10. Prenez-vous des somnifères?	❑	❑	❑
11. Est-ce que vous mangez beaucoup de fast food?	❑	❑	❑
12. Avez-vous des allergies?	❑	❑	❑
13. Est-ce que vous avez souvent des migraines et des maux de tête?	❑	❑	❑
14. Est-ce que vous bronzez (tan) sans protection?	❑	❑	❑
15. Etes-vous stressé(e)?	❑	❑	❑

C. Est-ce que les réponses de votre partenaire sont raisonnables ou pas? Regardez les évaluations suivantes (Félicitations, Pas mal, Il faut changer, Quelle horreur) et choisissez le meilleur message pour votre partenaire.

Félicitations!	Pas mal.	Il faut changer.	Quelle horreur!
Félicitations! Vous devez être fier! Ne changez pas vos habitudes. Vous allez probablement vivre très longtemps.	Pas mal. Vous avez peut-être de petits changements à faire mais votre espérance de vie est longue.	Si vous voulez changer vos habitudes, c'est le bon moment!	Quelle horreur! Vous n'allez pas voir vos petits-enfants si vous ne changez pas tout de suite votre style de vie!

D. Discutez les messages que vous avez choisis. Qui est en meilleure forme? Pourquoi? Rapportez votre décision à la classe.

Modèle:
Je suis en meilleure forme. Je prends toujours des vitamines, mais mon partenaire ne prend jamais de vitamines. Je fais souvent de la musculation, mais mon partenaire ne fait jamais de sport...

E. Devoirs. Est-ce que vous êtes d'accord avec votre partenaire? Pourquoi ou pourquoi pas? Ecrivez un paragraphe de 10 phrases. Qu'est-ce que vous ou votre partenaire devez faire pour être en meilleure forme et pour vivre plus longtemps?

Exercice 7. Les questions.

A. Décidez si les questions suivantes sont les questions d'un médecin, des parents de votre copain/copine, ou de quelqu'un d'autre.

	Médecin	Parents	Autre
1. Combien de frères et de soeurs avez-vous?	❑	❑	❑
2. Combien mesurez-vous?	❑	❑	❑
3. Quel est votre poids?	❑	❑	❑
4. De quelle couleur sont vos yeux?	❑	❑	❑
5. Vous habitez encore chez vos parents?	❑	❑	❑
6. Où est-ce que vous avez mal?	❑	❑	❑
7. Prenez-vous des somnifères?	❑	❑	❑
8. Quand est-ce que vous partez en vacances?	❑	❑	❑
9. Pourquoi est-ce que vous étudiez le français?	❑	❑	❑
10. Vous avez des allergies?	❑	❑	❑
11. Quels sont vos passe-temps préférés?	❑	❑	❑
12. Vous avez un lave-vaisselle chez vous?	❑	❑	❑
13. Est-ce que vous fumez?	❑	❑	❑
14. Comment s'appellent vos parents?	❑	❑	❑
15. Est-ce que votre mère achète vos sous-vêtements?	❑	❑	❑

B. Maintenant, avec votre partenaire, choisissez trois questions du tableau et posez-les à votre professeur ou à un nouveau partenaire.

Exercice 8. Est-ce que votre partenaire est sportif?

A. Posez les questions suivantes à votre partenaire et indiquez ses réponses.

1. Au lycée, qui t'énervait le plus?
   a. le prof de sport
   b. le prof de maths
2. En voiture, qui te dérange le plus?
   a. les cyclistes
   b. les autres voitures
3. Qui est ce que tu admires le plus?
   a. Lance Armstrong
   b. le président des Etats-Unis
4. Qu'est-ce qui t'amuse?
   a. Jouer au basket
   b. Jouer aux jeux vidéos
5. Qu'est-ce que tu fais le dimanche matin?
   a. tu fais du jogging
   b. tu dors
6. Qu'est-ce qui te détend le plus?
   a. la natation
   b. la télé
7. Qu'est-ce que tu préfères?
   a. faire de l'escalade
   b. faire de la peinture
8. Qui est-ce que tu respectes le plus?
   a. les sportifs
   b. les intellos
9. Avec qui est-ce que tu as envie de dîner?
   a. Tiger Woods
   b. Oprah
10. De quoi est-ce que tu parles le plus souvent?
   a. du football américain
   b. des études

B. Décidez si votre partenaire est sportif (majorité de a) ou non (majorité de b). Rapportez vos résultats à la classe.

Modèle:
Mon/ma partenaire est sportif/sportive parce qu'il/elle fait du footing le dimanche matin.
Mon/ma partenaire n'est pas sportif/sportive parce qu'il/elle parle souvent des études.

Exercice 9. Person or thing? Subject or object?

A. With a partner look at the questions in Items 1-4 and decide whether the first **qui** or **que** represents a person or a thing, and then whether the second **qui** or **que** represents the subject or object of the verb. (The responses to the questions are given as contextual clues.) Circle the appropriate responses in the chart below.

1. Au lycee, **qui est-ce qui** t'enervait? Le prof de sport m'énervait.	**qui** **person / thing**	**...est-ce...**	**qui** **subject / object**
2. Qui est-ce que tu preferes? Je préfère Lance Armstrong	**qui** **person / thing**	**...est-ce...**	**que** **subject / object**
3. Qu'est-ce qui t'amuse? Le vélo m'amuse	**que** **person / thing**	**...est-ce...**	**qui** **subject / object**
4. Qu'est-ce que tu fais le dimanche matin? Je fais du jogging	**que** **person / thing**	**...est-ce...**	**que** **subject / object**

B. Now look at the questions in items 5 and 6 and decide whether the person or thing is represented by **qui** or **quoi** in a question beginning with a preposition (de, à, avec). Also, indicate which preposition has been used.

5. De quoi est-ce que tu parles le plus souvent? Je parle le plus souvent de la mode.	**preposition =** ________	**quoi** **person / thing**
6. Avec qui est-ce que tu as envie de dîner? J'ai envie de dîner avec Oprah.	**preposition =** ________	**qui** **person / thing**

C. Now as a class, fill in the charts below to represent interrogative pronouns based on your responses above.

First part of interrogative			**Second part of interrogative**	
________	(person)	**...est-ce...**	________	(subject)
			________	(object)
________	(thing)	**...est-ce...**	________	(subject)
			________	(object)

Preposition	**First part of interrogative**		**Second part of interrogative**
à, avec, chez, de, pour, etc.	________	(person)	**est-ce que...**
	________	(thing)	**est-ce que...**

At home, please go to the Français interactif website. Read the following grammar points in Tex's French Grammar and complete all Texercises which you will turn in to your instructor.

10.1 mettre (remettre, promettre, admettre, permettre)

je	**mets**
tu	**mets**
il *elle* *on* }	**met**
nous	**mettons**
vous	**mettez**
ils *elles* }	**mettent**
Past participle:	**mis**

Exercice 10. Discrimination auditive avec mettre.

A. Ecoutez et décidez si le verbe est au singulier ou au pluriel. Ensuite écrivez la phrase.

	singulier	pluriel
Modèle: Vous entendez: Elle met la table tous les soirs. ___________	√	❑
1. ____	❑	❑
2. ____	❑	❑
3. ____	❑	❑
4. ____	❑	❑
5. ____	❑	❑
6. ____	❑	❑

Exercice 11. La vérité sur le professeur et les étudiants! D'accord ou pas d'accord?

	d'accord	pas d'accord
1. Le professeur met souvent des vêtements branchés pour aller en classe.	❑	❑
2. Les étudiants ne mettent jamais de vêtements décontractés.	❑	❑
3. Le professeur permet souvent aux étudiants de parler anglais en classe.	❑	❑
4. Les étudiants n'admettent pas les mauvaises notes (**grades**) aux examens.	❑	❑
5. Le professeur ne permet pas aux étudiants d'envoyer des textos en classe.	❑	❑
6. Les étudiants promettent souvent à leurs parents d'être plus sérieux.	❑	❑

Exercice 12. Quelle est la conséquence?

______1. Bette avait envie de dîner avec Tex.	a. Elle l'a mise pour son anniversaire .
______2. Les enfants de Rita voulaient sortir.	b. Il a admis qu'il était toxicomane (**addict**).
______3. Joe-Bob avait un compte-rendu (**paper**) d'histoire.	c. Elle leur a permis d'aller au cinéma.
______4. Tammy a acheté une nouvelle robe.	d. Il lui a promis une soirée à Chuy's.
______5. Corey consommait trop d'insecticide.	e. Il l'a remis hier.

Exercice 13. Découvrez votre style vestimentaire.

A. Lisez les phrases suivantes et choisissez la réponse qui vous convient le mieux.

1. Pour aller en cours, je mets plutôt
   a. une chemise blanche et un pantalon / un chemisier blanc et une jupe
   b. un tee-shirt noir et un jean noir
   c. un tee-shirt et un short
   d. une chemise à fleurs / une robe longue

2. Quand je sors en boite, je mets plutôt
   a. un costume et une cravate / une robe élégante
   b. une chemise noire et un pantalon en cuir (**leather**) / une jupe en cuir
   c. un survêtement
   d. un tee-shirt et un jean / une robe à fleurs

3. Quand il fait froid, je mets plutôt
   a. un manteau
   b. un imperméable sombre
   c. un anorak
   d. une écharpe en laine

4. En été, je mets plutôt
   a. un bermuda et un polo
   b. un jean noir
   c. un short et un tee-shirt
   d. un tee-shirt et short décontracté / un maillot de bain et une jupe

5. Dans un magasin de chaussures, j'achète
   a. des chaussures en cuir / des talons hauts
   b. des bottes noires
   c. des baskets / des tennis
   d. des sandales / des tongs

6. Qu'est-ce que vous portez en hiver?
   a. un pull
   b. une veste en cuir
   c. un sweat / un corsaire
   d. un cardigan

7. Mon accessoire préféré :
   a. des lunettes de soleil
   b. une ceinture large
   c. une casquette
   d. un chapeau

8. Mes sous-vêtements préférés sont
   a. un caleçon à carreaux (**plaid**)
   b. un slip / un soutien-gorge noir
   c. un boxer uni
   d. un caleçon / une culotte à pois (**polka dot**)

NOTE CULTURELLE

La mode

Spécialement pour les jeunes, suivre la mode est important. En général, les Français font attention aux vêtements qu'ils portent, surtout dans les grandes villes. Dans les villes françaises, il y a beaucoup de boutiques au centre-ville. Dans les grandes villes il y a aussi des grands magasins comme Le Printemps ou les Galeries Lafayettes qui proposent un grand choix de marques et de couturiers populaires.

Deux fois par an, en été (juin) et en hiver (janvier), il y a les soldes (sales). Les dates des soldes sont fixées par l'Etat. Les gens attendent les soldes pour acheter des vêtements bon marché.

B. Calculez combien de a, b, c, d vous avez au total:

Vous avez une majorité de a	Vous avez une majorité de b	Vous avez une majorité de c	Vous avez une majorité de d
Vous adoptez plutôt le style BCBG qui est classique, parfois habillé mais jamais de mauvais goût.	Il est clair que vous aimez le noir et les couleurs sombres. Votre style est gothique et le cuir est un élément important dans votre look.	Très actif et toujours prêt à faire de l'exercice, vous êtes sportif et aimez les vêtements qui vous permettent de faire des activités physiques.	Vous préférez être à l'aise (**comfortable**) et choisissez des vêtements décontractés. Le style baba cool vous va très bien.

C. Comparez vos résultats avec votre partenaire. Quel est le style de votre partenaire ? Expliquez.

Exercice 14. Avez-vous un look habillé, branché ou décontracté?

A. Quels vêtements associez-vous avec:

un look habillé: ______________________________

un look branché: ______________________________

un look décontracté: ______________________________

B. Posez les questions suivantes à un partenaire.

1. Qu'est-ce que tu mets pour aller à un mariage?
2. Qu'est-ce que tu mets quand tu sors avec des amis?
3. Qu'est-ce que tu mets quand tu restes chez toi le week-end?
4. Qu'est-ce que tu mets pour aller en cours?

C. Décidez si votre partenaire a un look plutôt habillé, branché ou décontracté. Rapportez votre résultat à la classe.

D. Devoirs: Etes-vous d'accord? Quel est votre look? Ecrivez un paragraphe de 8 phrases.

Exercice 15. Défilé de mode.

Avec vos camarades de classe, organisez un petit défilé de mode. Choisissez des étudiants dans la classe qui ont des looks différents. Décrivez leurs vêtements et les couleurs qu'ils portent.

Exercice 16. Qu'est-ce que tu fais en général?

Posez les questions suivantes à un nouveau partenaire.

1. En général, qu'est-ce que tu fais le week-end?
2. En général, qu'est-ce que tu prends au petit-déjeûner?
3. En général, qu'est-ce que tu regardes à la télé?
4. En général, qu'est-ce que tu portes pour aller en classe?
5. En général qu'est-ce que tu achètes souvent en vacances?

Exercice 17. Devinettes.

Posez les questions suivantes à un nouveau partenaire.

1. Qu'est-ce qui est rouge et liquide et que les Français adorent?
2. Qu'est-ce qui est rond et orange et qui produit du jus?
3. Qu'est-ce qui est de plusieurs couleurs et qui parfume?
4. Qu'est-ce qui est doré et liquide et que les étudiants adorent?
5. Qu'est-ce qui est haut, en métal, très célèbre et qui se trouve en Europe?
6. A votre tour! Ecrivez une ou deux devinettes pour vos camarades de classe.

Exercice 18. Les Français et les étudiants du Français interactif.

Posez les questions suivantes à un partenaire:

Parmi les personnes du Français interactif,
1. Qui est-ce que tu aimes bien?
2. Qui-est ce que tu comprends toujours?
3. Qui est-ce que tu trouves drôle?
4. Qui est-ce que tu trouves sérieux?
5. Qui est-ce que tu veux rencontrer?

Exercice 19. Quiz sportif.

1. Qui a gagné le championnat de football américain universitaire en 2006?
2. Qui a gagné le Tour de France de 1999 à 2005?
3. A votre tour! Ecrivez une question pour vos camarades de classe.

At home, please go to the Français interactif website. Read the following grammar points in Tex's French Grammar and complete all Texercises which you will turn in to your instructor.

10.2 interrogative pronouns

•Questions about people
Qui/qui est-ce qui
Qui est-ce que
Preposition + qui

•Questions about things
Qu'est-ce qui
Qu'est-ce que
Preposition + quoi

Exercice 20. Les interviews fictives des célébrités

Avec un partenaire, choisissez A ou B. L'étudiant A va lire les extraits d'une interview. L'autre étudiant (B) va lui poser les questions sur l'interview et va noter ses réponses. Maintenant changez de rôle pour l'autre interview.

Exercice 21. D'autres questions pour des célébrités

A. Utilisez **qui**, **que**, ou **quoi** pour compléter les questions suivantes.

1. _______ est-ce que vous respectez?
   Je respecte beaucoup mon mari.
2. _______ est-ce que vous respectez?
   Je respecte l'honnêté et la franchise!
3. Qu'est ce _______ vous regardez à la télé?
   Je regarde des feuilletons américains.
4. Avec _______ est-ce que vous aimez jouer aux échecs?
   Avec mon frère.
5. De _______ est-ce que vous discutez souvent?
   Je discute souvent des émissions de variété
6. Qu'est ce _______ vous amuse?
   Faire du sport!

B. Complétez les questions suivantes avec les pronoms interrogatifs appropriés.

1. ______________________________ vous portez pour des soirées élégantes?
   Une robe et des talons
2. ______________________________ vous donne mal à la tête?
   Trop de sport!
3. ______________________________vous voulez rencontrer?
   Le president américain!
4. ______________________________ vous téléphone souvent?
   Ma mère.
5. ______________________________ se passe (happens) après les matchs?
   On fait la fête
6. ______________________________ vous faites pour combattre le stress?
   Je fume!
7. ______________________________ vous passez vos vacances?
   Avec mes parents.
8. ______________________________on joue au basket?
   Avec un ballon!
9. ______________________________ vous mangez avant les matchs?
   De la viande et des pâtes!

Exercice 22. Pardon? Je n'ai pas compris.

Vous n'avez pas compris! Quelle question devez-vous poser?

> **Modèle:**
> J'aime manger XXX
> → Pardon, qu'est-ce que tu aimes manger?

1. XXX m'énerve! Il est paresseux!

Pardon, ____?

2. Je suis passé chez XXX.

Pardon, ____?

3. Pour y aller, je vais prendre XXX.

Pardon, ____?

4. J'ai vu XXX. Elle est très mignonne!

Pardon, ____?

5. Faire XXX m'amuse.

Pardon, ____?

6. J'ai parlé de XXX avec mon frère. Il adore cette émission!

Pardon, ____?

Exercice 23. Interviewez votre célébrité préférée!

A. Choisissez une célébrité et imaginez que vous pouvez l'interviewer. Quelles questions est-ce que vous avez envie de lui poser? Ecrivez 6 questions.

1. ____?
2. ____?
3. ____?
4. ____?
5. ____?
6. ____?

B. En classe, comparez vos questions.

Exercice 24. Les passe-temps d'Audrey et de Camille.

Regardez la video (Chapitre 2) et traduisez les questions suivantes en bon français. Ensuite répondez aux questions selon la vidéo.

1. Who likes to play in the park?

_______________ ? _______________ .

2. What amuses Audrey?

_______________ ? _______________ .

3. Who does Audrey kiss?

_______________ ? _______________ .

4. Who does Camille look for?

_______________ ? _______________ .

5. What is Audrey reading?

_______________ ? _______________ .

6. What does Camille hate?

_______________ ? _______________ .

7. Who does Audrey telephone?

_______________ ? _______________ .

8. What does Camille play with?

_______________ ? _______________ .

Exercice 25. Vrai ou faux?

	Vrai	Faux
1. Il faut étudier le français tous les jours.	❑	❑
2. Pour être en bonne forme, il est essentiel de boire un verre de vin rouge tous les jours.	❑	❑
3. Il est difficile de ne pas parler anglais en classe.	❑	❑
4. Il est amusant de faire du sport.	❑	❑
5. Il est important de mettre un anorak quand il fait chaud.	❑	❑
6. Il n'est pas fatigant de faire du sport tous les jours.	❑	❑
7. Pour mincir, il vaut mieux ne jamais manger de chocolat.	❑	❑
8. Il ne faut pas fumer dans les avions.	❑	❑

Exercice 26. Chez le médecin.

Vous allez entendre quelques monologues de personnes qui parlent de leurs problèmes de santé. Choisissez la réponse logique.

1.
   a. Il faut faire plus d'exercice.
   b. Il est indispensable de manger plus.
   c. Il vaut mieux prendre des somnifères.

2.
   a. Il faut arrêter de fumer.
   b. Il est essentiel de vous lever plus tard.
   c. Il est nécessaire de faire du sport.

3.
   a. Il est important de faire de l'exercice.
   b. Il faut prendre des médicaments.
   c. Il ne faut pas manger de chocolat.

4.
   a. Il ne faut pas parler à vos amis.
   b. Il est nécessaire de faire de la planche à voile.
   c. Il vaut mieux faire de la natation.

5.
   a. Il faut prendre des somnifères.
   b. Il faut mincir.
   c. Il est nécessaire de vous reposer.

6.
   a. Il est important de prendre des vitamines.
   b. Il faut faire un régime.
   c. Il est nécessaire de grossir.

7.
   a. Il faut travailler plus.
   b. Il n'est pas essentiel de se détendre.
   c. Il est nécessaire de ne pas travailler le week-end.

8.
   a. Il ne faut pas porter de lunettes de soleil.
   b. Il est essentiel de porter des lunettes.
   c. Il est indispensable de lire beaucoup.

Exercice 27. Corey, alors!

Corey n'est pas très sage! Avec un partenaire donnez-lui des conseils. Complétez les phrases avec les infinitifs suivants:

_____1. Corey est très stressé. Il est indispensable de ...
_____2. Corey est malade. Il est important de ...
_____3. Corey fait la fête tous les soirs. Il vaut mieux. ..
_____4. Corey ne mange pas bien. Il est essentiel de ...
_____5. Corey grossit. Il est nécessaire de ...
_____6. Corey fume en classe. Il faut ...
_____7. Corey ne fait jamais d'exercice mais il commence à faire de l'escalade. Il est important de ...
_____8. Corey porte des vêtements démodés. Il faut ...

a. respecter les règles de l'université
b. faire une activité sportive raisonnable
c. ne pas sortir pendant la semaine
d. se détendre
e. mettre des vêtements plus branchés
f. consulter un médecin
g. manger plus de fruits et de légumes
h. faire des promenades et de manger moins

At home, please go to the Français interactif website. Read the following grammar points in Tex's French Grammar and complete all Texercises which you will turn in to your instructor.

10.3 impersonal verbs and expressions: il faut, il est important,...

Impersonal Expressions

Il faut + [infinitive]
Il faut étudier pour l'examen.

Il vaut mieux + [infinitive]
Il vaut mieux faire du sport pour combattre le stress.

Il est + [adjective] + de + [infinitive] **
Il est essentiel de parler français!

Exercice 28. Réussir sa vie à l'université

Quels conseils est-ce que vous avez envie de donner pour réussir sa vie à l'université?
Complétez les phrases avec une expression impersonnelle différente pour chaque phrase:

> **Modèle:**
> Il est essentiel d'apprendre ses leçons.
> Il n'est pas essentiel de sortir en boîte.
> Il est essentiel de ne pas sécher (**skip**) les cours.

1. ______________________________ rencontrer de nouveaux amis.
2. ______________________________ faire la fête tous les soirs.
3. ______________________________ étudier 6 heures par jour.
4. ______________________________ boire trop d'alcool!
5. ______________________________ faire tous ses devoirs.
6. ______________________________ écouter les conseils des profs.
7. ______________________________ dormir 8 heures par nuit.
8. ______________________________ se détendre de temps en temps.

Exercice 29. La nécessité.

Complétez les phrases avec une expression impersonnelle d'obligation à l'affirmatif et au négatif:

> **Modèle:**
> Pour avoir des amis…
> il est important de se brosser les dents régulièrement
> et il ne faut pas être intolérant.

1. Pour réussir aux examens, ______________________________.
2. Pour mincir, ______________________________.
3. Pour aller à Paris, ______________________________.
4. Quand on est malade, ______________________________.
5. Pour avoir un(e) petit(e) ami(e), ______________________________.
6. Pour être à la mode, ______________________________.
7. Pour ne pas être trop stressé(e), ______________________________.
8. Pour ne pas avoir froid en hiver, ______________________________.

Exercice 30. Qu'est-ce qu'il faut faire pour combattre le stress?

A. Faites une liste de trois conseils pour combattre le stress. Utilisez des expressions impersonnelles:

> **Modèle:**
> Il vaut mieux parler de ses problèmes avec ses amis.

1. ______________________________
2. ______________________________
3. ______________________________

B. En groupes de 4, échangez vos conseils et techniques pour combattre le stress. Ecrivez-les:

1. ______________________________
2. ______________________________
3. ______________________________
4. ______________________________

C. Quel est le meilleur conseil de votre groupe? Rapportez votre décision à la classe.

D. Devoirs pour demain. Lisez le email de Pierre (le petit frère de Franck) ci-dessous et donnez-lui des conseils. Pierre vient de finir ses études universitaires et il cherche un travail. Employez les expressions impersonnelles. Ecrivez un paragraphe de 8 phrases.

> **Modèle:**
> Il ne faut pas être stressé.

To: *pierre@example.fr*
Cc:

Subject: *Salut!*

Attachments: Browse

Salut!

C'est moi. Qu'est-ce que je suis stressé en ce moment! D'abord, j'ai des migraines tout le temps et je ne peux pas dormir. En plus, je n'ai plus envie de faire du sport. Deuxièmement, j'ai un entretien demain pour un job et je ne sais pas quoi mettre. Et pour finir, ma copine m'a dit qu'elle sort avec un autre mec (guy) et qu'elle ne veut plus sortir avec moi!

Pour combattre mon stress, je fume un paquet de cigarettes par jour, je bois beaucoup de vin rouge, et je regarde la télé sans arrêt. Mais je suis toujours très stressé. Je ne comprends pas. Je ne sais pas quoi faire! Tu peux me donner des conseils?

A très bientôt.

At home, please go to the Français interactif website. Read the following grammar points in Tex's French Grammar and complete all Texercises which you will turn in to your instructor.

10.4 disjunctive pronouns

- moi
- toi
- lui / elle / (soi)
- nous
- vous
- eux / elles

Exercice 31. Avec qui?

Faites la correspondance entre les deux colonnes.

______1.	Tex sort avec elle.	a. avec mes amis et moi
______2.	Joe-Bob parle avec nous.	b. avec Fiona et Rita
______3.	Corey et Trey dansent avec elles.	c. avec Tammy
______4.	Fiona ne s'entend pas avec eux.	d. avec Tex
______5.	Bette veut se marier avec lui.	e. avec Joe-Bob et Tex.

Exercice 32. Quelle est votre réponse?

1. Mes amis et moi passons la plupart du temps...	❑ chez moi ❑ chez eux
2. Mon copain / Ma copine et moi, nous sommes souvent...	❑ chez moi chez lui / chez elle
3. Mes parents vont en vacances. Je préfère y aller...	❑ avec eux ❑ sans eux
4. Mon / Ma colocataire fait la cuisine et...	❑ moi, je fais la vaisselle. ❑ lui aussi, il fait la vaisselle. ❑ elle aussi, elle fait la vaisselle.
5. Qui est responsable pour votre succès? Vous, les étudiants, ou nous, les profs?	❑ C'est nous, les étudiants. ❑ C'est vous, les professeurs.

Exercice 33. Devinettes.

Modèle:
Le professeur parle français avec **eux**. → Le prof parle avec les étudiants.

1. **Eux**, ils détestent les devoirs.
2. Les enfants achètent des cadeaux pour **elles** en mai.
3. Quand on était jeune, on partait en vacances avec **eux**.
4. **Lui**, il a gagné Le Tour de France en 2005.
5. **Elle**, c'est la femme du président.
6. Franck part en vacances avec **elles**.

Exercice 34. Etes-vous d'accord ou pas d'accord?

A. Lisez les phrases suivantes et décidez si la phrase vous décrit ou non. Vous allez répondre avec moi aussi ou bien pas moi.

	moi aussi	pas moi
1. Tammy veut habiter en France.	❑	❑
2. Bette est née en mai.	❑	❑
3. Corey dîne avec ses parents mercredi soir.	❑	❑
4. Joe-Bob offre des fleurs à son chien pour la Saint-Valentin.	❑	❑

B. Maintenant lisez les phrases suivantes et décidez si la phrase vous décrit ou non. Vous allez répondre avec moi non plus ou bien moi si.

	moi non plus	moi si
1. Edouard ne reçoit pas beaucoup d'emails.	❑	❑
2. Paw-Paw ne sort jamais le vendredi soir.	❑	❑
3. Corey n'a pas d'amis.	❑	❑
4. Bette ne met jamais de tee-shirts.	❑	❑

C. What do you notice in the responses above? How do they differ in section A and section B?

Exercice 35. Et toi?

Posez les questions suivantes à un partenaire et comparez vos réponses.

Modèle:
Je fume. Et toi? **Moi aussi,** je fume. OU **Pas moi**, je ne fume pas.
Je ne fume pas. Et toi? **Moi non plus,** je ne fume pas. OU **Moi si**, je fume.

1. J'aime voyager / Je n'aime pas voyager. Et toi?
2. Je danse chez moi / Je ne danse jamais chez moi. Et toi?
3. Je suis sorti(e) hier soir / Je ne suis pas sorti(e) hier soir. Et toi?
4. Je fais un sport extrême / Je ne fais pas de sport extrême. Et toi?
5. Imaginez une autre situation.

Dictogloss 2. Pour être en forme.

Formez des groupes de 3 ou 4 personnes. Ecoutez le texte lu par votre professeur. Complétez les phrases suivantes et donnez le plus de détails possibles.

Je ne suis pas Superman, mais je suis assez sportif. Pour être en forme, ______________________ ______________________ avec mes amis. ___________________, je ne suis pas motivé et ______________________. D'habitude, je vais chez Jean-Charles. Il y a un beau lac à côté de ______________________ et on y fait ______________________ ensemble. ___________________, ___________________ trop le footing, mais ______________ c'est amusant. On court, on discute, on s'amuse quoi!

Après, quand je rentre ____________, ma femme et mes filles sont là. Je dîne ____________ ________________________. C'est bien parce que ma femme prépare toujours un bon repas __________________ ...pas de fast food chez nous! Comme ça, nous n'avons jamais besoin ____________________________.

11 Les études

In this chapter we will talk about secondary education and university life in France.

Vocabulaire

- *les études secondaires et supérieures*
- *les matières et les cours*
- *adjectifs*
- *verbes*

Phonétique

- *le e muet (silent e)*

Grammaire

- *11.1 savoir vs. connaître*
- *11.2 re verbs (irregular) like suivre, vivre*
- *11.3 -il y a, ago*
- *11.4 regular subjunctive*
- *11.5 irregular subjunctive*
- *11.6 subjunctive usage: obligation*

- *testez-vous!, chapitre 11*
- *verb conjugation reference*
- *verb practice*

Vidéos

Vocabulaire en contexte

- *les études*

Interviews

- *au lycée*
- *depuis quand?*
- *villes et langues*
- *à l'université*
- *les universités*

Culture

- *l'université Jean Moulin Lyon 3*

Vocabulaire

Préparation du vocabulaire

Be sure to download the pdf vocabulary preparation template from the FI website to complete Exercises B, E, and F.

! Your instructor will collect this homework.

Les études secondaires et supérieures	**High school and university studies**
la rentrée	beginning of school year
le collège	junior high, middle school
le lycée	high school
un lycéen / une lycéenne	high school student
la seconde	first year of high school
la première	second year of high school
la terminale	final year of high school
le baccalauréat / le bac	baccalaureate exam
un bachelier / une bachelière	student who has passed the bac
un concours (d'entrée)	competitive entrance exam
la fac	college, university
la Faculté des Beaux-Arts	school of fine arts
la Faculté de Lettres et des Sciences Humaines	school of humanities/liberal arts
la Faculté de Médecine	school of medicine
la Faculté de Pharmacie	school of pharmacy
la Faculté des Sciences	school of sciences
la Faculté de Droit	law school
L'Ecole de Commerce (f)	business school
les Grandes Écoles (f)	elite professional schools
une résidence universitaire	dormitory
un restaurant universitaire (un restau-U)	university cafeteria
une cafétéria	cafeteria
un amphithéâtre / un amphi	amphitheater
une salle de classe	classroom
un cours (de maths…)	a class (math class…)
un cours magistral (des cours magistraux)	large lecture class
un laboratoire / un labo	laboratory / lab
une bibliothèque	library
les devoirs (m)	homework
une copie	student paper
un exposé oral	oral presentation
un examen	test, exam
une note	grade
les résultats	results, grades
un bulletin de notes	grade report
un emploi du temps	schedule
une carte d'étudiant	student ID card
un stage	internship
un diplôme	a diploma, degree

Vocabulaire

Les matières et les cours	Subjects and classes
l'architecture (f)	architecture
l'art (m)	art
le dessin	drawing, design
la musique	music
la peinture	painting
la communication	communications
la comptabilité	accounting
le droit	law
l'économie (f)	economics
la géographie	geography
l'histoire (f)	history
l'informatique (f)	computer science
les langues (f)	languages
le chinois	Chinese
l'allemand (m)	German
l'anglais (m)	English
l'espagnol (m)	Spanish
le français	French
l'italien (m)	Italian
le latin	Latin
la linguistique	linguistics
la littérature	literature
les mathématiques (f) / les maths	math
la médecine	medicine
la pharmacie	pharmacy
la philosophie	philosophy
la psychologie	psychology
les sciences (f)	sciences
la biologie	biology
la chimie	chemistry
la physique	physics
les sciences politiques	political science
la sociologie	sociology

Adjectifs	Adjectives
chargé(e)	full, busy (referring to schedule)
occupé(e)	busy
prochain(e)	next
dernier / dernière	last

Verbes	Verbs
s'inscrire (à la fac, au ciné-club…)	to register, enroll (in)
régler (les frais d'inscription)	to pay (one's tuition/fees)

Vocabulaire

suivre	to take (a course), to follow
aller en cours	to attend class
faire ses devoirs	to do one's homework
faire un effort	to make an effort
faire des progrès	to improve
se renseigner	to find out about, to get information
apprendre	to learn
comprendre	to understand
passer un examen	to take an exam
réussir (à) un examen	to pass (an exam), to succeed (in)
réussir à + infinitif	to succeed at ...
avoir la moyenne	to receive a passing grade
recevoir son diplôme	to graduate, to complete one's studies
être bonne / bon en…	to be good in/at…
être mauvais(e) en...	to be bad in/at…
être nul(le) en… [slang]	to suck in/at…
se décourager	to be discouraged
sécher un cours	to skip a class
rater	to fail
redoubler	to repeat a grade/course
quitter	to leave (something, someone or some place)

Phonétique

Go to the website for a complete explanation and practice exercises.

Introduction

Regardons la video ensemble pour répondre aux questions suivantes: Qui présente le chapitre? Où est-il/elle? Quels sont les thèmes du chapitre?

Exercice 1. Vrai ou faux?

Discutez les phrases suivantes avec un(e) partenaire. Est-ce que les phrases sont vraies ou fausses pour vous?

	Vrai	Faux
1. J'ai raté mon premier examen de 507.	❑	❑
2. Je suis nul / nulle en maths.	❑	❑
3. J'ai un cours d'histoire ce semestre.	❑	❑
4. Mon emploi du temps est très chargé.	❑	❑
5. Je réussis toujours bien quand je fais un effort.	❑	❑
6. Quand j'ai un bon bulletin de notes, mes parents sont heureux.	❑	❑
7. Je suis bon / bonne en dessin.	❑	❑
8. Je vais recevoir mon diplôme cette année.	❑	❑

Exercice 2. Tes études

1. Est-que tu as toujours la moyenne à tes examens? ______________________
2. Est-ce que tu veux étudier à l'étranger? ______________________
3. Est-ce que tu sèches souvent tes cours ? ______________________
4. Est-ce que tu as souvent des exposés oraux à faire? ______________________
5. Est-ce que tu te décourages facilement? ______________________
6. Est-ce que tu fais tes devoirs à la bibliothèque? ______________________
7. Est-ce que tu passes beaucoup d'examens? ______________________
8. Est-ce que tu aimes les cours magistraux? ______________________

! Utilisez uniquement le français! Si la réponse est "OUI", demandez la signature de cette personne. Changez de camarade pour chaque question. Ecoutez attentivement les questions qu'on vous pose. Ne répondez pas à des questions incomplètes.

Exercice 3. Quel type de bac pour vous?

A. Votre professeur va vous donner des questions, A ou B. Posez vos questions, A ou B, à votre partenaire pour déterminer le type de bac qui lui convient. Notez les réponses de votre partenaire dans le tableau.

	Type of bac	Oui	Non
1.	S	❑	❑
2.	ES	❑	❑
3.	L	❑	❑
4.	L	❑	❑
5.	S	❑	❑
6.	S	❑	❑
7.	ES	❑	❑
8.	L	❑	❑
9.	S	❑	❑
10.	ES	❑	❑
11.	ES	❑	❑
12.	L	❑	❑

B. Maintenant regardez les résultats. Pour toutes les réponses avec 'oui' encerclez le type de bac et déterminez si votre partenaire a la majorité de réponses ES, L ou S. Quel bac convient à votre partenaire?

Majorité de ES	Majorité de L	Majorité de S
Le bac sciences économiques et sociales est pour toi. Tu aimes l'économie, la sociologie, l'histoire et la géographie. Tu t'intéresses à l'actualité et tu n'es pas mauvais en maths ou en langues étrangères.	Le bac littéraire est pour toi. Tu aimes la littérature, la philosophie. Tu aimes apprendre des langues étrangères. Tu es nul en maths et tu sèches les cours de sciences.	Le bac scientifique est pour toi. Tu es excellent en maths et tu adores la physique, la chimie, la biologie et la géologie. Tu n'aimes pas trop la littérature ou les sciences humaines.

C. Est-ce que vous êtes d'accord avec ces résultats? Est-ce que vous suivez la même filière (**track**) à UT?

Exercice 4. Qu'est-ce que tu étudies?

A. Discutez avec votre partenaire et complétez la phrase.

J'étudie le/la/les...

philosophie	linguistique
français	psychologie
espagnol	droit
littérature	comptabilité
biologie	informatique
sociologie	sciences politiques
maths	physique

B. Comparez avec votre partenaire

Quelle(s) matières est-ce que tu aimes? Pourquoi ?
Quelle(s) matières est-ce que tu détestes? Pourquoi ?

Exercice 5. Votre emploi du temps.

A. Remplissez votre emploi du temps pour cette semaine. Mettez vos cours et les heures où vous étudiez et/ou travaillez et vos autres obligations (sport, clubs, etc.)

	lundi	mardi	mercredi	jeudi	vendredi
9.00-10.00					
10.00-11.00					
11.00-12.00					
12.00-13.00					
13.00-14.00					
14.00-15.00					
15.00-16.00					
17.00-18.00					
18.00-19.00					
20.00-21.00					
21.00-22.00					
22.00-23.00					

B. Répondez aux questions suivantes avec un partenaire.

1. Quelle est ta journée la plus chargée?
2. Est-ce qu'il y a un jour que tu préfères? Pourquoi ?

C. Devoirs: Ecrivez un paragraphe de 8 phrases.

Qu'est-ce que vous faites pendant votre journée la plus chargée? Est-ce que vous suivez les mêmes cours que votre partenaire? Qui a l'emploi du temps le plus chargé? Pourquoi ? Etc.

Exercice 6. Etudiant modèle, moyen, ou nul?

Décidez si les phrases ci-dessous sont vraies ou fausses pour vous et votre partenaire.

Vos habitudes au lycée...	Moi	Mon partenaire
1. Je rêvais toujours pendant mes cours.	❑ Vrai ❑ Faux	❑ Vrai ❑ Faux
2. Je n'ai jamais séché de cours.	❑ Vrai ❑ Faux	❑ Vrai ❑ Faux
3. Je faisais mes devoirs tous les jours.	❑ Vrai ❑ Faux	❑ Vrai ❑ Faux
4. Je réussissais toujours mes examens.	❑ Vrai ❑ Faux	❑ Vrai ❑ Faux
5. J'allais en cours de temps en temps.	❑ Vrai ❑ Faux	❑ Vrai ❑ Faux

Est-ce que vous étiez un(e) élève modèle, moyen(ne), ou nul(le)? Et votre partenaire? Expliquez.

Exercice 7. Le système éducatif français

A. D'après ces informations, avec un partenaire, trouvez les écoles ou diplômes qui correspondent à chaque description à la page suivante.

AGE	Classe	Ecole	
25	Bac+8	Doctorat	
24	Bac+7		
23	Bac+6		
22	Bac+5	Master	
21	Bac +4		Grandes Ecoles
20	Bac +3	Licence	Concours
19	Bac +2	Université	Classes Préparatoires
18	Bac +1		
		BAC	
17	Terminale	Lycée	
16	1ère		
15	2nde		
		Examen: BREVET	
14	3ème	Collège	
13	4ème		
12	5ème		
11	6ème		
10	CM2	Ecole	
9	CM1		
8	CE2		
7	CE1		
6	CP		
5			
4			
3			

NOTE CULTURELLE

L'éducation en France

En France, l'éducation est obligatoire jusqu'à 16 ans. Il y a d'abord l'école primaire (6-10 ans), puis le collège (11-14 ans) et enfin le lycée (15-17 ans). A la fin du lycée, on passe l'examen final du Baccalauréat (le bac). On choisit sa préférence pour le bac pendant le lycée : les sciences (S), la littérature et les langues (L) ou l'économie et les sciences sociales (ES). Avec le bac, on peut aller à l'université.

A l'université, on obtient une Licence (3 ans après le bac), un Master (5 ans) et un Doctorat (8 ans ou plus).

Si on est bon élève au lycée, on peut passer des concours pour entrer dans une Grande Ecole. Les Grandes Ecoles sont des institutions spécialisées et élitistes. Les plus importantes sont Polytechniques (X), Sciences-Politiques (Sciences-Po) et Ecole Normale Supérieure (l'ENS).

At home, please go to the Français interactif website. Read the following grammar points in Tex's French Grammar and complete all Texercises which you will turn in to your instructor.

11.1 savoir vs. connaître/ present tense

Savoir 'to know (a fact)'
Connaître 'to know, to be acquainted with'

je	**sais** **connais**
tu	**sais** **connais**
il *elle* *on*	**sait** **connaît**
nous	**savons** **connaissons**
vous	**savez** **connaissez**
ils *elles*	**savent** **connaissent**
Past participle:	**su** **connu**

1. On va dans cette école pour préparer le bac: ______________________.
2. On quitte cette école avec le brevet: ______________________.
3. On entre dans cette école au CP: ______________________.
4. C'est un diplôme de formation générale qu'on obtient à l'université après le bac en 3 ans: ______________________.
5. C'est une formation de 2 ans qu'on prépare au lycée pour le concours d'entrée aux grandes écoles: ______________________.
6. C'est une formation professionnelle qu'on suit au lycée après le bac et qui dure 2 ans: ______________________.
7. C'est une formation de 8 ans pour devenir docteur des universités: ______________________.
8. C'est un diplôme de 2 ans qu'on prépare après la licence: ______________________.
9. C'est une formation professionnelle de 2 ans qu'on suit à l'université après le bac: ______________________.
10. Ce sont des écoles d'élites où on étudie les sciences de l'ingénieur et le commerce: ______________________.

B. Quelles sont les différences et les points communs entre le système éducatif français et le système éducatif américan? Discutez en anglais, si vous voulez.

Modèle:
En France, le doctorat dure 3 ans. Aux Etats-Unis, le "PhD" dure 5 ans. En France, il y a un examen à la fin du collège. Aux Etats-Unis il n'y a pas d'examen à la fin de "Junior High"

Exercice 8. Discrimination auditive avec savoir et connaître.

Ecoutez et décidez si le verbe est au singulier ou au pluriel.

	singulier	pluriel
Modèle: Il connaît la littérature anglaise.	√	❑
1. ______________________	❑	❑
2. ______________________	❑	❑
3. ______________________	❑	❑
4. ______________________	❑	❑
5. ______________________	❑	❑
6. ______________________	❑	❑

Exercice 9. Qu'est-ce que vous savez?

Posez les questions suivantes à un/une partenaire. Il faut répondre avec "**Oui, je le sais**" ou "**Non, je ne le sais pas**". Si vous savez, donnez les réponses.

1. Est-ce que tu sais si le Texas est plus grand que la France?
2. Est-ce que tu sais comment s'appelle le président français?
3. Est-ce que tu sais combien d'habitants il y a à Austin?
4. Est-ce que tu sais d'où vient le professeur de français?
5. Est-ce que tu sais la date de l'examen final?
6. Est-ce que tu sais former l'imparfait du verbe "être"?

Exercice 10. Vous le saviez?

Répondez aux questions avec "**Oui, je le savais**" ou "**Non, je ne le savais pas**."

1. Est-ce que tu savais que ce sont des Français, les frères Lumière, qui ont inventé le cinéma?
2. Est-ce que tu savais que c'est un Français, Cavelier de la Salle, qui a découvert la Louisiane?
3. Est-ce que tu savais que c'est un Français, Frédéric-Auguste Bartholdi, qui a sculpté la Statue de la Liberté?
4. Est-ce que tu savais que certains lycéens français ont 35 heures de cours par semaines?
5. Est-ce que tu savais que certains étudiants français ont 6 mois de vacances par an?

A votre tour! Complétez la phrase suivante et posez la question à votre partenaire:

6. Est-ce que tu savais que____ ?

Exercice 11. Bac blanc. Est-ce que vous pouvez avoir le bac?

A. Votre professeur va vous distribuer une liste de questions pour chaque bac. Choisissez un bac et posez les questions à votre partenaire. Comptez 2 points par bonne réponse.

B. Résultats

20/20 19/20 18/20	17/20 16/20	15/20 14/20	13/20 12/20	11/20 10/20	9/20 8/20	7/20 - 1/20
Vous avez votre bac avec la mention très bien et les félicitations du jury.	Vous avez votre bac avec la mention très bien.	Vous avez votre bac avec la mention bien.	Vous avez votre bac avec la mention assez bien.	Vous avez votre bac avec la mention passable.	Vous pouvez avoir votre bac si vous réussissez un examen oral.	Vous avez raté votre bac.
A+	A	A-	B	C	D	F

NOTE CULTURELLE

Le bac

Le bac est un examen national, inventé par Napoléon I en 1808, que tous les lycéens français doivent réussir pour pouvoir aller à l'université. Contrairement au SAT ou ACT, il y a plusieurs types de bac. Les lycéens français se spécialisent au lycée, et ils passent le bac qui détermine leurs futurs études. Les questions sur le bac ne sont pas non plus des questions à choix multiples. Par contre, les étudiants écrivent plusieurs dissertations et passent aussi des examens oraux. Plus difficile et plus spécialisé que le ACT et le SAT, réussir son bac est une étape importante dans la vie française.

Exercice 12. Qu'est-ce qu'on sait faire?

Tout le monde sait faire quelque chose, mais quoi exactement? Soyez créatif/créative et indiquez ce que les personnes suivantes savent faire. Faites attention aux temps des verbes.

> **Modèle**:
> Virginie est française. ➜ Elle sait parler français.

1. Nous sommes étudiants.
2. Tex est poète.
3. Churchill était orateur.
4. Audrey et Camille adorent aller à la piscine.
5. Le professeur aide les étudiants de 507.
6. Mozart était compositeur.
7. Franck a une voiture et un permis de conduire.
8. Stéphanie aime faire des marathons.

Exercice 13. Qu'est-ce que vous connaissez?

A. Complétez les phrases suivantes.

Les choses qu'on connaît:

Je connais ________________________________ . (une ville américaine)

Je connais ________________________________ . (une ville étrangère)

Je connais personnellement ______________________. (une personne célèbre)

Je connais ________________________________ . (un site touristique)

Par contre:

Je ne connais pas ____________________________ . (une ville américaine)

Je ne connais pas ____________________________ . (une ville étrangère)

Je ne connais pas ____________________________ . (un site touristique)

B. Ensuite, comparez vos réponses avec celles d'un partenaire.

Modèle:

Je connais Boston.	➔	Moi aussi, je connais Boston!/ Pas moi, mais je connais Chicago.
Je ne connais pas Lyon.	➔	Moi si, je connais Lyon, mais je ne connais pas Paris.

Exercice 14. Monsieur le Président.

A. Complétez les questions suivantes sur la vie du Président.

	Est-ce que vous savez...	Est-ce que vous connaissez...	
1.	❑	❑	...où le président habite?
2.	❑	❑	... son époux/épouse?
3.	❑	❑	... la date de son anniversaire?
4.	❑	❑	... quand il est devenu président?
5.	❑	❑	... à quelle heure il se réveille en général?
6.	❑	❑	... s'il est honnête?
7.	❑	❑	... sa ville natale?
8.	❑	❑	... s'il a un chat ou un chien?

B. En classe, en groupes de 3 personnes, posez les questions à vos 2 camarades de classe. Combien de personnes dans votre groupe savent toutes les bonnes réponses aux questions?

Exercice 15. Grammaire interactive. Le bulletin de notes d'Alexandre.

A. Alexandre, le neveu de Franck, est un lycéen en seconde. Avec un partenaire, regardez les bulletins.

LE BULLETIN DE NOTES

NOM Guilloteau PRENOM Alexandre
DATE 02 / 08 / 2013

SUJET	NOTE de L'ÉLÈVE	MOYENNE de la CLASSE	COMMENTAIRES
FRANÇAIS M. Adem	12	8,9	Assez bons résultants. Élève curieux et motivé qui s'intéresse beaucoup à la littérature.
MATHÉMATIQUES Mme Hervé	5,13	10,27	Les resultats sont très mauvais. Il ne faut pas se décourager!
ANGLAIS LV1 Mme Détrie	18	10,5	Excellent élève. Très bonne participation en cours. Continuez ainsi!
ALLEMAND LV2 Mme Roubach	14,33	9,3	Bon trimestre dans l'ensemble. Mais Alexandre a raté le dernier contrôle.
ESPAGNOL LV3 M. Poquet	16,5	11,5	Très bon élève. Alexandre a fait un excellent exposé oral.
HISTOIRE-GÉOGRAPHIE M. Pezot	10,5	9,7	Ensemble moyen. Alexandre n'apprend pas toujours ses leçons et ne fait pas souvent ses devoirs!
SCIENCES DE LA VIE ET DE LA TERRE Mme Dufour	6,5	10,3	Les résultats sont très insuffisants! Il est essentiel que Alexandre fasse des efforts si il ne veut pas redoubler!
SCIENCES PHYSIQUES M. Orange	1,25	9,8	Les notes sont CATASTROPHIQUES! Alexandre doit faire ses T.P. au labo et il faut qu'il sache ses formules de chimie!
SCIENCES ECONOMIQUES ET SOCIALES M. Durand	11	8,4	Assez bon élève. Alexandre a fait des progrès. Il rend souvent de très bonnes copies, mais il ne réussit pas toujours ses examens.
EDUCATION PHYSIQUE ET SPORTIVE Mme Anquetil	ABS	12,5	Alexandre est toujours absent! Il est nécessaire que Alexandre comprenne que le sport est oligatoire!

1. Quel type d'élève est Alexandre? Expliquez.
2. Quels conseils est-ce que vous pouvez donner à Alexandre?

Modèle:
Il vaut mieux savoir ses formules de chimie.

3. Quel type de bac est fait pour Alexandre? Expliquez.

B. Link the following sentences to their equivalent

_____1.	Il est essentiel qu'il fasse	a. Il faut **savoir**
_____2.	Il faut qu'il sache	b. Il est nécessaire de **comprendre**
_____3.	Il est nécessaire qu'il comprenne	c. Il est essentiel de **faire**

1. What is the third person singular present indicative conjugation of savoir, comprendre and faire:
   savoir : il ________ comprendre: il ________ faire : il ________

   Now look at the verbs in column A above. Notice how these forms differ from the verb forms you just conjugated. The verbs in column A are conjugated in what is called the **subjunctive**.

2. Now look at the verbs in column A and column B? How do they differ?

3. What do the impersonal expressions **il est essentiel**, **il faut**, **il est nécessaire** express: desire, obligation, certainty or emotion?

4. Select the correct underlined item to complete the following sentences.
   a. After impersonal expressions of obligation, we use an **infinitive** when there is a subject / no subject.
   b. After impersonal expressions of obligation, we use the **subjunctive** when there is a subject / no subject.

Exercice 16. Discrimination auditive avec suivre et vivre.

Ecoutez et décidez si le verbe est au singulier ou au pluriel.

	singulier	pluriel
Modèle: Franck suit l'émission American Chopper.	√	❑
1. ________________________	❑	❑
2. ________________________	❑	❑
3. ________________________	❑	❑
4. ________________________	❑	❑
5. ________________________	❑	❑
6. ________________________	❑	❑

Exercice 17. Logique ou illogique.

A. Déterminez si les phrases suivantes sont logiques ou illogiques.

	logique	illogique
1. Pour devenir ingénieur, on suit beaucoup de cours d'art.	❑	❑
2. Si on est étudiant dans la Faculté de Médecine, on suit des cours de sciences.	❑	❑
3. Si on rêve en classe, on ne suit pas la leçon.	❑	❑
4. Pour bien suivre les actualités, on écoute les infos tous les jours.	❑	❑
5. Si on suit trois cours, on a un emploi du temps très chargé!	❑	❑
6. A l'école, on suit des cours d'histoire, d'anglais et d'architecture.	❑	❑

B. Posez les questions suivantes à un partenaire. Quels cours est-ce que tu suis ce semestre? Quels cours est-ce que tu as suivi au lycée?

Exercice 18. Les différents sens du verbe vivre.

A. Vrai ou faux? Indiquez si les phrases suivantes sont vraies ou fausses.

	Vrai	Faux
1. Einstein a vécu au 19ème siècle.	❑	❑
2. Thomas Jefferson a vécu aux Etats-Unis et en France.	❑	❑
3. Madonna vit à Los Angeles.	❑	❑
4. Johnny Depp et Vanessa Paradis vivent en France.	❑	❑

B. Posez les questions suivantes à un/une partenaire. Avez-vous des choses en commun?

1. Où est-ce que tu vis ce semestre?
2. Où est-ce que tu vivais à l'âge de 5 ans?
3. Est-ce que tu as déjà vécu à l'étranger (**abroad**)?

Exercice 19. Connaissez-vous l'histoire internationale?

Trouvez la date correcte de l'événement historique et ensuite complétez les phrases.

_____1. Christophe Colomb a découvert l'Amérique il y a _______ siècles. a. 1997

_____2. Les Etats-Unis ont déclaré leur indépendance il y a _______ ans. b. 1989

_____3. Le mur de Berlin est tombé il y a _______ ans. c. 1789

_____4. La princesse Diana est morte à Paris il y a _______ ans. d. 1492

_____5. La Révolution française a eu lieu il y a _______ ans. e. 1776

Exercice 20. Votre parcours scolaire

Posez les questions suivantes à votre partenaire. Répondez avec une phrase complète en utilisant "il y a".

1. Quand est-ce que tu es entré(e) à l'école primaire?
2. Quand est-ce que tu t'es inscrit(e) à UT?
3. Quand est-ce que tu as commencé à apprendre le français?
4. Pensez à une question originale à poser à vos camarades de classe.

At home, please go to the Français interactif website. Read the following grammar points in Tex's French Grammar and complete all Texercises which you will turn in to your instructor.

11.2 -re verbs (irregular) like suivre, vivre

Suivre 'to follow, to take a course, to be interested in or keep up with'
Vivre 'to live, to be alive'

je	**suis** **vis**
tu	**suis** **vis**
il *elle* *on*	**suit** **vit**
nous	**suivons** **vivons**
vous	**suivez** **vivez**
ils *elles*	**suivent** **vivent**
Past participle:	**suivi** **vécu**

Remember not to confuse the first person conjugation of être 'je suis' with the first person conjugation of suivre 'je suis'. The difference is determined by the context.

Exercice 21. Bon ou mauvais conseil?

Lisez les conseils de votre professeur. Est-ce qu'il/elle vous donne de bons ou de mauvais conseils?

	bons conseils	mauvais conseils
1. Il faut que vous **séchiez** souvent vos cours.	❑	❑
2. Il est nécessaire que vous **dépensiez** tout votre argent.	❑	❑
3. Il vaut mieux que vous **sortiez** sur la sixième rue tous les soirs.	❑	❑
4. Il faut que vous **étudiiez** pendant le week-end.	❑	❑
5. Il est important que vous **attendiez** la fin des cours pour partir en vacances.	❑	❑
6. Il est préférable que vous vous **détendiez** de temps en temps.	❑	❑
7. Il est essentiel que vous **finissiez** vos devoirs avant de faire la fête.	❑	❑
8. Il est indispensable que vous **choisissiez** bien vos cours le semestre prochain.	❑	❑

Exercice 22. Encore des conseils.

Jean-Charles donne des conseils à son cousin qui vient étudier à l'Université du Texas. Identifiez le mode de chaque verbe (indicatif, impératif ou subjonctif). Si le verbe est à l'indicatif, indiquez le temps du verbe aussi (passé composé, imparfait ou présent).

	Indicatif	Impératif	Subjonctif
Modèle: Ne **sèche** pas tes cours.	❑ passé composé ❑ imparfait ❑ présent	√	❑
1. Il est nécessaire que tu **suives** le professeur.	❑ passé composé ❑ imparfait ❑ présent	❑	❑
2. Il ne faut pas que tu **fumes** en classe.	❑ passé composé ❑ imparfait ❑ présent	❑	❑
3. Tu as **réglé** les frais d'inscription?	❑ passé composé ❑ imparfait ❑ présent	❑	❑
4. Tu **avais** toujours la moyenne au lycée, n'est-ce pas?	❑ passé composé ❑ imparfait ❑ présent	❑	❑
5. Ne te **décourage** pas!	❑ passé composé ❑ imparfait ❑ présent	❑	❑
6. Il est indispensable que tu **étudies** tous les jours.	❑ passé composé ❑ imparfait ❑ présent	❑	❑

At home, please go to the Français interactif website. Read the following grammar points in Tex's French Grammar and complete all Texercises which you will turn in to your instructor.

11.3 il y a [+ time expression]

When il y a is followed by a time expression, it means 'ago' (ex. il y a 2 jours…)

11.4 regular subjunctive

Present subjunctive of
–er verbs: parler
–ir verbs: finir
–re verbs: attendre

que j'(e)	**parle** **finisse** **attende**
que tu	**parles** **finisses** **attendes**
qu'il *qu'elle* *qu'on*	**parle** **finisse** **attende**
que nous	**parlions** **finissions** **attendions**
que vous	**parliez** **finissiez** **attendiez**
qu'ils *qu'elles*	**parlent** **finissent** **attendent**

Exercice 23. D'accord ou pas d'accord?

Quelles phrases sont vraies pour vous?

	Vrai	Faux
1. Il faut que je sois stressé pour réussir mes études.	❑	❑
2. Il est important que j'aie la moyenne à tous mes examens.	❑	❑
3. Il est indispensable que j'aille à la bibliothèque tous les jours.	❑	❑
4. Il vaut mieux que je fasse des devoirs tous les jours.	❑	❑
5. Il est important que je puisse étudier en silence.	❑	❑
6. Il est indispensable que je sache parler français avant la fin de mes études.	❑	❑

Exercice 24. Est-ce que vous connaissez votre partenaire?

Qu'est-ce qu'il est nécessaire que votre partenaire fasse pour être heureux? Qu'est-ce qu'il n'est pas nécesaire qu'il fasse pour être heureux?

A. Complétez les phrases avec une expression impersonnelle d'obligation à l'affirmatif ou au négatif.

Pour être heureux,

1. ______________________________ qu'il/elle dorme beaucoup.
2. ______________________________ qu'il/elle parte souvent en vacances.
3. ______________________________ qu'il/elle sorte tous les jours.
4. ______________________________ qu'il/elle écrive des paragraphes de français.
5. ______________________________ qu'il/elle lise des romans d'amour.
6. ______________________________ qu'il/elle mette des vêtmements branchés.
7. ______________________________ qu'il/elle connaisse beaucoup d'amis.
8. ______________________________ qu'il/elle suive un cours de sciences politiques.

B. En classe lisez les phrases à votre partenaire. Comptez un point par bonne réponse. Qui a le plus de points?

At home, please go to the Français interactif website. Read the following grammar points in Tex's French Grammar and complete all Texercises which you will turn in to your instructor.

11.5 irregular subjunctive

Avoir
Etre

que j'(e)	aie sois
que tu	aies sois
qu'il qu'elle qu'on	ait soit
que nous	ayons soyons
que vous	ayez soyez
qu'ils qu'elles	aient soient

Don't forget to go to Tex to read about double stem verbs (venir, devoir, prendre, boire, voir, croire), irregular double stem verbs (aller & vouloir) and irregular one stem verbs (faire, pouvoir, savoir)

Exercice 25. Qu'est-ce qu'il faut faire pour réussir le bac?

A. Conjuguez les verbes au subjonctif et mettez les phrases dans un ordre chronologique.

_____ Il est essentiel que tu ________________ (étudier) bien dans toutes les matières.

_____ Il est indispensable que tu ________________ (réviser) la philosophie en premier.

_____ Il vaut mieux que tu ____ (sortir) avec tes amis après les examens pour te détendre.

_____ Il ne faut pas que tu ____________________ (redoubler) la classe de première.

_____ Il vaut mieux que tu ____ (attendre) les résultats du bac avant de t'inscrire à la fac.

_____ Il est nécessaire que tu ___________________ (dormir) beaucoup avant le bac.

_____ Il est préférable que tu ____ (choisir) bien ta spécialité après la classe de seconde.

_____ Il est important que tu ___________________________ (ne pas se décourager).

B. En classe, vous allez comparer vos ordres chronologiques.

Exercice 26. Le subjonctif des verbes irréguliers.

Complétez les formes suivantes:

aller	...que j' ________________	...que nous ________________
avoir	...que j' ________________	...que nous ________________
boire	...que je ________________	...que nous ________________
croire	...que je ________________	...que nous ________________
devoir	...que je ________________	...que nous ________________
être	...que je ________________	...que nous ________________
faire	...que je ________________	...que nous ________________
mourir	...que je ________________	...que nous ________________
pouvoir	...que je ________________	...que nous ________________
prendre	...que je ________________	...que nous ________________
savoir	...que je ________________	...que nous ________________
venir	...que je ________________	...que nous ________________
voir	...que je ________________	...que nous ________________
vouloir	...que je ________________	...que nous ________________

NOTE CULTURELLE

Les grèves (Strikes)

Les grèves font parties de la vie universitaire française. Les étudiants et les profs manifestent souvent, par exemple pour les salaires compétitifs des profs ou contre les frais de scolarité qui montent. Quand il y a la grève, il n'y a plus de cours pour les étudiants, la fac est bloquée, fermée. Quelquefois, le blocage peut durer longtemps, même quelques semaines.

Exercice 27. Qu'est-ce que vous en pensez?

Avec un partenaire réagissez aux affirmations suivantes.

Modèle:
Il faut que vous fassiez du sport pour vous détendre.
C'est vrai! Il faut que je fasse du sport pour me détendre!
C'est faux! Il n'est pas nécessaire que je fasse de sport pour me détendre.

1. Il est indispensable que vous voyiez vos amis pour vous amuser.
2. Il est nécessaire que vous preniez le bus pour venir à l'université.
3. Il vaut mieux que vous buviez de l'alcool pour faire la fête.
4. Il faut que vous veniez à l'université tous les jours.
5. Il est essentiel que vous croyiez en vous pour réussir.
6. Il est important que vous alliez à la bibliothèque pour étudier.
7. Il est bizarre que vous deviez étudier plus à l'université qu'au lycée.
8. Il est bizarre que vous vouliez sortir en boîte le week-end.

Exercice 28. Vos mauvaises habitudes.

A. Quels sont vos mauvaises habitudes? Ecrivez 5 phrases.

Modèle:
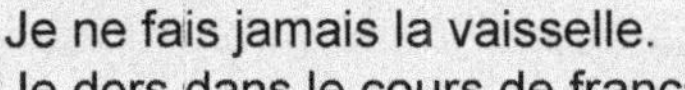
Je ne fais jamais la vaisselle.
Je dors dans le cours de français.

1. ______________________________
2. ______________________________
3. ______________________________
4. ______________________________
5. ______________________________

B. Ecoutez les mauvaises habitudes de votre partenaire et donnez-lui des conseils.

Modèle:
Il faut que tu fasses la vaisselle.
Il ne faut pas que tu dormes dans le cours de français.

Exercice 29. Des conseils pour les étudiants.

A. Le professeur donne des conseils pendant la classe. Décidez si ces conseils sont pour tous les étudiants en général (à l'infinitif) ou pour un étudiant en particulier (au subjonctif).

	Pour tous les étudiants	Pour un étudiant
Modèle: Il ne faut pas dormir en classe.	√	❑
1. ____________________	❑	❑
2. ____________________	❑	❑
3. ____________________	❑	❑
4. ____________________	❑	❑
5. ____________________	❑	❑
6. ____________________	❑	❑

Exercice 30. Logique ou illogique.

A. Imaginez que vous partiez à Lyon pour étudier pendant l'été. Décidez si les phrases suivantes sont logiques ou illogiques.

	logique	**illogique**
1. Il est nécessaire que nous réussissions nos examens avant d'aller à Lyon.	❑	❑
2. Il est indispensable que nous parlions français tout le temps.	❑	❑
3. Il est essentiel que nous fassions la grève avec les étudiants français.	❑	❑
4. Il est préférable que nous suivions des cours de maths pendant l'été.	❑	❑
5. Il vaut mieux que nous nous détendions aussi.	❑	❑
6. Il faut que nous soyons sérieux en classe.	❑	❑

B. Avec un partenaire, écrivez 2 phrases : qu'est-ce qu'il faut que vous fassiez avant votre départ ?

1. ______________________________

2. ______________________________

At home, please go to the Français interactif website. Read the following grammar points in Tex's French Grammar and complete all Texercises which you will turn in to your instructor.

11.6 subjunctive usage: obligation

The following impersonal expressions of obligation require the subjunctive:

Il faut que
Il est important que
Il est nécessaire que
Il est essentiel que
Il est inévitable que
Il vaut mieux que
Il est préférable que
Il est indispensable que

Exercice 31. Qu'est-ce qu'il faut faire pour...?

Ecoutez les situations que votre professeur va lire, et choisissez la réponse logique.

1.
   a. Il faut qu'on aille sur la sixième rue.
   b. Il ne faut pas qu'on fume en classe.
   c. Il est nécessaire qu'on fasse ses devoirs.

2.
   a. Il est essentiel qu'on arrive en retard.
   b. Il faut qu'on s'inscrive à UT.
   c. Il est indispensable qu'on ait la moyenne.

3.
   a. Il est important qu'on aille voir les TA.
   b. Il vaut mieux qu'on ne parle pas espagnol.
   c. Il est préférable qu'on étudie de temps en temps.

4.
   a. Il est essentiel qu'on soit bon en maths.
   b. Il vaut mieux qu'on se couche de bonne heure.
   c. Il est nécessaire qu'on soit sérieux.

5.
   a. Il ne faut pas qu'on sache parler français.
   b. Il est inévitable qu'on suive des cours de littérature.
   c. Il est préférable qu'on n'étudie pas trop.

Exercice 32. Les responsabilités.

Il faut que les personnes suivantes fassent certaines choses. Lisez les phrases qui sont construites avec des expressions impersonnelles, et transformez-les au subjonctif.

> **Modèle:**
> Décrivez la vie d'un scientifique.
> Il faut lire des revues scientifiques. ➔ Il faut qu'il lise des revues scientifiques.

1. Décrivez la vie d'un(e) étudiant(e) modèle.

Il faut aller en cours tous les jours. ____________________

Il faut finir toujours les devoirs. ____________________

Il ne faut pas sécher de cours. ____________________

2. Décrivez la vie d'un professeur.

Il ne faut pas être en retard en classe. ____________________

Il faut suivre les progrès de ses étudiants. ____________________

Il faut connaître les leçons. ____________________

Exercice 33. Tout le monde ou les étudiants?

Pour chaque expression verbale, décidez si cela concerne tout le monde ou les étudiants? Ecrivez cinq conseils pour tout le monde et cinq conseils pour les étudiants en employant une expression verbale et une expression d'obligation.

Expressions d'obligation	**Expressions verbales**
il faut	ne pas fumer
il est important	aller à la bibliothèque
il vaut mieux	faire les devoirs
il est nécessaire	faire du sport
il est essentiel	manger équilibré
il est indispensable	ne pas sécher les cours
il est important	sortir le week-end
	savoir les leçons
	ne pas boire trop d'alcool
	se détendre de temps en temps

Tout le monde (cinq phrases)

> **Modèle: Expressions verbales:** ~~se reposer~~
> Il faut se reposer..

Les étudiants (cinq phrases)

> **Modèle: Expressions verbales:** ~~étudier~~
> Il faut que les étudiants étudient.

Exercice 34. Donnez des conseils à Gilles.

A. Lisez l'email ci-dessous que Gilles a envoyé à son grand cousin Franck.

To: *franck@example.fr*
Cc:

Subject: *Salut!*

Attachments: Browse

Salut Franck!

Comment vas-tu? Moi, bof! Ça ne va pas très bien. J'ai beaucoup de problèmes à la fac et je ne réussis pas très bien ma première année.
D'abord, il y a beaucoup de bruit dans la résidence universitaire, et je ne peux pas me concentrer…impossible d'étudier!!! De plus, mon camarade de chambre se réveille à 6 heures du matin et il commence à jouer de la guitare!!! Il est fou! Je crois que je vais vendre sa guitare pendant qu'il est en cours demain. Bonne idée, n'est-ce pas? Deuxièmement, mon professeur de maths ne parle pas bien français, donc je ne comprends rien! Je pense que je dois lui dire qu'il a besoin de pratiquer son français. De plus, il y a une fille dans mon cours de maths qui est très belle, sympa et intelligente. Je crois qu'elle veut me parler, mais je suis trop timide. Et pour finir, je mange très mal. La cuisine dans le restau-U est mauvaise, donc je mange chez Mac Do tous les jours. Je commence à grossir et je dépense tout mon argent! Je ne sais pas quoi faire. Je crois que je vais rater tous mes cours si ça continue comme ça. Qu'est-ce que tu en penses?

A plus, Gilles

B. Ecrivez trois conseils pour Gilles.

1. ____________________________________
2. ____________________________________
3. ____________________________________

C. En classe, comparez vos conseils avec un partenaire. Qui a les meilleurs conseils ?

D. Devoirs: Ecrivez un paragraphe avec 8 conseils pour Gilles. Variez vos expressions et le vocabulaire.

Dictogloss 1. L'Université en France.

Formez des groupes de 3 ou 4 personnes. Ecoutez le texte lu par votre professeur. Complétez les phrases suivantes et donnez le plus de détails possibles.

Il est vrai que la vie universitaire en France est assez différente de la vie universitaire américaine. Au début de leurs études, il faut que les étudiants français _ immédiatement. Il est aussi important ______________________________ dans la faculté de leur choix quand ils reçoivent leurs _________________________. Les étudiants sont heureux parce que l'université en France est gratuite (même s'il faut qu'ils paient entre _____ et ______ euros pour une année scolaire).

L'année universitaire commence en général ______________________________________ et se termine ______________. Les étudiants _____________________________________ des cours magistraux dans des amphis. Bien sûr il est indispensable _________________ en cours régulièrement et __________________________ leurs devoirs.

Contrairement aux Etats-Unis, le sport n'a pas de place importante dans _______________ ________________. L'université est principalement un endroit pour __________________ et ___________________________________.

Les étudiants français ________________souvent chez leurs parents mais ils vivent aussi en ____________________________________, dans des appartements ou dans des chambres. Comme les étudiants américains, il est souvent nécessaire ______________________ un travail à mi-temps pour pouvoir payer leur loyer ou partir en vacances

NOTE CULTURELLE

La vie universitaire

La vie universitaire en France est centrée autour des cours et des études. Il n'y a pas d'équipes de sport ou beaucoup de clubs au campus. L'université est presque gratuite en France. En général, les étudiants vont dans l'université de leur ville et ils habitent souvent chez leurs parents pendant leurs études.

Vocabulaire

- *le monde du travail*
- *les métiers*
- *adjectifs*
- *verbes*

Phonétique

- *la liaison*

Grammaire

- *12.1 subjunctive usage: doubt*
- *12.2 depuis, pendant, pour: 'for'*
- *12.3 adverbs: formation and placement*
- *12.4 comparative and superlative of adverbs*
- *12.5 bon / meilleur vs bien / mieux*
- *12.6 simple future: regular*
- *12.7 simple future: irregular*
- *testez-vous!, chapitre 12*
- *verb conjugation reference*
- *verb practice*

Vidéos
Vocabulaire en contexte

- *métiers et occupations*

Interviews

- *les métiers*
- *le métier pour vous*
- *les vacances*
- *le métier pour vous*

12 *La vie professionnelle*

In this chapter we will talk about professions and working conditions in France.

Vocabulaire

Préparation du vocabulaire

Be sure to download the pdf vocabulary preparation template from the FI website to complete Exercises B, E, and F.

! Your instructor will collect this homework.

Le monde du travail	**The working world**
les affaires (f pl)	business
une entreprise / une boîte [slang]	firm, business
un bureau	office
un client / une cliente	client, customer
un métier	profession
un emploi / un travail / un job / un boulot [slang]	job
un poste à mi-temps/à plein temps	half-time / full-time position
un chômeur / une chômeuse	unemployed person
le marché du travail	job market
les petites annonces (f pl)	classified ads
un curriculum vitae (un CV)	résumé
un entretien	interview
les avantages sociaux (m)	benefits (health insurance, retirement plan, etc.)
un salaire	salary
les congés	vacation days
une promotion	promotion
la retraite	retirement
un retraité / une retraitée	retired person

Les métiers	**Professions**
un/une fonctionnaire	civil servant, government worker
un facteur	mail carrier
un militaire	person in the armed services
un policier	police officer
un pompier	firefighter
un enseignant / une enseignante	teacher
une assistante sociale	social worker
un médecin	doctor, physician
un/une dentiste	dentist
un infirmier / une infirmière	nurse
un kinésithérapeute / un kiné	chiropractor, physical therapist
un/une psychologue	psychologist
un opticien / une opticienne	optician
un pharmacien / une pharmacienne	pharmacist
un avocat / une avocate	lawyer

Vocabulaire

un banquier / une banquière	banker
un chef d'entreprise	company head, business owner
un patron / une patronne	boss
un P.D.G. (Président Directeur Général)	CEO
un cadre	executive
un/une comptable	accountant
un publicitaire	advertising agent
un/une secrétaire	secretary
un employé / une employée (de bureau)	employee (office employee)
un ouvrier / une ouvrière	blue collar worker
une usine	factory
un informaticien / une informaticienne	computer scientist
un ingénieur	engineer
un chercheur	researcher
un technicien / une technicienne	technician
un/une propriétaire	owner
un commerçant / une commerçante	shopkeeper, store owner
un vendeur / une vendeuse	salesperson
un caissier / une caissière	cashier
un restaurateur	restaurant owner
un cuisinier / une cuisinière	cook
un serveur / une serveuse	wait person
un boulanger / une boulangère	a baker
un couturier / une couturière	fashion designer, seamstress
un coiffeur / une coiffeuse	hairdresser
un critique (de films, d'art, etc.)	critic (film, art, etc.)
un écrivain	writer
un journaliste	reporter, journalist
un peintre / une peintre	painter
un musicien / une musicienne	musician
un voyagiste / un agent de voyage	travel agent
une femme au foyer	housewife

Vocabulaire

Adjectifs	Adjectives
dur(e) / difficile	hard, tough, difficult
dynamique	dynamic
honnête	honest
passionnant(e)	enthralling, fascinating
utile	useful
inutile	useless
d'occasion (une voiture d'occasion)	second-hand, used

Verbes	Verbs
chercher une situation	to look for a job
faire une demande d'emploi	to apply for a job
prendre un rendez-vous	to make an appointment
remplir un formulaire	to fill out a form
embaucher / être embauché(e)	to hire / to be hired
gérer	to manage, to direct, to organize
gagner sa vie / gagner de l'argent	to earn a living / to earn money
payer des impôts	to pay taxes
être au chômage	to be unemployed
être à la retraite	to be retired

Phonétique

Go to the website for a complete explanation and practice exercises.

Introduction

Regardons la video ensemble pour répondre aux questions suivantes: Qui présente le chapitre? Où est-il/elle? Quels sont les thèmes du chapitre?

Exercice 1. Lieux de travail. (work places)

Regardez les lieux de travail, et décidez qui ne travaille pas dans ce lieu. Marquez ces personnes par un X.

1. **un lycée**: une banquière, un facteur, un enseignant, un cadre, une assistante sociale
2. **une entreprise**: une vendeuse, un médecin, un cadre, un chef d'entreprise, un avocat
3. **une banque**: un banquier, un psychologue, un fonctionnaire, un cadre, une assistante sociale
4. **un cabinet médical**: une dentiste, un professeur, un médecin, une infirmière, un journaliste
5. **un magasin**: une commerçante, une avocate, un ouvrier, une couturière, un vendeur
6. **un hôpital**: une informaticienne, un médecin, un secrétaire, un écrivain, un infirmier

Exercice 2. Quelle matières?

A tour de role, posez les questions suivantes à un/une partenaire dans la classe.

> **Modèle**:
> Qu'est-ce qu'il faut étudier pour devenir ... biologiste?
> → Il faut étudier la biologie et les maths.

1. … avocat?
2. … médecin?
3. … peintre?
4. ... architecte?
5. ... géographe?
6. ... publicitaire?

Exercice 3. Classez les métiers.

Quels métiers associez-vous avec les catégories suivantes?

1. Les métiers où on doit être courageux...
2. Les métiers où on a beaucoup de responsabilités...
3. Les métiers où on travaille seul...
4. Les métiers où on trouve beaucoup de femmes...
5. Les métiers où on n'a pas besoin de diplôme universitaire...
6. Les métiers où on travaille la nuit...
7. Les métiers où on a beaucoup de congés...
8. Les métiers où on a beaucoup de contact avec le public...

Exercice 4. Grammaire interactive. Votre avis sur les métiers.

A. D'accord ou pas d'accord. Avec un partenaire décidez si vous êtes d'accord ou pas avec les phrases suivantes.

1. Je pense que le métier de médecin est intéressant.
2. Je crois que le métier d'enseignant convient à (**suits**) ma personalité.
3. Je doute que le métier de comptable soit passionnant.
4. Je ne crois pas que le métier de fonctionnaire convienne à ma personnalité.

B. Highlight the verbs in the sentences above which are in the subjunctive. Look at all four sentences and hypothesize why certain verbs are in the indicative and others are in the subjunctive.

Exercice 5. Quelle profession choisir?

1. Quelle profession choisir si on est très organisé(e)?
2. Quelle profession choisir si on aime écrire?
3. Quelle profession choisir si on veut aider les personnes malades ou blessées (**injured**)?
4. Quelle profession choisir si on est dynamique et éloquent?
5. Quelle profession choisir si on sait bien cuisiner?
6. Quelle profession choisir si on est très créatif/créative?

Exercice 6. Indicatif ou subjonctif?

Ecoutez votre professeur et décidez si le deuxième verbe conjugué dans les phrases suivantes est à l'indicatif ou au subjonctif.

	indicatif	subjonctif
Modèle: Je sais que tu es intelligent.	√	❑
1. ____________________	❑	❑
2. ____________________	❑	❑
3. ____________________	❑	❑
4. ____________________	❑	❑
5. ____________________	❑	❑
6. ____________________	❑	❑

Exercice 7. Des problèmes.

La copine de Léonard a beaucoup de problèmes. Il essaie d'expliquer ses problèmes à ses amies. Faites correspondre les informations entre les 2 colonnes.

_____1. Je doute qu'elle s'entende avec ses parents…
_____2. Je ne pense pas qu'elle soit malade…
_____3. Il est possible qu'elle ait des problèmes d'argent…
_____4. Je doute qu'elle vienne danser avec nous ce soir…
_____5. Je ne crois pas que nous puissions l'aider…
_____6. Je ne crois pas qu'elle veuille me parler…
_____7. Je pense qu'elle a raté son examen de français…
_____8. Je suis sûr qu'elle prend beaucoup de somnifères…

a. Je l'ai vue dans un café il y a deux heures.
b. Elle n'a pas étudié avant l'examen.
c. Elle n'a pas réglé ses frais d'inscription.
d. Elle a besoin de voir un psychologue.
e. Elle s'endort en classe.
f. Ils sont très désagréables.
g. Elle ne répond pas au téléphone quand je l'appelle.
h. Elle n'a jamais envie de sortir.

At home, please go to the Français interactif website. Read the following grammar points in Tex's French Grammar and complete all Texercises which you will turn in to your instructor.

12.1 subjunctive usage: doubt

Use the subjunctive with expressions of doubt:

il est possible que…
il est impossible que…
il est incroyable que…

douter que
ne pas penser que
ne pas croire que

Exercice 8. Quelques conseils pour Léonard.

Les amies de Léonard lui donnent des conseils pour mieux comprendre les problèmes de sa copine. Identifiez le mode de chaque verbe (indicatif, impératif ou subjonctif). Si le verbe est à l'indicatif, indiquez le temps du verbe aussi (passé composé, imparfait ou présent).

	Indicatif	Impératif	Subjonctif
Modèle: Ne lui **téléphone** plus!	❑ passé composé ❑ imparfait ❑ présent	√	❑
1. Il est possible qu'elle n'**ait** plus envie d'être avec toi.	❑ passé composé ❑ imparfait ❑ présent	❑	❑
2. Tu penses qu'elle t'**aime** toujours?	❑ passé composé ❑ imparfait ❑ présent	❑	❑
3. Est-ce que tu **es sorti** avec elle récemment?	❑ passé composé ❑ imparfait ❑ présent	❑	❑
4. Il est incroyable qu'elle ne **réponde** pas au téléphone.	❑ passé composé ❑ imparfait ❑ présent	❑	❑
5. Ne **sois** pas triste!	❑ passé composé ❑ imparfait ❑ présent	❑	❑
6. Il est essentiel que tu lui **parles** bientôt.	❑ passé composé ❑ imparfait ❑ présent	❑	❑
7. Nous pensons qu'elle **est** snob.	❑ passé composé ❑ imparfait ❑ présent	❑	❑
8. Elle n'**était** jamais très gentille avec toi.	❑ passé composé ❑ imparfait ❑ présent	❑	❑
9. Nous doutons qu'elle **change**.	❑ passé composé ❑ imparfait ❑ présent	❑	❑
10. Il faut que tu **trouves** une autre copine.	❑ passé composé ❑ imparfait ❑ présent	❑	❑

Exercice 9. A ton avis?

Quelle est votre opinion sur la France et les Français? Répondez aux questions suivantes:

Modèle :
Est-ce que tu crois que la France est un beau pays?
Oui, je crois que la France est un beau pays.
Non, je ne crois pas que la France soit un beau pays.

1. Est- ce que tu penses que les Français sont paresseux?
2. Est-ce que tu crois qu'on doit travailler plus en France qu'aux Etats-Unis?
3. Est-ce que tu crois qu'on peut partir à la retraite à 40 ans en France?
4. Est- ce que tu penses qu'il y a moins de chômage en France qu'aux Etats-Unis?
5. Est-ce que tu crois que tous les Français savent parler anglais?

NOTE CULTURELLE

Les Vacances

Les Français ont le droit à 5 semaines de congés payés par an. Normalement, on prend les vacances vers la fin de l'été et surtout en août. Ils ont aussi plusieurs congés payés pendant l'année, surtout en mai. En plus, il faut comprendre que les Français ne travaillent que 35 heures par semaine.

Exercice 10. L'infinitif, l'indicatif ou le subjonctif?

Remplacez les blancs avec le verbe à l'infinitif ou conjugué à l'indicatif ou au subjonctif.

1. Pour réussir un entretien professionnel, il est important de ______________________ (s'habiller) bien.
2. Il est possible de/d' ______________________ (être) chef d'entreprise si on veut travailler beaucoup.
3. Tout le monde sait que le chomage ______________________ (devenir) l'un des problèmes les plus sévères du monde.
4. Il est incroyable que les Français ______________________ (prendre) cinq semaines de vacances.
5. Pour combattre le stress il est préférable de ______________________ (travailler) moins.
6. Il n'est pas sûr que les politiciens américains ______________________ (pouvoir) s'entendre.
7. Les Américains doutent que les politiciens ______________________ (être) honnêtes.
8. Il est évident qu'un PDG ______________________ (avoir) un travail stressant.

Exercice 11. Cherchons une situation.

D'habitude, on ne trouve pas de poste sans effort; il y a une certaine progression. Mettez les activités suivantes dans l'ordre logique (1 à 8).

_____	préparer un CV	_____	avoir un entretien
_____	choisir une profession	_____	travailler beaucoup
_____	être embauché(e)	_____	profiter des congés
_____	obtenir son diplôme	_____	faire une demande d'emploi

Exercice 12. Joe-Bob cherche un travail en France.

Joe-Bob a envie de travailler en France, mais ce n'est pas facile pour un Américain.

A. Avec un partenaire, lisez le dialogue entre Joe-Bob et la secrétaire d'un PDG d'une grande compagnie en France.

Joe-Bob:	Bonjour Madame. Je veux parler avec le PDG de la compagnie, s'il vous plaît.
La secrétaire:	Monsieur, le PDG est très occupé!
Joe-Bob:	Mais vous ne comprenez pas, Madame. Je suis américain et je veux travailler en France.
La secrétaire:	Avez-vous un visa pour travailler en France?
Joe-Bob:	Non, mais je suis très intelligent. Je suis étudiant à l'Université Texas A & M aux Etats-Unis.
La secrétaire:	Oui, mais si vous n'avez pas de visa...
Joe-Bob:	Ne vous inquiétez pas, Madame. On peut me payer en espèces (**cash**). Et je veux gagner beaucoup d'argent!
La secrétaire:	Monsieur, vous ne comprenez rien! Vous êtes un Américain sans visa! Vous ne pouvez pas travailler en France, et vous ne pouvez pas non plus voir le PDG! Laissez-moi tranquille, s'il vous plaît! J'ai du travail à faire!

B. Complétez les phrases suivantes avec votre partenaire. Faites attention! Il faut employer l'infinitif, l'indicatif, ou le subjonctif. Employez des sujets variés (Joe-Bob, la secrétaire, le PDG, etc.). Soyez créatif/créative!

1. Nous doutons que...
2. Nous savons que...
3. Nous ne croyons pas que...
4. Il faut...
5. Nous sommes certain(e)s que...
6. Il est impossible que...

C. Discutez ce que vous avez écrit avec la classe.

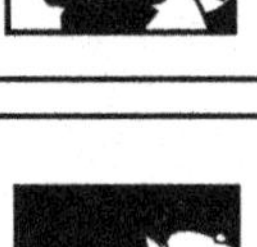

Exercice 13. On parle de quel métier?

Lisez les descriptions et indiquez le métier qui correspond à la description.

Modèle: Quelqu'un qui travaille dans un journal est journaliste.

1. Quelqu'un qui est âgé et ne travaille plus est ____________________.
2. Quelqu'un qui a perdu son travail et qui cherche un emploi est ____________________.
3. Quelqu'un qui travaille pour l'état est ____________________.
4. Quelqu'un qui travaille dans l'Armée ou l'Armée de l'Air est ____________________.
5. Quelqu'un qui soigne des gens avec des maladies mentales est ____________________.
6. Quelqu'un qui reste à la maison, fait le ménage, et s'occupe des enfants est __________.
7. Un artiste qui peint est ____________________.
8. Quelqu'un qui travaille dans une usine est ____________________.

Exercice 14. Des étudiants typiques ou pas typiques?

		typique	pas typique
1.	Il étudie le latin **depuis** l'âge de 5 ans.	❑	❑
2.	Ils utilisent des ordinateurs **depuis** 1997.	❑	❑
3.	Il connaît ses profs **depuis** le premier jour du semestre.	❑	❑
4.	Il surfe sur internet **depuis** 2005.	❑	❑
5.	Il étudie le français **depuis** cinq heures ce matin.	❑	❑
6.	Ils conduisent **depuis** dix ans.	❑	❑

At home, please go to the Français interactif website. Read the following grammar points in Tex's French Grammar and complete all Texercises which you will turn in to your instructor.

12.2 depuis, pendant

Depuis

Used with an event that began in the past and is continuing into the present

Pendant

Used with all tenses to mean 'during'

Exercice 15. Votre emploi du temps.

Pour chaque phrase, remplissez le premier blanc avec une activité que vous faites et le deuxième avec le temps correspondant.

A. Depuis combien de temps...? (nombre de mois, d' années, de jours, etc.).

1. Je fais du/de la (sport) ____________________ depuis ________________________ .
2. Je fais partie du club de ____________________ à UT depuis ____________________ .
3. Je joue du/de la (instrument musical) ________________ depuis _______________ .

B. Depuis quand...? (une date précise, un mois précis, l'âge de 5 ans, etc.)

4. Je suis des cours de ____________________ depuis ________________________ .
5. Je conduis une/un (moyen de transport) ______________ depuis ______________ .
6. J'habite dans un/une (sorte de résidence) ______________ depuis ______________ .

C. Comparez vos réponses avec un partenaire et rapportez les résultats à la classe.

Exercice 16. Les habitudes de vos camarades de classe.

En groupes de trois ou quatre, posez les questions suivantes et comparez vos réponses. N'oubliez pas la différence entre "Depuis quand" et " Depuis combien de temps". Avez-vous des choses en commun avec vos camarades?

1. Depuis quand est-ce que tu travailles? (date)
2. Depuis quand est-ce que tu bois du café?
3. Depuis quand est-ce que tu as ton permis de conduire?
4. Depuis combien de temps est-ce que tu es à l'université? (période de temps)
5. Depuis combien de temps est-ce que tu utilises un ordinateur?

Exercice 17. C'est fini ou ça continue?

Indiquez si les actions suivantes sont finies ou si elles continuent.

	c'est fini	ça continue
1. J'étudie le français depuis un an.	❑	❑
2. J'ai passé un mois en France.	❑	❑
3. Je corresponds avec des amis français depuis mon retour.	❑	❑
4. Mes parents habitent leur maison depuis 10 ans.	❑	❑
5. Depuis le mois de juillet, nous suivons des cours.	❑	❑
6. Ce matin j'ai attendu le professeur pendant trente minutes.	❑	❑

Exercice 18. Joe-Bob est bizarre ou normal?

	bizarre	normal
1. Joe-Bob a travaillé **pendant** 12 heures hier.	❑	❑
2. Il lit le journal **pendant** les cours.	❑	❑
3. Il a nagé **pendant** l'hiver.	❑	❑
4. Quand il était petit, il parlait avec son psychologue **pendant** des heures.	❑	❑
5. Il a vécu avec ses parents **pendant** les vacances d'été.	❑	❑

Exercice 19. Pendant combien de temps?

Pour chaque phrase, remplissez les blancs avec la durée du temps qui correspond avec l'activité.

1. Hier, j'ai étudié le français pendant ________________ .
2. Ce matin, j'ai attendu le bus pendant ________________ .
3. Tous les jours, je regarde la télé pendant ________________ .
4. Je surfe sur internet pendant ________________ tous les jours.
5. Demain, je vais étudier pendant ________________ .
6. Ce soir, je vais dormir pendant ________________ .

Exercice 20. Vos habitudes.

A. Remplissez les blancs suivants pour former des questions.

B. En classe, posez des questions à un partenaire et comparer vos réponses. Attention: Où est-ce que vous mettez l'indication de temps dans votre réponse?

1. Pendant combien de temps est-ce que tu ______________________________?
2. Depuis quand est-ce que tu ______________________________________?
3. Pendant combien de temps est-ce que tu ____________________ chaque jour?
4. Depuis combien de temps est-ce que tu ______________________________?
5. Pendant combien de temps est-ce que tu as __________________________?
6. Pendant combien de temps est-ce que tu vas _________________________?

Dictogloss 1. Toño cherche un travail.

Formez des groupes de 3 ou 4 personnes. Ecoutez le texte lu par votre professeur. Complétez les phrases suivantes et donnez le plus de détails possibles.

Depuis quelques mois, Toño cherche ____________________________________

qui offre beaucoup _______________. Le problème, c'est qu'_______________

_____________________ comme professeur. Mais, un professeur est quelqu'un qui a

______________ ____________________, et Toño n'a pas encore son diplôme.

De plus, Toño n'a jamais travaillé et on cherche toujours des gens ______________

______________. Donc il a besoin de ___________________________________

pour se préparer pour ____.

Exercice 21. Logique ou illogique?

At home, please go to the Français interactif website. Read the following grammar points in Tex's French Grammar and complete all Texercises which you will turn in to your instructor.

12.3 adverbs: formation and placement

Add -ment to the feminine singular form of the adjective.

heureux (heureuse) --> heureusement

Refer to Tex for exceptions and placement.

		logique	illogique
1.	Les gens qui sont en forme font **régulièrement** du sport.	❑	❑
2.	Les enfants préfèrent qu'on leur parle **calmement**.	❑	❑
3.	Les étudiants aiment les profs qui expliquent **impatiemment**.	❑	❑
4.	Les étudiants qui étudient **sérieusement** ratent tous leurs examens.	❑	❑
5.	Dans un entretien professionnel, il faut parler aux gens **brusquement**.	❑	❑
6.	Il est important de dormir **suffisamment** avant un examen.	❑	❑
7.	Quand les vacances arrivent, les étudiants quittent **immédiatement** Austin.	❑	❑
8.	On mange **bien** en France.	❑	❑

Exercice 22. Quel verbe?

Quels adverbes associez-vous avec les verbes suivants?

Modèle:
s'habiller élégamment

~~élégamment~~	lentement	sérieusement
bien	rapidement	profondément
mal	poliment	suffisamment
doucement	franchement	fréquemment
attentivement	souvent	brillamment
énormément	intelligemment	

1. conduire
2. écouter
3. parler
4. travailler
5. répondre
6. chanter
7. dormir
8. aimer

Exercice 23. Les adverbes.

Formez des adverbes à partir des adjectifs masculins ci-dessous.

1. heureux ______________________
2. attentif ______________________
3. rapide ______________________
4. régulier ______________________
5. franc ______________________
6. facile ______________________
7. sérieux ______________________
8. fréquent ______________________
9. lent ______________________
10. énorme ______________________

Exercice 24. Tes habitudes.

Posez des questions à vos camarades.

1. Est-ce que tu étudies facilement? ______________________
2. Est-ce que tu préfères travailler indépendamment? ______________________
3. Est-ce que tu parles français rapidement? ______________________
4. Est-ce que tu attends la fin du semestre impatiemment? ______________________
5. Est-ce que tu fais tes devoirs régulièrement? ______________________
6. Est-ce que tu parles franchement? ______________________
7. Est-ce que tu danses bien? ______________________
8. Est-ce que tu manges mal? ______________________

Exercice 25. Quelques comparaisons. Vrai ou faux?

		vrai	faux
1.	Les étudiantes sortent aussi fréquemment que les étudiants.	❑	❑
2.	Les adultes conduisent plus prudemment que les adolescents.	❑	❑
3.	Les Texans s'habillent aussi élégamment que les Parisiens.	❑	❑
4.	Le professeur de français parle français plus couramment que les étudiants.	❑	❑
5.	Les hommes conduisent plus vite que les femmes.	❑	❑
6.	Il pleut moins fréquemment à Austin qu'à El Paso.	❑	❑

Exercice 26. Votre avis sur les stéréotypes.

Formez des phrases en employant le comparatif des adverbes.

> **Modèle:**
> Les Français / Les Américains (suivre le Tour de France /+ - =/ attentivement)
> ➜ Les Américains suivent le Tour de France moins attentivement que les Français.

1. Les Français / Les Américains (aller en vacances /+ - =/ fréquemment)

   ____.

2. Les Parisiens / Les New-Yorkais (parler /+ - =/ rapidement)

   ____.

3. Les Français / les Américains (boire du vin /+ - =/ régulièrement

   ____.

4. Les Français / les Américains (faire le marché /+ - =/ souvent)

   ____.

Exercice 27. Encore des stéréotypes. D'accord ou pas d'accord?

A. Si vous n'êtes pas d'accord, expliquez pourquoi.

		d'accord	pas d'accord
1.	Les Italiennes, les Françaises, les Américaines: Des trois nationalités, ce sont les Françaises qui s'habillent le plus élégamment.	❑	❑
2.	Les Parisiens, les New-Yorkais, les Texans: De ces trois groupes, ce sont les Texans qui parlent le moins vite.	❑	❑
3.	Les Français, les Espagnols, les Allemands Des trois nationalités, ce sont les Espagnols qui travaillent le plus sérieusement.	❑	❑
4.	Les Français, les Américains, les Italiens: De toutes ces personnes, ce sont les Français qui mangent des pâtes le plus fréquemment.	❑	❑

B. Maintenant avec deux ou trois partenaires, écrivez deux autres stéréotypes avec le superlatif des adverbes. Soyez créatif!

1. ______________________________
2. ______________________________

Exercice 28. Le meilleur et le pire d'Austin selon vous!

A. Complétez les phrases suivantes.

1. A Austin, le meilleur restaurant pour les étudiants est ______________
2. A Austin, le pire restaurant pour les étudiants est ______________
3. A Austin, les meilleures margaritas se trouvent (**are found**) à ______________
4. A Austin, la plus mauvaise station de radio est ______________
5. A Austin, le plus mauvais café est ______________
6. A Austin, le meilleur endroit (**place**) pour écouter de la musique ______________

B. En classe, comparez vos réponses.

Exercice 29. Les stéréotypes.

Complétez les phrases suivantes avec une nationalité selon votre opinion.

Modèle: Les Français cuisinent le mieux.

1. ______________________________ jouent au foot le mieux.
2. ______________________________ s'habillent le mieux.
3. ______________________________ conduisent le moins bien.
4. ______________________________ mangent le moins bien.

At home, please go to the Français interactif website. Read the following grammar points in Tex's French Grammar and complete all Texercises which you will turn in to your instructor.

12.4 comparative and superlative of adverbs

comparative of adverbs: **indicating more, less, or equality**

superlative of adverbs: **indicating the most, the least**

At home, please go to the Français interactif website. Read the following grammar points in Tex's French Grammar and complete all Texercises which you will turn in to your instructor.

12.5 bon/meilleur vs bien/mieux

adjective :
bon / meilleur

adverb :
bien / mieux

superlative forms :
le meilleur / le mieux

Exercice 30. Le top!

A. Etudiez le tableau.
B. Ecrivez 3 phrases en employant le comparatif (plus/aussi/moins) et le superlatif (le plus/le moins).

	Joe-Bob	Bette	Paw-Paw
Modèle: sort souvent?	★★★	★★	★
1. conduit vite?	★★★	★★★	★
2. parle lentement?	★★	★	★★★
3. mange bien?	★★	★	★★★

Modèle:
Bette sort plus souvent que Paw-Paw, mais Joe-Bob sort le plus souvent des trois.
OU
Bette sort moins souvent que Joe-Bob, mais Paw-Paw sort le moins souvent des trois.

1. ______________________________.
2. ______________________________.
3. ______________________________.

Exercice 31. Pour impressionner mon professeur de français!

A. Choisissez l'adverbe approprié qui **mieux** décrit vos efforts pour impressionner votre prof de français pour les activités suivantes. Remplissez colonne A.

Voici des adverbes utiles pour cet exercice:

jamais **rarement** **quelquefois** **souvent** **toujours**

Noms	**A:** moi	**B:**________	**C:**________
Modèle: dormir en classe	rarement	jamais	quelquefois
1. faire les devoirs			
2. parler français en classe			
3. participer aux activités en classe			
4. aller au labo après la classe			
5. sécher le cours			
6. passer mes examens			
7. rater mes examens			

B. En groupes de trois personnes, comparez votre participation aux activités .

Modèle:
dormir en classe
Etudiant A: Pour impressionner mon prof, je dors rarement en classe.
Etudiant B: Pour impressionner mon prof, je ne dors jamais en classe.
Etudiant C: Pour impressionner mon prof, je dors quelquefois en classe.
Conclusion:
De nous trois, Etudiant C dort le plus souvent en classe.
De nous trois, Etudiant B dort le moins souvent en classe.

C. **Devoirs:** Ecrivez un paragraphe de 8 phrases en employant le superlatif des adverbes d'après l'activité que vous venez de faire. De vous trois, qui impressionne le professeur le plus régulièrement et pourquoi?

Modèle:
Etudiant B impressionne le professeur le plus régulièrement parce que de nous trois, c'est lui qui dort le moins souvent en classe.

Dictogloss 2. Une augmentation de salaire.

A. Formez des groupes de 3 ou 4 personnes. Ecoutez le texte lu par votre professeur. Complétez les phrases suivantes et donnez le plus de détails possibles.

Lucien Dolifère, vendeur en informatique, a pris rendez-vous avec Mme Zemour, la responsable du magasin, pour lui demander une augmentation (**raise**).

At home, please go to the Français interactif website. Read the following grammar points in Tex's French Grammar and complete all Texercises which you will turn in to your instructor.

12.6 Simple future: regular

The future endings are the same for all verbs:

-ai -as -a -ons -ez -ont

Future of regular...
–er verbs: voyager
–ir verbs: choisir
–re verbs: répondre

je	**voyagerai choisirai répondrai**
tu	**voyageras choisiras répondras**
il / elle / on	**voyagera choisira répondra**
nous	**voyagerons choisirons répondrons**
vous	**voyagerez choisirez répondrez**
ils / elles	**voyageront choisiront répondront**

M. Dolifère:	Bonjour, Madame. Merci de me recevoir. ______________________?
Mme Zemour:	Très bien, merci. Et vous?
M. Dolifère:	Bien merci. ______________________ vous voir pour vous parler d'une éventuelle ______________________. Je sais que mes deux collègues, Jean-Luc et Chantal viennent d'en recevoir une et je me ______________________, moi ______________________.
Mme Zemour:	Ah oui... une augmentation de salaire, hein? Et bien, vous voyez mon cher Dolifère, vos collègues sont ______________________ qui ____________ ici. En plus ce sont des employés extraordinaires ______________________ deux ans avant vous. Mais vous...
M. Dolifère:	Mais, qu'est-ce qu'ils font exactement, les autres? A mon avis, ils travaillent ______________________ ______________________.
Mme Zemour:	Voyons...Alors...Chantal parle ______________________ aux clients. Et Chantal et Jean-Luc, ils viennent au travail ____________ ______________________.
M. Dolifère:	Mais non. Ce n'est pas du tout le cas Madame. C'est moi qui parle ___ ______________________ de nos mauvais ordinateurs! Mes clients n'achètent jamais rien. Donc, c'est moi qui les aide ______________________!

B. A votre avis.

1. Qu'est-ce que vous pensez de Monsieur Dolifère?
2. Est-ce qu'il mérite une augmentation de salaire ou pas? Expliquez.
3. Est-ce qu'il parle trop franchement avec son patron?
4. Est-ce que M Dolifère va perdre son travail?

Exercice 32. Futur ou pas?

Ecoutez chaque phrase et décidez si le verbe est au présent ou au futur. Ecoutez une deuxième fois et écrivez la phrase.

	présent	futur
Modèle: Nous voyagerons à Paris	❑	√
1. __________	❑	❑
2. __________	❑	❑
3. __________	❑	❑
4. __________	❑	❑
5. __________	❑	❑
6. __________	❑	❑
7. __________	❑	❑
8. __________	❑	❑

Irregular verbs that are regular in the future:

sortir (je sortirai) partir (je partirai) dormir (je dormirai) boire (je boirai) dire (je dirai) écrire (j'écrirai) lire (je lirai) mettre (je mettrai) prendre (je prendrai) suivre (je suivrai).

Exercice 33. Cet été.

Posez ces questions à vos camarades de classe.

Cet été...

1. Est-ce que tu partiras en vacances? __________
2. Est-ce que tes amis resteront à Austin? __________
3. Est-ce que toi et tes amis, vous sortirez tous les soirs __________
4. Est-ce que tu te réveilleras à midi tous les jours? __________
5. Est-ce que tu suivras un cours? __________
6. Est-ce que tu voyageras en France? __________
7. Est-ce que tes parents te donneront de l'argent? __________
8. Est-ce que ton copain/ta copine te rendra visite tous les jours ? __________

! Utilisez uniquement le français! Si la réponse est "OUI", demandez la signature de cette personne. Changez de camarade pour chaque question. Ecoutez attentivement les questions qu'on vous pose. Ne répondez pas à des questions incomplètes.

At home, please go to the Français interactif website. Read the following grammar points in Tex's French Grammar and complete all Texercises which you will turn in to your instructor.

12.7 Simple future: irregular

irregular future stems :

être	ser-
avoir	aur-
aller	ir-
courir	courr-
devoir	devr-
envoyer	enverr-
faire	fer-
falloir	faudr-
mourir	mourr-
pleuvoir	pleuvr-
pouvoir	pourr-
recevoir	recevr-
savoir	saur-
venir	viendr-
voir	verr-
vouloir	voudr-

Most –er verbs with spelling changes (préférer, manger, commencer) have regular future stems. Others add –r to the present tense je form to create their future stems:

appeler	appeller-
employer	emploier-
acheter	achèter-

Exercice 34. Dans 50 ans.

Comment sera votre vie dans 50 ans? Est-ce que vous pensez que les phrases suivantes sont vraies ou fausses?

	vrai	faux
1. Je serai retraité(e).	❑	❑
2. J'aurai des petits-enfants.	❑	❑
3. J'irai en France une fois par an.	❑	❑
4. Je ferai de l'escalade.	❑	❑
5. Il faudra que j'aille souvent chez le médecin.	❑	❑
6. Je devrai payer beaucoup d'impôts.	❑	❑
7. Je ne pourrai plus lire.	❑	❑
8. Je saurai parler français couramment.	❑	❑
9. Je reviendrai à UT pour les matchs de football américain.	❑	❑
10. Je ne verrai plus mes amis de UT	❑	❑

Exercice 35. Est-ce que vous pouvez lire l'avenir?

A. A quelle date est-ce que vous pensez que ces événements (**events**) auront lieu.

Modèle:
- partir d'Austin
Je partirai d'Austin en 2020
Je ne partirai jamais d'Austin.

1. (aller en France) ______________________________
2. (recevoir son diplôme) ______________________________
3. (faire une demande d'emploi) ______________________________
4. (acheter une maison) ______________________________
5. (avoir des enfants) ______________________________
6. (être grand-père/grand-mère) ______________________________
7. (pouvoir prendre sa retraite) ______________________________
8. (devenir président(e) des Etats-Unis) ______________________________

B. Maintenant devinez à quelle date ces évènements seront vrais pour votre partenaire.

> **Modèle:**
> - partir d'Austin
> Il/elle partira d'Austin en 2030
> Il/elle ne partira jamais d'Austin.

1. (aller en France) ____________________
2. (recevoir son diplôme) ____________________
3. (faire une demande d'emploi) ____________________
4. (acheter une maison) ____________________
5. (avoir des enfants) ____________________
6. (être grand-père/grand-mère) ____________________
7. (pouvoir prendre sa retraite) ____________________
8. (devenir president des Etats-Unis) ____________________

C. Lisez vos phrases à votre partenaire. Est- ce que vous avez réussi à prédire (**predict**) l'avenir de votre partenaire?

Exercice 36. Votre profession préférée.

A. Choisissez une profession pour votre partenaire:

avocat(e)	**cadre**	**enseignant(e)**	**femme (homme) au foyer**
ingénieur	**médecin**	**militaire**	**musicien(ne)**

B. Décrivez ce que votre partenaire fera ou ne fera pas:

> **Modèle:** (avoir des congés):
> Tu auras beacoup de congés.
> Tu n'auras pas beaucoup de congés.

1. ____________________ (avoir beaucoup de congés)
2. ____________________ (voyager souvent)
3. ____________________ (gérer des employés)
4. ____________________ (aller souvent au tribunal)
5. ____________________ (faire des concerts)
6. ____________________ (savoir aider des malades)
7. ____________________ (être excellent en sciences)
8. ____________________ (voir souvent tes enfants)

C. Lisez les phrases à votre partenaire. Votre partenaire doit deviner la profession que vous avez choisie pour lui/elle.

NOTE CULTURELLE

La Retraite

Normalement, les Français ont le droit de prendre leur retraite à l'âge de 60 ans. Par contre, s'ils travaillent pour l'un des régimes spéciaux de retraite, comme la Société Nationale de Chemins de Fer (SNCF), ils peuvent prendre leur retraite plus tôt, même à l'âge de 57.5 ans. Les femmes avec 3 enfants ou plus, ont le droit de prendre la retraite plus tôt aussi. Les générations du baby boom arrivent à l'âge de la retraite, et la France doit reformuler le système de retraite pour pouvoir les financer.

13 L'amour et l'argent

In this chapter we will talk about the future in terms of love and finances

Vocabulaire

- *les finances*
- *la bourse*
- *adjectifs*
- *verbes - les finances*
- *les amours*
- *verbes - les amours*
- *l'horoscope - horoscope*

Phonétique

- *les groupes rythmiques*

Grammaire

- *13.1 future: usage*
- *13.2 subjunctive usage: will, emotion, desire*
- *13.3 conditional*
- *13.4 si clauses*

- *testez-vous!, chapitre 13*
- *verb conjugation reference*
- *verb practice*

Vidéos

Vocabulaire en contexte

- *l'amour*
- *les finances*

Interviews

- *dans 5 ans ...*
- *si ...*

Culture

- *votre signe*

Vocabulaire

Préparation du vocabulaire

Be sure to download the pdf vocabulary preparation template from the FI website to complete Exercises B, E, and F.

! Your instructor will collect this homework.

Les finances	**Finances**
une banque	bank
une caisse d'épargne	savings and loan association
un compte (bancaire)	(bank) account
un distributeur (automatique de billets)	ATM (automatic teller machine)
un guichet automatique	
l'euro	euro (currency)
un héritage	inheritance
les dépenses (f pl)	expenses
les factures (f pl)	bills
le logement	housing
le loyer	rent
l'alimentation	food
le divertissement / les loisirs	entertainment
la facture de téléphone	telephone bill
les frais (m) de scolarité	tuition, education expenses
l'emprunt-étudiant (m)	student loan
l'assurance (f)	insurance
l'essence (f)	gas
les charges	utilities
les impôts (m pl)	taxes
les dettes (f pl)	debts

La bourse	**The stock market**
des actions (f pl)	stocks
un portefeuille	portfolio (also, wallet)

Adjectifs	**Adjectives**
généreux / généreuse	generous
dépensier / dépensière	spendthrift
radin / radine [slang]	miserly, stingy
économe	economical, frugal
bon marché / pas cher	inexpensive
être en solde	to be on sale
un prix intéressant	a good price
cher / chère	expensive
être fauché(e) [slang]	to be broke
être aisé(e)	to be well off
satisfait(e)	satisfied, fulfilled

Vocabulaire

Verbes – Les finances	Verbs - Finances
coûter	to cost
dépenser	to spend
rembourser	to reimburse
emprunter	borrow
avoir les moyens de	to have the means to
louer	to rent
faire un budget	to establish a budget
dépasser son budget	to go beyond one's budget
avoir des dettes	to have debts
gaspiller	to waste
faire des économies	to save money
offrir	to give, to offer

Les amours	Love life
un couple	couple
le coup de foudre	love at first sight
l'amour passion (m)	passionate love
le grand amour	the love of one's life
un rendez-vous	date (also an appointment)
une relation	relationship
les fiançailles (f pl)	engagement
un fiancé / une fiancée	fiancé / fiancée
le mariage	marriage, wedding
la compatibilité	compatibility / matching
l'apparence physique	physical appearance
le bonheur	happiness
la communication	interaction / communication
le sens de l'humour	sense of humor
le respect	respect
l'honnêteté (f)	honesty
le romantisme	romanticism

Verbes – Les amours	Verbs – Love life
draguer	to try to pick up, to hit on someone, to flirt
être amis	to be friends
vivre ensemble	to live together
s'embrasser	to kiss each other
s'aimer	to love each other

Vocabulaire

se pacser	to enter a PACS contract
se fiancer	to get engaged
se marier	to get married
rompre	to break up
divorcer	to get divorced
tromper	to cheat on

Phonétique

Go to the website for a complete explanation and practice exercises.

Introduction

Regardons la video ensemble pour répondre aux questions suivantes: Qui présente le chapitre? Où est-il/elle? Quels sont les thèmes du chapitre?

Exercice 1. Les amours.

A. Est-ce que vous êtes d'accord ou pas avec les idées suivantes. Pourquoi?

1. Le coup de foudre n'existe pas.
2. Le grand amour? On peut en avoir 2 ou 3!
3. L'amour passion est dangereux.
4. On doit se fiancer au moins un an avant le mariage.
5. Les couples ne doivent pas vivre ensemble avant le mariage.
6. On ne doit pas se marier avant l'âge de 30 ans.
7. Divorcer n'est jamais la meilleure solution.

B. Discutons ensemble!!!
Quelles sont les choses les plus importantes dans une relation?

C. Décrivez le premier rendez-vous de rêve.

Exercice 2. Les finances.

A. Indiquez la fréquence avec laquelle (**with which**), vous faites les activités suivantes.

Activité:	**toujours**	**quelquefois**	**jamais**
1. Je fais un budget.	❑	❑	❑
2. Je dépasse mon budget.	❑	❑	❑
3. Je fais des économies.	❑	❑	❑
4. Je suis fauché(e).	❑	❑	❑
5. J'achète uniquement ce qui est en solde.	❑	❑	❑

NOTE CULTURELLE

L'Argent

En général, c'est considéré comme impoli de parler en France à propos d'argent en public. En fait, les gens sont plus enclins de parler de leur vie sexuelle que d'argent. Par exemple, on peut connaître quelqu'un pendant des années sans savoir ce qu'il/elle fait dans la vie ou ce qu'il/elle gagne comme salaire.

B. Maintenant, interviewez votre partenaire sur ses activités.

Modèle: Est-ce que tu fais un budget? Je fais souvent un budget.

Activité:	toujours	quelquefois	jamais
1. Il/elle fait un budget.	❑	❑	❑
2. Il/elle dépasse son budget.	❑	❑	❑
3. Il/elle fait des économies.	❑	❑	❑
4. Il/elle est fauché(e).	❑	❑	❑
5. Il/elle achète uniquement ce qui est en solde.	❑	❑	❑

C. Et votre budget... Faites la liste des choses qui sont importantes dans votre budget. Et votre partenaire? Quelles sont les choses qui sont importantes dans son budget?

Modèle: 1. le loyer, 2. la voiture, etc.

Moi	**Mon partenaire**
1. ______________________	1. ______________________
2. ______________________	2. ______________________
3. ______________________	3. ______________________

D. Ecrivez dix phrases pour décrire vos habitudes financières. Est-ce que vous avez les mêmes tendances que votre partenaire? Est-ce que vos finances vous posent beaucoup de problèmes? Pourquoi ou pourquoi pas?

Exercice 3. Logique ou illogique?

	logique	illogique
1. Si on achète des choses en solde, on dépensera moins d'argent.	❑	❑
2. Si on est fauché(e), on pourra payer ses factures.	❑	❑
3. Si on reçoit un héritage, on n'aura plus besoin de travailler.	❑	❑
4. Si on est aisé(e), on voyagera beaucoup.	❑	❑
5. Si on va en France, on dépensera beaucoup d'euros.	❑	❑

Exercice 4. Madame Irma.

A. Madame Irma a prédit votre avenir. Décidez si vous pensez que ses prédictions seront vraies ou fausses.

		oui	non
1.	Quand vous aurez 30 ans, vous serez marié(e).	❑	❑
2.	Vous aurez des enfants dès que vous recevrez votre diplôme.	❑	❑
3.	Lorsque vous serez à la retraite, vous serez aisé(e).	❑	❑
4.	Dès que vous aurez un emploi, vous serez dépensier(-ière).	❑	❑
5.	Dans 20 ans vous irez souvent en France.	❑	❑
6.	En 2020, vous courrez un marathon.	❑	❑
7.	Quand vous aurez 40 ans, vous reviendrez à UT pour les matchs de football américain.	❑	❑
8.	Quand vous aurez 60 ans, vous vivrez au Texas.	❑	❑

B. A votre tour de prédire l'avenir. Ecrivez 3 prédictions sur votre partenaire:

1. ____________________
2. ____________________
3. ____________________

C. Etes-vous d'accord avec les prédictions de votre partenaire?

Exercice 5. Quand...

Complétez les phrases suivantes.

1. J'irai en France quand ____________________ .
2. Je serai heureux/heureuse dès que ____________________ .
3. ____________________ lorsque je serai riche.

Exercice 6. Cet été.

Traduisez le paragraphe suivant sur les étudiants du programme de Lyon.

The students will leave as soon as they take their final exams. When they arrive in Paris, they will visit many monuments and museums. After Paris they will go to Lyon and they will meet their families.

At home, please go to the Français interactif website. Read the following grammar points in Tex's French Grammar and complete all Texercises which you will turn in to your instructor.

13.1 Future: usage

See Tex for an explanation of the usage of the future.

Conjunctions which require future:

dès que, aussitôt que, lorsque, quand

Exercice 7. L'avenir de Pierre et sa copine Maria.

A. Pierre, le petit frère de Franck parle de son avenir avec sa copine. Lisez le dialogue suivant avec un partenaire.

Maria:	Tu sais, mes parents ont bien commencé les préparatifs pour fêter nos fiançailles. La soirée commencera avec un apéritif dans le jardin et puis mes parents inviteront tout le monde à table dans la salle à manger pour un dîner intime. Dès qu'on décidera le menu pour la soirée, ma mère fera le nécessaire pour tout acheter et…
Pierre:	Mais attends, attends. J'ai une meilleure idée, moi. Au lieu de se fiancer, tu ne préfères pas qu'on se pacse? Ce sera plus pratique et moins compliqué si jamais on décide de rompre ou…
Maria:	Mais ça va pas, non? J'ai déjà annoncé à toutes mes copines que nous nous marierons l'année prochaine et maintenant, tu…
Pierre:	Oh écoute! Même si nous serons fiancés en décembre, je n'ai jamais dit que je voulais me marier l'année prochaine!
Maria:	Oh les hommes! Vous ne comprenez rien! En tout cas, je ne me pacserai jamais! C'est le mariage ou rien. Si tu décides d'être plus raisonnable, on en parlera. Mais pour l'instant, je n'ai plus envie d'être avec toi! Je m'en vais.

B. Répondez aux questions que votre professeur vous pose.

1. ______________________________
2. ______________________________
3. ______________________________
4. ______________________________
5. ______________________________

Exercice 8. L'argent ou l'amour?

Décidez si les phrases suivantes correspondent à quelqu'un qui s'intéresse plus à **l'argent** ou à **l'amour**.

1. Mes parents veulent que je sorte avec quelqu'un qui est d'une famille aisée.
2. Je souhaite faire des économies. Ma copine est triste que je ne veuille pas me fiancer.
3. Je ne veux pas que mon copain me fasse de cadeaux! Je préfère qu'il m'écrive un poème de temps en temps.
4. Je suis surpris que ma colocataire trompe son copain. Il est riche!
5. Je suis heureuse que mon copain et moi vivions ensemble. Nous n'avons pas d'argent, mais on passe beaucoup de temps ensemble.

NOTE CULTURELLE

Le PACS

Le pacte civil de solidarité (PACS) est un contrat entre deux personnes majeures, de même sexes ou de sexes différents, pour organiser leur vie commune. Depuis sa création en France en novembre 1999, plus de 300 000 couples ont conclu un PACS, hétérosexuels comme homosexuels. Le concubinage est devenu officiel par le PACS. Comme les couples mariés, les couples qui se sont pacsés profitent des avantages fiscaux et légaux à cause de leur statut.

Exercice 9. Le monde de Tex.

Faites correspondre les phrases suivantes.

______1. Fiona s'est fiancée récemment.	a.	Il est urgent qu'il rembourse ses emprunts.
______2. Bette tombe souvent amoureuse.	b.	Il est necéssaire qu'ils achètent des vêtements en solde.
______3. Corey et Joe-Bob sont souvent fauchés.	c.	Ses amis sont surpris qu'elle ne fasse pas d'économies.
______4. Tex a des dettes.	d.	Tex et Tammy sont ravis qu'elle se marie cet été.
______5. Rita a besoin d'emprunter souvent de l'argent.	e.	Leurs amis ont peur qu'ils rompent.
______6. Tex a récemment trompé Tammy.	f.	Nous sommes étonnés qu'elle ne croie pas au coup de foudre.

Exercice 10. Vrai ou faux?

		vrai	faux
1.	Il est important que les étudiants fassent des économies.	❑	❑
2.	Il est essentiel qu'on vive ensemble avant de se marier.	❑	❑
3.	Mes parents ont peur que je n'aie pas les moyens de payer mes frais de scolarité.	❑	❑
4.	Il vaut mieux qu'on lise son horoscope tous les jours.	❑	❑
5.	Mes amis doutent que je trouve bientôt le grand amour.	❑	❑
6.	Le professeur est surpris que nous soyons fatigués aujourd'hui.	❑	❑
7.	Mes parents exigent que je parte en vacances avec eux.	❑	❑
8.	Le professeur ne pense pas que nous réussissions l'examen final.	❑	❑

Exercice 11. Qui le connaît le mieux?

A. Choisissez un(e) étudiant(e) dans la classe que tout le monde connaît assez bien. Cette personne va s'asseoir dans le couloir pendant que les autres étudiants font cet exercice

B. En groupes de 3 ou 4, écrivez le nom de cette personne dans le premier blanc. Puis, complétez chaque phrase.

1. Les étudiants dans la classe ont peur que ____________ sorte ________________ .
2. Il faut que ____________ soit ____ .
3. Il est impossible que ____________ ait ________________________________ .
4. Il ne faut pas que ____________ boive ________________________________ .
5. Nous sommes contents que ____________ puisse __________________________ .

C. Chaque groupe donne leurs phrases au professeur qui va lire les copies devant la classe et devant l'étudiant(e) qu'on a choisi de décrire. Si la personne répond "C'est vrai," le groupe qui a complété la phrase reçoit un point. Quel groupe connaît cette personne le mieux?

At home, please go to the Français interactif website. Read the following grammar points in Tex's French Grammar and complete all Texercises which you will turn in to your instructor.

13.2 Subjunctive usage: will, emotion, desire

Please refer to Tex for verbs and expressions of will, emotion, and desire, which require the subjunctive.

Exercice 12. Tex et ses amis.

Faites les correspondances logiques.

_____1. Les parents de Joe-Bob veulent que...
_____2. Joe-Bob est ravi que...
_____3. Mais il est triste de...
_____4. Tammy a peur que...
_____5. Tex souhaite que...
_____6. Bette est mécontente de...
_____7. Il est dommage que...
_____8. Il est bon de...

i. ...Tex sorte avec Bette.
j. ...pouvoir s'amuser avec ses amis.
k. ...Edouard fasse la cuisine pour lui ce soir.
l. ...ne pas être la copine de Tex.
m. ...Joe-Bob réussisse ses études et sa vie.
n. ...Joe-Bob boive du vin blanc avec du bœuf.
o. ...le semestre soit bientôt terminé.
p. ...devoir passer beaucoup d'examens à la fin du semestre.

Exercice 13. Les émotions et les désirs des autres.

Complétez les phrases suivantes.

1. Mes parents sont ravis que ______________________________ .
2. Ma mère a peur que ______________________________ .
3. Mon meilleur ami est surpris que ______________________________ .
4. Mes camarades de classe veulent que ______________________________ .
5. Mes amis souhaitent que ______________________________ .
6. Mes parents espèrent que ______________________________

(Attention: espérer n'exige pas le subjonctif!)

Exercice 14. Mes émotions et désirs.

1. Je suis ravi(e) que ______________________________.
2. J'ai peur de ______________________________.
3. Je suis surpris(e) que ______________________________.
4. Je veux ______________________________.
5. Je suis triste de ______________________________.

Exercice 15. Un peu de traduction.

Traduisez les phrases suivantes.

1. I'm surprised to be here. ______________________________ .
2. I'm surprised you are here. ______________________________ .
3. I want you to be happy. ______________________________ .
4. I want to be happy.______________________________ .
5. What do you want me to do? ______________________________ .
6. What do you want to do? ______________________________ .
7. I'm afraid that he's not here. ______________________________ .
8. I'm afraid to go to bed. ______________________________ .

Dictogloss 1. Cédric, le cousin de Franck.

A. Formez des groupes de 3 ou 4 personnes. Ecoutez le texte lu par votre professeur. Complétez les phrases suivantes et donnez le plus de détails possibles.

Cédric, le cousin de Franck, et sa copine sont venus à Austin pour faire leurs études à l'université du Texas

Cédric a quitté le lycée l'année dernière et il a du mal à s'adapter à la vie universitaire. D'abord, il veut que ses profs ______________________________ . De plus, il faut qu' il ________________tous les soirs, mais il a plutôt ____________________ avec ses copains.

Il a aussi des problèmes dans sa vie personnelle. Il est content que sa copine __________ à l'université, mais il doute qu' ______________________________ avec lui. Elle ne lui téléphone plus jamais, et elle n'est jamais chez elle. Il est triste qu' __ avec ses amis et pas avec lui.

Pour oublier tous ses problèmes, Cédric commence à sortir avec ses amis un peu. Ses copains veulent qu' ______________________________ à la sixième rue, mais Cédric déteste danser et boire. Il préfère qu' ________________ au restaurant ou au cinéma.

Comme il est tellement déprimé, il est possible que Cédric ________________ ses cours à l'université. Franck et ses parents ont peur qu' ________________ quitter l'université.

Et vous? Est-ce que vos parents sont contents (ou mécontents) que vous soyez à l'Université du Texas? Qu'est-ce qu'ils veulent que vous fassiez? (étudier plus, leur rendre visite plus souvent, devenir médecin, faire des économies, etc.) Est-ce qu'ils ont peur que vous ne réussissiez pas vos études? (que vous ne vous mariiez pas, que vous n'ayez jamais d'enfants, etc.) Soyez créatif/créative et imaginez leurs désirs et craintes! Ecrivez au moins 10 bonnes phrases!

NOTE CULTURELLE

Dating

En général, les jeunes Français sortent en groupe plus souvent qu'en couple. L'idée de 'dating' est un phénomène particulièrement américain.

At home, please go to the Français interactif website. Read the following grammar points in Tex's French Grammar and complete all Texercises which you will turn in to your instructor.

13.3 Conditional

The stem used to form the conditional is the same as the stem of the future (usually the infinitive).

The conditional endings are -ais, -ais, -ait, -ions, -iez, -aient (These are also the imperfect endings).

Exercice 16. Futur ou conditionnel?

Ecoutez et décidez si les phrases sont au futur ou au conditionnel.

	future	conditionnel
Modèle: Il ira en France. ______	√	❑
1. ______	❑	❑
2. ______	❑	❑
3. ______	❑	❑
4. ______	❑	❑
5. ______	❑	❑
6. ______	❑	❑

Exercice 17. Poli ou pas?

Ecoutez chaque phrase et décidez si c'est Joe-Bob qui parle (verbe au présent) ou Edouard (verbe au conditionnel). Ecoutez une deuxième fois et écrivez la phrase.

	Joe-Bob	Edouard
Modèle: Je veux un café. ______	√	❑
1. ______	❑	❑
2. ______	❑	❑
3. ______	❑	❑
4. ______	❑	❑
5. ______	❑	❑
6. ______	❑	❑

Exercice 18. La fin du semestre.

A. Complétez les phrases suivantes.

Pendant les vacances,

1. je voudrais (+ infinitif) ______
2. je voudrais que ______
3. le professeur aimerait (+ infinitif) ______
4. le professeur aimerait que ______
5. mes amis et moi devrions ______
6. je pourrais ______

B. Comparez vos réponses avec un partenaire.

Exercice 19. Si....

A. La loterie.

1. Si je gagnais à la loterie, j'irais ______________________.
2. Si je gagnais à la loterie, j'achèterais ______________________.
3. Si je gagnais à la loterie, je ne ferais plus de ______________________.
4. A votre tour ! Si je gagnais à la loterie, ______________________.

B. L'université.

1. Si nous pouvions changer l'université, les étudiants auraient ______________________
2. Si nous pouvions changer l'université, les profs seraient ______________________
3. Si nous pouvions changer l'université, les cours seraient ______________________
4. A votre tour ! Si nous pouvions changer l'université, ______________________

C. Comparez vos réponses avec la classe.

Exercice 20. Si il était millionnaire....

Qu'est-ce qu'il ferait si il était millionnaire?

A. Choisissez un(e) étudiant(e) dans la classe que tout le monde connaît assez bien. Cette personne va s'asseoir dans le couloir pendant que les autres étudiants font cet exercice.

B. En groupes de 3 ou 4, écrivez le nom de cette personne dans le premier blanc. Puis, complétez chaque phrase.

Si ______________________ (l'étudiant[e]) était millionnaire...

1. il/elle n'irait jamais ______________________.
2. il/elle n'achèterait jamais ______________________.
3. il/elle ne ferait jamais ______________________.
4. il/elle mangerait ______________________.
5. il/elle pourrait ______________________.

C. Chaque groupe donne ses phrases au professeur qui va lire les copies devant la classe et devant l'étudiant(e) qu'on a choisi de décrire. Si la personne répond "C'est vrai," le groupe qui a complété la phrase reçoit un point. Quel groupe connaît cette personne le mieux?

D. **Devoirs.** Et vous? Si vous étiez millionnaire, est-ce que vous feriez des économies? Est-ce que vous offririez des cadeaux à votre famille? Est-ce que vous partiriez pour la France? Ecrivez au moins 10 phrases pour décrire ce que vous feriez avec un million d'euros.

At home, please go to the Français interactif website. Read the following grammar points in Tex's French Grammar and complete all Texercises which you will turn in to your instructor.

13.4 Si clauses

You have already seen the use of si clauses in the present to express possible conditions:

• The conditional is used to express the result of a hypothetical situation in a si clause with a verb in the imparfait.

si + imparfait => conditional

Exercice 21. Portrait chinois…

En grouopes de 3, posez les questions suivantes à vos camarades de classe et notez leurs réponses. Qui vous ressemble le plus? Expliquez pourquoi.

1. Si tu étais un animal, quel animal serais-tu? ______________________
2. Si tu étais un fruit, quel fruit serais-tu ? ______________________
3. Si tu étais un sport, quel sport serais-tu?______________________
4. Si tu étais une fête française, quelle fête serais-tu ? ______________________
5. Si tu étais un meuble, quel meuble serais-tu ? ______________________
6. Si tu étais un genre de film, quel genre de film serais-tu ? ______________________
7. Si tu étais une matière scolaire, quelle matière serais-tu ? ______________________
8. Si tu étais une profession, quelle profession serais-tu?______________________

Exercice 22. Connaissez-vous bien votre partenaire ?

A. Complétez les phrases sur votre partenaire.

1. Si il/elle recevait un héritage, il/elle ______________________
2. Si il/elle ______________________ , il/elle serait satisfait(e) de sa vie.
3. Si il/elle ______________________, il/elle se mariera.
4. Il/elle rendra visite à ses parents, lorsqu'il/elle ______________________
5. Si il/elle dépasse son budget, ______________________
6. Si il/elle était radin(e), ______________________
7. Quand il/elle aura 60 ans, il/elle ______________________
8. Si son copain/sa copine ______________________, il/elle romprait.

B. Lisez votre phrase à votre partenaire. Comptez un point par bonne réponse. Soyez honnête! Qui connaît mieux l'autre?

Modèle:
→ Si tu gagnais à la loterie, tu irais en France.
- C'est vrai! Si je gagnais à la loterie, j'irais en France! (1 point)
- C'est faux! Si je gagnais à la loterie, j'irais aux Bahamas! (0 points)

Exercice 23. Vos parents.

A. Est-ce que vos parents sont contents que vous soyez à l'université? Complétez les phrases suivantes.

1. Mes parents sont contents que je ________________
2. Mes parents seraient contents, si je ________________
3. Mes parents seront contents, si je ________________
4. Mes parents seront contents quand je ________________
5. Mes parents seront contents dès que je ________________

B. Discutez vos réponses avec la classe.

Exercice 24. Traduction.

Traduisez les phrases suivantes.

1. If I finish my homework, we will go to the movies. ________________
2. As soon as I finish my homework, we will go to the movies. ________________
3. If she has enough money, she will travel to Europe. ________________
4. If she had enough money, she would travel to Europe. ________________
5. When she has enough money, she will travel to Europe. ________________
6. What do you want your friends to do? ________________
7. It is important for students to study. ________________
8. It is important to study. ________________

Exercice 25. Formes verbales: temps et modes

Ecoutez et choisissez le temps ou le mode des verbes suivants. (Choose the proper tense/mood for the verbs listed below in their infinitive forms.)

Modèle: Il vaut mieux que vous parliez français.

	présent	passé composé	imparfait	futur proche	futur simple	conditionnel	subjonctif	impératif
Modèle: parler	❑	❑	❑	❑	❑	❑	√	❑
1. avoir	❑	❑	❑	❑	❑	❑	❑	❑
2. aller	❑	❑	❑	❑	❑	❑	❑	❑
3. naître	❑	❑	❑	❑	❑	❑	❑	❑
4. habiter	❑	❑	❑	❑	❑	❑	❑	❑
5. visiter	❑	❑	❑	❑	❑	❑	❑	❑
6. aller	❑	❑	❑	❑	❑	❑	❑	❑
7. faire	❑	❑	❑	❑	❑	❑	❑	❑
8. pleuvoir	❑	❑	❑	❑	❑	❑	❑	❑

GLOSSAIRE

FRANÇAIS - ANGLAIS

à carreaux / une chemise à carreaux: plaid / plaid shirt, **10**
à fleurs / une robe à fleurs: floral (print), with flowers / floral print dress, **10**
à la mode: in fashion, **10**
abonnement: *m.* subscription, **9**
achat / faire des achats: *m.* purchase / to go shopping, **8**
acheter: to buy, **3**
acteur / actrice: *m / f.* actor / actress, **1, 9**
actif / active : active, **4**
actionnaire: *m, f.* shareholder, **13**
actions : *f pl,* , stocks, **13**
activité: *f.* activity, **2, 3**
actualité: *f.* current events, **9**
adjectif / adjectifs qui précèdent le nom : *m.* adjective / adjectives which precede the noun, **4**
administration économique et sociale: *f.* AES - public affairs, **11**
adorer: to adore, **2**
adverbe: *m.* adverb, **2**
aérobique / faire de l'aérobique: *f.* aerobics / to do aerobics, **10**
aéroport: *m.* airport, **6**
affaire / affaires: *f.* a business / business (in general), **12**
affiche: *f.* poster, **1**
africain(e): African, **2**
Afrique: *f.* Africa, **2**
âge: *m.* age, **2**
agent de voyage: *m.* travel agent, **12**
agréable: pleasant, **4**
ail: *m.* garlic, **5**
aimer: to like, to love, **2**
s'aimer: to love each other, **13**
album: *m.* album, **9**
alcoolisé(e) / boisson alcoolisée (f): alcoholic / alcoholic beverage, **5**
Algérie: *f.* Algeria , **2**
algérien(ne): Algerian, **2**
Allemagne: *f.* Germany, **2**
allemand: *m.* German, **11**
allemand(e): German, **2**
aller: to go, **3, 6**
aller à l'université: to go to the university, **3**
aller à pied: to go on foot, **6**
aller au cinéma: to go to the movies, **3**
aller au concert: to go to a concert, **3**
aller au parc: to go to the park, **3**
aller bien: to fit well, **10**
aller en boîte: to go to a nightclub, dance club, **3**
aller en cours: to attend class, **11**
aller en discothèque: to go to a nightclub, dance club, **3**
aller mal: to fit poorly, **10**
allergie: *f.* allergy, **10**
Allô...: Hello..., **9**
Alpes: *f pl,* Alps, **3**
alphabet: *m.* alphabet, **pré**
alphapage: *m.* pager, **9**
Alsace: *f.* Alsace, **3**
ambitieux / ambitieuse: ambitious, **4**
amener: to bring somebody (along), **3**
américain(e): American, **2**
Amérique: *f.* America, **2**
Amérique du Nord: *f.* North America, **2**
Amérique du Sud: *f.* South America, **2**
ami / amie: *m / f.* friend, **2**
amour / grand amour: *m.* love / the love of one's life, **13**
amour passion: *m.* infatuation-type love, **13**
amours: *m pl,* love life, **13**
amphithéâtre / amphi: *m.* amphitheater, **11**
amusant(e) / Il est amusant de: funny, amusing / It is fun (to)..., **4, 10**
s'amuser: to have, fun, **4, 8**
analyste-programmeur: *m.* analyst-programmer, **12**
ancien(ne): old, **8**
anglais: *m.* English, **pré, 11**
anglais(e): English, **2**
Angleterre: *f.* England, **2**
année: *f.* year, **1**
anniversaire / Bon (Joyeux) anniversaire!: *m.* birthday, anniversary / Happy Birthday!, **7**
anniversaire de mariage: *m.* wedding anniversary, **7**
annonceur / annonceuse: *m / f.* announcer, **9**
annuaire (téléphonique): *m.* phone book, **9**
anorak: *m.* parka, **10**
août: *m.* August, **1**
apéritif: *m.* cocktail (before dinner drink), **5**
appartement: *m.* apartment, **8**
apprendre: to learn, **5, 11**
apprendre à quelqu'un: to teach someone, **5**
après-midi: *m, f.* afternoon, **1**
architecte: *m.* architect, **1**
architecture: *f.* architecture, **11**
argent: *m.* money, **13**
Armistice, le 11 novembre: *m.* Armistice Day, **7**
armoire: *f.* armoire, **8**
arriver: to arrive, **6**
arrogant(e): arrogant, **4**
arrondissement: *m.* administrative district in a large city (e.g. Paris), **6**
art: *m.* art, **11**
artisan / artisane: *m / f.* craftsman, **12**
Ascension: *f.* Ascension Day, **7**
asiatique: Asian, **2**
Asie: *f.* Asia, **2**
asperge: *f.* asparagus, **5**
aspirateur / passer l'aspirateur: *m.* vacuum cleaner / to pass the vacuum cleaner, **8**
assez de: enough, **5**
assiette / une assiette de: *f.* plate / a plate of, a plateful, **5**
assistante sociale: *f.* social worker, **12**
assister (à): to attend, **11**
Assomption, le 15 août: *f.* feast of the Assumption, **7**
assurance: *f.* insurance, **13**
attendre: to wait for, **6**
Au revoir: Goodbye, **1**
aubergine: *f.* eggplant, **5**

auditeur / auditrice: *m / f.* listener, **9**
aujourd'hui: today, **1**
aussi: also, **2**
Australie: *f.* Australia, **2**
australien(ne): Australian, **2**
automne / en automne: *m.* fall / in the fall, **3**
autre: other, **4, 6**
avantages sociaux: *m pl*, benefits (health insurance, retirement plan, etc.), **12**
avare: miserly, **13**
avenue: *f.* avenue, **6**
avion / en avion: *m.* plane / by plane, **3**
avocat / avocate: *m / f.* lawyer, **12**
avoir: to have, **2**
avoir besoin de: to need, **2**
avoir envie de: to feel like (to want to), **2**
avoir faim: to be, hungry, **5**
avoir l'intention de: to intend (to), **2**
avoir la moyenne: to receive a passing grade, **11**
avoir les moyens de: to have the means to **13**
avoir mal à / (avoir mal à la tête, au dos, aux pieds, etc): to hurt (body part) / (to have a headache, a backache, sore feet, etc), **10**
avoir soif: to be, thirsty, **5**
avril / premier avril : *m.* April / April Fool's Day, **1, 7**
baccalauréat / bac: *m.* baccalaureate exam, **11**
bachelier / bachelière: *m / f.* student who has passed the bac , **11**
baguette: *f.* baguette, **5**
baignoire: *f.* bathtub, **8**
Balance: *f.* Libra, **13**
balcon: *m.* balcony, **8**
banane: *f.* banana, **5**
bande-dessinée: *f.* comic strip, **9**
banlieue: *f.* suburbs, **6**
banque: *f.* bank, **6, 13**
banquier / banquière: *m / f.* banker, **12**
basket: *m.* basketball, **2**
baskets: *f pl*, basketball shoes, **10**
bateau / en bateau: *m.* boat / by boat, **3**
bâtiment: *m.* building, **6**
beau / bel / belle: beautiful, **4**
beau / Il fait beau.: nice (weather) / It's nice (weather)., **3**
beaucoup / beaucoup de: a lot / a lot (of), **2, 5**
belge: Belgian, **2**
Belgique: *f.* Belgium, **2**
Bélier: *m.* Aries, **13**
beurre: *m.* butter, **5**
bibliothèque: *f.* library, **6, 11**
bicyclette: *f.* bicycle, bike, **3**
bientôt / à bientôt: soon / see you soon, **1**
bière: *f.* beer, **5**
biologie: *f.* biology, **pré, 11**
blague: *f.* joke, **7**
blanc / blanche: white, **4**
bleu(e): blue, **4**
blond / blonde: blond, **4**
blouson: *m.* short jacket, leather jacket, **10**
boeuf: *m.* beef, **5**
boire: to drink, **5**
boisson / boisson non-alcoolisée / boisson alcoolisée: *f.* drink, beverage / non-alcoholic beverage / alcoholic beverage, **5**
boîte / une boîte de: *f.* can / a can of, **5**
boîte [slang]: *f.* firm, business, **12**
boîte aux lettres: *f.* mailbox, **6**
boîte de nuit: *f.* nightclub, dance club, **3, 6**
bol / un bol de: *m.* bowl / a bowl of, a bowlful, **5**
Bon (Joyeux) anniversaire!: Happy Birthday!, **7**
bon / bonne: good, **4**
Bon appétit!: have a nice meal!, **5**
bon marché: inexpensive, **13**
Bonjour: Good day (Hello), **1**
Bonne Année!: Happy New Year!, **7**
Bonne fête!: Happy Saint's Day!, **7**
Bonsoir: Good evening, **1**
botte: *f.* boot, **10**
bouche: *f.* mouth, **4, 10**
boucher / chez le boucher: *m.* butcher / at the butcher's, **5**
boucherie / à la boucherie: *f.* butcher shop / at the butcher shop, **5, 6**
bouclé(e): curly, **4**
bougie: *f.* candle, **7**
boulanger / boulangère / chez le boulanger: *m / f.* baker / at the baker's, **5, 12**
boulangerie: *f.* bakery, **6**
boulangerie-pâtisserie / à la boulangerie-pâtisserie: *f.* bakery-pastry shop / at the bakery-pastry shop, **5**
boulevard: *m.* boulevard, **6**
boulot [slang]: *m.* job, **12**
bourguignon (ne): from Burgundy, **5**
Bourgogne: *f.* Burgundy, **3**
bourse / bourse (de Paris): *f.* stock market / (Paris) stock market, **13**
bout / au bout (de): *m.* end / at the far end (of), **6**
bouteille / une bouteille de: *f.* bottle / a bottle of, **5**
boutique: *f.* boutique, **6**
branché(e): in fashion, **10**
bras: *m.* arm, **10**
Bretagne: *f.* Brittany, **3**
bricoler: to make, home repairs or improvements, **8**
brioche: *f.* brioche, **5**
se brosser les cheveux: to brush your hair, **4**
se brosser les dents: to brush your teeth, **4**
brouillard / Il y a du brouillard. : *m.* fog / It's foggy., **3**
brun / brune: brown (hair), brunette, **4**
bûche de Noël: *f.* Yule log (also a cake in the shape of a Yule log), **7**
budget / faire un budget / dépasser son budget: *m.* budget / to establish a budget / to go beyond one's budget, **13**
buffet: *m.* hutch, buffet, **8**
bulletin de notes: *m.* grade report, **11**
bureau / sur le bureau: *m.* desk, office / on the desk, **1, 6, 8, 12**
bureau de poste: *m.* post office, **6**
bureau de tabac: *m.* tobacco shop, **6**
bus / en bus: *m.* bus / by bus, **3**
cabine téléphonique: *f.* phone booth, telephone booth, **6, 9**

cadeau: *m.* gift, **7**
cadre: *m.* executive, **12**
cafard: *m.* cockroach, **pré**
café / au café: *m.* coffee, café / at the café, **5, 6**
cafétéria: *f.* cafeteria, **11**
cahier: *m.* notebook, **1**
caisse d'épargne: *f.* savings and loan association, **13**
caissier / caissière : *m / f.* cashier, **12**
calendrier / calendrier français : *m.* calendar / French calendar, **1, 7**
calme : calm, **4**
camarade: *m, f.* friend, **2**
campagne: *f.* country, **3**
Canada: *m.* Canada, **2**
canadien(ne): Canadian, **2**
canapé: *m.* couch, **8**
canard: *m.* duck, **5**
Cancer: *m.* Cancer, **13**
canoë / faire du canoë: *m.* canoeing / to go canoeing, **10**
Capricorne: *m.* Capricorn, **13**
car / en car: *m.* tour bus / by tour bus (from city to city), **3**
cardinal / cardinale / cardinaux / cardinales: cardinal, **1**
Carnaval (Mardi Gras): *m.* Mardi Gras, Carnival, **7**
carotte: *f.* carrot, **5**
carré(e): square, **4**
carrefour / au carrefour (de): *m.* intersection / at the intersection of, **6**
carrière: *f.* career, **12**
carte (du monde) / jouer aux cartes: *f.* card, map (of the world) / to play cards, **1, 2**
carte d'étudiant: *f.* student ID card, **11**
carte de voeux: *f.* greeting card, **7**
carte postale virtuelle: *f.* virtual postcard, **9**
carte téléphonique: *f.* phone card, **9**
casquette: *f.* cap, **10**
cathédrale: *f.* cathedral, **3, 6**
cave: *f.* cellar, wine cellar, **8**
cédérom / CD-rom: *m.* CD-rom, **9**
ceinture: *f.* belt, **10**
célèbre: famous, **9**
célébrer: to celebrate, **7**
célébrité: *f.* celebrity, **9**
cent / deux cents: hundred (one hundred) / two hundred, **3**
centre / au centre: *m.* center / in the center, **3, 6**
centre commercial: *m.* shopping center, mall, **6, 10**
centre-ville: *m.* downtown, **6**
céréales: *f pl*, cereal, **5**
cérémonie: *f.* ceremony, **7**
cerise: *f.* cherry, **5**
chaîne: *f.* channel, **9**
chaîne-stéréo: *f.* stereo, **8**
chaise: *f.* chair, **1, 8**
chambre / dans la chambre...: *f.* bedroom / in the bedroom…, **8**
champagne: *m.* champagne, **5, 7**
champignon: *m.* mushroom, **5**
Chandeleur, le 2 février: *f.* Candlemas, **7**
changer: to change, **3**
chanson: *f.* song, **9**
chanter: to sing, **2, 9**
chanteur / chanteuse: *m / f.* singer, **1, 9**
chapeau: *m.* hat, **10**
chapitre: *m.* chapter,
charcuterie / à la charcuterie: *f.* pork butcher shop, delicatessen / at the pork butcher shop/delicatessen , **5, 6**
charcutier / charcutière / chez le charcutier: *m / f.* pork butcher / at the pork butcher's, **5**
chargé(e): full/busy (referring to schedule), **11**
chat / chatte: *m / f.* cat, **pré**
châtain (invariable): light brown, chestnut, **4**
château: *m.* castle, **3**
chaud(e) / Il fait chaud.: hot / It's hot (weather)., **3**
chaussette: *f.* sock, **10**
chaussure: *f.* shoe, **10**
chef d'entreprise: *m.* company head, business owner, **12**
chemise: *f.* man's shirt, **10**
chemisier: *m.* blouse, **10**
cher / chère: expensive, dear, **13**
chercher: to look for, **2**
chercher une situation: to look for a job, **12**
chercheur: *m.* researcher, **12**
cheveux / se brosser les cheveux / De quelle couleur sont vos cheveux?: *m pl*, hair / to brush your hair / What color is your hair?, **4**
cheville: *f.* ankle, **10**
chez: at someone's house, **6**
chimie: *f.* chemistry, **pré, 11**
Chine: *f.* China, **2**
chinois: *m.* Chinese, **11**
chinois(e): Chinese, **2**
choisir: to choose, **5**
chômage: *m.* unemployment, **12**
chômeur / chômeuse: *m / f.* unemployed person, **12**
chou: *m.* cabbage, **5**
cicatrice: *f.* scar, **4**
cinéma / aller au cinéma: *m.* movie theater, cinema / to go to the movies, **3, 6, 9**
cinq: five, **1**
cinquante: fifty, **1**
cinquième: fifth, **6**
citron: *m.* lemon, **5**
clair(e): bright, full of light, **8**
classe / en classe / la salle de classe: *f.* class / in class / classroom, **1**
clavier: *m.* keyboard, **9**
client / cliente: *m / f.* client, customer, **12**
cliquer: to click, **9**
coca-cola: *m.* cola, **5**
coiffeur / coiffeuse: *m / f.* hair dresser, **1, 12**
coiffure / Comment est-il coiffé?: *f.* hairstyle / What is his hair like?, **4**
coin / au coin (de): *m.* corner / at the corner of, **6**
collège: *m.* junior high, middle school, **6, 11**
comédie: *f.* comedy (movie, play), **9**
comédie musicale: *f.* musical comedy, **9**
comique: funny, **9**
commander / au café, on commande…: to order / at the café, you order…, **5**

comment: how, **2**
commerçant / commerçante: *m / f.* shopkeeper, store owner, **12**
commerce / petits commerces: *m.* business, trade / small businesses, **pré, 6**
commode: *f.* chest of drawers, **8**
communication: *f.* communications (subject matter), **11**
communications: *f pl*, communications, **9**
compétitif / compétitive: competitive, **4**
comprendre: to understand, **1, 5, 11**
comptabilité: *m / f.* accounting, **pré, 11**
comptable: *m.* accountant, **12**
compte (bancaire): *m.* account, (bank) account, **13**
concert / aller au concert: *m.* concert / to go to a concert, **3, 9**
concombre: *m.* cucumber, **5**
concours (d'entrée): *m.* competitive entrance exam, **11**
concubinage: *m.* living together out of wedlock, **13**
confortable: comfortable, **8**
congé: *m.* vacation day, **12**
congélateur: *m.* freezer, **8**
continent: *m.* continent, **2**
continuer: to continue, **6**
contrôle: *m.* test, exam, **11**
copain / copine: *m / f.* friend; boyfriend / girlfriend, **2**
copie: *f.* student paper, **11**
coq au vin: *m.* chicken (rooster) stewed in red wine, **5**
corps (invariable): *m.* body, **10**
corriger: to correct, **11**
corsaire: *m.* crop pants, **10**
Corse: *f.* Corsica, **3**
costume: *m.* costume / man's suit, **7, 10**
côté / à côté (de): *m.* side / beside, next to **6**
côte / sur la côte: *f.* coast / on the coast, **3**
Côte d'Azur: *f.* the Riviera, **3**
côtelette / une côtelette de porc: *f.* cutlet, chop / a pork chop, **5**
cou: *m.* neck, **4, 10**
se coucher: to go to bed, **4**
coude: *m.* elbow, **10**
couleur: *f.* color, **4**
couloir: *m.* hallway, **8**
coup de foudre: *m.* love at first sight, **13**
couple: *m.* couple, **13**
courgette: *f.* zucchini, **5**
courrier électronique: *m.* e-mail, **9**
cours (invariable) / cours (de maths…) / aller en cours: *m.* class, course / class (math class…) / to attend class, **11**
cours magistral / des cours magistraux: *m.* large lecture class, **11**
course / faire des courses: *f.* errand / to do errands, **8**
course à pied / faire de la course à pied: *f.* running / to go running, **10**
court(e): short, **4**
couteau / un couteau de: *m.* knife / a knife of, a knifeful, **5**
coûter: to cost, **13**
coutume: *f.* custom, **7**
couturier / couturière: *m / f.* fashion designer, seamstress, **12**
craie: *f.* chalk, **1**
cravate: *f.* tie, **10**
crayon: *m.* pencil, **1**
créatif / créative : creative, **4**
crème brûlée: *f.* crème brûlée, **5**
crème caramel: *f.* caramel custard, **5**
crêpe: *f.* crepe, **7**
critique (de films, d'art, etc.): *m, f.* critic (film, art, etc.), **12**
croire: to believe, **5**
croissant: *m.* croissant, **5**
croque-madame: *m.* croque -monsieur with a fried egg, **5**
croque-monsieur: *m.* toasted cheese sandwich with ham, **5**
crudités: *f.pl*, raw vegetables with vinaigrette, **5**
cuillère / une cuillère de: *f.* spoon / a spoonful of, **5**
cuisine / dans la cuisine / faire la cuisine: *f.* kitchen, cooking / in the kitchen / to cook, **5, 8**
cuisinier / cuisinière: *m / f.* cook, **12**
cuisinière: *f.* stove, **8**
curieux / curieuse: curious, **4**
curriculum vitae (CV): *m.* résumé, **12**
cyclisme / faire du cyclisme: *m.* cycling / to go cycling, **10**
danser: to dance, **2**
date / Quelle est la date?: *f.* date / What's the date?, **1**
débrouillard(e): resourceful, **4**
décembre: *m.* December, **1**
décontracté(e): casual, **10**
se décourager: to be discouraged, **11**
décrocher: to pick up/answer (the phone), **9**
défilé (militaire): *m.* parade, (military) parade, **7**
défilé de mode: *m.* fashion show, **10**
déjeuner: *m.* lunch, **5**
déjeuner: to have lunch, **5**
délicieux / délicieuse: delicious, **5**
demain / à demain: tomorrow / see you tomorrow, **1**
demande d'emploi / faire une demande d'emploi: *f.* job application / to apply for a job, **12**
demander: to ask (for), **6**
déménager: to move (change residences), **8**
dépenses : expenses, **13**
démodé(e): out of style, **10**
dent / dents / se brosser les dents: *f.* tooth / teeth / to brush your teeth, **4**
dentiste: *m, f.* dentist, **1, 12**
dépasser son budget: to go beyond one's budget, **13**
se dépêcher: to hurry, **4, 8**
dépenser: to spend, **13**
dépensier / dépensière: *m / f.* spendthrift, **13**
se déplacer (en ville): to get around (town), **6**
dernier / dernière: last, **1, 11**
derrière: behind, **6**
derrière: *m.* rear, behind, **10**
désagréable: unpleasant, **4**
descendre: to go down, to go downstairs, **6**
désordre / en désordre: *m.* disorderliness / messy, **8**
dessert: *m.* dessert, **5**
dessin: *m.* drawing, design, **11**

dessin animé: *m.* cartoon, **9**
se détendre: to relax, **10**
détester: to detest, **2**
deux: two, **1**
deuxième: second, **6**
devant: in front of, **6**
devoirs: *m pl*, homework, **1, 11**
dialoguer en direct: to chat on-line, **9**
dictionnaire: *m.* dictionary, **1**
difficile / Il est difficile de: difficult / It is difficult (to)..., **10**
dimanche: *m.* Sunday, **1**
dinde: *f.* turkey, **5**
dîner: *m.* dinner, supper, **5**
dîner: to have dinner, **5**
diplôme: *m.* diploma, degree, **11**
discipliné(e): disciplined, **10**
disc-jockey / DJ: *m.* dee-jay, **9**
discothèque: *f.* dance club, disco, nightclub, **3, 6**
se disputer: to argue (with one another), **8**
distributeur (automatique de billets): *m.* ATM (automatic teller machine), **13**
divorcer: to divorce, to get divorced, **13**
dix: ten, **1**
dix-huit: eighteen, **1**
dix-huitième: eighteenth, **6**
dixième: tenth, **6**
dix-neuf: nineteen, **1**
dix-neuvième: nineteenth, **6**
dix-sept: seventeen, **1**
dix-septième: seventeenth, **6**
DJ / disc-jockey: *m.* dee-jay, **9**
documentaire: *m.* documentary, **9**
doigt: *m.* finger, **10**
donner: to give, **7**
dormir: to sleep, **3**
dos: *m.* back, **10**
douche: *f.* shower, **8**
douzaine / une douzaine d'oeufs: *f.* dozen / a dozen eggs, **5**
douze: twelve, **1**
douzième: twelfth, **6**
draguer: to try to pick up, to hit on, to flirt, **13**
drame: *m.* drama, **9**
droit: *m.* law, **11**
droit(e) / à droite (de), sur votre droite / tout droit: right / on the right / straight ahead, **6**
drôle: funny, **4**
dur(e): hard, tough, **12**
durer: to last, **9**
dynamique: dynamic, **12**
eau / eau minérale: *f.* water / mineral water, **5**
échecs / jouer aux échecs: *m pl*, chess / to play chess, **10**
école: *f.* school, **6**
Ecole de commerce: *f.* business school, **11**
e-commerce: *m.* e-commerce, **9**
économe: economical, frugal, **13**
économie: *f.* economics, **11**
écouter: to listen to…, **2**
écouter en direct: to listen to a live broadcast, **9**
écran: *m.* monitor, **9**
écrivain: *m.* writer, **12**
écureuil: *m.* squirrel, **pré**
église: *f.* church, **6**
égoïste: selfish, **4**
email : *m.* e-mail, **9**
embaucher / être embauché(e): to hire / to be hired, **12**
embrasser : to kiss, **2**
s'embrasser: to kiss each other, **13**
émission: *f.* show, **9**
émission de variétés: *f.* variety show, **9**
emmener: to take somebody (along), **3**
emploi: *m.* job, **12**
emploi du temps: *m.* schedule, **11**
employé / employée (de bureau): *m / f.* employee (office employee), **12**
emprunt-étudiant : *m.* student loan, **13**
emprunt-logement: *m.* mortgage, **13**
enfant: *m, f.* child, **2**
en-ligne: online, **9**
s'ennuyer: to be, bored, **4, 8**
ennuyeux / ennuyeuse: boring, **4, 9**
enseignant: *m.* teacher, **12**
entendre: to hear, **6**
s'entendre: to get along (with one another), **8**
enthousiaste: enthusiastic, **4**
entrée: *f.* first course, **5**, entranceway, **8**
entreprise: *f.* firm, business, **12**
entrer: to enter, **6**
entretien: *m.* interview, **12**
épice: *f.* spice, **5**
épicé(e): spicy, **5**
épicerie / à l'épicerie: *f.* grocery store / at the grocery store, **5, 6**
épicier / épicière / chez l'épicier : *m / f.* grocer / at the grocer's, **5**
épinard: *m.* spinach, **5**
EPS (éducation physique et sportive) : *f.* physical education, **11**
escalade / faire de l'escalade: *f.* rock-climbing / to go rock-climbling, **10**
escalier: *m.* staircase, stairs, **8**
escargot: *m.* snail, **pré**
Espagne: *f.* Spain, **2**
espagnol: *m.* Spanish, **pré, 11**
espagnol(e): Spanish, **2**
espérer: to hope, **3**
essayer: to try, **3**
essentiel / essentielle / Il est essentiel de: essential / It is essential (to), **10**
est / dans l'est, à l'est: *m.* east / in the east, **3**
étagère: *f.* bookcase, **8**
Etats Unis: *m pl*, United States, **2**
été / en été: *m.* summer / in the summer, **3**
étranger / étrangère: foreign, **9**
être accro à (l'internet, à la télé…)[slang]: to be, addicted, to have a habit, **9**
être au régime: to be on a diet, **10**
être bon(ne) en: to be good in/at, **11**
être de bonne humeur : to be in a good mood, **4**
être de mauvaise humeur: to be in a bad mood, **4**
être embauché(e): to be hired, **12**

être en forme: to be in shape, **10**
être en solde: to be on sale, **13**
être fauché(e) [slang]: to be broke, **13**
être licencié(e): to be laid off, **12**
être mauvais(e) en: to be bad in/at, **11**
être mis(e) à la porte: to be fired, **12**
être muté(e): to be transferred, **12**
être nul(le) en [slang]: to to suck in/at [slang], **11**
étude / études secondaires / études supérieures: *f.* study / high school studies / university studies, **11**
étudiant / étudiante / Je suis étudiant(e) en... (français, maths, etc.): *m / f.* student / I am a student in...(French, math, etc.), **pré**
étudier: to study, **2**
euro: *m.* euro (currency), **13**
Europe: *f.* Europe, **2**
européen(ne): European, **2**
évier: *m.* sink, **8**
examen: *m.* test, exam, **1, 11**
exercice: *m.* exercise, **1**
exposé oral: *m.* paper / presentation, **11**
exposition: *f.* exhibition, show, **3**
expression / expressions de quantité: *f.* expression / expressions of quantity, **5**
expression impersonnelle: *f.* impersonal expression, **10**
fac: *f.* college, university, **11**
face / en face (de): *f.* side, face / facing, opposite, **6**
se fâcher: to get, angry, **4, 8**
facile / Il est facile de: easy / It is easy (to)..., **10**
facteur: *m.* mail carrier, **12**
facture / facture de téléphone: *f.* bill / telephone bill, **13**
Faculté de droit: *f.* law school, **11**
Faculté de médecine: *f.* school of medicine, **11**
Faculté de pharmacie: *f.* school of pharmacy, **11**
Faculté des Beaux-Arts: *f.* school of fine arts, **11**
Faculté des lettres et des sciences humaines: *f.* school of humanities/liberal arts, **11**
Faculté des sciences: *f.* school of sciences, **11**
faire de l'aérobique: to do, aerobics, **10**
faire de l'escalade: to go, rock-climbling, **10**
faire de la bicyclette: to go, bicycle riding, **3**
faire de la course à pied: to go, running, **10**
faire de la musculation: to train with weights, **10**
faire de la natation: to go, swimming, **10**
faire de la peinture: to paint (art), **10**
faire de la planche à voile: to go, windsurfing, sailboarding, **3, 10**
faire de la randonnée: to go, hiking, **10**
faire de la voile: to go, sailing, **3**
faire des achats: to go, shopping, **8**
faire des courses: to do, errands, **8**
faire des économies: to save money, **13**
faire des progrès: to improve, **11**
faire des randonnées: to go, hiking, **3**
faire du bateau: to go, boating, **3**
faire du canoë: to go, canoeing, **10**
faire du cyclisme: to go, cycling, **10**
faire du footing: to go, running, **10**
faire du kayak: to go , kayaking, **10**
faire du roller: to go , roller blading, **10**
faire du ski: to go, skiing, **3, 10**
faire du sport: to exercise, **10**
faire du vélo: to go, cycling, **3**
faire la cuisine: to cook, **5, 8**
faire la fête: to party, **7**
faire la lessive: to do laundry, **8**
faire la vaisselle: to do the dishes, **5, 8**
faire le lit: to make the bed, **8**
faire le marché: to do the grocery shopping, **5, 8**
faire le ménage: to do housework, **8**
faire le pont: literally 'to make a bridge' - The French often take an extra day off from work when a holiday falls on Tuesday or Thursday. If the holiday falls on Tuesday, they take Monday off, and if the holiday falls on Thursday, they take Friday off thus, **7**
faire ses devoirs: to do one's homework, **11**
faire un budget: to establish a budget, **13**
faire un don: to make a donation, **13**
faire un effort: to make an effort, **11**
faire un poisson d'avril: to play a joke (on someone), **7**
faire un régime: to be on a diet, **5, 10**
faire une demande d'emploi: to apply for a job, **12**
faire une promenade: to go for a, walk, to take a walk, **3, 10**
falloir / Il faut + infinitive: to be, necessary, must, have to (obligation) / It is necessary (to), **10**
famille: *f.* family, **2**
famille étendue: *f.* extended family, **2**
fatigant(e) / Il est fatigant de: tiring, annoying / It is tiring/annoying (to)..., **10**
fauteuil: *m.* armchair, **8**
femme: *f.* woman, wife, **2**
femme au foyer: *f.* housewife, **12**
fenêtre: *f.* window, **1, 8**
fesses: *f pl*, buttocks, **10**
fête / fêtes / Bonne fête!: *f.* saint's day, celebration, party / holidays / Happy Saint's Day!, **7**
fête des mères: *f.* Mother's Day, **7**
fête des pères: *f.* Father's Day, **7**
fête du Travail, le 1er mai: *f.* Labor Day, **7**
fête nationale, le 14 juillet: *f.* Bastille Day, French National Day, **7**
fêter: to celebrate, **7**
feuilleton: *m.* series, **9**
feux d'artifice: *m pl*, fireworks, **7**
février: *m.* February, **1**
fiançailles : *pl*, engagement, **13**
fiancé / fiancée: *m / f.* fiancé / fiancée, **2**
se fiancer: to get engaged, **13**
fiche d'identité: *f.* identification form, **2**
fille: *f.* daughter, **2**
fille unique: *f.* only child (female), **2**
film: *m.* movie, **9**
film d'amour: *m.* romantic movie, **9**
film d'aventures: *m.* adventure movie, **9**
film d'épouvante: *m.* horror movie, **9**
film d'action: *m.* action film, **9**
film de science-fiction: *m.* science-fiction movie, **9**
film d'horreur: *m.* horror movie, **9**
film policier: *m.* detective/police movie, **9**
fils: *m.* son, **2**

fils unique: *m.* only child (male), **2**
finances: *f pl*, finances, **13**
finir: to finish, **5**
fleuve: *m.* major river (that flows to the sea), **3, 6**
fonctionnaire: *m, f.* civil servant, government worker, **12**
fondant au chocolat: *m.* rich chocolate flourless cake, **5**
football: *m.* soccer, **2**
footing / faire du footing: *m.* running / to go running, **2, 10**
forêt: *f.* forest, **3**
formation: *f.* education, training, **12**
forme / Quelle est la forme de son visage?: *f.* form, shape, fitness / What's the shape of his face?, **4, 10**
formulaire: *m.* form, **12**
forum: *m.* bulletin board, newsgroup, **9**
fou / folle : crazy, **4**
four: *m.* oven, **8**
four à micro-ondes: *m.* microwave, **8**
fourchette / une forchette de: *f.* fork / a forkful of, **5**
fourmi: *f.* ant, **pré**
frais: *m pl*, fees, **13**
frais / fraîche: fresh, **5**
frais / Il fait frais.: cool (weather) / It's cool (weather)., **3**
frais de crèche: *m pl*, child-care expenses, **13**
frais de garderie: *m pl*, child-care expenses, **13**
frais de scolarité: *m pl*, tuition, education expenses, **13**
fraise: *f.* strawberry, **5**
framboise: *f.* raspberry, **5**
franc: *m.* franc (currency), **13**
franc / franche : frank, **4**
français: *m.* French, **pré, 11**
français(e): French, **2**
France: *f.* France, **2**
frère: *m.* brother, **2**
frigo: *m.* fridge, **8**
froid(e) / Il fait froid.: cold / It's cold (weather)., **3**
fromage: *m.* cheese, **5**
front: *m.* forehead, **4**
fruit: *m.* fruit, **5**
fumer: to smoke, **10**
gagner / gagner sa vie / gagner de l'argent: to earn, to win / to earn a living / to earn money, **12**
garage: *m.* garage, **8**
gare: *f.* train station, **6**
Garonne: *f.* Garonne (river), **3**
gaspiller: to waste, **13**
gâteau / gâteau au chocolat: *m.* cake / chocolate cake, **5, 7**
gauche / à gauche (de), sur votre gauche: left / on the left, **6**
Gémeaux: *m pl*, Gemini, **13**
généreux / généreuse: generous, **4, 13**
genou: *m.* knee, **10**
gens: *m pl,* people, **4**
gentil / gentille: kind, nice, **4**
géographie: *f.* geography, **pré, 3, 11**
gérer: to manage, direct, organize, **12**
gestion: *f.* management, **12**
gilet: *m.* button-up sweater, **10**
glace: *f.* ice cream, **5**
golf: *m.* golf, **2**
gorge: *f.* throat, **10**
goûter: *m.* snack, **5**
gramme / 50 grammes de: *m.* gram / 50 grams of , **5**
grand amour: *m,* the, love of one's life, **13**
grand(e): tall, big, **4**
grande école: *f.* elite professional school, **11**
grandir: to grow up, **5**
grand-mère: *f.* grandmother, **2**
grand-père: *m.* grandfather, **2**
grands-parents: *m pl*, grandparents, **2**
gratuit(e): free, **9**
grenier: *m.* attic, **8**
grillé(e): grilled, **5**
grippe: *f.* the flu, **10**
gris(e): gray, **4**
gros / grosse : big, fat, **4**
grossir: to gain weight, **5, 10**
gui: *m.* mistletoe, **7**
guitare / jouer de la guitare: *f.* guitar / to play the guitar, **2**
guyanais(e) : Guyanese, **2**
Guyane française: *f.* French Guyana, **2**
habillé(e): dressy, **10**
s' habiller: to dress (oneself), to get dressed, **4, 10**
habiter: to live, **2**
haché(e): chopped, **5**
hall d'entrée: *m.* foyer, **8**
Halloween: Halloween, **7**
Hanouka: Hannukah, **7**
haricot vert*: *m.* green bean, **5**
héritage: *m.* inheritance, **13**
heure / l'heure officielle: *f.* time (the), hour / official time, **2**
heureux / heureuse : happy, **4**
Hexagone: *m.* France, **3**
hip-hop: *m.* hip-hop, **2**
histoire: *f.* history, **pré, 11**
hiver / en hiver: *m.* winter / in the winter, **3**
homme: *m.* man, **2**
honnête: honest, **4, 12**
hôpital: *m.* hospital , **6**
horoscope: *m.* horoscope, **13**
hôtel: *m.* hotel, **6**
hôtel de ville : *m.* city hall, mayor's office, **6**
huile: *f.* oil, **5**
huit: eight, **1**
huitième: eighth, **6**
humeur / être de bonne humeur / être de mauvaise humeur: *f.* mood, humor / to be in a good mood / to be in a bad mood, **4**
hypocrite: hypocritical, **4**
idéaliste: idealistic, **4**
Il y a: There is, there are…, **1**
Ile de France (la région parisienne): *f.* Ile de France (Parisian region), **3**
immeuble: *m.* apartment building, **6**
imperméable: *m.* raincoat, **10**
important(e) / Il est important de: important / It is important (to), **10**

impôt / payer des impôts: *m.* tax / to pay taxes, **12, 13**
incapable: incapable, incompetent, **4**
indices (i.e., le CAC 40): *m pl*, indices (i.e., DJIA, NASDAQ), **13**
indifférent(e): indifferent, **4**
indispensable / Il est indispensable de: essential / It is essential (to), **10**
infirmier / infirmière: *m / f.* nurse, **12**
informaticien / informaticienne: *m / f.* computer scientist, **12**
informations: *f pl*, news, **9**
informatique: *f.* computer science, **pré, 11**
ingénieur: *m.* engineer, **1, 12**
s' inquiéter: to worry, **8**
s' inscrire (à la fac, au ciné-club…): to register/enroll (in college, in the film club...), **11**
instituteur / institutrice: *m / f.* teacher (elementary school), **12**
intelligent(e): intelligent, **4**
intéressant(e): interesting, **4**
internaute: *m.* internet user, **9**
internet: *m.* internet, **9**
interrogatif / interrogative: interrogative, **2**
inutile: useless, **12**
inviter: to invite, **7**
Italie: *f.* Italy, **2**
italien: *m.* Italian, **11**
italien(ne): Italian, **2**
jambe: *f.* leg, **10**
jambon: *m.* ham, **5**
janvier: *m.* January, **1**
Japon: *m.* Japan, **2**
japonais(e): Japanese, **2**
jardin / jardin public: *m.* garden, yard / park, large garden, **6, 8**
jaune: yellow, **4**
jazz: *m.* jazz, **2**
jean: *m.* jeans, **10**
jeu télévisé: *m.* game show, **9**
jeudi: *m.* Thursday, **1**
jeune: young, **4**
job: *m.* job, **12**
joli(e): pretty, **4**
joue: *f.* cheek, **4**
jouer…au foot / au tennis / aux cartes / aux échecs / de la guitare / du piano / : to play… soccer / tennis / cards / chess / guitar / piano, **2, 10**
jour: *m.* day, **1**
Jour de l'An, le premier janvier / Bonne Année!: *m.* New Year's Day / Happy New Year!, **7**
jour férié: *m.* national holiday, **7**
journal (national, régional): *m.* news, newspaper (national, regional), **9**
journaliste: *m, f.* reporter, journalist, **1, 12**
Joyeuses Pâques!: Happy Easter!, **7**
Joyeux Noël!: Merry Christmas! , **7**
juillet: *m.* July, **1**
juin: *m.* June, **1**
jupe: *f.* skirt, **10**
Jura: *m.* Jura (mountains), **3**
juriste: *m, f.* attorney, **12**
jus / jus de fruit: *m.* juice / fruit juice, **5**
kayak / faire du kayak: *m.* kayaking / to go kayaking, **10**
kilo / un kilo de: *m.* kilo / a kilo of, **5**
kinésithérapeute: *m.* chiropractor, physical therapist, **12**
kiné: *m.* chiropractor, physical therapist, **12**
kiosque (à journaux): *m.* news stand, **9**
laboratoire / labo / au labo: *m.* laboratory / lab / in the lab, **1, 11**
lac: *m.* lake, **3**
laisser: to leave, **9**
lait: *m.* milk, **5**
laitue: *f.* lettuce, **5**
lampe: *f.* lamp, **8**
langue: *f.* language, **pré, 11**
latin: *m.* Latin, **11**
lavabo: *m.* sink, **8**
lave-linge: *m.* washing machine, **8**
se laver: to wash (oneself), **4**
laverie: *f.* launderette, **6**
lave-vaisselle: *m.* dishwasher, **8**
légume: *m.* vegetable, **5**
lessive / faire la lessive: *f.* laundry detergent / to do laundry, **8**
lettre de motivation: *f.* cover letter (to accompany a CV), **12**
se lever: to get up, **4**
librairie : *f.* bookstore , **6**
licencier / être licencié(e): to lay off / to be laid off, **12**
lien: *m.* link, **9**
lieu: *m.* place, **3**
lingerie / dans la lingerie: *f.* laundry room / in the laundry room, **8**
linguistique: *f.* linguistics, **11**
Lion: *m.* Leo, **13**
lire: to read, **2**
lit / faire le lit: *m.* bed / to make the bed, **8**
litre / un litre de: *m.* liter / a liter of, **5**
littérature: *f.* literature, **pré, 11**
living: *m.* living room, **8**
livre: *m.* book, **1, 9**
logement: *m.* housing, **13**
loin (de): far, **6**
Loire: *f.* Loire (river), **3**
long / longue: long, **4**
Lorraine: *f.* Lorraine, **3**
louer: to rent, **13**
loyer: *m.* rent, **13**
lundi: *m.* Monday, **1**
lunettes: *f pl*, glasses, **4**
lunettes de soleil: *f pl*, sunglasses, **10**
lycée: *m.* high school, **6, 11**
lycéen / lycéenne: *m / f.* high school student, **11**
Madame / Mesdames: *f.* Ma'am (Mrs.) / ladies, **1**
Mademoiselle / Mesdemoiselles: *f.* Miss / ladies (unmarried), **1**
magasin (de musique, de vidéo, etc.): *m.* store (music, video, etc.), **6**
magazine: *m.* magazine, **9**

magazine d'actualités (à la télévision): *m.* news show, **9**
magnétoscope: *m.* videocassette recorder, VCR, **9**
mai: *m.* May, **1**
maigre: thin, skinny, **4**
maigrir: to lose weight, **5**
mail: *m.* e-mail, **9**
maillot de bain: *m.* swimsuit, **10**
main: *f.* hand, **10**
maintenant: now, **2**
mairie : *f.* city hall, mayor's office, **6**
maison / à la maison: *f.* house / at home, **6, 8**
malade / tomber malade: sick / to get sick, **10**
maladie: *f.* illness, **10**
malhonnête: dishonest, **4**
Manche: *f.* English Channel, **3**
manger: to eat, **3**
manteau: *m.* coat, **10**
se maquiller: to put on make-up, **4**
marché / au marché: *m.* market / at the market, **5**
marché du travail: *m.* job market, **12**
marcher: to walk, **6**
mardi: *m.* Tuesday, **1**
mari: *m.* husband, **2**
mariage: *m.* marriage, wedding, **13**
se marier: to marry, to get married, **13**
Maroc: *m.* Morocco, **2**
marocain(e): Moroccan, **2**
marque: *f.* brand, **10**
marrant(e): funny, **9**
marron (invariable): brown, **4**
mars: *m.* March, **1**
Massif Central: *m.* Massif Central, **3**
mathématiques / maths: *f pl*, math, **pré, 11**
matière: *f.* subject (school), **pré, 11**
matin: *m.* morning, **1**
mauvais(e) / Il fait mauvais.: bad / It's bad (weather)., **3, 4**
mayonnaise: *f.* mayonnaise, **5**
médecin: *m.* doctor, physician, **1, 12**
médecine: *f.* medicine, **11**
médias: *m pl*, media, **9**
médicament: *m.* medicine, **10**
Meilleurs Voeux!: Best wishes!, **7**
mémoire: *m.* term paper, **11**
ménage / faire le ménage: *m.* housekeeping, **8**
menton: *m.* chin, **4**
mer: *f.* sea, **3**
mer Méditerranée: *f.* Mediterranean Sea, **3**
mercredi: *m.* Wednesday, **1**
mère: *f.* mother, **2**
message: *m.* message, **9**
messe: *f.* mass, **7**
météo: *f.* weather report, **9**
métier: *m.* profession, career, job, **12**
métro / en métro: *m.* metro / by metro, **3**
mettre: to put (on), **10**
mettre à jour: to update, **13**
mettre à la porte / être mis(e) à la porte: to fire / to be fired, **12**
mettre de côté: to put aside, to save, **13**
meuble / meubles: *m.* piece of furniture / furniture, **8**
mexicain(e): Mexican, **2**
Mexique: *m.* Mexico, **2**
mignon / mignonne: cute, **4**
migraine: *f.* migraine headache, **10**
militaire: *m.* person in the armed services, **12**
million (1.000.000): *m.* million (one million), **3**
mince : thin, slender, **4**
mincir: to lose weight, **10**
ministre: *m.* government minister, **12**
minitel: *m.* terminal connected to the French telecommunications system, **9**
miroir: *m.* mirror, **8**
mode / à la mode: *f.* fashion / in fashion, **10**
moderne: modern, **8**
mois: *m.* month, **1**
monde / monde du travail: *m.* world / working world, **12**
Monsieur / Messieurs: *m.* Sir / gentlemen, **1**
montagne: *f.* mountain, **3**
monter: to go up, to go upstairs, to climb, **6**
montrer: to show, **9**
monument: *m.* monument , **3**
moquette: *f.* carpet (wall to wall), **8**
morceau / un morceau de: *m.* piece / a piece of, **5**
mosquée: *f.* mosque, **6**
mot / mots interrogatifs: *m.* mot / interrogative words, **2**
mot de passe: *m.* password, **9**
moteur de recherche: *m.* search engine, **9**
moto / à moto : *f.* motorcycle / by motorcycle, **3**
mourir: to die, **6**
mousse au chocolat: *f.* chocolate mousse, **5**
moutarde: *f.* mustard, **5**
moyenne: *f.* passing grade, **11**
muguet: *m.* lily of the valley, **7**
musculation / faire de la musculation: *f.* weight training / to train with weights, **10**
musée: *m.* museum, **3, 6**
musicien / musicienne: *m / f.* musician, **12**
musique / musique classique: *f.* music / classical music, **pré, 2, 11**
nager: to swim, **2, 3**
naïf / naïve: naive, **4**
naître: to be , born, **6**
natation / faire de la natation: *f.* swimming / to go swimming, **10**
nationalité: *f.* nationality, **2**
naviguer: to navigate, **9**
ne...jamais: never (Refer to Tex's French Grammar: Negation – Alternate forms of negation for correct formation and use.), **2**
nécessaire / Il est nécessaire de: necessary / It is necessary (to), **10**
neiger / Il neige.: to snow / It's snowing., **3**
nerveux / nerveuse: nervous, **4**
neuf: nine, **1**
neuvième: ninth, **6**
neveu: *m.* nephew, **2**
nez: *m.* nose, **4, 10**
nièce: *f.* niece, **2**
noces: *f pl*, wedding, **7**

Noël, le 25 décembre / Joyeux Noël!: *m.* Christmas / Merry Christmas! , **7**
noir(e): black, **4**
noix: *f.* walnut, **5**
nom (de famille): *m.* last name, **2**
nombre / nombres cardinaux / nombres ordinaux: *m.* number / cardinal numbers / ordinal numbers, **1, 3, 6**
non-alcoolisé(e) / boisson non-alcoolisée (f): non-alcoholic / non-alcoholic beverage, **5**
nord / dans le nord, au nord: *m.* north / in the north, **3**
Normandie: *f.* Normandy, **3**
note: *f.* grade, **11**
noter: to assign a grade, **11**
nouveau / nouvel / nouvelle: new, **4**
novembre: *m.* November, **1**
nuage / Il y a des nuages.: *m.* cloud / It's cloudy., **3**
numéro de téléphone: *m.* phone number, **9**
obéir à: to obey, **5**
(d') **occasion:** second-hand, **12**
occupé(e): busy, **11**
océan: *m.* ocean, **3**
océan Atlantique: *m.* Atlantic Ocean, **3**
Océanie: *f.* Oceania (the South Sea Islands), **2**
octobre: *m.* October, **1**
œil / yeux: *m.* eye / eyes, **4, 10**
oeuf: *m.* egg, **5**
office du tourisme: *m.* chamber of commerce, **6**
officiel / officielle: official, **1**
offrir: to give, to offer, **7, 13**
oignon: *m.* onion, **5**
omelette (aux fines herbes, au fromage, etc): *f.* omelette (with herbs, cheese), **5**
oncle: *m.* uncle, **2**
onze: eleven, **1**
onzième: eleventh, **6**
opticien / opticienne: *m / f.* optician, **12**
optimiste: optimistic, **4**
orage / Il y a des orages.: *m.* storm / There are storms., **3**
orange: *f.* orange, **5**
orange (invariable): orange (color), **4**
ordinateur: *m.* computer, **1, 8, 9**
ordre / en ordre: *m.* order / straightened up, **8**
oreille: *f.* ear, **4, 10**
s' orienter: to get your bearings, **6**
où: where, **2**
oublier: to forget, **2**
ouest / dans l'ouest, à l'ouest: *m.* west / in the west, **3**
ouvrier / ouvrière: *m / f.* blue collar worker, **12**
ouvrir: to open, **7**
P.D.G. (Président Directeur Général): *m.* CEO, **12**
PACS: *m.* PACS contract, **13**
se pacser: to enter a PACS contract , **13**
page d'accueil: *f.* homepage, **9**
pain: *m.* bread, **5**
pamplemousse: *m.* grapefruit, **5**
pantalon: *m.* pants (a pair of), **10**
papeterie: *f.* paper/stationery store, **6**
pâque juive / Pessach: *f.* Passover, **7**
Pâques / Joyeuses Pâques!: *m, f pl,* Easter / Happy Easter!, **7**
parc: *m.* park, **3, 6**
parce que: because, **2**
parents: *m pl,* parents, relatives , **2**
paresseux / paresseuse: lazy, **4**
parfois: at times, **2**
parking: *m.* parking lot, **6**
parler: to speak, **2**
se parler: to talk to (one another), **8**
partager: to share, **3**
partir: to leave, **3, 6**
pas / à deux pas (de): *m.* step / just a step from, **6**
passer: to pass, to go by (intransitive), to spend (time), **6, 9**
se passer de: to do without, **13**
passer l'aspirateur: to vacuum, to pass the vacuum cleaner, **8**
passer les vacances: *f pl,* spend a vacation, **3**
passer un examen: to take an exam, **11**
passe-temps (invariable): *m.* pastime, **2, 10**
passionnant(e): enthralling, fascinating, **12**
pâté: *m.* pâté, **5**
patient(e): patient, **4**
pâtisserie: *f.* pastry, pastry shop, **5, 6**
pâtissier / pâtissière / chez le pâtissier: *m / f.* pastry chef / at the pastry chef's, **5**
patron / patronne: *m / f.* boss, **12**
payer / payer des impôts: to pay / to pay taxes, **12**
pays: *m.* country, **2**
pêche: *f.* peach, **5**
peintre: *m.* painter, **12**
peinture: *f.* painting, **11**
peinture / faire de la peinture: *m.* painting / to paint (art), **10**
perdre: to lose, **6**
père: *m.* father, **2**
Père Noël: *m.* Santa Claus, **7**
personnalité (de la télévision, du cinéma, de la radio…): *f.* celebrity, **9**
personne: *f.* person, **3**
personnel / personnelles: personal, **2**
peser / Combien pesez-vous? (Je fais 55 kilos.): to weigh / How much do you weigh? (I weigh 55 kilos.), **4**
Pessach / la pâque juive: Passover, **7**
pessimiste: pessimistic, **4**
petit déjeuner: *m.* breakfast, **5**
petit pain: *m.* roll, **5**
petit(e): little, **4**
petite annonce: *f.* classified ad, **9, 12**
petit-enfant: *m.* grandchild, **2**
petits commerces: *m pl,* small businesses, **6**
petits pois: *m pl,* peas, **5**
peu / un peu / un peu de : little / a little / a little (+ noun), **2, 5**
pharmacie: *f.* pharmacy, **6, 11**
pharmacien /pharmacienne: *m / f.* pharmacist, **12**
philosophie: *f.* philosophy, **pré, 11**
physique: physical, **4**
physique: *f.* physics, **11**
piano / jouer du piano: *m.* piano / to play the piano, **2**

pichet / un pichet de: *m.* pitcher / a pitcher of, **5**
pièce: *f.* room (general term), **8**
pied / à pìed: *m.* foot / on foot, **3, 10**
piercing: *m.* body piercing, **4**
pique-nique: *m.* picnic, **7**
placard: *m.* closet, cabinet, **8**
place: *f.* public square, **6**
plage : *f.* beach, **3**
plaisanter: to joke, **7**
planche à voile / faire de la planche à voile: *f.* sailboarding, windsurfing / to go sailboarding/windsurfing, **3, 10**
plat principal: *m.* main course, **5**
pleuvoir / Il pleut.: to rain / It's raining., **3**
plus tard: later, **2**
poignet: *m.* wrist, **10**
points cardinaux: *m pl,* points of the compass, **3**
pointu(e) / Il a le nez pointu.: pointed / He has a snub nose., **4**
poire: *f.* pear, **5**
poireau: *m.* leek, **5**
poisson: *m.* fish, **5**
Poisson d'avril!: April Fool!, **7**
poissonnerie / à la poissonnerie: *f.* seafood shop / at the seafood shop, **5**
poissonnier / poissonnière / chez le poissonnier: *m / f.* fish merchant / at the fish merchant's, **5**
Poissons: *m pl,* Pisces, **13**
poitrine: *f.* chest, **10**
poivre: *m.* pepper, **5**
poivron vert: *m.* green pepper, **5**
policier: *m.* police officer, **12**
polo: *m.* polo shirt, **10**
pomme: *f.* apple, **5**
pomme de terre: *f.* potato **5**
pont: *m.* bridge, **6**
porc: *m.* pork, **5**
portable: *m.* laptop, **9**
porte: *f.* door, **1**
portefeuille: *m.* portfolio (also, wallet), **13**
porter: to wear, **10**
portrait / le portrait physique / le portrait moral: *m.* portrait, description / physical description / psychological description , **4**
poste / poste à plein temps / poste à mi-temps: *m.* position, post / full-time position / half-time position, **12**
poubelle: *f.* trash can, **8**
poulet: *m.* chicken, **5**
pourquoi: why, **2**
pratique: practical, **8**
préférer: to prefer, **2**
préliminaire: preliminary, **pré**
premier avril / Poisson d'avril: *m.* April Fool's Day / April Fool!, **7**
premier, première: first, **6**
première (la): *f.* second year of high school (lycée), **11**
prendre: to take, **5**
prendre le métro, un taxi, etc. : to take the metro, a taxi, etc. , **6**
prendre un rendez-vous: to make an appointment, **12**
prendre un repas: to have a meal, **5**
prénom(s): *m.* first (and middle) name(s), **2**
près (de) / tout près: near, close / nearby, **6**
présentateur / présentatrice: *m / f.* newscaster, **9**
présentation: *f.* introduction, **1**
presse: *f.* press (the), **9**
prétentieux / prétentieuse: pretentious, **4**
printemps / au printemps: *m.* spring / in the spring, **3**
prix / prix intéressant: *m.* price / good price, **13**
prochain(e): next, **1, 11**
produit laitier: *m.* dairy product, **5**
professeur: *m.* teacher, professor, **1**
profession: *f.* profession, **2**
programme: *m.* television schedule, **9**
promenade / faire une promenade: *f.* walk / to go for a walk, to take a walk, **3, 10**
se promener: to take a, walk, to go for a walk, **4**
promotion: *f.* promotion, **12**
propre: clean, own, **8**
propriétaire: *m, f.* owner, **12**
Provence: *f.* Provence, **3**
province: *f.* province, **3**
psychologie: *f.* psychology, **pré, 11**
psychologue: *m, f.* psychologist, **12**
publicitaire: *m.* advertising agent, **12**
publicité / pub: *f.* commercial, **9**
pull: *m.* sweater, **10**
Pyrénées: *f pl,* Pyrenees, **3**
quand: when, **2**
quantité: *f.* quantity, **5**
quarante: forty, **1**
quartier: *m.* neighborhood, **6**
quatorze: fourteen, **1**
quatorzième: fourteenth, **6**
quatre: four, **1**
quatre-vingt-dix: ninety, **3**
quatre-vingt-dix-huit: ninety-eight, **3**
quatre-vingt-dix-neuf: ninety-nine, **3**
quatre-vingt-dix-sept : ninety-seven, **3**
quatre-vingt-douze: ninety-two, **3**
quatre-vingt-onze: ninety-one, **3**
quatre-vingt-quatorze: ninety-four, **3**
quatre-vingt-quinze: ninety-five, **3**
quatre-vingts: eighty, **3**
quatre-vingt-seize: ninety-six, **3**
quatre-vingt-treize: ninety-three, **3**
quatre-vingt-un: eighty-one, **3**
quatrième: fourth, **6**
quel / quelle / quels / quelles: which, **2**
quelquefois: sometimes, **2**
question / questions personnelles: *f.* question / personal questions, **2**
qui: who, **2**
quiche (lorraine, au saumon, etc): *f.* quiche (lorraine, with salmon, etc), **5**
quinze: fifteen, **1**
quinzième: fifteenth, **6**
quitter: to leave, **9, 11**
raccrocher: to hang up (the phone), **9**
radin / radine [slang]: miserly, stingy, **13**
radio: *f.* radio, **2, 9**
raide: straight, **4**

raisin: *m.* grape, **5**
Ramadan: *m.* Ramadan, **7**
randonnée / faire de la randonnée: *f.* a walk, hiking / to go hiking, **3, 10**
ranger : to straighten up, **8**
rappeler : to call back, **9**
rarement: rarely, **2**
se raser: to shave, **4**
rater: to fail, **11**
rayé(e) / un tee-shirt rayé: striped / striped T-shirt, **10**
réaliser (un projet): to accomplish / to finish a project, **12**
réaliste: realistic, **4**
recevoir: to receive, **7**
recevoir son diplôme: to graduate, to complete one's studies, **11**
redoubler: to repeat a grade/course, **11**
réfléchir à: to reflect (on), **5**
réfrigérateur: *m.* refrigerator, **8**
regarder la télévision: to watch television, **2**
région: *f.* region, **3**
régisseur: *m.* stage manager, **12**
régler (les frais d'inscription): to pay (one's tuition/fees), **11**
relation: *f.* relationship, **13**
rembourser: to reimburse, **13**
remplir un formulaire: to fill out a form, **12**
rencontrer: to meet, **2**
rendez-vous: *m.* appointment, date, **12, 13**
rendre: to hand in, give back, **6**
rendre visite à quelqu'un: to visit someone, **6**
renseignement: *m.* information, piece of information, **9**
se renseigner: to find out about, to get information, **11**
rentrée: *f.* beginning of school year, **11**
rentrer: to go home, to go back, **6**
repas: *m.* meal, **5**
repasser: to iron, **8**
répondeur (automatique): *m.* answering machine, **9**
répondre: to answer, **6**
reporter: *m.* reporter, **9**
se reposer: to rest, **4, 10**
réservé(e): reserved, **4**
résidence actuelle: *f.* current address, **2**
résidence universitaire: *f.* dormitory, university dorm, **8, 11**
restaurant: *m.* restaurant, **6**
restaurant universitaire (restau-U): *m.* university cafeteria, **11**
restaurateur: *m.* restaurant owner, **12**
rester / rester à la maison: to stay / to stay at home, **2, 6**
résultats: *m pl*, results, grades, **11**
retourner: to return, **6**
retraite: *f.* retirement, **12**
retraité / retraitée: *m / f.* retired man/woman, **1, 12**
retroussé(e) / Il a le nez retroussé: snub / He has a snub nose., **4**
réussir (à) (un examen): to pass an exam, to succeed (in), **11**
se réveiller: to wake up, **4**
réveillon: *m.* Christmas Eve or New Year's Eve party, **7**
réveillonner: to celebrate Christmas or New Year's Eve, **7**
rêver: to dream, **2**
rez-de-chaussée: *m.* ground floor, first floor, **8**
Rhône: *m.* Rhône (river), **3**
rhume: *m.* a cold, **10**
rite: *m.* ritual, **7**
robe: *f.* dress, **10**
roller / faire du roller: *m.* roller blading / to go roller blading, **10**
roman: *m.* novel, **9**
rompre: to break up, **13**
rond(e): round, **4**
Rosh Hashana: Rosh Hashana, **7**
rôti / un rôti de bœuf: *m.* roast / a beef roast, **5**
rouge: red, **4**
roux / rousse: red (hair), red-head, **4**
rue: *f.* street, **6**
sabbat / le shabbat: *m.* sabbath , **7**
sac à dos: *m.* backpack, **1**
Sagittaire: *m.* Sagittarius, **13**
Saint-Sylvestre, le 31 décembre: *f.* New Year's Eve, **7**
Saint-Valentin, le 14 février: *f.* Valentine's Day, **7**
saison: *f.* season, **3**
salade: *f.* salad, lettuce, **5**
salaire: *m.* salary, **12**
sale: dirty, **8**
salé(e): salty, **5**
salle à manger / dans la salle à manger...: *f.* dining room / in the dining room…, **8**
salle de bains / dans la salle de bains...: *f.* bathroom / in the bathroom…, **8**
salle de classe: *f.* classroom, **1, 11**
salle de séjour / dans la salle de séjour...: *f.* living room / in the living room…, **8**
salle de tchatche: *f.* chat room, **9**
salon: *m.* living room, **8**
Salut!: Hi!, **1**
salutation: *f.* greeting, **1**
samedi: *m.* Saturday, **1**
sandales: *f.* sandal, **10**
sandwich (jambon beurre): *m.* sandwich (with ham and butter), **5**
santé: *f.* health, **10**
sapin de Noël: *m.* Christmas tree, **7**
satisfait(e): satisfied, fulfilled, **13**
saucisse: *f.* sausage, **5**
saucisson: *m.* hard sausage, **5**
saumon: *m.* salmon, **5**
science: *f.* science, **pré, 11**
sciences politiques: *f pl*, political science, **pré, 11**
Scorpion: *m.* Scorpio, **13**
séance de T.D. (travaux dirigés) / un T.D: *f.* small discussion section, **11**
séance de T.P. (travaux pratiques) / un T.P: *f.* lab section, **11**
sèche-linge: *m.* dryer, **8**
sécher un cours: to skip a class, **11**

seconde (la): *f.* first year of high school (lycée), **11**
secrétaire: *m, f.* secretary, **12**
Seine: *f.* Seine (river), **3**
seize: sixteen, **1**
seizième: sixteenth, **6**
séjour: *m.* living room, **8**
sel: *m.* salt, **5**
semaine / la semaine prochaine / la semaine dernière: *f.* week / next week / last week, **1**
Sénégal: *m.* Senegal, **2**
sénégalais(e): Senegalese, **2**
sensible : sensitive, **4**
sept: seven, **1**
septembre: *m.* September, **1**
septième: seventh, **6**
série: *f.* series, **9**
sérieux / sérieuse: serious, **4**
serveur / serveuse: *m / f.* wait person, **12**
shabbat / le sabbat : *m.* sabbath, **7**
short: *m.* shorts, **10**
signe / Quel est ton signe?: *m.* sign, **13**
signet: *m.* bookmark, **9**
sincère: sincere, **4**
site: *m.* website, **9**
situation: *f.* position (employment), **12**
six: six, **1**
sixième: sixth, **6**
ski (alpin, nautique) / faire du ski: *m.* ski, skiing (snow, water) / to go skiing, **3, 10**
soap: *m.* soap opera, **9**
sociable: sociable, **4**
sociologie: *f.* sociology, **11**
soeur: *f.* sister, **2**
sofa: *m.* couch, **8**
soir: *m.* evening, **1**
soixante: sixty, **1**
soixante et onze: seventy-one, **3**
soixante-dix: seventy, **3**
soixante-dix-huit: seventy-eight, **3**
soixante-dix-neuf: seventy-nine, **3**
soixante-dix-sept : seventy-seven, **3**
soixante-douze: seventy-two, **3**
soixante-quatorze: seventy-four, **3**
soixante-quinze: seventy-five, **3**
soixante-seize: seventy-six, **3**
soixante-treize: seventy-three, **3**
sole: *f.* sole, **5**
soleil / Il y a du soleil.: *m.* sun / It's sunny., **3**
sombre: dark, **8**
somme / somme importante: *f.* amount / substantial amount, **13**
somnifère: *m.* sleeping pill, **10**
sortir: to go out, **3, 6**
souffler: to blow out (candles), **7**
soupe (à l'oignon): *f.* (onion) soup, **5**
sourcil: *m.* eyebrow, **4**
souris: *f.* mouse, **9**
sous: under, **6**
se souvenir (de): to remember, **8**
souvent: often, **2**
se spécialiser en… (langues, maths, etc): to major in…, **11**
sport: *m.* sports, **2**
sportif / sportive: athletic, **4, 10**
stade: *m.* stadium, **6**
stage: *m.* internship, **11**
stagiaire: *m, f.* intern, **1**
star: *f.* celebrity, **9**
station: *f.* radio station, **9**
steak-frites: *m.* steak and French fries, **5**
stressé(e): stressed , **10**
stylo: *m.* pen, **1**
sucré(e): sweet, **5**
sud / dans le sud, au sud: *m.* south / in the south, **3**
Suisse: *f.* Switzerland, **2**
suisse: Swiss, **2**
suivre: to take (a course), to follow, **11**
supermarché / au supermarché: *m.* supermarket / at the supermarket, **5, 6**
sur: on, **6**
surfer: to surf (the web), **9**
surprendre: to surprise, **5**
sweat: *m.* running suit, **10**
synagogue: *f.* synagogue, **6**
tabac: *m.* tobacco, **10**
table / à table : *f.* table / at the table, **5, 8**
table basse: *f.* coffee table, **8**
tableau: *m.* painting, **8**
tableau (noir): *m.* blackboard, **1**
tâches domestiques: *f pl*, household chores, **8**
taille / de taille moyenne / Quelle est votre taille? (Je fais 1 m. 60.): *f.* height, size / of medium height / What's your height? (I'm one meter 60.), **4**
tailleur: *m.* woman's suit, **10**
talon: *m.* heel, **10**
tante: *f.* aunt, **2**
tapis: *m.* area rug or carpet, **8**
tarte / tarte à la fraise / tarte au citron / tarte aux pommes: *f.* tart / strawberry tart / lemon tart / apple tart, **5**
tasse / une tasse de: *f.* cup / a cup of, a cupful, **5**
tatou: *m.* armadillo, **pré**
tatouage: *m.* tattoo, **4**
Taureau: *m.* Taurus, **13**
taxi / en taxi: *m.* taxi / by taxi, **3**
technicien / technicienne: *m / f.* technician, **12**
techno: *f.* techno, **2**
tee-shirt: *m.* T-shirt, **10**
télécharger: to download, **9**
télécommande: *f.* remote control, **9**
téléphone / au téléphone: *m.* telephone / on the phone, **8, 9**
téléphone portable: *m.* cell phone, **9**
téléphoner à : to telephone, **2**
téléspectateur / téléspectatrice : *m / f.* television spectator, **9**
télévision / télé: *f.* television / TV, **1, 8, 9**
temple: *m.* temple, **6**
temps: *m.* weather, **3**
tennis: *m.* tennis, **2**
tennis: *f pl*, tennis shoes, **10**
tennis / jouer au tennis: *m.* tennis / to play tennis, **2**
terminale (la): *f.* final year of high school (lycée), **11**
(se) terminer: to end, **9**

terrasse: *f.* terrace, **8**
tête: *f.* head, **4, 10**
têtu/ têtue: stubborn, **4**
thé: *m.* tea, **5**
théâtre: *m.* theater, **6**
thon: *m.* tuna, **5**
timide: shy, timid, **4**
toilettes: *f pl*, toilet, **8**
tolérant(e): tolerant, **4**
tomate: *f.* tomato **5**
tomber: to fall, **6**
tomber amoureux (de)/ amoureuse : to fall in love, **2**
tomber malade: to get sick, **10**
toujours: always, **2**
tourner: to turn, **6**
Toussaint, le 1er novembre: *f.* All Saints' Day , **7**
tout droit: straight ahead, **6**
tout près: nearby, **6**
tragique: tragic, **9**
train / en train: *m.* train / by train, **3**
traiteur: *m.* deli, catering shop, **6**
tranche / une tranche de: *f.* slice / a slice of, **5**
transports: *m pl*, means of transport, **3**
travail / au travail: *m.* work, job / to at work, **3, 12**
travailler: to work, **2**
travailleur / travailleuse: *m / f.* hard-working, **4**
traverser: to cross, **6**
treize: thirteen, **1**
treizième: thirteenth, **6**
trente: thirty, **1**
trois: three, **1**
troisième: third, **6**
tromper: to cheat on, **13**
trop de: too much (too many), **5**
se trouver: to be found/to be located, **6**
trouver : to find, **2**
Tunisie: *f.* Tunisia, **2**
tunisien(ne): Tunisian, **2**
un, une: one, **1**
université: *f.* university, **3, 6**
utile: useful, **12**
vacances / passer les vacances: *f pl,* vacation / to spend a vacation, **3**
vaisselle - See 'faire la vaiselle': , **8**
Vallée de la Loire: *f.* Loire Valley, **3**
valoir / Il vaut mieux + infinitive: to be, worth / It is advisable (to), It is better (to), **10**
veau: *m.* veal, **5**
vedette: *f.* celebrity, **9**
vélo / à vélo: *m.* bicycle, bike / by bicycle, **3**
vendeur / vendeuse: *m / f.* salesperson, **12**
vendre: to sell, **6**
vendredi: *m.* Friday, **1**
vent / Il y a du vent. : *m.* wind / It's windy., **3**
ventre: *m.* stomach, **10**
verbe / verbe pronominal / verbe réfléchi / verbe réciproque: *m.* verb / pronominal verb / reflexive verb / reciprocal verb, **4, 8**
verre / un verre de: *m.* glass / a glass of, a glassful, **5**
Verseau: *m.* Aquarius, **13**
vert(e): green, **4**
veste: *f.* jacket, **10**
viande: *f.* meat, **5**
Victoire 1945, le 8 mai: *f.* VE Day (Victory in Europe), **7**
vie / Que faites-vous dans la vie? : *f.* life / What do you do for a living?, **12**
vie professionnelle: *f.* professional life, **12**
Vierge: *f.* Virgo, **13**
Vietnam: *m.* Vietnam, **2**
vietnamien(ne): Vietnamese, **2**
vieux / vieil / vieille: old, **4**
ville / en ville: *f.* city, town / in the city, **3, 6**
vin / du vin blanc (du blanc) / du vin rosé (du rosé) / du vin rouge (du rouge): *m.* wine / white wine / rosé wine / red wine, **5**
vinaigre: *m.* vinegar, **5**
vingt: twenty, **1**
vingtième: twentieth, **6**
violent(e): violent, **9**
violet / violette: purple, **4**
visage: *m.* face, **4**
visiter… (un lieu, pas une personne): to visit… (a place, not a person), **3**
vitamine: *f.* vitamin, **10**
vivre ensemble: to live together , **13**
vocabulaire: *m.* vocabulary,
Voici : Here is … (here are…), This is…, **1**
Voilà: There is… (there are…), **1**
voile: *f.* sail, **3**
voiture / en voiture: *f.* car / by car, **3**
Vosges: *f pl* , Vosges, **3**
voyager: to travel, **2**
voyagiste: *m.* travel agent, **12**
W.C.: *m pl* , toilet, **8**
web: *m.* the Web, **9**
western: *m.* western, **9**
yaourt: *m.* yogurt, **5**
yeux / un œil: *m pl*, eyes / eye, **4, 10**
Yom Kippour: *m.* Yom Kippur, **7**

ENGLISH - FRENCH

a lot / a lot (of) : beaucoup / beaucoup de
to **accomplish / to finish a project :** réaliser (un projet)
account, (bank) account : compte (bancaire) *m*
accountant : comptable *m / f*
accounting : comptabilité *f*
action film : film d'action *m*
active : actif / active
activity : activité *f*
actor / actress : acteur / actrice *m / f*
to be **addicted, to have a habit :** être accro à (l'internet, à la télé…)[slang]
adjective / adjectives which precede the noun : adjectif / adjectifs qui précèdent le nom *m*
administrative district in a large city (e.g. Paris) : arrondissement *m*
to **adore :** adorer
adventure movie : film d'aventures *m*
adverb : adverbe *m*
advertising agent : publicitaire *m*

to do **aerobics** : faire de l'aérobique
aerobics / to do aerobics : aérobique / faire de l'aérobique *f*
AES - Public affairs : administration économique et sociale *f*
Africa : Afrique *f*
African : africain(e)
afternoon : après-midi *m, f*
age : âge *m*
airport : aéroport *m*
album : album *m*
alcoholic / alcoholic beverage : alcoolisé(e) / boisson alcoolisée (f)
Algeria : Algérie *f*
Algerian : algérien(ne)
All Saints' Day : Toussaint, le 1er novembre *f*
allergy : allergie *f*
alphabet : alphabet *m*
Alps : Alpes *f pl*
Alsace : Alsace *f*
also : aussi
always : toujours
ambitious : ambitieux / ambitieuse
America : Amérique *f*
American : américain(e)
amount / substantial amount : somme / somme importante *f*
amphitheater : amphithéâtre / amphi *m*
analyst-programmer : analyste-programmeur *m*
to get **angry** : **se** fâcher
ankle : cheville *f*
announcer : annonceur / annonceuse *m / f*
to **answer** : répondre
answering machine : répondeur (automatique) *m*
ant : fourmi *f*
apartment : appartement *m*
apartment building : immeuble *m*
apple : pomme *f*
to **apply for a job** : faire une demande d'emploi
appointment, date : rendez-vous *m*
April: avril *m*
April Fool! : Poisson d'avril!
April Fool's Day : premier avril *m*
Aquarius : Verseau *m*
architect : architecte *m*
architecture : architecture *f*
area rug or carpet : tapis *m*
to **argue (with one another)** : **se** disputer
Aries : Bélier *m*
arm : bras *m*
armadillo : tatou *m*
armchair : fauteuil *m*
Armistice Day : Armistice, le 11 novembre *m*
armoire : armoire *f*
to **arrive** : arriver
arrogant : arrogant(e)
art : art *m*
Ascension Day : Ascension *f*
Asia : Asie *f*
Asian : asiatique
to **ask (for)** : demander
asparagus : asperge *f*
to **assign a grade** : noter
at someone's house : chez
at times : parfois
athletic : sportif / sportive
Atlantic Ocean : océan Atlantique *m*
ATM (automatic teller machine) : distributeur automatique de billets *m*
to **attend** : assister (à)
to **attend class** : aller en cours
attic : grenier *m*
attorney : juriste *m, f*
August : août *m*
aunt : tante *f*
Australia : Australie *f*
Australian : australien(ne)
avenue : avenue *f*
baccalaureate exam : baccalauréat / bac *m*
back : dos *m*
backpack : sac à dos *m*
bad / It's bad (weather). : mauvais(e) / Il fait mauvais.
to **be bad in/at** : être mauvais(e) en
baguette : baguette *f*
baker / at the baker's : boulanger / boulangère / chez le boulanger *m / f*
bakery : boulangerie *f*
bakery-pastry shop / at the bakery-pastry shop : boulangerie-pâtisserie / à la boulangerie-pâtisserie *f*
balcony : balcon *m*
banana : banane *f*
bank : banque *f*
banker : banquier / banquière *m / f*
basketball : basket *m*
basketball shoes : baskets *f pl*
Bastille Day, French National Day : fête nationale, le 14 juillet *f*
bathroom / in the bathroom... : salle de bains / dans la salle de bains... *f*
bathtub : baignoire *f*
beach : plage *f*
beautiful : beau / bel / belle
because : parce que
bed / to make the bed : lit / faire le lit *m*
bedroom / in the bedroom... : chambre / dans la chambre... *f*
beef : boeuf *m*
beer : bière *f*
beginning of school year : rentrée *f*
behind : derrière
Belgian : belge
Belgium : Belgique *f*
to **believe** : croire
belt : ceinture *f*
benefits (health insurance, retirement plan, etc.) : avantages sociaux *m pl*
Best wishes! : Meilleurs Voeux!
to go **bicycle riding** : faire de la bicyclette
bicycle, bike : bicyclette *f*
bicycle, bike / by bicycle : bicyclette *f*; vélo *m*. / à vélo *m*
big, fat : gros / grosse
bill / telephone bill : facture / facture de téléphone *f*

biology : biologie *f*
birthday, anniversary / Happy Birthday! : anniversaire / Bon (Joyeux) anniversaire! *m*
black : noir(e)
blackboard : tableau (noir) *m*
blond : blond / blonde
blouse : chemisier *m*
to **blow out (candles)** : souffler
blue : bleu(e)
blue collar worker : ouvrier / ouvrière *m* / *f*
boat / by boat : bateau / en bateau *m*
to go **boating** : faire du bateau
body : corps (invariable) *m*
body piercing : piercing *m*
book : livre *m*
bookcase : étagère *f*
bookmark : signet *m*
bookstore : librairie *f*
boot : botte *f*
to be **bored** : **s'** ennuyer
boring : ennuyeux / ennuyeuse
to be **born** : naître
boss : patron / patronne *m* / *f*
bottle / a bottle of : bouteille / une bouteille de *f*
boulevard : boulevard *m*
boutique : boutique *f*
bowl / a bowl of, a bowlful : bol / un bol de *m*
brand : marque *f*
bread : pain *m*
to **break up** : rompre
breakfast : petit déjeuner *m*
bridge : pont *m*
bright, full of light : clair(e)
to **bring somebody (along)** : amener
brioche : brioche *f*
Brittany : Bretagne *f*
to **be broke** : être fauché(e) [slang]
brother : frère *m*
brown : marron (invariable)
brown (hair), brunette : brun / brune
light brown, chestnut : châtain (invariable)
to **brush your hair** : se brosser les cheveux
to **brush your teeth** : se brosser les dents
budget : budget
to **establish a budget** : faire un budget
to go **beyond one's budget** : dépasser son budget *m*
building : bâtiment *m*
bulletin board, newsgroup : forum *m*
Burgundy : Bourgogne *f*
from **Burgundy** : bourguignon (ne)
bus / by bus : bus / en bus *m*
a **business / business (in general)** : affaire / affaires *f*
business school : Ecole de commerce *f*
business, trade / small businesses : commerce / petits commerces *m*
busy : occupé(e)
butcher / at the butcher's : boucher / chez le boucher *m*
butcher shop / at the butcher shop : boucherie / à la boucherie *f*
butter : beurre *m*
buttocks : fesses *f pl*
button-up sweater : gilet *m*
to **buy** : acheter
cabbage : chou *m*
cafeteria : cafétéria *f*
café / at the café: café *m.* / au café
cake / chocolate cake : gâteau / gâteau au chocolat *m*
calendar / French calendar : calendrier / calendrier français *m*
to **call back** : rappeler
calm : calme
can / a can of : boîte / une boîte de *f*
Canada : Canada *m*
Canadian : canadien(ne)
Cancer : Cancer *m*
candle : bougie *f*
Candlemas : Chandeleur, le 2 février *f*
canoeing / to go canoeing : canoë / faire du canoë *m*
cap : casquette *f*
Capricorn : Capricorne *m*
car / by car : voiture / en voiture *f*
caramel custard : crème caramel *f*
card, map (of the world) / to play cards : carte (du monde) / jouer aux cartes *f*
cardinal : cardinal / cardinale / cardinaux / cardinales
career : carrière *f*
carpet (wall to wall) : moquette *f*
carrot : carotte *f*
cartoon : dessin animé *m*
cashier : caissier / caissière *m* / *f*
castle : château *m*
casual : décontracté(e)
cat : chat / chatte *m* / *f*
cathedral : cathédrale *f*
CD-rom : cédérom / CD-rom *m*
to **celebrate** : célébrer
to **celebrate** : fêter
to **celebrate Christmas or New Year's Eve** : réveillonner
celebrity : célébrité *f*, personnalité (de la télévision, du cinéma, de la radio…) *f*, star *f*, vedette *f*.
cell phone : téléphone portable *m*
cellar, wine cellar : cave *f*
center / in the center : centre / au centre *m*
CEO : P.D.G. (Président Directeur Général) *m*
cereal : céréales *f pl*
ceremony : cérémonie *f*
chair : chaise *f*
chalk : craie *f*
chamber of commerce : office du tourisme *m*
champagne : champagne *m*
to **change** : changer
channel : chaîne *f*
chapter : chapitre *m*
to **chat on-line** : dialoguer en direct
chat room : salle de tchatche *f*
to **cheat on** : tromper
cheek : joue *f*
cheese : fromage *m*
chemistry : chimie *f*
cherry : cerise *f*

chess / to play chess : échecs *m pl* / jouer aux échecs
chest : poitrine *f*
chest of drawers : commode *f*
chicken : poulet *m*
chicken (rooster) stewed in red wine : coq au vin *m*
child : enfant *m, f*
child-care expenses : frais de crèche *m pl*
child-care expenses : frais de garderie *m pl*
chin : menton *m*
China : Chine *f*
Chinese : chinois *m*
Chinese : chinois(e)
chiropractor: kinésithérapeute; kiné *m*
chocolate mousse : mousse au chocolat *f*
to **choose** : choisir
chopped : haché(e)
Christmas / Merry Christmas! : Noël, le 25 décembre / Joyeux Noël! *m*
Christmas Eve or New Year's Eve party : réveillon *m*
Christmas tree : sapin de Noël *m*
church : église *f*
city hall, mayor's office : hôtel de ville *m*, mairie *f*
city, town / in the city : ville / en ville *f*
civil servant, government worker : fonctionnaire *m, f*
class / in class / classroom : classe *f* / en classe / la salle de classe
class, course / class (math class…) / to attend class : cours (invariable) *m* / cours (de maths…) / aller en cours
classified ad : petite annonce *f*
classroom : salle de classe *f*
clean : propre
to **click** : cliquer
client, customer : client / cliente *m / f*
closet, cabinet : placard *m*
cloud / It's cloudy. : nuage / Il y a des nuages. *m*
coast / on the coast : côte / sur la côte *f*
coat : manteau *m*
cockroach : cafard *m*
cocktail (before dinner drink) : apéritif *m*
coffee table : table basse *f*
coffee : café *m*
cola : coca-cola *m*
a **cold** : rhume *m*
cold / It's cold (weather). : froid(e) / Il fait froid.
college, university : fac *f*
color : couleur *f*
comedy (movie, play) : comédie *f*
comfortable : confortable
comic strip : bande-dessinée *f*
commercial : publicité / pub *f*
communications : communications *f pl*
communications (subject matter) : communication *f*
company head, business owner : chef d'entreprise *m*
competitive : compétitif / compétitive
competitive entrance exam : concours (d'entrée) *m*
computer : ordinateur *m*
computer science : informatique *f*
computer scientist : informaticien / informaticienne *m / f*
concert / to go to a concert : concert / aller au concert *m*
continent : continent *m*
to **continue** : continuer
cook : cuisinier / cuisinière *m / f*
to **cook** : faire la cuisine
cool (weather) / It's cool (weather). : frais / Il fait frais.
corner / at the corner of : coin / au coin (de) *m*
to **correct** : corriger
Corsica : Corse *f*
to **cost** : coûter
costume : costume *m*
couch : canapé *m* , sofa *m*
country : campagne *f*
country : pays *m*
couple : couple *m*
cover letter (to accompany a CV) : lettre de motivation *f*
craftsman : artisan / artisane *m / f*
crazy : fou / folle
creative : créatif / créative
crème brûlée : crème brûlée *f*
crepe : crêpe *f*
critic (film, art, etc.) : critique (de films, d'art, etc.) *m, f*
croissant : croissant *m*
crop pants : corsaire *m*
croque -monsieur with a fried egg : croque-madame *m*
to **cross** : traverser
cucumber : concombre *m*
cup / a cup of, a cupful : tasse / une tasse de *f*
curious : curieux / curieuse
curly : bouclé(e)
current address : résidence actuelle *f*
current events : actualité *f*
custom : coutume *f*
cute : mignon / mignonne
cutlet, chop / a pork chop : côtelette / une côtelette de porc *f*
to go **cycling** : faire du cyclisme, faire du vélo
cycling : cyclisme *m*
dairy product : produit laitier *m*
to **dance** : danser
dance club, disco, nightclub : discothèque *f*
dark : sombre
date / What's the date? : date / Quelle est la date? *f*
daughter : fille *f*
day : jour *m*
dear: cher chère
December : décembre *m*
dee-jay : disc-jockey / DJ *m*
deli, catering shop : traiteur *m*
delicious : délicieux / délicieuse
dentist : dentiste *m, f*
desk, office / on the desk : bureau / sur le bureau *m*
dessert : dessert *m*
detective/police movie : film policier *m*
to **detest** : détester

dictionary : dictionnaire *m*
to **die** : mourir
to be on a **diet** : être au régime; faire un régime
difficult / It is difficult (to)... : difficile / Il est difficile de
dining room / in the dining room… : salle à manger / dans la salle à manger... *f*
dinner, supper : dîner *m*
diploma, degree : diplôme *m*
dirty : sale
disciplined : discipliné(e)
to **be discouraged** : **se** décourager
to **do the dishes** : faire la vaisselle
dishonest : malhonnête
dishwasher : lave-vaisselle *m*
disorderliness / messy : désordre / en désordre *m*
to **divorce, to get divorced** : divorcer
doctor, physician : médecin *m*
documentary : documentaire *m*
door : porte *f*
dormitory, university dorm : résidence universitaire *f*
to **download** : télécharger
downtown : centre-ville *m*
dozen / a dozen eggs : douzaine / une douzaine d'oeufs *f*
drama : drame *m*
drawing, design : dessin *m*
to **dream** : rêver
dress : robe *f*
to **dress (oneself)** : **s'** habiller
to **dress, to get dressed** : **s'** habiller
dressy : habillé(e)
to **drink** : boire
drink, beverage / non-alcoholic beverage / alcoholic beverage : boisson / boisson non-alcoolisée / boisson alcoolisée *f*
dryer : sèche-linge *m*
duck : canard *m*
dynamic : dynamique
ear : oreille *f*
to **earn / to earn a living / to earn money** : gagner / gagner sa vie / gagner de l'argent
east / in the east : est / dans l'est, à l'est *m*
Easter / Happy Easter! : Pâques / Joyeuses Pâques! *m, f pl*
easy / It is easy (to)... : facile / Il est facile de
to **eat** : manger
e-commerce : e-commerce *m*
economical, frugal : économe
economics : économie *f*
education, training : formation *f*
egg : oeuf *m*
eggplant : aubergine *f*
eight : huit
eighteen : dix-huit
eighteenth : dix-huitième
eighth : huitième
eighty : quatre-vingts
eighty-one : quatre-vingt-un
elbow : coude *m*
eleven : onze
eleventh : onzième
elite professional school : grande école *f*
e-mail : courrier électronique *m*, email *m*, mail *m*
employee (office employee) : employé / employée (de bureau) *m / f*
to **end** : **(se)** terminer
end / at the far end (of) : bout / au bout (de) *m*
engagement : fiançailles *pl*
engineer : ingénieur *m*
England : Angleterre *f*
English : anglais *m*
English : anglais(e)
English Channel : Manche *f*
enough : assez de
to **enter** : entrer
to **enter a PACS contract** : se pacser
enthralling, fascinating : passionnant(e)
enthusiastic : enthousiaste
entranceway : entrée *f*
errand / to do errands : course / faire des courses *f*
to do **errands** : faire des courses
essential / It is essential (to) : essentiel / essentielle / indispensable / Il est essentiel de / Il est indispensable de
euro (currency) : euro *m*
Europe : Europe *f*
European : européen(ne)
evening : soir *m*
executive : cadre *m*
exercise : exercice *m*
to **exercise** : faire du sport
exhibition, show : exposition *f*
expenses : dépenses *m pl*
expensive : cher / chère
expression / expressions of quantity : expression / expressions de quantité *f*
extended family : famille étendue *f*
eye / eyes : œil / yeux *m*
eyebrow : sourcil *m*
eyes : yeux *m pl*
face : visage *m*
to **fail** : rater
to **fall** : tomber
fall / in the fall : automne / en automne *m*
to **fall in love** : tomber amoureux (de)/ amoureuse
family : famille *f*
famous : célèbre
far : loin (de)
fashion : mode *f*
in fashion : à la mode; branché(e)
fashion designer, seamstress : couturier / couturière *m / f*
fashion show : défilé de mode *m*
father : père *m*
Father's Day : fête des pères *f*
feast of the Assumption : Assomption, le 15 août *f*
February : février *m*
fees : frais *mpl.*
to **feel like (to want to)** : avoir envie de
fiancé / fiancée : fiancé / fiancée *m / f*
fifteen : quinze
fifteenth : quinzième

fifth : cinquième
fifty : cinquante
to **fill out a form** : remplir un formulaire
final year of high school (lycée) : terminale (la) *f*
finances : finances *f pl*
to **find** : trouver
to **find out about, to get information** : **se** renseigner
finger : doigt *m*
to **finish** : finir
to **fire** : mettre à la porte
to **be fired** : être mis(e) à la porte
fireworks : feux d'artifice *m pl*
firm, business : entreprise *f;* boîte [slang] *f*
first : premier, première
first (and middle) name(s) : prénom(s) *m*
first course : entrée *f*
first year of high school (lycée) : seconde (la) *f*
fish : poisson *m*
fish merchant / at the fish merchant's : poissonnier / poissonnière / chez le poissonnier *m / f*
to **fit poorly** : aller mal
to **fit well** : aller bien
five : cinq
floral (print), with flowers / floral print dress : à fleurs / une robe à fleurs
the **flu** : grippe *f*
fog / It's foggy. : brouillard / Il y a du brouillard. *m*
foot / on foot : pied / à pied *m*
forehead : front *m*
foreign : étranger / étrangère
forest : forêt *f*
to **forget** : oublier
fork / a forkful of : fourchette / une forchette de *f*
form : formulaire *m*
form: forme *f*
forty : quarante
to **be found/to be located** : **se** trouver
four : quatre
fourteen : quatorze
fourteenth : quatorzième
fourth : quatrième
foyer : hall d'entrée *m*
franc (currency) : franc *m*
France : France *f;* Hexagone *m*
frank : franc / franche
free : gratuit(e)
freezer : congélateur *m*
French : français *m*
French : français(e)
French Guyana : Guyane française *f*
fresh : frais / fraîche
Friday : vendredi *m*
fridge : frigo *m*
friend : ami / amie *m / f*; camarade *m, f*
friend (boyfriend / girlfriend) : copain / copine *m / f*
fruit : fruit *m*
full/busy (referring to schedule) : chargé(e)
to have **fun** : **s'** amuser
funny : comique, drôle, marrant(e)
funny, amusing / It is fun (to)... : amusant(e) / Il est amusant de
piece of furniture / furniture : meuble / meubles *m*
to **gain weight** : grossir
game show : jeu télévisé *m*
garage : garage *m*
garden, yard / park, large garden : jardin / jardin public *m*
garlic : ail *m*
Garonne (river) : Garonne *f*
Gemini : Gémeaux *m pl*
generous : généreux / généreuse
geography : géographie *f*
German : allemand *m*
German : allemand(e)
Germany : Allemagne *f*
to **get along (with one another)** : **s'** entendre
to **get around (town)** : **se** déplacer (en ville)
to **get engaged** : **se** fiancer
to **get sick** : tomber malade
to **get up** : **se** lever
to **get your bearings** : **s'** orienter
gift : cadeau *m*
to **give** : donner
to **give, to offer** : offrir
glass / a glass of, a glassful : verre / un verre de *m*
glasses : lunettes *f pl*
to **go** : aller
to **go beyond one's budget** : dépasser son budget
to **go down, to go downstairs** : descendre
to **go home, to go back** : rentrer
to **go on foot** : aller à pied
to **go out** : sortir
to **go to a concert** : aller au concert
to **go to a nightclub, dance club** : aller en boîte; aller en discothèque
to **go to bed** : **se** coucher
to **go to the movies** : aller au cinéma
to **go to the park** : aller au parc
to **go to the university** : aller à l'université
to **go up, to go upstairs, to climb** : monter
golf : golf *m*
good : bon / bonne
to **be good in/at** : être bon(ne) en
Good day (Hello) : Bonjour
Good evening : Bonsoir
Goodbye : Au revoir
government minister : ministre *m*
grade : note *f*
grade report : bulletin de notes *m*
to **graduate, to complete one's studies** : recevoir son diplôme
gram / 50 grams of : gramme / 50 grammes de *m*
grandchild : petit-enfant *m*
grandfather : grand-père *m*
grandmother : grand-mère *f*
grandparents : grands-parents *m pl*
grape : raisin *m*
grapefruit : pamplemousse *m*
gray : gris(e)
green : vert(e)
green bean : haricot vert* *m*
green pepper : poivron vert *m*
greeting : salutation *f*
greeting card : carte de voeux *f*

grilled : grillé(e)
grocer / at the grocer's : épicier / épicière / chez l'épicier *m / f*
to **do the grocery shopping** : faire le marché
grocery store / at the grocery store : épicerie / à l'épicerie *f*
ground floor, first floor : rez-de-chaussée *m*
to **grow up** : grandir
guitar / to play the guitar : guitare / jouer de la guitare *f*
Guyanese : guyanais(e)
hair / to brush your hair / What color is your hair? : cheveux / se brosser les cheveux / De quelle couleur sont vos cheveux? *m pl*
hair dresser : coiffeur / coiffeuse *m / f*
hairstyle / What is his hair like? : coiffure / Comment est-il coiffé? *f*
Halloween : Halloween
hallway : couloir *m*
ham : jambon *m*
hand : main *f*
to **hand in, give back** : rendre
to **hang up (the phone)** : raccrocher
Hannukah : Hanouka
happy : heureux / heureuse
Happy Birthday! : Bon (Joyeux) anniversaire!
Happy Easter! : Joyeuses Pâques!
Happy New Year! : Bonne Année!
Happy Saint's Day! : Bonne fête!
hard, tough : dur(e)
hard-working : travailleur / travailleuse *m / f*
hat : chapeau *m*
to **have** : avoir
to **have a meal** : prendre un repas
have a nice meal! : Bon appétit!
to **have dinner** : dîner
to **have lunch** : déjeuner
to **have the means to** : avoir les moyens de
head : tête *f*
health : santé *f*
to **hear** : entendre
heel : talon *m*
height, size / of medium height / What's your height? (I'm one meter 60.) : taille / de taille moyenne / Quelle est votre taille? (Je fais 1 m. 60.) *f*
Hello... (phone) : Allô...
Here is ... (here are...), This is... : Voici
Hi! : Salut!
high school : lycée *m*
high school student : lycéen / lycéenne *m / f*
to go **hiking** : faire des randonnées
hip-hop : hip-hop *m*
to **hire / to be hired** : embaucher / être embauché(e)
history : histoire *f*
to make **home repairs or improvements** : bricoler
homepage : page d'accueil *f*
homework : devoirs *m pl*
to **do one's homework** : faire ses devoirs
honest : honnête
to **hope** : espérer
horoscope : horoscope *m*
horror movie : film d'épouvante *m;* film d'horreur *m*
hospital : hôpital *m*
hot / It's hot (weather). : chaud(e) / Il fait chaud.
hotel : hôtel *m*
house / at home : maison / à la maison *f*
household chores : tâches domestiques *f pl*
housekeeping : ménage / faire le ménage *m*
housewife : femme au foyer *f*
to **do housework** : faire le ménage
housing : logement *m*
how : comment
hundred (one hundred) / two hundred : cent / deux cents
to be **hungry** : avoir faim
to **hurry** : se dépêcher
to **hurt (body part) / (to have a headache, a backache, sore feet, etc)** : avoir mal à / (avoir mal à la tête, au dos, aux pieds, etc)
husband : mari *m*
hutch, buffet : buffet *m*
hypocritical : hypocrite
ice cream : glace *f*
idealistic : idéaliste
identification form : fiche d'identité *f*
Ile de France (Parisian region) : Ile de France (la région parisienne) *f*
illness : maladie *f*
impersonal expression : expression impersonnelle *f*
important / It is important (to) : important(e) / Il est important de
to **improve** : faire des progrès
in front of : devant
incapable, incompetent : incapable
indices (such as... Dow Jones Industrial Average (DJIA), NASDAQ) : indices (i.e., le CAC 40) *m pl*
indifferent : indifférent(e)
inexpensive : bon marché
infatuation-type love : amour passion *m*
information, piece of information: renseignement *m*
inheritance : héritage *m*
insurance : assurance *f*
intelligent : intelligent(e)
to **intend (to)** : avoir l'intention de
interesting : intéressant(e)
intern : stagiaire *m, f*
internet : internet *m*
internet user : internaute *m*
internship : stage *m*
interrogative : interrogatif / interrogative
intersection / at the intersection of : carrefour / au carrefour (de) *m*
interview : entretien *m*
introduction : présentation *f*
to **invite** : inviter
to **iron** : repasser
Italian : italien *m*
Italian : italien(ne)
Italy : Italie *f*
jacket : veste *f*
short jacket, leather jacket : blouson *m*
January : janvier *m*
Japan : Japon *m*
Japanese : japanese *m*

Japanese : japonais(e)
jazz : jazz *m*
jeans : jean *m*
job : emploi *m;* job *m;* boulot [slang] *m*
job application / to apply for a job : demande d'emploi / faire une demande d'emploi *f*
job market : marché du travail *m*
joke : blague *f*
to **joke** : plaisanter
juice / fruit juice : jus / jus de fruit *m*
July : juillet *m*
June : juin *m*
junior high, middle school : collège *m*
Jura (mountains) : Jura *m*
to go **kayaking** : faire du kayak
kayaking : kayak *m*
keyboard : clavier *m*
kilo / a kilo of : kilo / un kilo de *m*
kind, nice : gentil / gentille
to **kiss** : embrasser
to **kiss each other** : s' embrasser
kitchen, cooking / in the kitchen / to cook : cuisine / dans la cuisine / faire la cuisine *f*
knee : genou *m*
knife / a knife of, a knifeful : couteau / un couteau de *m*
lab section : séance de T.P. (travaux pratiques) / un T.P *f*
Labor Day : fête du Travail, le 1er mai *f*
laboratory / lab / in the lab : laboratoire / labo / au labo *m*
to **be laid off** : être licencié(e)
lake : lac *m*
lamp : lampe *f*
language : langue *f*
laptop : portable *m*
large lecture class : cours magistral / des cours magistraux *m*
last : dernier / dernière
to **last** : durer
last name : nom (de famille) *m*
later : plus tard
Latin : latin *m*
launderette : laverie *f*
laundry detergent : lessive *f*
to **do laundry** : faire la lessive
laundry room / in the laundry room : lingerie / dans la lingerie *f*
law : droit *m*
law school : Faculté de droit *f*
lawyer : avocat / avocate *m / f*
to **lay off / to be laid off** : licencier / être licencié(e)
lazy : paresseux / paresseuse
to **learn** : apprendre
to **leave** : laisser, partir, quitter
leek : poireau *m*
left / on the left : gauche / à gauche (de), sur votre gauche
leg : jambe *f*
lemon : citron *m*
Leo : Lion *m*
lettuce : laitue *f*
Libra : Balance *f*
library : bibliothèque *f*
life / What do you do for a living? : vie / Que faites-vous dans la vie? *f*
to **like, to love** : aimer
lily of the valley : muguet *m*
linguistics : linguistique *f*
link : lien *m*
to **listen to a live broadcast** : écouter en direct
to **listen to...** : écouter
listener : auditeur / auditrice *m / f*
liter / a liter of : litre / un litre de *m*
literature : littérature *f*
little : petit(e)
little / a little / a little (+ noun) : peu / un peu / un peu de
to **live** : habiter
to **live together** : vivre ensemble
living room : living *m;* salon *m;* séjour *m*
living room / in the living room... : salle de séjour / dans la salle de séjour... *f*
living together out of wedlock : concubinage *m*
Loire (river) : Loire *f*
Loire Valley : Vallée de la Loire *f*
long : long / longue
to **look for** : chercher
to **look for a job** : chercher une situation
long holiday weekend : faire le pont
Lorraine : Lorraine *f*
to **lose** : perdre
to **lose weight** : maigrir, mincir
love / the love of one's life : amour / grand amour *m*
love at first sight : coup de foudre *m*
to **love each other** : s' aimer
love life : amours *m pl*
the **love of one's life** : grand amour *m*
lunch : déjeuner *m*
Ma'am (Mrs.) / ladies : Madame / Mesdames *f*
magazine : magazine *m*
mail carrier : facteur *m*
mailbox : boîte aux lettres *f*
main course : plat principal *m*
to **major in...** : se spécialiser en... (langues, maths, etc)
major river (that flows to the sea) : fleuve *m*
to **make a donation** : faire un don
to **make an appointment** : prendre un rendez-vous
to **make an effort** : faire un effort
to **make the bed** : faire le lit
man : homme *m*
man's shirt : chemise *f*
to **manage, direct, organize** : gérer
management : gestion *f*
March : mars *m*
Mardi Gras, Carnival : Carnaval (Mardi Gras) *m*
market / at the market : marché / au marché *m*
marriage, wedding : mariage *m*
to **marry, to get married** : se marier
mass : messe *f*
Massif Central : Massif Central *m*
math : mathématiques / maths *f pl*
May : mai *m*

mayonnaise : mayonnaise *f*
meal : repas *m*
means of transport : transports *m pl*
meat : viande *f*
media : médias *m pl*
medicine : médecine *f*
medicine : médicament *m*
Mediterranean Sea : mer Méditerranée *f*
to **meet** : rencontrer
Merry Christmas! : Joyeux Noël!
message : message *m*
metro / by metro : métro / en métro *m*
Mexican : mexicain(e)
Mexico : Mexique *m*
microwave : four à micro-ondes *m*
migraine headache : migraine *f*
milk : lait *m*
million (one million) : million (1.000.000) *m*
mirror : miroir *m*
miserly : avare
miserly, stingy : radin / radine [slang]
Miss / ladies (unmarried) : Mademoiselle / Mesdemoiselles *f*
mistletoe : gui *m*
modern : moderne
Monday : lundi *m*
money : argent *m*
monitor : écran *m*
month : mois *m*
monument : monument *m*
mood, humor: humeur *f*
to **be in a bad mood** : être de mauvaise humeur
to **be in a good mood** : être de bonne humeur
morning : matin *m*
Moroccan : marocain(e)
Morocco : Maroc *m*
mortgage : emprunt-logement *m*
mosque : mosquée *f*
mot / interrogative words : mot *m* / mots interrogatifs
mother : mère *f*
Mother's Day : fête des mères *f*
motorcycle / by motorcycle : moto *f* / à moto
mountain : montagne *f*
mouse : souris *f*
mouth : bouche *f*
to **move (change residences)** : déménager
movie : film *m*
movie theater, cinema / to go to the movies : cinéma *m* / aller au cinéma
museum : musée *m*
mushroom : champignon *m*
music / classical music : musique / musique classique *f*
musical comedy : comédie musicale *f*
musician : musicien / musicienne *m / f*
mustard : moutarde *f*
naive : naïf / naïve
national holiday : jour férié *m*
nationality : nationalité *f*
to **navigate** : naviguer
near, close / nearby : près (de) / tout près
nearby : tout près
necessary / It is necessary (to) : nécessaire / Il est nécessaire de
to be **necessary, must, have to (obligation) / It is necessary (to)** : falloir / Il faut + infinitive
neck : cou *m*
to **need** : avoir besoin de
neighborhood : quartier *m*
nephew : neveu *m*
nervous : nerveux / nerveuse
never: ne...jamais
new : nouveau / nouvel / nouvelle
New Year's Day / Happy New Year! : Jour de l'An *m*, le premier janvier / Bonne Année!
New Year's Eve : Saint-Sylvestre *f*, le 31 décembre
news : informations *f pl*
news show : magazine d'actualités (à la télévision) *m*
news stand : kiosque (à journaux) *m*
news, newspaper (national, regional) : journal (national, régional) *m*
newscaster : présentateur / présentatrice *m / f*
next : prochain(e)
nice (weather) / It's nice (weather). : beau / Il fait beau.
niece : nièce *f*
nightclub, dance club : boîte de nuit *f*
nine : neuf
nineteen : dix-neuf
nineteenth : dix-neuvième
ninety : quatre-vingt-dix
ninety-eight : quatre-vingt-dix-huit
ninety-five : quatre-vingt-quinze
ninety-four : quatre-vingt-quatorze
ninety-nine : quatre-vingt-dix-neuf
ninety-one : quatre-vingt-onze
ninety-seven : quatre-vingt-dix-sept
ninety-six : quatre-vingt-seize
ninety-three : quatre-vingt-treize
ninety-two : quatre-vingt-douze
ninth : neuvième
non-alcoholic / non-alcoholic beverage : non-alcoolisé(e) / boisson non-alcoolisée (f)
Normandy : Normandie *f*
north / in the north : nord / dans le nord, au nord *m*
North America : Amérique du Nord *f*
nose : nez *m*
notebook : cahier *m*
novel : roman *m*
November : novembre *m*
now : maintenant
number / cardinal numbers / ordinal numbers : nombre / nombres cardinaux / nombres ordinaux *m*
nurse : infirmier / infirmière *m / f*
to **obey** : obéir à
ocean : océan *m*
Oceania (the South Sea Islands) : Océanie *f*
October : octobre *m*
official : officiel / officielle
often : souvent
oil : huile *f*
old : ancien(ne)
old : vieux / vieil / vieille

omelette (with herbs, cheese) : omelette (aux fines herbes, au fromage, etc) *f*
on : sur
one : un, une
onion : oignon *m*
online : en-ligne
only child (female) : fille unique *f*
only child (male) : fils unique *m*
to **open** : ouvrir
optician : opticien / opticienne *m / f*
optimistic : optimiste
orange : orange *f*
orange (color) : orange (invariable)
to **order / at the café, you order…** : commander / au café, on commande…
order / straightened up : ordre *m* / en ordre
other : autre
out of style : démodé(e)
oven : four *m*
owner : propriétaire *m, f*
PACS contract : PACS *m*
pager : alphapage *m*
to **paint (art)** : faire de la peinture
painter : peintre *m*
painting : peinture *f*
painting : tableau *m*
painting / to paint (art) : peinture *m* / faire de la peinture
pants (a pair of) : pantalon *m*
paper / presentation : exposé oral *m*
paper/stationery store : papeterie *f*
parade, (military) parade : défilé (militaire) *m*
parents, relatives : parents *m pl*
park : parc *m*
parka : anorak *m*
parking lot : parking *m*
to **party** : faire la fête
to **pass an exam, to succeed (in)** : réussir (à) (un examen)
to **pass, to go by (intransitive), to spend (time)** : passer
passing grade : moyenne *f*
Passover : pâque juive / Pessach *f*
password : mot de passe *m*
pastime : passe-temps (invariable) *m*
pastry chef / at the pastry chef's : pâtissier / pâtissière / chez le pâtissier *m / f*
pastry, pastry shop : pâtisserie *f*
pâté : pâté *m*
patient : patient(e)
to **pay (one's tuition/fees)** : régler (les frais d'inscription)
to **pay / to pay taxes** : payer / payer des impôts
peach : pêche *f*
pear : poire *f*
peas : petits pois *m pl*
pen : stylo *m*
pencil : crayon *m*
people : gens *m pl*
pepper : poivre *m*
person : personne *f*
personal : personnel / personnelle
pessimistic : pessimiste
pharmacist : pharmacien /pharmacienne *m / f*
pharmacy : pharmacie *f*
philosophy : philosophie *f*
phone book : annuaire (téléphonique) *m*
phone booth, telephone booth : cabine téléphonique *f*
phone card : carte téléphonique *f*
phone number : numéro de téléphone *m*
physical : physique
physical education : EPS (éducation physique et sportive) *f*
physical therapist : kinésithérapeute; kiné *m*
physics : physique *f*
piano / to play the piano : piano / jouer du piano *m*
to **pick up/answer (the phone)** : décrocher
to try to **pick up, to hit on, to flirt** : draguer
picnic : pique-nique *m*
piece / a piece of : morceau / un morceau de *m*
body **piercing** : piercing *m.*
Pisces : Poissons *m pl*
pitcher / a pitcher of : pichet / un pichet de *m*
place : lieu *m*
plaid / plaid shirt : à carreaux / une chemise à carreaux
plane / by plane : avion / en avion *m*
plate / a plate of, a plateful : assiette / une assiette de *f*
to **play an April Fools joke (on someone)** : faire un poisson d'avril
to **play… soccer / tennis / cards / chess / guitar / piano** : jouer…au foot / au tennis / aux cartes / aux échecs / de la guitare / du piano /
pleasant : agréable
pointed / He has a snub nose. : pointu(e) / Il a le nez pointu.
points of the compass : points cardinaux *m pl*
police officer : policier *m*
political science : sciences politiques *f pl*
polo shirt : polo *m*
pork : porc *m*
pork butcher / at the pork butcher's : charcutier / charcutière / chez le charcutier *m / f*
pork butcher shop, delicatessen / at the pork butcher shop/delicatessen : charcuterie / à la charcuterie *f*
portfolio (also, wallet) : portefeuille *m*
portrait, description / physical description / psychological description : portrait / le portrait physique / le portrait moral *m*
position (employment) : situation *f*
position, post / full-time position / half-time position : poste / poste à plein temps / poste à mi-temps *m*
post office : bureau de poste *m*
poster : affiche *f*
potato : pomme de terre *f*
practical : pratique
to **prefer** : préférer
preliminary : préliminaire
press (the) : presse *f*
pretentious : prétentieux / prétentieuse

pretty : joli(e)
price / good price : prix / prix intéressant *m*
profession : profession *f*
profession, career, job : métier *m*
professional life : vie professionnelle *f*
promotion : promotion *f*
Provence : Provence *f*
province : province *f*
psychologist : psychologue *m, f*
psychology : psychologie *f*
public square : place *f*
purchase / to go shopping : achat / faire des achats *m*
purple : violet / violette
to **put (on)** : mettre
to **put aside, to save** : mettre de côté
to **put on make-up** : se maquiller
Pyrenees : Pyrénées *f pl*
quantity : quantité *f*
question / personal questions : question / questions personnelles *f*
quiche (lorraine, with salmon, etc) : quiche (lorraine, au saumon, etc) *f*
radio : radio *f*
radio station : station *f*
to **rain / It's raining.** : pleuvoir / Il pleut.
raincoat : imperméable *m*
Ramadan : Ramadan *m*
rarely : rarement
raspberry : framboise *f*
raw vegetables with vinaigrette : crudités *f.pl*
to **read** : lire
realistic : réaliste
rear, behind : derrière *m*
to **receive** : recevoir
to **receive a passing grade** : avoir la moyenne
red : rouge
red (hair), red-head : roux / rousse
to **reflect (on)** : réfléchir à
refrigerator : réfrigérateur *m*
region : région *f*
to **register/enroll (in college, in the film club...)** : s'inscrire (à la fac, au ciné-club…)
to **reimburse** : rembourser
relationship : relation *f*
to **relax** : se détendre
to **remember** : se souvenir (de)
remote control : télécommande *f*
to **rent** : louer
rent : loyer *m*
to **repeat a grade/course** : redoubler
reporter : reporter *m*
reporter, journalist : journaliste *m, f*
researcher : chercheur *m*
reserved : réservé(e)
resourceful : débrouillard(e)
to **rest** : se reposer
restaurant : restaurant *m*
restaurant owner : restaurateur *m*
results, grades : résultats *m pl*
résumé : curriculum vitae (CV) *m*
retired man/woman : retraité / retraitée *m / f*
retirement : retraite *f*
to **return** : retourner
Rhône (river) : Rhône *m*
right / on the right / straight ahead : droit(e) / à droite (de), sur votre droite / tout droit
ritual : rite *m*
the **Riviera** : Côte d'Azur *f*
roast / a beef roast : rôti / un rôti de bœuf *m*
rock-climbing / to go rock-climbling : escalade / faire de l'escalade *f*
roll : petit pain *m*
roller blading : roller *m*
to go **roller blading:** faire du roller
romantic movie : film d'amour *m*
room (general term) : pièce *f*
Rosh Hashana : Rosh Hashana
round : rond(e)
to go **running** : faire de la course à pied
to go **running** : faire du footing
running / to go running : course à pied *f*; footing / faire de la course à pied / faire du footing
running suit : sweat *m*
sabbath : shabbat / le sabbat *m*
Sagittarius : Sagittaire *m*
sail : voile *f*
sailboarding, windsurfing / to go sailboarding/windsurfing : planche à voile / faire de la planche à voile *f*
to go **sailing** : faire de la voile
saint's day, celebration, party / holidays / Happy Saint's Day! : fête / fêtes / Bonne fête! *f*
salad, lettuce : salade *f*
salary : salaire *m*
to **be on sale** : être en solde
salesperson : vendeur / vendeuse *m / f*
salmon : saumon *m*
salt : sel *m*
salty : salé(e)
sandal : sandales *f*
sandwich (with ham and butter) : sandwich (jambon beurre) *m*
Santa Claus : Père Noël *m*
satisfied, fulfilled : satisfait(e)
Saturday : samedi *m*
sausage : saucisse *f*
hard **sausage** : saucisson *m*
to **save money** : faire des économies
savings and loan association : caisse d'épargne *f*
scar : cicatrice *f*
schedule : emploi du temps *m*
school : école *f*
school of fine arts : Faculté des Beaux-Arts *f*
school of humanities/liberal arts : Faculté des lettres et des sciences humaines *f*
school of medicine : Faculté de médecine *f*
school of pharmacy : Faculté de pharmacie *f*
school of sciences : Faculté des sciences *f*
science : science *f*
science-fiction movie : film de science-fiction *m*
Scorpio : Scorpion *m*
sea : mer *f*

seafood shop / at the seafood shop : poissonnerie / à la poissonnerie *f*
search engine : moteur de recherche *m*
season : saison *f*
second : deuxième
second year of high school (lycée) : (la) première *f*
second-hand : (d') occasion
secretary : secrétaire *m, f*
Seine (river) : Seine *f*
selfish : égoïste
to **sell** : vendre
Senegal : Sénégal *m*
Senegalese : sénégalais(e)
sensitive : sensible
September : septembre *m*
series : feuilleton *m*; série *f*
serious : sérieux / sérieuse
seven : sept
seventeen : dix-sept
seventeenth : dix-septième
seventh : septième
seventy : soixante-dix
seventy-eight : soixante-dix-huit
seventy-five : soixante-quinze
seventy-four : soixante-quatorze
seventy-nine : soixante-dix-neuf
seventy-one : soixante et onze
seventy-seven : soixante-dix-sept
seventy-six : soixante-seize
seventy-three : soixante-treize
seventy-two : soixante-douze
to **be in shape** : être en forme
to **share** : partager
shareholder : actionnaire *m, f*
to **shave** : **se** raser
shoe : chaussure *f*
shopkeeper, store owner : commerçant / commerçante *m / f*
to go **shopping** : faire des achats
shopping center, mall : centre commercial *m*
short : court(e)
shorts : short *m*
show : émission *f*
to **show** : montrer
shower : douche *f*
shy, timid : timide
sick / to get sick : malade / tomber malade
side / beside, next to : côté / à côté (de) *m*
side, face / facing, opposite : face / en face (de) *f*
sign / What is your sign? : signe / Quel est ton signe? *m*
sincere : sincère
to **sing** : chanter
singer : chanteur / chanteuse *m / f*
sink (kitchen) : évier *m*
sink (bathroom) : lavabo *m*
Sir / gentlemen : Monsieur / Messieurs *m*
sister : soeur *f*
six : six
sixteen : seize
sixteenth : seizième
sixth : sixième
sixty : soixante
ski, skiing (snow, water) / to go skiing : ski (alpin, nautique) / faire du ski *m*
to **skip a class** : sécher un cours
skirt : jupe *f*
to **sleep** : dormir
sleeping pill : somnifère *m*
slice / a slice of : tranche / une tranche de *f*
small businesses : petits commerces *m pl*
small discussion section : séance de T.D. (travaux dirigés) / un T.D *f*
to **smoke** : fumer
snack : goûter *m*
snail : escargot *m*
to **snow / It's snowing.** : neiger / Il neige.
snub / He has a snub nose. : retroussé(e) / Il a le nez retroussé
soap opera : soap *m*
soccer : football *m*
sociable : sociable
social worker : assistante sociale *f*
sociology : sociologie *f*
sock : chaussette *f*
soldier : militaire *m*
sole : sole *f*
sometimes : quelquefois
son : fils *m*
song : chanson *f*
soon / see you soon : bientôt / à bientôt
(onion) soup : soupe (à l'oignon) *f*
south / in the south : sud / dans le sud, au sud *m*
South America : Amérique du Sud *f*
Spain : Espagne *f*
Spanish : espagnol *m*
Spanish : espagnol(e)
to **speak** : parler
to **spend** : dépenser
spend a vacation : passer les vacances *f pl*
spendthrift : dépensier / dépensière *m / f*
spice : épice *f*
spicy : épicé(e)
spinach : épinard *m*
spoon / a spoonful of : cuillère / une cuillère de *f*
sports : sport *m*
spring / in the spring : printemps / au printemps *m*
square : carré(e)
squirrel : écureuil *m*
stadium : stade *m*
stage manager : régisseur *m*
staircase, stairs : escalier *m*
to **stay / to stay at home** : rester / rester à la maison
steak and French fries : steak-frites *m*
step / just a step from : pas / à deux pas (de) *m*
stereo : chaîne-stéréo *f*
stock market / (Paris) stock market : bourse / bourse (de Paris) *f*
stocks : actions *f pl*
stomach : ventre *m*
store (music, video, etc.) : magasin (de musique, de vidéo, etc.) *m*
storm / There are storms. : orage / Il y a des orages. *m*

stove : cuisinière *f*
straight : raide
straight ahead : tout droit
to **straighten up** : ranger
strawberry : fraise *f*
street : rue *f*
stressed : stressé(e)
striped / striped T-shirt : rayé(e) / un tee-shirt rayé
stubborn : têtu/ têtue
student / I am a student in...(French, math, etc.) : étudiant / étudiante / Je suis étudiant(e) en... (français, maths, etc.) *m / f*
student ID card : carte d'étudiant *f*
student paper : copie *f*
student who has passed the bac : bachelier / bachelière *m / f*
to **study** : étudier
study / high school studies / university studies : étude / études secondaires / études supérieures *f*
subject (school) : matière *f*
subscription : abonnement *m*
suburbs : banlieue *f*
to **suck in/at [slang]** : être nul(le) en [slang]
man's **suit** : costume *m*
woman's **suit** : tailleur *m*
summer / in the summer : été / en été *m*
sun / It's sunny. : soleil / Il y a du soleil. *m*
Sunday : dimanche *m*
sunglasses : lunettes de soleil *f pl*
supermarket / at the supermarket : supermarché / au supermarché *m*
to **surf (the web)** : surfer
to **surprise** : surprendre
sweater : pull *m*
sweet : sucré(e)
to **swim** : nager
to go **swimming** : faire de la natation
swimming / to go swimming : natation / faire de la natation *f*
swimsuit : maillot de bain *m*
Swiss : suisse
Switzerland : Suisse *f*
synagogue : synagogue *f*
table / at the table : table / à table *f*
to **take** : prendre
to **take (a course), to follow** : suivre
to **take an exam** : passer un examen
to **take somebody (along)** : emmener
to **take the metro, a taxi, etc.** : prendre le métro, un taxi, etc.
to **talk to (one another)** : se parler
tall, big : grand(e)
tart / strawberry tart / lemon tart / apple tart : tarte / tarte à la fraise / tarte au citron / tarte aux pommes *f*
tattoo : tatouage *m*
Taurus : Taureau *m*
tax / to pay taxes : impôt / payer des impôts *m*
taxi / by taxi : taxi / en taxi *m*
tea : thé *m*
to **teach someone** : apprendre à quelqu'un
teacher : enseignant *m*
teacher (elementary school) : instituteur / institutrice *m / f*
teacher, professor : professeur *m*
technician : technicien / technicienne *m / f*
techno : techno *f*
to **telephone** : téléphoner à
telephone / on the phone : téléphone / au téléphone *m*
television / TV : télévision / télé *f*
television schedule : programme *m*
television spectator : téléspectateur / téléspectatrice *m / f*
temple : temple *m*
ten : dix
tennis / to play tennis : tennis / jouer au tennis *m*
tennis shoes : tennis *f pl*
tenth : dixième
term paper : mémoire *m*
terminal connected to the French telecommunications system : minitel *m*
terrace : terrasse *f*
test, exam : contrôle *m*, examen *m*
theater : théâtre *m*
There is, there are… : Il y a
There is… (there are…) : Voilà
thin, skinny : maigre
thin, slender : mince
third : troisième
to be **thirsty** : avoir soif
thirteen : treize
thirteenth : treizième
thirty : trente
three : trois
throat : gorge *f*
Thursday : jeudi *m*
tie : cravate *f*
time (the), hour / official time : heure / l'heure officielle *f*
tiring, annoying / It is tiring/annoying (to)... : fatiguant(e) / Il est fatiguant de
toasted cheese sandwich with ham : croque-monsieur *m*
tobacco : tabac *m*
tobacco shop : bureau de tabac *m*
today : aujourd'hui
toilet : toilettes *f pl;* W.C. *m pl*
tolerant : tolérant(e)
tomato : tomate *f*
tomorrow / see you tomorrow : demain / à demain
too much (too many) : trop de
tooth / teeth / to brush your teeth : dent / dents / se brosser les dents *f*
tour bus / by tour bus : car *m* / en car
tragic : tragique
train / by train : train / en train *m*
train station : gare *f*
to **train with weights** : faire de la musculation
to **be transferred** : être muté(e)
trash can : poubelle *f*
to **travel** : voyager
travel agent : agent de voyage *m*, voyagiste *m*
to **try** : essayer

T-shirt : tee-shirt *m*
Tuesday : mardi *m*
tuition, education expenses : frais de scolarité *m pl*
tuna : thon *m*
Tunisia : Tunisie *f*
Tunisian : tunisien(ne)
turkey : dinde *f*
to **turn** : tourner
twelfth : douzième
twelve : douze
twentieth : vingtième
twenty : vingt
two : deux
uncle : oncle *m*
under : sous
to **understand** : comprendre
unemployed person : chômeur / chômeuse *m / f*
unemployment : chômage *m*
United States : Etats Unis *m pl*
university : université *f*
university cafeteria : restaurant universitaire (restau-U) *m*
unpleasant : désagréable
to **update** : mettre à jour
useful : utile
useless : inutile
vacation / to spend a vacation : vacances / passer les vacances *f pl*
vacation day : congé *m*
vacuum cleaner : aspirateur *m*
to **vacuum** : passer l'aspirateur
Valentine's Day : Saint-Valentin, le 14 février *f*
variety show : émission de variétés *f*
VE Day (Victory in Europe) : Victoire 1945, le 8 mai *f*
veal : veau *m*
vegetable : légume *m*
verb / pronominal verb / reflexive verb / reciprocal verb : verbe / verbe pronominal / verbe réfléchi / verbe réciproque *m*
videocassette recorder, VCR : magnétoscope *m*
Vietnam : Vietnam *m*
Vietnamese : vietnamien(ne)
vinegar : vinaigre *m*
violent : violent(e)
Virgo : Vierge *f*
virtual postcard : carte postale virtuelle *f*
to **visit someone** : rendre visite à quelqu'un
to **visit... (a place)** : visiter... (un lieu)
vitamin : vitamine *f*
vocabulary : vocabulaire *m*
Vosges : Vosges *f pl*
to **wait for** : attendre
waiter / waitress : serveur / serveuse *m / f*
to **wake up** : se réveiller
a **walk** : randonnée *f*, promenade *f*
to **walk** : marcher
to go for a walk, to take a walk : faire une promenade *f*, se promener; **to go hiking** : faire des randonnées *f*
walnut : noix *f*
to **wash (oneself)** : se laver
washing machine : lave-linge *m*
to **waste** : gaspiller
to **watch television** : regarder la télévision
water / mineral water : eau / eau minérale *f*
to **wear** : porter
weather : temps *m*
weather report : météo *f*
the **web** : web *m*
website : site *m*
wedding : noces *f pl*
wedding anniversary : anniversaire de mariage *m*
Wednesday : mercredi *m*
week / next week / last week : semaine / la semaine prochaine / la semaine dernière *f*
to **weigh / How much do you weigh? (I weigh 55 kilos.)** : peser / Combien pesez-vous? (Je fais 55 kilos.)
weight training / to train with weights : musculation / faire de la musculation *f*
west / in the west : ouest / dans l'ouest, à l'ouest *m*
western : western *m*
when : quand
where : où
which : quel / quelle / quels / quelles
white : blanc / blanche
who : qui
why : pourquoi
wind / It's windy. : vent / Il y a du vent. *m*
window : fenêtre *f*
to go **windsurfing, sailboarding** : faire de la planche à voile
wine / white wine / rosé wine / red wine : vin / du vin blanc (du blanc) / du vin rosé (du rosé) / du vin rouge (du rouge) *m*
winter / in the winter : hiver / en hiver *m*
to do **without** : **se** passer de
woman, wife : femme *f*
to **work** : travailler
work, job / to, at work : travail / au travail *m*
world / working world : monde / monde du travail *m*
to **worry** : **s'** inquiéter
to be **worth / It is advisable (to), It is better (to)** : valoir / Il vaut mieux + infinitive
wrist : poignet *m*
writer : écrivain *m*
year : année *f*
yellow : jaune
yogurt : yaourt *m*
Yom Kippur : Yom Kippour *m*
young : jeune
Yule log (also a cake in the shape of a Yule log) : bûche de Noël *f*
zucchini : courgette *f*

Made in the USA
Columbia, SC
06 January 2023

75708990R00193